The Birth of Judicial Politics in France

The Birth of Judicial Politics in France

The Constitutional Council in Comparative Perspective

ALEC STONE

New York   Oxford
OXFORD UNIVERSITY PRESS
1992

This book is dedicated
to my mother and friend, Elsie Stone.

Oxford University Press

Oxford   New York   Toronto
Delhi   Bombay   Calcutta   Madras   Karachi
Petaling Jaya   Singapore   Hong Kong   Tokyo
Nairobi   Dar es Salaam   Cape Town
Melbourne   Auckland

and associated companies in
Berlin   Ibadan

Copyright © 1992 by Oxford University Press, Inc.

Published by Oxford University Press, Inc.,
200 Madison Avenue, New York, New York 10016

Oxford is a registered trademark of Oxford University Press.

Library of Congress Cataloging-in-Publication Data
Stone, Alec.
The birth of judicial politics in France : the Constitutional
Council in comparative perspective / Alec Stone.
p.   cm.   Includes bibliographical references and index.
ISBN 0-19-507034-8
1. Judicial review—France.   2. Political questions and judicial
power—France.   3. France.   Conseil constitutionnel.
4. Constitutional courts—France.   I. Title.
KJV4392.S76 1992   347.44'012—dc20
[344.40712]   91-29245

1 3 5 7 9 8 6 4 2

Printed in the United States of America
on acid-free paper

ACKNOWLEDGMENTS

This book began as a paper written for Professor John T. S. Keeler's French Politics seminar during my first year in the doctoral program at the University of Washington in Seattle. At that time, no French or English social science research on the Constitutional Council existed, despite the fact that the council's impact on French national politics had become quite obvious. In the past thirty-five years, comparative politics had all but lost its once thriving interest in foreign courts and constitutions. The public law field was abandoned to academic lawyers, who themselves were not much interested in comparative work. Thus when I began this research, I hoped, among other things, to demonstrate the importance of French constitutional law to the general concerns of comparative politics.

I soon discovered, for reasons that will become clear, that I had an interest in engaging some of the concerns of public lawyers. For most comparative-politics people, lawyerly discourse is insular, often arcane, and largely distinct from what is considered to be the normal (interest- and power-based) language of politics. Two individuals, working in radically different scholarly traditions, encouraged me to look closely at doctrinal and other legal materials. Both helped me to see how these materials could be integrated into what I insisted must remain a work primarily addressed to the comparative-politics field. In 1987, in one of the most fortunate events of my graduate schooling, I met Professor Martin Shapiro, of Boalt Law School (the University of California, Berkeley). During a year in which we both lived in Paris, Professor Shapiro, gently and with great patience, introduced me to how modern political scientists have studied constitutional law. Whatever success I have had in contributing to such study is due largely to Professor Shapiro's influence. I must also single out Dean Louis Favoreu, professor of law at the University of Aix-en-Provence-Marseille, for his extraordinary dedication to the study of the Constitutional Council. As is all too evident in the book, his work inspired and in many respects provoked my own. Over the past six years, I have come to respect Professor Favoreu and his scholarship far more than I disagree with his interpretive conclusions.

The book is an abridged version of a much longer doctoral dissertation. Cutting the dissertation for publication (more than one-quarter of the orginal text) was extremely painful, a kind of self-amputation. I am particularly grateful to my wife, Tamar Gutner, for her help in this process. Armed with a very red pen, she read the entire dissertation and then had the courage and persistence to force and cajole me to make the necessary deletions. At Oxford University Press, I wish to thank Valerie Aubry, her assistant Niko Pfund, and my editor, Carole Sollis-Cohen, for shepherding the manuscript to completion, and Sharon Lahaye for her careful and laborious copyediting. They suffered but forgave the many faults and errors for which I was responsible.

Finally, I would like to express my gratitude to the people and institutions who encouraged and assisted my research and writing at the dissertation stage. Foremost, I owe a huge debt to Professor Keeler, my dissertation advisor, whose advice and criticism sustained, and often restored, my enthusiasm for what at times seemed to be a never-ending project. I relied on him, and his contagious devotion to the study of comparative and French politics, far more than he realizes. I look forward to repaying this debt during what I hope and expect to be a lifetime of friendship and collaboration. Along with Professor Keeler, Professors Michael W. McCann and Daniel S. Lev of the Department of Political Science, University of Washington, read and made invaluable comments at every stage of the writing of the manuscript, as did Professor Martin Shapiro. Access to the library and archives of the French National Assembly was obtained with the kind assistance of Professor Guy Carcas-sonne, of the University of Paris X, and Françoise Monet, of the National Assembly. Access to the resources of the University of Aix-en-Provence-Marseilles was obtained with the assistance of Dean Louis Favoreu. A number of institutions provided financial and logistic support. I wish to thank: the Camargo Foundation (Cassis, France) and its director, Michael Pretina, for a research fellowship in 1986; the French government and the *Bourse Chateaubriand* for a research fellowship in 1987–1988 (Paris); the Graduate School of the University of Washington, which provided support for both research (Paris, 1985, 1987) and writing (Seattle, 1989); and the Department of Political Science at the University of Oregon, where I taught while completing the dissertation. For the most important support of all, that which I received by virtue of love and friendship, I thank Manuel and Aurélia Mestre of Paris, France; Simone Lemaire of Busset, France; Elsie Stone of Bellingham, Washington; Lona Badgett, Kristina Lynn Case, John Keeler, Julie Sakahara, and Joe Vinikow of Seattle; and Tamar Gutner of Cambridge, Massachusetts.

Middlebury, VT.   Alec Stone Sweet
August 1991

CONTENTS

The Birth of Judicial Politics in France

INTRODUCTION

Where Judicial Politics
Are Legislative Politics

"If we allow the Constitutional Council's jurisprudence to develop as it has recently," the French minister of justice complained, "we will find ourselves in a situation where the governments of tomorrow . . . will no longer have anything to do."[1] Albin Chalandon's voice was only one in a chorus of protests orchestrated by the majority during the 1986 parliamentary sessions and directed at the French constitutional court. The view, expressed as forcefully on the Right as on the Left in the 1980s, holds that policymakers are in danger of losing their power to legislate, power being restricted by a constantly expanding spiral of constitutional constraint, jurisprudential precedent, and legal debate.

Reformers in the new Chirac government were understandably frustrated. The opposition had attacked their program at nearly every stage of the legislative process, quoting extensively from what one minister called the Socialist's "bible"—"a litany of Council decisions"[2]—and warning of impending damnation. During that first year (1986), the Socialists referred more than one in every three pieces of legislation to the Council for a ruling, and more than half of these were judged to be in whole or in part unconstitutional. By late summer, the Council was being decried as a "deviation" and a "new kind of legislator"[3] possessing "discretionary power" over laws voted by parliament;[4] the presidents of the National Assembly and the Senate even called a press conference to denounce one ruling (of 23 January 1987) as "unacceptable," "a veritable attack on national sovereignty," and an "amputation of the power of parliamentarians."[5]

These events, however, were not indicative of new developments, but of an extraordinary and nearly continuous judicial-political confrontation which first flared more than five years before. In the spring of 1981, when Mitterrand forces took control of the presidency, the National Assembly, and the government, the Council—hailed as the "last rampart against Socialism"—became the only effective source of institutional opposition available to a routed

3

Right.[6] The latter referred virtually every major piece of the government's reform program to the Council, and with impressive results: an unprecedented number of laws were censured, and some of the most important pieces of the Socialist reform program were struck down, significantly altered, or delayed by Council decisions or the threat of future censure. The Council—long ignored even by French legal specialists and virtually unknown to the general public—suddenly found itself on center stage and the object of harsh attacks by disgruntled politicians.

By 1986, five years of tenacious opposition had demonstrated that the systematic referral of important pieces could have a crucial impact on final legislative outcomes. On the eve of the 1986 legislative elections in March, and with every poll predicting imminent defeat for the Left, the Socialists prepared themselves for opposition by building their strength in the new politics of the constitution. In late February, Mitterrand appointed his minister of justice, Robert Badinter, to the presidency of the Council—after another Socialist appointee had agreed to vacate the office (while staying on as a member of France's constitutional court).[7] Pledging to use the Council's offices in full measure, the party also returned to opposition armed with a permanent, in-house constitutional specialist—a law professor and an expert on the Council's jurisprudence as well as parliamentary procedure and activity.[8] As one director of cabinet summed up the situation in those early days of the Chirac government: "Constitutional preoccupation is permanent."[9]

Because the Council is convened only by politicians—in practice exclusively by the opposition—and because the Council rules on the constitutionality of legislation *after* it has been definitively adopted by parliament but *before* it may be promulgated, the mere threat of petition can *juridicize* the legislative process. That is, the opposition may use such threats to enforce or cajole changes in proposed legislation, and the government may be obliged to work to insulate a bill from future constitutional censure by compromising its policy objectives. The Chirac government's problems were compounded because its ambitious reform program was designed to abrogate and then replace legal regimes established by the previous Parliament but which had themselves been the subject of the most important juridicized debates and most controversial Council rulings. Put differently, the Right had from 1981 to 1985 participated in building obstacles, which it was then forced to confront when it returned to power in 1986.

French judicial politics are legislative politics by any other name. So true is this that the policymaking process in France can no longer be understood without taking into account the direct and indirect influence of the Council on legislative outcomes. Moreover, the development of constitutional review has transformed the customs, habits, and conduct of ministries and parliament. Striking confirmation of this point was recently provided by Michel Rocard in his first official act as prime minister, a statement (a *circulaire* of May 1988) elaborating a general code of conduct for his new government. In stark contrast to the traditional French model of parliamentary sovereignty and the deep aversion to "legalism" evident in the early years of the Fifth Republic,

Rocard called the "respect for the state of law (*l'état de droit*)" his government's first priority, and ordered his ministers to do "everything" possible to "eliminate the risks of unconstitutionality"—even for bills which they did *not* expect to see referred to the Council. As important, he urged that constitutional vigilance be maintained as bills make their way through parliamentary committees and onto the parliamentary floor.[10] The juridicization of policymaking processes in France was now official.

Between 1980 and 1988 French judicial politics were born; they then matured and were institutionalized. The reform mania which dominated French politics from 1981 to 1987 concentrated and harnessed partisan to ideological energies, and transformed Parliament into a battleground for radically opposed social agenda. It also transformed constitutional politics into high politics—as constitutional law gradually emerged as an important and at times crucial element of political discourse, and the Council—for the first time—was systematically implicated in the day-to-day struggles of Parliament. This book is in part the story of these remarkable developments, and of how an originally weak and deferential institution became a powerful actor in a political environment extraordinarily hostile to judicial review. More broadly, it argues that comparativists can no longer ignore the politics of courts and constitutions, at least in Europe. Parliamentarians and ministers take constitutional courts seriously; the press regularly devotes front page coverage to important decisions; and academic lawyers are increasingly involved in noisy doctrinal disputes about the status, coherence, and import of constitutional jurisprudence. Political scientists are alone, it seems, in failing to take notice. We have everything to gain by "bringing the courts back in," by undertaking careful, empirical research into their behavior and impact on national political systems and processes, and in working to organize these studies in a theoretically significant manner.

Rediscovering Courts

In recent years judicial review has exploded into prominence in Western Europe: since 1950, the European Community, France, Greece, Portugal, Spain, and Sweden joined Austria, West Germany, and Italy as polities with established review mechanisms. Yet prior to that time, the control of legislation by European constitutional courts was virtually unknown (the notable exceptions being in Austria and in Germany during the Weimar Republic). Political scientists have not taken stock of these developments. Although the review activities of the U.S. Supreme Court have spawned a massive literature, our knowledge of judicial review elsewhere suffers from astonishing inattention.

How can the paucity of research interest in judicial institutions be explained? In part, it appears to be a result of anti-institutional biases which accompanied the demise of a comparative politics said to have been, in Macridis's terms, "excessively formalistic."[11] By the end of the 1950s, the field had all but abandoned "formal-legalism"—the study of constitutions and the formal rules and structures of the state—turning instead to questions of social power, political behavior, and decision making, and embracing methodologies developed in other less literary social sciences.[12] So extensive was this anti-institutionalist correction that in 1968 Macridis himself was moved to complain that comparativists now studied "everything but the machinery of the state and its organizational structures." "The state of the discipline can be summed up in one phrase," he wrote: "the gradual disappearance of the political."[13]

In a recent survey and analysis of the subject matters of articles published in the comparative field from 1968 to 1981, Sigelman and Gadbois concurred, concluding that "exceptionally little work has been done on the basic structural aspects of government." Courts and constitutions—perhaps the most "formal," "the most legal" of institutions—have suffered the worst, finishing "in a tie for last place" among the twenty-nine substantive categories into which articles and research notes were coded. They asked:

> Have we gained such a complete understanding of the structural aspects of politics that comparative research on governmental institutions is no longer needed? No serious student of comparative politics would be willing to answer in the affirmative, and yet we see no signs of resurgence of interest in formal governmental institutions.[14]

Since their survey, no article relating to either courts or constitutions has appeared to date (October 1991) in either *Comparative Politics* or *Comparative Political Studies*.

The neglect of judicial institutions may also be a consequence of the inherent difficulties of comparative research—language problems and logistic support, for example—compounded by the formalist, professional-technical nature of legal discourse, and the sparseness or nonexistence of native scholarship. Whereas a field of inquiry devoted to "political jurisprudence," or even more roughly to "judicial politics," has become a kind of orthodoxy in the United States—and has even penetrated into law school curricula[15]—an equivalent field does not exist in Europe.[16] The case of France, where *no major book or journal article on the Constitutional Council has been produced by a French social scientist*, is an extraordinary example. But in all European countries, academic discourse on law and courts is the privileged domain of law professors. In this discourse, the notion that courts are political actors at all is resisted, and the interaction of courts with other governmental institutions is largely ignored. In consequence, we have slight ideographic[17]—and no comparative—understanding of how European constitutional courts actually function within their respective governmental systems.

Recent developments in comparative research would seem to encourage such a project. As has been by now extensively documented,[18] there has been "a sudden upsurge of interest in the state." Social scientists—and notably comparativists—are in the process of rediscovering institutions, and studying their origins, subsequent development, and impact on other official and non-official structures, public policy, and social relationships. This "New Institutionalism" largely rejects putative "mainstream behavioral and pluralist" conceptions of governmental structures as relatively neutral "arenas within which political behavior, driven by more fundamental factors, occurs,"[19] as well as an alleged "Marxist" conception of the state as a simple reflection or instrument of ruling class interests. Instead, state agencies are considered to have unique capacities to generate and direct their own preferred agenda, and to shape social politics; and these capacities are considered to be endogenous to the State itself. March and Olsen put it this way:

> Without denying the importance of both the social context of politics and the motives of individual actors, the new institutionalism insists on a more autonomous role for political institutions. . . . The ideas deemphasize the dependence of the polity on society in favor of an interdependence between relatively autonomous social and political institutions.[20]

That said, the "new institutionalists" have not provided much guidance for research on courts. Although Skocpol and March and Olsen review how the number and quality of studies on legislatures, bureaucracies, and policymaking, and the organization and formation of interest groups have grown in the past decade, neither their discussions nor their bibliographies contain references to judicial institutions.

Focus on policymaking is rightly one of the general methodological or strategic biases of new institutionalist work and theory-building, not least because it directs analytical attention to the concrete relationships among and between social and political structures, and provides the empirical means by which to verify their respective strength and mutual impact. As Macridis—who sounded what is perhaps the earliest sustained call to comparativists to return to the study of the State "stripped of all its metaphysical settings"—has written, "The study of the impact of the decisions made by government can provide us with an excellent laboratory for comparative analysis. Conflict-policies-decisions-consequences, this is the heart of political life."[21]

My work on what has been called (if somewhat awkwardly) the *juridicization* of policymaking is an example of why judicial politics matter to who gets what, when, and how. More precisely, it demonstrates how the increasingly intense interaction between a constitutional court and governments and parliamentarians has structured political choices and shaped policy outcomes.[22] Constitutional courts and their jurisprudence are treated as important independent and mediating variables in the legislative process. Such a focus takes courts well beyond what might be considered the narrow, orthodox concerns of classic jurisprudence and constitutionalism. Constitutional courts produce legal language and doctrinal commentary, but they are also governmental institutions which are shaped by and in turn shape the political environment. It is in this environment that these courts endeavor to survive, to compete for power, and to prosper.

The Constitutional Council and the
Juridicized Legislative Process

French republican tradition manifests itself most often in reverence for the sovereignty of the parliamentary act—*la loi*—conceived as a kind of constitutional reification of the Rousseauian notion of the "expression of the general will." In this tradition, judicial review is explicitly precluded, and no court since the Revolution has ever invalidated or otherwise refused to apply a statute on the grounds that it was unconstitutional. The constitution of the Fifth Republic does not undermine this constitutional orthodoxy, at least not technically. Once promulgated, a law may not be challenged or made subject to any jurisidictional control other than that of parliament itself. But the 1958 constitution does provide for what is effectively a priori control over the constitutionality of legislation, and created an institution—the Constitutional Council—to exercise it.

The political aspects of this control can not be overemphasized, and are part and parcel of the Council's structural mandate. First, the body's nine members, the majority of whom have served in parliaments or governments, are politically appointed (by the president of the Republic, and the presidents of the Senate and the National Assembly). These appointments may not be obstructed or set aside: there is neither a confirmation process, nor established mechanisms of consultation with political and social groups. Second, *the Council rules only on the constitutionality of bills which have been definitively adopted by parliament but not yet promulgated by the executive.* Legislation may not be challenged by private citizens, nor can legal controversies percolate up to the Council through the judicial system. The control is thus a priori and abstract rather than a posteriori and concrete as in the American model. Third, only politicians—the president, the prime minister, the presidents of the two chambers of parliament and, since 1974, any sixty senators or National Assembly deputies—have the authority to refer bills to the Council for a ruling. There are also judicial aspects to the Council's mandate. As is the case with all French judicial bodies, the Council's internal deliberations are formally secret, dissenting opinions are not allowed, and votes are not published. Its decisions too generally follow standard judicial practice: they are published and must be based on legal materials, for example. In short, because much more will be said about this issue later, the Council can be considered at least quasi-judicial to the extent that it produces a jurisprudence; moreover, this jurisprudence constitutes the only public record of its behavior.

Constitutional review in France is not technically "judicial" in other ways, most notably by virtue of the fact that the Council is formally detached from the greater judicial system. In fact, its impact is concentrated *exclusively* on the legislature and on legislative outcomes. As a matter of form, each Council decision necessarily constitutes the final, substantive stage of the policymaking process, and is itself an integral element of a referred bill's legislative history. If we take as our point of reference the referral itself, how and why this is the case becomes readily apparent. A referral *automatically suspends* a bill duly adopted by parliament and *requires* the Council to make a ruling. This ruling may impact this suspension in one of several ways, which can be summarized as follows: (1) if a bill is judged not to be unconstitutional, the suspension is lifted and the bill is promulgated; (2) if judged to be unconstitutional, the bill remains in permanent suspension, vetoed; (3) a bill judged to be in part unconstitutional (a partial annulment) may be promulgated, but only after it has been "amputated" of the offending provisions (which remain in permanent suspension); or, (4) a bill may be judged to be only in part unconstitutional but nonpromulgable nevertheless. In this final case, the Council may rule that the offending provisions are "inseparable" from the whole and that, in conse-quence, the bill possesses no separate constitutional integrity as law without them. In the latter two cases, legislators may elect, or be obliged, to go through the whole legislative process again in order to "correct" or "revise" the bill by incorporating the Council's prescriptions into new legislation. While I have translated the terms of this impact from the language of constitutional law to that of practical policymaking, they are constitutionally derived and may only be altered by constitutional amendment.[23]

When the Council rules on the constitutionality of legislative provisions, its impact on policy outcomes is direct. As mentioned earlier, however, the Council can also have extraordinary influence of an indirect kind when legis-lators sacrifice policy preferences *before* referrals as a means of avoiding con-stitutional censure. This indirect impact too might be said to constitute the court's policymaking behavior, or impact. Taken together, we can say that the legislative process is *juridicized* to the extent that the Council's decisions, the pedagogical authority of its past jurisprudence, and the threat of future censure alter legislative outcomes.

From an institutionalist perspective, focus on the phenomenon of *juridicization* yields distinct advantages. The most important of these derive from the fact that research is structured by the extensive and concrete inter-action of institutions within a relatively closed and controlled systemic context, in this case, that of policymaking. Political actors and the groups to which they belong behave purposefully, but such behavior is state-bounded—confined to institutional space, and conditioned by meaningful structural settings. The deemphasis of cultural variables reflects an institutionalist bias, but is appro-priate given the fact that there is no formal link between the Council and the greater society; the Council interacts only with official policymakers. Such research need not be irrelevant to students of political culture and society. As with any focus on policymaking, the roads to and from state and society are many, and are constantly being traveled in both lanes.[24] As will be shown in chapter 6, not only partisan interests but stockholder's interests were affected when the Council ruled on the constitutionality of nationalization or privatiza-tion legislation—and party programs and the composition of bank boards were redrawn afterwards. Moreover, institutions which exercise judicial review may possess capacities to shape political beliefs and cultural norms beyond immediate policy impact, and at the same time are subject to these same values. Thus, the Council's decision on the Socialists nationalization program in 1982 may constitute a potentially formative explication of the meaning of property rights in France, but at the same time can not be divorced from certain long-standing French attitudes to property. Finally, it is important to note that the salient problem of much of the institutionalist literature, the extent to which the state can be said to be autonomous from society, is not problematic, or does not arise—at least not in the same form. The remarkable changes described in this book occurred without significant input from society, but were instead a result of official interaction at the heart of the French State.

Speaking to and Learning from American "Public Law"

At a recent symposium convened to assess the virtues and shortcomings of *political jurisprudence*, and to comment on its likely and most productive future directions, several participants lamented the dearth of studies in public law on foreign courts. The lack of interest need not be belabored and should not surprise, since public law is virtually a subfield of American politics. Still Shapiro, among others, proposed that a "movement toward comparative law and courts" would be a promising direction of new inquiry:

> We now know just enough about comparative law and courts to begin a more scholarly, less interventionist [than the earlier "law and development"] course of study—the same course pursued by comparative politics more generally. We are prepared to choose relatively modest, mid-range theories and test them against a number of legal-political systems at roughly the same level of socio-economic development. While we cannot expect comparative politics people to become interested in law, law-oriented political scientists can easily improve their competencies and enter the comparative field.[25]

Speaking as a comparativist, one important premise of my research was that my field can learn from public law, and that developments in public law merit our attention. Once convinced that courts are worthy of sustained, systematic study, comparativists have an interest in acquainting themselves with what their public law colleagues have been saying about the politics of law and courts. Indeed, there is a good chance that we will find useful conceptual guidance to the extent that 1) institutions are comparable generally, and that 2) the political behavior of European courts and judges can be compared to that of their American counterparts in particular. Comparativists in turn, and as directly as possible, should attempt to engage relevant debates in public law—by underlining the contributions which comparative studies can make to the understanding of the relationships between law and politics, but also by weighing carefully research strategies developed by public law scholars against the needs of a given comparative project. This interaction will be fruitful only to the extent that audiences are addressed explicitly, and from the outset.

Important concerns of this work and of contemporary public law scholarship dovetail at several crucial points. First, since students of the U.S. Supreme Court, whether academic lawyers or political scientists, have been enormously preoccupied with normative debate about the legitimacy of judicial review, studies of the creation and development of review elsewhere will likely be of immediate interest. In fact, current controversies surrounding the protracted judicial-political confrontation in France bear striking resemblance to traditional American debates: in the 1980s, politicians raised the cry of "*gouvernement des juges*" with regularity; comparisons of the confrontation with one between the Supreme Court and President Roosevelt in the United States were debated in Parliament and the press; and academic lawyers came to view themselves as militant if unofficial advocates for the Council and constitutional review.

Yet a closer examination of the respective terms of normative debate about the legitimacy, utility, and desirability of constitutional review reveals profound differences among cases. In the American case, the legitimacy of review, although periodically problematic, is far more easily defended than in France. This is due to a number of factors: the longevity of the constitutional regime, a flexible separation of powers doctrine which asserts, as a basis for democratic theory, equality in the authority of the three branches of government, and a historical tradition of a judge-made common law. As chapter 1 will make much more clear, advocates of judicial review in France were hampered, in the end fatally so, by the revolutionary ideology of the *general will*. In contrast to the American, the French separation of powers tradition manifests itself principally in reverence for statute and in unmitigated hostility to judicial review. The creation of the Constitutional Council did not overthrow this doctrine. On the contrary, the founders of the Fifth Republic charged the Council with reviewing legislation *before* it became law, that is, before the legislative act is invested with sovereignty. A great deal more will be said on these points later.

A second evident point of intersection between my concerns and those of American public law is with that of political jurisprudence. While the demise of formal legalism might have led comparative political science to abandon the study of judicial institutions, American public law simply underwent the same discursive transformation occurring in the discipline as a whole.[26] The more speculative scholarly enterprises associated with traditional public law studies—attacks on or the defense of judicial independence, the synthesis or deconstruction of doctrine—lost their salience, and were replaced by behavioral concerns for judicial process, power, and decision making.

"Not wed to any theory or method,"[27] early approaches to political jurisprudence varied widely. Using tools originally developed for research on legislatures and bureaucracies, public law behavioralists worked to determine how and why judges decide the way they do.[28] Some correlated personal background with voting records and published opinions and dissents.[29] Others treated courts as small, elite groups, looked for evidence of subgroups and voting blocs, and identified stable or shifting patterns of leadership within the group.[30] A court's formal pronouncements—its jurisprudence—was often only of secondary concern. Still another strain sought to describe the properties of judicial process and policymaking and then to situate these within the greater sociopolitical context. These scholars openly accepted pluralist models of macropolitics, with legal institutions functioning as sites for micropolitical conflict. In their studies, a court's jurisprudence was relatively more important, to the extent that legal language is the medium through which social conflict is communicated to judges, and through which judges seek to implement their own policy choices.[31]

Notwithstanding the diversity of methodological commitments and substantive concerns, there was consensus on the necessity of treating courts and judges as official decision makers who, by passing on judicial controversies, necessarily make public policy. Like other governmental officials, judges make authoritative distributive decisions: interests are advantaged or disadvantaged, public and private resources are allocated, social values are identified or reinforced. "Their point," Stumph writes, "was simply that one gets a good deal closer to reality by conceptualizing courts as political agencies than was the case in the old jurisprudential view, namely that courts are purely legal agencies whereas the executive and legislative departments are political."[32] Political jurisprudence broadcast this message over and over, not least, because of the significant resistance—and cries of heresy—which the message elicited from traditionalists and law professors.

The conscious demystification of things "legal" constitutes perhaps the most important contribution of political jurisprudence to comparative work such as my own. Political jurisprudence, by denying any fundamental distinction between law and politics, opened up judicial institutions to empirical scrutiny from perspectives "external" to the law itself. It then insisted that judges were, first and foremost, policymakers. Both steps—and they are not really separable—are essential ones to take if we are to gain even the most elementary understanding of how courts function anywhere. Much of this book is a confirmation of these essential lessons of political jurisprudence: that analysts ought to develop and defend perspectives external to "the law," and ought to identify "judicial power" as "policy-making capacity," and judges as decision makers. Moreover, these lessons, at least, are perfectly compatible with new institutionalist biases.

Third, certain concerns of this study might be said, at least in part, to converge with what is identified as a critique of and a reaction to political jurisprudence. The extraordinary pluralism—one might even call it the fragmentation—of present day public law research testifies to the breakdown of consensus around certain tenets of political jurisprudence. Most important, the positivist's insistence on maintaining rigid "external" positions was increasingly criticized as too restrictive and, ultimately, counterproductive to the understanding of the behavior of judicial actors and institutions. As Pritchett counseled in 1969,

> Political scientists who have done so much to put the "political" in "political jurisprudence" need to emphasize that it is still "jurisprudence." It is judging in a political context, but it is still judging, and judging is something different from legislating and administering.[33]

Much of the contemporary work in public law is an effort to elaborate on this difference, which often, if not necessarily, combines with a new and self-conscious concern for normative theory. Debates about judicial review among and between political scientists and academic lawyers have shifted from focus on the countermajoritarian difficulty[34] to hermeneutics,[35] and to the importance of intellectual and discursive structures and properties which *restrain* judges' discretion in constitutional interpretation, and in their conception of their political roles. These latter efforts include movements toward "normative jurisprudence,"[36] "law and language,"[37] and "critical legal studies."[38]

In a recent leading article, Rogers Smith has attempted to pull the diverse strands of this reaction to political jurisprudence together by, among other things, tying them to broader new institutionalist critiques and concerns.[39] Like the new institutionalists, Smith identifies an underlying dissatisfaction in his field with the notion that the behavior of institutions and of the actors within them—courts and judges, for example—can be wholly understood as by-products of societal forces and conflict. In "Pluralist" and (traditional) "Marxist" views that deny the legal system's "relative autonomy" from society, the critique goes,[40] "judicial decision-making . . . inevitably seems a tedious, crassly self-interested, and rather ineffectual game among programmed players."[41] And both views, it is alleged, deemphasize or deny the role the legal system may play in shaping the perspectives and political behavior of judges.

Smith argues—as I have argued earlier, if for different reasons—that courts, like other important governmental organizations, can and should be studied in their structural environments. But following Gordon,[42] Smith further proposes that a society's "legal tradition" might be profitably conceived as a relatively autonomous "cognitive structure." According to this view, *law and legal discourse ought to be conceived as an institution in its own right, and studied as one of the coherent and long-term repertoires of thought and behavior that determine political outcomes.* The conceptualization of legal discourse (or for that matter any *cognitive*, i.e., nonconcrete, *structure*) as an "institution" might appear problematic at first glance. For comparativists, it may be helpful to state the proposition in more familiar terms: *comparativists have an interest in taking legal communities and their traditions seriously to the extent that how relevant elites think, are socialized, and interact with other elites makes a difference.* Similarly, the analysis of the social consciousness of any expert elite might usefully inform many different kinds of studies (of physicists in research on nuclear regulatory politics, of doctors in research on public health care systems). But underlying Smith's argument is the assertion that legal structures may be even more autonomous, that is, less determined and more insulated from both concrete social interests and from political struggle taking place in other state institutions, than are other such cognitive structures.This "relative autonomy," counsels Gordon,

> means that [legal forms and practices] can't be explained completely by reference to external political/social/economic factors. To some extent they

are independent variables in social experience and therefore may require study elaborating their peculiar internal structures with the aim of finding out how these structures feed back upon social life.[43]

It may certainly be important to know if and how "non-legal" considerations, such as a judge's party affiliation or ideological profile affects his decision making; and these concerns—and many others—should not be thrown out with the proverbial political jurisprudence and behavioral bathwater. "But," as Smith writes, "if legal discourse truly displays some 'relative autonomy,' then it will at times play more than [a] justificatory role."[44] "Judges," for example, "may decide in part out of a concern to mitigate internal tensions in legal doctrines"[45]; law professors may seek to reinforce or destabilize interpretation and the production of jurisprudence by doctrinal advocacy; and this advocacy may be governed by rules of acceptable behavior and discourse specific to forms of legal consciousness itself.

Integrating concern for legal discourse into the study of courts and their interaction with other institutions may be all the more relevant in the European case. Scholarly research and writing on courts in Europe is virtually monopolized by law professors who, as a matter of basic epistomological commitment, carry on their work "almost entirely divorced from socioeconomic history on the one hand, and from the discussion of the origin and development of specific legal institutions on the other."[46] Stated differently, European legal scholars are fiercely committed to maintaining—at least in published work—their "relative autonomy" from "politics." The implications of this monopoly and substantive myopia for institutionalist projects are not all negative. On the contrary. Students of comparative law insist on the extent to which legal discourse in the civil law-European tradition is dominated not by judges but by academic lawyers. So true is this that doctrinal materials may not be divorced from both general and specific outcomes—the production of a jurisprudence, for example. As Merryman writes,

> . . . the legal scholar is the great man of the civil law. Legislators, executives, administrators, judges, lawyers all come under his influence. He molds the civil law tradition and the formal materials of the law into a model of the legal system. He teaches this model to law students and writes about it in books and articles. . . . [I]t is reasonably accurate to say that the law in a civil law tradition is what the scholars say it is.[47]

In short, the materials produced by this community may provide the researcher with a rich source of evidence for autonomy. That this community is homegenous, insular, and most important, politically meaningful, makes the argument for taking seriously its study a compelling one.

One explicit working assumption of this work, borne out I believe at a number of crucial points in the evolution of the Council into both a "courtlike" institution and a powerful lawmaker, is that the benefits of integrating doctrinal materials into research far outweigh liabilities. Furthermore, potential problems might be mitigated if we qualify how these materials are to be used in at least two ways. First, there is always the potential that in speaking to and from doctrine and jurisprudence the study of judicial politics will be given back to formalism, to words chasing words. This danger is especially acute in studies of European courts, where there is an enormous body of doctrinal work, virtually no political science literature, and where the lessons of legal realism and of behavioralism are unknown or regarded as heretical. "The trick," as Shapiro would have it, is to be able to integrate legal materials "while maintaining an outsider's perspectives."[48] It may go without saying that the maintenance of "observer status" may be especially important to comparativists, because most work on foreign courts is already doctrinal and participatory, but also because active intervention has, for sound reasons, largely been discredited. This is not the same thing as claiming that normative issues are unimportant, or that an observer is or can be "neutral."

Second, focus on cognitive structures—those "patterns of rhetorical legitimation characteristic of certain traditions of political discourse or the sorts of associated values found in popular 'belief systems'"[49]—threatens to reinvent the political culture dilemma. Society was once filled with groups acting according to a variety of conflicting interests; this view has now given way to one of a world of cognitive structures which political actors—whether official or not—presumably carry around in their heads and which shape their behavior. We might ask: Is there any social interest or political behavior *not* associated with a cognitive structure? If the answer is no, the novelty of this aspect of new institutionalism is semantic not theoretical. The solution must be found in research design, in bounding the relevant political universe. Cognitive structures are in essence ideologies—norms of behavior and values which not only shape activity, but also help to explain, and to justify it. *For this study*, at least, *of special importance are politicolegal ideologies that may be said to dwell in institutional space, and to cluster around points of institutional interaction.* By grounding ideological issues in meaningful structural settings, the contours of normative debate are made more visible, and the terms of that debate more significant.

The Birth of Judicial Politics in France

What follows constitutes the first in-depth case study of the political behavior and impact of the French Constitutional Council. Before turning to the structural organization of the book, a number of preliminary remarks are in order. First, the absence of a social science literature on French constitutional politics presents the American political scientist with certain critical choices. On the one hand, one could proceed along lines already traced by American public lawyers, using the French case to validate, refute, or otherwise refine hypotheses and conceptual constructs developed in literature on the U.S. Supreme Court and judicial review. On the other hand, one could approach the French Constitutional Council more skeptically, as potentially more unlike than like the U.S. Supreme Court. I have chosen the second way. New institutions are often new because they do not easily fit into the theoretical paradigms or orthodox classifications derived from scholarly work on older institutions. This should not surprise: many modern institutions—the Council of the European Community and the U.S. Federal Trade Commission, for example—do not. My contention is that a certain theoretical naivety is in order. That is, we may come much closer to the truth about the European constitutional courts if we do not impose such categories and concepts as separation of powers, judicial review, judicial independence, parliamentary sovereignty, and so on, from the outside and from the outset. Each may indeed be useful analytic and descriptive tools. But they are also heavily laden with resonances built up in non-European contexts, and some of these the Europeans themselves sought quite consciously to transcend. Still, important scholarly debates about American judicial policymaking and review are explicitly assessed from a comparative perspective in virtually every chapter.

Second, the French Constitutional Council first attracted my attention in 1985 precisely because it was clearly in the throes of profound transformation from a passive, even docile body to an assertive and powerful policymaker. To some extent, rapid institutional change subverts certain tenets of orthodox, social science research design. A central concern of political science is, of course, the building of empirical theory by the generation of hypotheses; these hypotheses are then tested against bodies of data chosen for their potential to yield deviant outcomes. Causal hypotheses are, however, necessarily put forward in an "all other things being equal" form. That is, in a world of multiple causations, we may have confidence that X caused Y only to the extent that we are able to hold other potentially independent variables constant. Political scientists have relied a great deal on institutions to provide this control. That is, institutions—by which I mean certain regularities of thought and behavior—have provided us with relatively fixed and known settings for the study of political interaction. It follows that in many instances a relatively thorough understanding of institutions is prerequisite to hypothesis formation and testing. It also follows that in the absence of such an understanding, the social scientist must undertake careful, sometimes descriptive, research into the origins and development of the institution under study. This is all the more true if political scientists wish to nominate institutions and institutional interaction as themselves independent variables, and individual political behavior and policy outputs as dependent variables.

For both of these reasons, the research presented here was not therefore driven by existent theory. Rather my central purpose was to examine the birth and subsequent evolution of a new institution. As this institution developed and was brought into closer and more sustained interaction with other, long-established institutions, an entirely new, relatively stable repertoire of political ideas and behaviors emerged. In carefully examining these regularities, I am (1) laying the groundwork for forming and testing hypotheses about French constitutional politics, and (2) establishing how and to what extent the French experience can and ought to be compared with other constitutional courts found in the world.

The book is divided into three parts. Part I establishes the historical setting and contextual backdrop to the study. Chapter 1 focuses on the 1789–1958 period, identifies two meaningful cognitive structures, and describes their interaction. These institutional ideologies are shown to be coherent, long-lived, and relatively autonomous from each other. At the same time, they are not separate, since each yields radically opposed conceptions of (1) the proper relationship between legal and political authority, and (2) the role and function of the judiciary. The first is called simply the ideology of the *general will*. According to this ideology, sovereignty is expressed most concretely by statute, and judicial review is therefore explicitly precluded: judges are expected to apply statutes in the course of resolving legal conflicts, but they may not "interpret" the work of legislators. The second ideology, a founding, constitutive component of French legal consciousness, is that of *constitutionalism*: the belief that statutes must conform to a judicially elaborated higher law if they are to be valid and therefore legally binding. In roughly 1890, when public law became an autonomous branch of the law in France, law professors actively began to resist the principle of statutory sovereignty, to articulate a set of super-legislative legal norms and principles, and to call upon judges to assert powers of judicial review in order to defend them. The movement largely failed, but the creation of the Constitutional Council in 1958 brought these two ideologies in open and direct confrontation.

Chapters 2 and 3 examine the creation, constitutional mandate, and subsequent evolution of the Constitutional Council. Chapter 2 focuses in detail on the framers intentions in establishing the Council in 1958, and on the body's structural characteristics, recruitment patterns, and jurisdiction. Chapter 3 traces the political evolution of the Council as a policymaker. In its first decade, the Council behaved as a dutiful servant of the executive, defending the president and his government against any incursion by parliament on executive prerogatives. The Council's second decade were dominated by two events which, taken together, transformed the Council's institutional role. In 1971, and for the first time, the Council declared a statute drafted and supported by the executive unconstitutional and, at the same time, incorporated into the constitution an extensive bill of rights. In 1974, a constitutional amendment granted the power to petition the Council for a ruling on pending legislation to opposition parliamentarians. In consequence, the post-1974 period is one of increasing judicial–political interaction, and of recurring judicial–political confrontation after the Socialist's victories of 1981. While focusing on these and other events, the chapter examines virtually every major Council decision during the 1958–87 period.

Chapter 4 examines the remarkable development of doctrinal attitudes toward the Council. In brief, the public law community moved from fundamental, organic opposition to this new form of Bonapartist "political review," to grudging support, and finally to militant defense. Supporters of the Council, heartened by its dramatic incorporation and development of a charter of rights and some notable displays of independence during the 1970s, worked first to convince a majority of the public law community that the body was more judicial than political. They then worked to convince politicians that the Council's role was an unambiguously positive one, even for those who protested the loudest against it. By the end of the 1981–87 period, the symbiotic relationship between the Council and the legal community was firmly established. For public lawyers, the Council provided the public law discipline with an institutional base for the founding of a dense doctrinal discourse, and therefore for the building of constitutional law. For the Council, the support of the legal community, manifested in doctrinal construction, increasingly became a primary source of legitimacy and of the defense of constitutional review—but only to the extent that the Council was attendant to established judicial norms. In this chapter and in the case studies contained in Part II, I show that the Council's jurisprudence, in both style (language and decision making) and substance (who wins, loses, and why), can not be understood absent attention to the influence of legal scholarship.

Chapter 4 is also devoted to an analysis and critique of existing literature which seeks to explain French constitutional politics. After examining the basic structure of this discourse, I focus on two prevalent "theses" concerning the Constitutional Council's role and impact during the crucial 1981–86 period. The first, originally formulated with reference to the 1982 nationalization decision, argues that the Council functions more as a legitimator of than as an obstacle to governmental reforms. I compare the "legitimation thesis" with its counterpart in U.S. public law discourse, situate the French version within its political context, and argue the contrary: namely, that policymakers perceived the Council not as a legitimator but as an obstacle, and that the Council did not possess the prestige necessary either to counteract countermajoritarian charges or to confer legitimacy. I develop my critique of this thesis in greater detail in chapter 6, which focuses on the Socialist nationalizations. The second thesis asserts that the Council has not only played a juridicizing role but a pacifying role; in consequence, the juridicized policymaking process is now a "pacified" one, in contradistinction to the obstructionism which is generally said to characterize French parliamentary life. I argue that in juridicized processes the constitution is indeed a site for partisan conflict, but that this conflict is no less passive or pacified for being waged in constitutional terms. Chapters 5 to 8 develop this view further, and I nominate the media pluralism decisions (1984–86) discussed in chapter 7 as a crucial case study test of the pacification thesis.

Part II is devoted to in-depth empirical inquiry and analysis into the phenomenon which I have termed the juridicization of the policymaking process. Before 1981, the interaction between the Council and legislative institutions was sparse and irregular; after 1981, the Council is integrated fully into the legislative process as a highly visible and powerful actor. Chapter 5 provides a conceptual overview of juridicization during, principally, the 1981–86 period. In chapters 6 and 7, French judicial–legislative relations are clarified by empirical studies of the Council's impact—direct and indirect—on policy outcomes in two legislative sectors: (1) nationalization and privatization of industry; and, (2) the pursuit of pluralism in the print and broadcast media. Both policy areas were the focus of extensive, nonincremental reforms undertaken by governments first on the Left and then on the Right. This impact is shown to be significant and multidimensional. In chapter 8, a central claim of the book, that *the Council functions, and should be studied, as a third legislative chamber*, is elaborated and defended.

In Part III, the French experience is employed as the basis for structured comparison with the three other European courts which exercise abstract constitutional review—those of Austria, West Germany, and Spain. I review the relevant published research on the creation, activity, and policymaking impact of these courts, and compare these findings with those made in my study of the French case. I then suggest a means of conceptualizing and comparing European with American constitutional review with reference to traditional separation of powers concepts and notions of judicial and political legitimacy. In its broad contours, the study thus constitutes the initial stages of an empirically driven, incremental, middle-range theory-building project, driven by research resembling, in Lijphart's typology, the "hypothesis-generating case-study,"[50] in Eckstein's terms, a "heuristic case-study."[51]

I

INVENTING CONSTITUTIONAL REVIEW IN FRANCE

1

The Historical Tension:
Politics v. *le droit*

The development of constitutional review of legislation[1] in France constitutes an extraordinary and transformative departure from an established constitutional orthodoxy long thought to have been utterly resistant to fundamental change. In this orthodoxy, *la loi* ("statute" or "legislation")—the product of public politics—is a concrete expression of sovereignty, sovereignty to which *le droit* ("a subject matter," things "juridical")—the work of the judiciary and of legal science—is an obedient, if at times, creative servant. "If the average Frenchmen," wrote a Fourth Republic critic, "were asked, 'what is democracy?,' he would not hesitate to answer: 'It's the sovereignty of the people whose will is expressed by the majority vote of the elected assemblies.'"[2] To recognize judge-made law is to diagnose pathology,[3] and judicial review is all but unthinkable.

> A fundamental principle of French law denies judges the power to declare a statute unconstitutional or the right to refuse to apply it on the basis of its violation of the Constitution. No one questions this principle. It is so well established that successive French constitutions have seen no need to state it.[4]

In the first part of this chapter, I briefly describe how and why the hostility to judicial review in France was institutionalized as a dominant ideological dogma of political life, structuring the development of modern French judicial institutions and judicial behavior.[5] Throughout the formative period of this ideology—roughly the first two decades after the Revolution—attitudes toward the practice of judicial review formed part of a general political animosity toward *le droit* itself, and this animosity has survived into the present. In the second part, I argue that active resistance to this ideology constituted *the* central focus of an autonomous French tradition of public law. According to this tradition, which dates from before the Revolution, legislation must either conform to legal norms which are superior to it, or be juridically invalid. The great problem of public law has long been how best to develop and enforce what was argued to be the essential "sovereignty of *le droit*" in a political system manifestly hostile to constitutional review.

As the introduction suggested, a principal objective of this study is to locate and describe institutionally embedded ideologies, in this case with respect to the relationship between law and politics. These ideologies provide politicians, judges, and legal scholars with divergent normative models of appropriate political behavior, and opposed standards for assessing political legitimacy. Because in France these models have proved both coherent and remarkably stable over time, the elaboration of their origins and subsequent evolution also provides a historico-structural contextual and analytical setting particularly sensitive to change. As will become clear in this and later chapters, the intensity of the judicial–political confrontations of the 1980s and of the polemical academic and doctrinal disputes about the proper role of the Constitutional Council which accompanied them are not easily understood outside of the context which preceded the advent of the Fifth Republic.

The Ideology of the "General Will"

The separation and then subordination of *le droit* to politics is one of the more resilient and enduring legacies of the French Revolution, inscribed in one form or another in each of France's fifteen written constitutions from 1791 to 1958. The basic organizing principle is a simple one: whichever public authority controls the production of *la loi* possesses de facto the authority of the sovereign state itself, authority to which all other public officials—not least of all, judges—must submit. This principle has survived intact the long-running institutional rivalry between parliament and executive, the salient saga of French constitutional history from the Revolution to 1958. But whether essential power is located in divided, relatively weak but sovereign parliaments, or in more powerful, authoritarian administrations headed by king's ministers, emperors, or generals, *its constitutive component—control over the production of* la loi—*remains constant.* Written constitutions only reflect important shifts in the struggle for power over the legislative process, and do not disturb in any fundamental way the status of *la loi*, upon which the juridical conception of the sovereignty of the French State rests. *Constitutions fail not only to provide judges with a source of independent jurisprudential authority, they also can not be considered to limit the substantive content of legislation, including in the area of public liberties and fundamental rights.*

From the first moments of the Revolution, the Rousseauian identification of legislation with the general will, and legislators with popular sovereignty, were constitutionally enshrined,[6] producing a separation of powers doctrine which rigidly circumscribed judicial authority. During this period[7] and for at least a century thereafter, legislators considered the judiciary a corrupt and reactionary enemy of social reform, and decried the "confusion of powers" wherein judicial and law-making functions were alleged to be indistinguishable. Not surprisingly, the *parlements*, judicial institutions which exercised a form of review over royal acts under the *ancien régime*, were an early casualty; they were, for all practical purposes, abolished by the National Assembly in a decree of 1789.[8] The law of 16–24 August 1790, which remains in force today, explicitly precluded judicial review, as did a series of written constitutions beginning with that of 1791:

> Courts can not interfere with the exercising of legislative powers, suspend the application of the laws, nor can they infringe on administrative functions, or take cognizance of administrative acts of any kind.[9]

As important, given the permanence of the Napoleonic codes relative to the ephemeral nature of French constitutions, judicial review was specified as a punishable offense in the penal code.[10] With the possibility of judicial review eliminated—and not to be seriously raised again for more than a century—the path was cleared for a complete restructuring of judicial institutions.

The Judicial Function

The modern French judicial system (which would fully emerge by 1804) was constructed on the principle—itself a virtual corollary of popular sovereignty—that judges must not directly, or indirectly through interpretation, make law. Democrats and generals, parliamentarians and imperialists, did not differ in their assessments of the intrinsic virtue of this principle.[11] The law was, following Rousseau, to be codified in "simple, non-technical, and straightforward" language.[12] As a consequence, politics would be made transparent, the legitimacy of the new social compact assured, and the multitude of intermediate institutions and social practices separating the people and State, and obscuring that fundamental relationship, could be cleared away or fatally undermined. *Le droit* was thought to be one of the more mystifying of these institutions, and it was hoped and expected that lawyers, and their penchant for doctrinal commentaries and formalist discourse, would gradually obsolesce.[13] Judges could then proceed in a straightforward manner, as civil servants applying the codes.

Although reformers recognized that insuperable problems of application might arise for judges, they worked to assure that only legislators could provide stable solutions. In 1799, one such reformer put it this way:

> Only the law-maker has the authority to interpret the law. . . . Without this principle, judges would embark on a vast, unobstructed course of interpreting statutes according to their imaginations, . . . and even their passions. Judicial institutions would thus be entirely deformed. Judges would be able to substitute their will for *la loi*, . . . and establish themselves as legislators.[14]

To ensure the successful functioning of the system, two special quasi-judicial structures—one within parliamentary and one within executive space—evolved. First, because lawmakers foresaw the possibility that parliament might become paralyzed by judicial controversy, the *Tribunal de cassation* (lit. "to break," or "to quash") was established. Its role, according to the constitution of 1795,[15] is to police the courts and to defend the separation of powers by rendering void judgments "which contain any manifest contradiction with *la loi*"; cases are then returned to the court of last instance. This body was thus originally "constituted not as a court but as part of the legislature."[16] In the event of judicial intransigence, the legislator provides an authoritative interpretation binding on all other public authorities. Second, because judges in the ordinary courts were enjoined from controlling acts of governmental officials, a set of administrative courts developed within the administration itself, and under the jurisdiction of the *Conseil d'Etat.*[17]

The judge's role in this fragmented but centralized system is subservient and bureaucratic: he is "an operator of a machine designed and built by legislators."[18] The codes, being clear, literal expressions of sovereignty, must be treated as providing a series of sovereign commands binding upon the whole of the body politique. The judge may be required to verify the existence and applicability of a command, but he may not investigate the work of the legislature any further. Once verified, the statute must be considered superior to any other legal norm and applied as such. A leading decision, *Paulin* (1833),[19] provides an illustration of a clear conflict between a constitutional provision and a statute adopted subsequent to it. In this case, the newspaper, *Le National*, appealed a judgment against it on the grounds that the trial had proceeded without a jury, according to procedures established by the law of 8 October 1830. Such a trial and the law which enabled it, however, contravened the dictates of the constitution of the day (the Charter of 14 August 1830), which explicitly guaranteed jury trials in cases involving violations of the press laws. The *Cour de cassation* ruled that the law of 8 October 1830 "binds the courts," and therefore "could not be attacked before them on the basis of its unconstitutionality." The *avocat général*, while admitting the possibility that legislators might have erred in adopting legislation contrary to the charter, argued that even if such an error had been committed, "it is not for courts to judge the work of the legislator, since they have to apply the laws, even bad laws, until they have been abrogated." This functional duty in the service of *la loi* was absorbed self-consciously by judges in the ordinary as well as in appellate (*cassation*) and administrative jurisdictions: no judicial body in France has ever declared a statute unconstitutional.

Although the terms of the decision in *Paulin* express rigid constitutional orthodoxy vis-à-vis the judicial system, important differences between the parliamentary and the Bonapartist-authoritarian constitutional traditions exist with respect to attitudes toward popular sovereignty and constitutional review. In schematic terms, the parliamentary tradition derives its professed legitimacy from the direct elections of deputies to the National Assembly. It admits to no limitations on the assembly's sovereignty, and views proposals to initiate any form of constitutional review as a priori illegitimate. The Bonapartist tradition claims legitimacy on the basis of the direct relationship between the people and a leader, and on the alleged popular mandate of the latter to tame an unruly parliament, and to restore civil order. Institutions which exercise *nonjudicial* constitutional review are acceptable to the extent that they facilitate the centralization of executive authority.

The Tradition of the Sovereign Parliament

Constitutional texts and practices governing the First (1792–99), Second (1848–52), Third (1875–1940), and Fourth (1946–58) Republics unambiguously enshrine the doctrine of absolute parliamentary sovereignty. Indeed, legislative and constituent powers are either fused explicitly or confused in practice, that is, constitutions can be revised by a simple majority vote of the National Assembly. During these periods, the doctrine did not go entirely unchallenged, but practical measures to limit legislative discretion as a means of protecting fundamental rights were rarely proposed from within parliament itself,[20] and virtually never discussed formally after having been introduced. In any event, such proposals were never made by dominant coalitions in the assembly, and quashing them was therefore a simple matter. They could either be kept off of the parliamentary agenda, or a formal motion called a *quéstion préalable* (lit. "preliminary question")—whose passage automatically suspends discussion, even before it begins, of what is judged to be an *illegitimate* subject matter for parliamentary debate—could be adopted. Even initiatives which sought to create *nonjudicial* mechanisms of constitutional review have elicited such responses. During the drafting of the 1793 constitution, for example, an amendment was offered to create an elected *Grand juré*, "to guarantee citizens against the oppression of the legislative body and the executive."[21] The *quéstion préalable*, which passed without dissent, was framed in these Rousseauian terms:

> . . . considering that a court of this type already exists—it's called public opinion—and that a new such court would be disastrous for the freedom of opinion of the legislative body . . . ; and considering that the People are always here, that they examine the conduct of their representatives and possess the power to punish them for their abuses; I insist that this amendment be rejected.[22]

During periods in which legislative representatives themselves were engaged in the writing of constitutions, debates on the establishment of some form of constitutional review have at times proved more open (if no more successful) than the *Grand juré* scheme. This was especially true of the debates on the drafting of the constitution of the Fourth Republic. As discussed later, throughout the first half of the twentieth century, legal scholarship had noisily championed the cause of judicial review, converting certain reactionary and openly *antiparliamentary* political forces along the way. These groups, alienated by what they thought to be the permanent dominance of parliament by socialist sympathizers, regularly introduced bills to establish an American-style supreme court.[23] The institution of judicial review had become, for them, a necessary means to protect the "indivisible trinity" proclaimed by the 1789

Declaration of the Rights of Man—"the Law, the Individual, and Property"[24]—against assaults from revolutionary syndicalism, anticlericals, nationalizations, and income taxes. The American experience of the late nineteenth and early twentieth centuries, at least as they understood it, was proof enough of the efficacy of such an arrangement.[25] None of these proposals were ever debated. Indeed, it was not until the drafting of the constitution of the Fourth Republic (by the 1945–46 constitutional assemblies) that proponents of constitutional review would have an opportunity to put forward their views.

The final text of the 1946 constitution is the product of a complicated set of compromises among more than two dozen political parties, each seeking to protect their electoral positions and institutional power bases.[26] For the most part, the compromises reached were inconclusive and, once in place, the regime quickly reverted to the Third Republic model of a flexible and evolving constitution. In fact, if not in word (given the existence of a new upper chamber of parliament, "the Council of the Republic"), the constitution enshrined the "sovereignty of the National Assembly to the exclusion of any other institution."[27] As will be discussed in greater detail later, substantive limitations on this sovereignty were discussed. In the end, a proposed declaration of rights contained in the first draft of the constitution was dropped entirely after that constitution's rejection in referendum, and a new text, reaffirming the "people's" commitment to the 1789 Declaration of the Rights of Man, was relegated to a preamble of dubious constitutional status. Although this was done at the insistence of the Right, the preamble also proclaimed fidelity to a long list of often contradictory social principles dear to the Left. Not least because the conflict over the preamble proved so explosive, no mechanism to ensure its respect gained acceptance.

The same pattern of inconclusive compromise gave birth to the bizarre Constitutional Committee, an institution created to exercise severely limited powers of what might be called constitutional review. The constitutional assemblies however did not call it that. In December 1945, a committee of the first assembly discussed a proposal to establish a supreme court, based largely on the American model. On what appears to be the first occasion of a vote to institute judicial review in France, proponents were overwhelmed, 39–2. In April 1946, elements within the Right again tried to gain support for a supreme court, this time to be composed of four politicians chosen by parliament, and four judges to be selected by the *Conseil d'Etat* and the *Cour de cassation*, with the president of the Republic acting as president and ninth member. This proposal was never brought to a vote. Opponents instead passed, 289–259, a vote explicitly repudiating the principle of "constitutional review" (*le contrôle de la constitutionnalité des lois*).[28]

If by 1946 *judicial* review had been hopelessly discredited as reactionary and "anti-democratic,"[29] a significant part of the second assembly was willing to admit that the constitutional text, at least in principle and in the context of the emergent Fourth Republic, enjoyed status superior to ordinary law.[30] For many, this admission did not offend traditional notions of popular sovereignty and social contract, not least, because of the special role accorded to the

People: after all, it was a referendum which had enabled the direct election of the constitutional assembly, and therefore the drafting of a constitution, and the assembly's work was to be subject to the people's approval in another referendum. On the other hand, the majority of the assembly had clearly refused to support any limitation of the legislative authority of the National Assembly. Curiously, if understandable to those who could follow the tortuously convoluted logic, a restricted notion of constitutional review was eventually linked to the constitutional revision process, and a series of proposals were introduced to institute a kind of "popular constitutional review," to be exercised ultimately by the people in referenda. By linking the promulgation of hypothetically "unconstitutional laws" to a successful amending process, the sovereign status of *la loi*, and therefore of parliament, could be preserved without undermining the regime's source of legitimacy.

The result was yet another tangled, ambiguous compromise, culminating in the creation of the Constitutional Committee—composed of thirteen politicians—with power, given certain conditions, to review the constitutionality of legislation.[31] The committee's mandate, however, was severely restricted by the fact that the constitution expressly excluded from its jurisdiction the whole of the preamble. André Philip had successfully argued that to do otherwise would "be dangerous for democracy," and would lead to referendums on the most controversial of legislative matters involving conflicts between social concerns and individual rights—"such as the press and nationalizations."[32] What was settled on might be characterized as merely a polite bow to the notion of "popular review," a cautious mechanism whose activation was dependent on an improbable series of events.

According to the constitutional provisions governing "Constitutional Revision", *if* a majority of the upper house believes that the National Assembly has passed legislation which violates the constitution, it could ask the president of the Republic to convene the Constitutional Committee. The committee then is required to seek a compromise between the two chambers but, *if* consultations fail, the committee must rule on the legislation's constitutionality. *If* the legislation is then judged to be unconstitutional by the committee, it is sent back to the National Assembly for a new reading. Finally, *if* the assembly subsequently adopts the original law a second time, then the constitution must be revised in order to enable its promulgation. The full revision process in the case of ineradicable conflict between the assembly and other institutions is nearly as conditional as the review procedure, but will ultimately result in a constitutional amendment which is submitted to the People in a popular referendum.[33]

Not surprisingly, the system was never required to go that far. The committee was convened on only one occasion: a compromise between the two chambers was worked out almost effortlessly, and no ruling as to the constitutionality of the proposed legislation was rendered.[34] Furthermore, although two revisions of the constitution did occur during the Fourth Republic, both were accomplished by the procedures fixed for the passage of ordinary legislation, that is, after majority votes of parliament.[35]

The Bonapartist Tradition

In the Bonapartist tradition, parliament is viewed as a source of instability whose work, in modern parlance, must be "rationalized"—brought under the centralized management of the executive. The representative legislature all but disappears as a focal point of state power: the *Conseil d'Etat*,[36] as the executive's advisory body, drafts legislation and controls parliament's right to amend it, and a superlegislative body (like the *Tribunat*) or a government *detached* from the legislative body controls the legislative agenda and the work of the assembly itself. In both periods of imperial ascendancy and rule (1799–1814 and 1852–75), a form of political constitutional review existed.

In 1799, the Abbé Sieyès, whose proposals to establish special constitutional bodies had been rejected in 1793 and 1795,[37] succeeded in enshrining review powers in a new institution, the Senate.[38] According to the constitutional acts of 1799 and 1804 (the latter of which established the empire),[39] the Senate—composed of eighty or so political appointees who served for life—was charged with the defense of "public liberties," and possessed the power "to annul any act referred to it as unconstitutional by the government or the *Tribunat*." Such referrals[40] would suspend the promulgation of legislation until the Senate ruled, but once promulgated the legislation was immune from scrutiny. Although it disappeared with the empire in 1815, Napoleon III revived the institution in nearly the same terms after the *coup d'état* of the eighteenth *Brumaire*, but the role and functioning of the two were virtually identical.[41]

The imperial Senate never annulled a law or executive act, despite the fact that decrees regularly violated constitution texts.[42] Bonaparte, however, *did* use the Senate, if for seemingly unconstitutional purposes—to overturn judicial decisions he did not like and "to fill in gaps in the constitution."[43] Indeed, its essential function was to reflect the power of the dictator himself, and to house a new aristocracy for postrepublican times.[44] Not surprisingly, constitutional specialists have unanimously condemned the experiment. The Senate, Deslandres lamented, "was to be the defender of the constitution, . . . seemingly the final holder of sovereignty. But with appearances, its powers stopped. It never exercised any positive function and participated in none. It was a body . . . without any contact with reality, operating in a void."[45] Thiry assesses the institution's work generally as "treasonous," but also reports that "an army general, a member of the Senate" once said to Bonaparte "that he would not have to ask for more than four men and a corporal to put the Senate at his feet."[46]

In summary, the ideology of the general will is founded on the organic unity of legislation and law, with its attendant confusion of legislative and constituent powers. *La loi*, accordingly, organizes the juridical framework of the French state. The judicial function is to defend the domain of *la loi*, not least, by guaranteeing the superiority of statute in any conceivable hierarchy of laws. While at different times the constitution has been considered an element of this hierarchy, legislative authorities alone possess the authority to ensure its viability as such. Institutions possessing the powers of constitutional review have at least in theory existed, but only for brief periods. Moreover, *such review institutions were explicitly denied a judicial function and did not subvert the separation of powers doctrine: they operated within legislative space, and no integration with the judicial system was intended or desired.* Although inoperant in practice, "political" review is not considered neutral; its introduction is instead a product of specific historicopolitical contexts. As seen by the Left and by advocates of parliamentary sovereignty, these review mechanisms form part of the Bonapartist, *coup d'état* constitutional tradition; as seen by certain elements of the Right and by enemies of parliament, they are instruments of stabilization for new, more centralized regimes after periods of social turbulence had allegedly debilitated parliament and discredited the French State.

The Ideology of Constitutionalism

According to French orthodoxy, it might appear that the judicial function can only be a negligible one: "Legislative positivism, the dogma of the separation of powers, the ideology of codification, the attitude toward interpretation of statutes . . . all these tend to diminish the judge and to glorify the legislator," writes Merryman in his work on the civil law tradition.[47] But as that author takes pains to point out, appearances can deceive. In the rest of this chapter, I describe and evaluate what will be shown to be a "relatively"—and meaningfully—"autonomous" French legal tradition. By relative autonomy, I mean the extent to which *le droit*—the complex interaction of legal institutions, jurisprudence, and legal scholarship—does not conform to the classical model described earlier, evolving, instead, its own internally derived set of moral and professional standards of conduct. A wide range of judicial activities may provide evidence of autonomy, each likely flowing from one common source: the deeply held philosophical attachment to a teleological notion of the law as a holistic system. Because the purpose of *le droit* is to perfect this system, it is thought both natural and necessary to insulate the law from the rest of the world. There is, accordingly, a deep animosity to the incursion of "politics"—partisan passions, goings-on in parliament, and the like—because politics threatens to undermine this effort at perfection.

This may explain to a large extent why public law—constitutional and administrative law—has long suffered from a relative lack of prestige within the ranks of the French legal community. Because private, especially economic, relations were traditionally considered to be outside the interference of government, the civil (or "private") law became the center of gravity for legal philosophy and science. Indeed, the civil code served almost "a constitutional function" for *le droit*, being "the area of law in which the sole function of government was the recognition and enforcement of private rights."[48] In the nineteenth century, judges and publicists working in this area identified and then consciously exploited the relationship between judicial authority and the defense of fundamental, that is, "natural," rights, and were largely successful in reestablishing judicial primacy over interpretation.[49] In contrast, the public lawyer's universe is a provisional one, continually being scrambled by first one manifestation of political power, and then recast by another. In it, a stable set of public liberties can be located only with great difficulty, and are seemingly impossible to defend.

If public law judges and publicists were in 1958 arguably the least autonomous part of the French legal community, their achievements had not been incidental. Due largely to their efforts, the special appellate and administrative organs first created to enforce the doctrine of the separation of powers are today unambiguously considered courts. Both the *Cour de cassation* and the *Conseil d'Etat* gradually expanded their control over a wide range of judicial activities, and their jurisprudence is considered to be a source of law.[50] Moreover, while seemingly dependent on the legislature for guidance and legitimacy, judges of the public law also struggled to insulate their activities from the vagaries of the political world.

The most visible evidence of the relative autonomy of public law is to be found in doctrinal materials. In France, as in other civil law countries, the ideology of codification did not succeed in eliminating legal discourse.[51] On the contrary, the legal scholar and not the judge or even the politician reemerged as the principal protagonist in the ongoing project to perfect the legal system, facilitated by the community's insularity. In fact, an extraordinary renaissance of public law occurred during the second decade of the Third Republic, and the discipline subsequently entered a golden age. I can only offer some tentative explanations for the causes of this renaissance. First, although the prior century was an unstable one—no constitution had lasted more than fourteen years—by at least the 1890s a remarkable consensus had developed on the utility of the constitutional laws of 1875 (perhaps because they were so flexible). By the early twentieth century, the Third Republic and its constitutional life had come to be seen as a natural state of affairs. Second, a series of laws which sought to guarantee what in France are called *public liberties* were passed—on free association, union membership, freedom of the press, and so on—and these came to be seen as performing the function of a judicially applicable bill of rights. Third, and partly in consequence of the above, the *Conseil d'Etat* was gradually shaping a more aggressive, even activist, judicial function of its own—it was expressly made a jurisdiction in 1872, and asserted for itself independence from the ministries in its case law in 1889;[52] it was thus able to shake off some of the taint of its imperial origins, and to provide a stable source of doctrinal commentary. Fourth, the stability of the constitutional regime during this period did not necessarily make for a period of social harmony; indeed, new social movements, particularly on the Left, were perceived by legal scholars as significant threats. Many of these scholars worked to show that a fundamental purpose of *le droit* was to develop, as a means to achieve social order, what was alleged to be the law's inherent function of social integration.[53]

In any event, during this time public law began to be taught as a separate branch of the law, and doctrine began to evolve independently. Specialized journals appeared, treatises multiplied and lengthened, and scholars, drifting away from projects oriented primarily to order the chaos of constitutional history, became consumed with the study of jurisprudence, especially the *Conseil d'Etat's*. As will be shown, *statutes ceased to be recognized as dominant sources of law*, freeing doctrinal commentary to lobby courts, often to convince judges to rebel against the traditional model of the judicial function and the strict separation of powers. In sum, this revival constituted no less than a self-conscious movement to increase the prestige of public law and the social power of public lawyers. The founder and first editor of the *Revue du droit public*, lamenting the fact that all too often politicians and journalists ignore *la doctrine*, explained the *Revue*'s "program" in the journal's inaugural issue (1884):

> We hope that the idea of public law, that the forms of public law, that the procedures of public law will penetrate more deeply, each and every day, into constitutional, administrative, and international matters. Then and only then can any institution acquire the force of resistance that will permit it to brave the storms which confront it.[54]

This formative period in the history and sociology of modern French public law[55] yielded a coherent argument for judicial autonomy, founded on the rejection of the ideology of the general will and its attendant prohibition against judicial review. This argument can be broken down into three main elements: (1) the belief, traceable to legal theorists of the *ancien régime*, that the constitution enjoys a special status as "higher law" in any hierarchy of legal norms, and that the effective protection of that hierarchy by constitutional review is essential to the achievement of social order; (2) the beliefs that judicial review, as exercised by the regular judiciary in the discharge of the normal judicial function of hearing litigation, is the only acceptable form of constitutional review, and that judges are morally and professionally required to begin doing so immediately; and (3) the effort to show, in doctrinal commentaries and treatises on constitutional law, that not only is the evolution toward judicial review both natural and inevitable, but judges have already begun doing judicial review without yet acknowledging it. Each of these elements will be examined. It is important to stress, however, that because this discussion focuses on the attitude of the public law community to the issue of judicial review—a unifying issue—the extent to which this community actively disputed many other matters of legal science, philosophy, and jurisprudence is obscured.

The Hierarchy of Legal Norms and the "Necessity" of Judicial Review

The inclination to construct and then secure hierarchies of legal norms is a central focus of French legal consciousness. The logical result of the statutory sovereignty is to make such efforts relatively simple: statute takes precedent over administrative decree, decree takes precedent over a local regulation, and so on. But this was not always the case—the pre-Revolutionary notion of limitations to absolute monarchical sovereignty, flowing from the scholarly development of "natural law," is an example. What is remarkable about modern (i.e., post-1890) legal discourse is the extent to which publicists embraced neo-natural law ideals, seizing upon the rejection of the official hierarchy as inimical to *le droit* itself. As Léon Duguit, arguably France's most influential public law scholar through the early decades of the twentieth century, wrote in 1917,

> . . . the persistent effort of French judicial doctrine has ever been, from 1789 to the present time, to find the true juristic basis for the legal limitation upon the power of the state, and to insure its sanction. Its conceptions have been diverse. . . . But the end in view has always been the same; namely, to prove that the powers of the state are limited by a jural principle (*une règle de droit*) superior to the state itself. Does there exist a jural principle superior to the state, which forbids it from doing certain things and commands it to do certain others? *If the answer is no, then there is no public law, since no act or refusal to act on the part of the state will be contrary to law* [parentheses in original translation, emphases added].[56]

And elsewhere:

> . . . we believe firmly that there is a rule of law above the individual and the state, above the rulers and the ruled; a rule which is compulsory on one and on the other; and we hold that if there is such a thing as sovereignty of the state it is juridically limited by this rule of law. . . . [T]o express this in words is that of legal art. If this is too much for legal science and legal art, their study is not worth a moment's effort.[57]

The major figures in public law scholarship during this period worked to reconstruct the foundations of their field by positing the existence of an overarching higher law, to be elaborated and refined by *le droit*, by scholarly activity. Although the pre-Revolutionary opposition of ideas of natural law and political sovereignty had seemingly been obliterated by the orthodoxy of the general will—which posits that legal and popular sovereignty can never conflict—these scholars grafted their project onto deep roots in the French legal tradition.

Certain physiocratic legal scholars, like Dupont, Le Trosne, Le Vauguyon, and Le Mercier, had refined fully developed theories of judicial authority based on just such notions before being overwhelmed by the events of the Revolution.[58] In these theories, "the laws of absolute and essential justice" were considered to be God's law, presocial and unwritten, which judges alone had the capacity to discover, interpret, and apply. In the domain of positive law, the constitutional laws—those which establish the organization of the State and the procedures for legislating—were thought supreme and the foundation of all social order, and thus no ordinary law could be considered to have legal status if it did not conform to them. This hierarchy structured conceptions of the judicial role: judges, it was argued, had an "inescapable," even "religious," duty to refuse to enforce unconstitutional laws. "Ignominy and disgrace would be heaped upon [their] heads"—worse, the social order would collapse—if they failed to fulfill this duty.[59] While these notions lost their force during the century after the Revolution, major figures such as the Abbé de Sieyès[60] and Benjamin Constant[61] gave them periodic salience. Both echoed Sieyes's famous phrase iterated before Marshall handed down *Marbury*: "A constitution is a body of obligatory laws, or it is nothing,"[62] and therefore must not be "reduced to [the status of] a chapter in the civil code."[63]

No major figure in French public law after 1890 took issue with the logic of Sieyes and Marshall. Doctrinal commentators on the *written* sources of law begin with the constitution—because it establishes and delegates public authority—and not the statute; Hauriou states,

> The national Constitution, being the most direct expression of national sovereignty is the supreme law of the land. This superiority consists of two elements: (1) the Constitution delegates powers to the representative institutions, which the Constitution has established; (2) the Constitution is superior to ordinary law, a superiority which logically leads to a system in which provisions of ordinary laws which are contrary to the text or the principles of the Constitution are invalid.[64]

This point is made dogmatically, even by treatise writers who *oppose* as a practical matter (because *not* in principle) the introduction of judicial review into France.

Given the almost fanatical worship of statute on the part of judges in the system, the reverence for *la loi* was viewed as the great obstacle to be overcome by *le droit*.[65] The enemy of the movement was Rousseau, "the father of 'Jacobin despotism,' and 'Caesarian dictatorship.'"[66] "We must attack at its root the belief in the absolute power of the general will," Hauriou writes. "Few false doctrines have had so evil an influence as that doctrine."[67] Duguit set about to show his colleagues that the orthodox, "metaphysical conception" of *la loi*, according to which statutes constitute "the formulated command of [indivisible] sovereign power," could no longer be sustained. By "metaphysical," Duguit simply meant the traditional doctrinal notion of the state as a sovereign unity, or "person," against which he offered his "realist" notion of the state as a bureaucratic organization made up of many individuals:

> A statute is simply the expression of the *individual will* of the men who make it, . . . the private members of a legislative body. Beyond that we are in the realm of fiction [emphases added].[68]

And Gaston Jèze, the editor of the *Revue du droit public* echoed Duguit in 1924:

> *La loi* is not the expression of the national will; in France, *la loi* is the manifestation of the will of the individuals—deputies and senators—who have voted for it. Deputies and senators say of course that they represent the national will. But this assertion can not change the reality of the situation. Juridically, *la loi* is only the manifestation of a certain number of individuals.[69]

This "realist" notion of the statute expresses a deep mistrust and a scarcely veiled animosity toward parliament, or what doctrine calls political authority. Because they are made by politicians—"whose technical competence might be mediocre and whose impartiality and spirit of justice might be questioned"— statutes, asserted Jèze, "no longer merit . . . the fetishism and the idolatry with which they have been invested."

The great difficulty with the movement's position flowed from the hard reality that the constitutional laws of 1875 were wholly inadequate as sources for the substantive limitation of legislative sovereignty. As sceptics pointed out, they contained no reference to any body of fundamental rights or general principles of law, "formulated no judicial rules," and were "vague and general" even as to procedural requirements. Worse, where they were quite explicit, they reinforced rather then eroded parliamentary sovereignty—simple legislation was all that was required to amend them, for example.[70] The movement countered by arguing that the constitution contained judicially discoverable, *nonwritten* provisions, as well as the 1789 Declaration of the Rights of Man. Hauriou's argument on the former is representative:

> It would be an error to believe that the principle of constitutional supremacy only included that which is written in the Constitution; it includes many other things, for example, . . . the principles of individualism [*l'ordre individual- iste*] which are at the foundation of the State. . . . These principles constitute a kind of constitutional legitimacy which take their place above even the written constitution.[71]

As for the declaration, Duguit argued that since it had been adopted before any written constitution, and had never been abrogated, it must be considered an immovable feature of the constitutional landscape.[72] Hauriou, for his part, called the declaration a constituent part of a permanent "social constitution," "the basis of public law," and thus higher than even the written, "political" constitution.[73]

No violence is done to this doctrinal movement by describing it in terms the physiocrats would recognize—in terms of natural law.[74] It is, in essence, a natural law renaissance.[75] For its proponents, the constitution is only partially and imperfectly written; the solemn function of *le droit* and judicial authority is to complete and perfect it by, in essence, "constitutionalizing" natural law. Once the constitution is expanded in this way, once higher law is made the source of all legitimate authority, all laws, including the constitutional text, must conform to them, or be themselves unconstitutional. And since the development of the unwritten, extra- or superconstitutional law is a domain wholly within the purview of *le droit*, *le droit* must be recognized as a sovereign authority in itself.[76] "This school does not recognize the sovereignty of the State, but only the sovereignty of *le droit*, and this formula deserves approval," wrote Roubier. From this perspective, neo-natural law doctrines may be char- acterized as functionally equivalent to rule of law notions in Anglo-American legal theory. That is, they both attempt to rationalize the coexistence of a system of judicially enforced limitations on public authority on the one hand with a sovereign lawmaker on the other (a task made more difficult for the French in the absence of the legitimizing notion, inherent in common law doctrines on the judicial function, that judges ought to and do participate in the making of constitutional law).

Against this onslaught, the traditional separation of powers doctrine crumbled and was swept away, and with it the illegitimate prohibition against judicial review. "Any unconstitutional law," Duguit asserted, "contrary to a superior principle of *le droit*, inscribed or not, . . . written or not . . . is a law without effect, a law without executive force," and one which people, most of all judges, ought to disobey.[77] Whereas opponents of judicial review had long argued that the review of legislation would lead to legal uncertainty and social chaos, Duguit and others turned the argument on its head: disorder is brought about by legislators who disregard and violate the "objective" norms discovered and developed by *le droit*.[78] Judicial review, on the other hand, has the power to reinforce or restore systemic legitimacy in the face of despotism. In the absence of review, legislation which violates "inalienable and imprescriptible natural rights" may be promulgated, and its enforcement might lead, or even require, citizens to exercise their natural right to revolt against an unjust regime.[79]

The dominant model of judicial authority for French public law specialists was provided by America.[80] *From at least 1890 until well after 1958, virtually every major figure in French public law had condemned the very idea of a special constitutional court detached from the judiciary, and instead praised the American system.*[81] "Political review," that exercised by *any* nonjudicial body without reference to concrete cases, was condemned as inadequate because hopelessly ineffective in the past. But as important, it was argued that if a special constitutional court was to be established, and was to operate effectively, the practice of constitutional review would be continuously embroiled in political and partisan controversy. It was therefore thought necessary that review be separated from the legislative function. Given the present state of constitutional politics in France, it is worth quoting Hauriou on the subject at length:

> We condemn absolutely any system of constitutional review by a political organ because such review must be both independent from and inoffensive to the government. . . . Such review, of whatever type, which occurs during the law-making process, *and which hinders or even delays a law's promulgation*, risks provoking the worst conflicts, because it confronts parliament in the heat of that process. One of the wisest policies of *le droit* consists in refusing to intervene . . . until after the fires have calmed, and political passions are no longer engaged. Premature intervention would lead to conflict without end, and would compromise the judge himself in [partisan] battles. We must therefore wait until the law has been promulgated, and sometimes long afterwards, before the question of its constitutionality is to be raised. . . . It's for this reason that we are obliged to turn toward the judge, if still taking precautions to see that his role does not become political, that is, by rigorously restricting it to the litigation process.[82]

American constitutional theory provided the movement with a powerful reinterpretation of the separation of powers. The classic texts (the law of 1790 and the constitution of 1791 quoted earlier), it was argued, were either no longer applicable to the "modern judiciary," or only prohibited a priori control by judges, that is, judges were enjoined from "suspending the execution" of duly adopted laws, quite a different thing from refusing to apply them in the judicial domain.[83] A posteriori control by ordinary or administrative judges in the normal discharge of their functions, however, violates no separation of powers principle—control constitutes instead that principle's fulfillment. The traditional American doctrine, as understood at that time, is imported in its entirety and applied to the contemporary situation in France; Duguit stated,

> It has long been accepted dogma that no court could accept a plea of unconstitutionality and refuse to apply a formal statute even where they considered it unconstitutional. . . . The principle of the separation of powers leads to an entirely different solution. A court which refuses to apply a statute on the grounds of unconstitutionality does not interfere with the exercise of legislative powers. It does not suspend its application. The law remains untouched. . . . It is simply because the judicial power is distinct from and independently equal to the two others that it cannot be forced to apply the statutes it deems unconstitutional.[84]

Duguit and his colleagues, believing that judges would be "led" by doctrine and "the sheer force of events to this conclusion,"[85] began to view the direct lobbying of judges to be an essential function of scholarly activity.

The movement worked to show judges that doctrine required that they exercise substantive judicial review, and that they had already begun doing so but apparently did not yet know it.[86] The most important line of decisions providing such an interpretation involved the right to strike of public employees heard before the *Conseil d'Etat*, beginning with *Winkell*, in 1909.[87] That case involved a provision of a 1905 law which required the government to notify certain state employees in writing of reasons for impending dismissal, before such dismissal could take place. Winkell was fired, along with a large number of his postal service colleagues, after having taken part in a postal strike, and he brought action on the grounds that he had received no prior notification. The *Conseil d'Etat*, appealing to no source of law and making no other attempt to justify its decision, ruled simply that the law was not applicable in cases of strikes involving public employees—despite the fact that the law contained no such exception.

Hauriou (whose influence was enormous, not least because he wrote the doctrinal notes on administrative jurisprudence published in the quasi-official *Recueil Sirey* and in the *Revue du droit public* for more than three decades) argued that, if correct, the decision to refuse to apply the law was understandable only if the *Conseil d'Etat* believed that the law violated higher, constitutional principles. Hauriou found these principles in certain articles of the constitutional law of 25 February 1875 which, *inter alia*, gave the executive authority to "name civil employees," and which, Hauriou inferred, charged it with the responsibility to ensure "the continuity of public service." Although in a long line of subsequent cases, the *Conseil d'Etat* did not admit that it had or was engaged in constitutional review, it appeared to adopt Hauriou's line of reasoning, and even his language. Hauriou, Duguit, and others then argued that the judges "without expressly admitting it, and perhaps without even admitting it to themselves, have opened the way to judicial review."[88]

In the 1920s, this campaign achieved an extraordinarily high degree of visibility, and began to be debated publicly in the press.[89] Outsiders took notice. In 1921, Edouard Lambert's study of American judicial politics—"The Government of Judges and the Struggle Against Social Legislation"—appeared, and quickly became essential reading.[90] Lambert's work radically departed from traditional French public law scholarship in that it eschewed formalist exegesis of jurisprudence and abstract legal categories. He focused instead on the socialization and ideological orientation of judges, and examined the social impact of a broad class of judicial decisions, notably those which had blocked whole categories of economic legislation—regulating the workplace and strikes, establishing workman's compensation, and the like—by a coherent if restrictive judicial reading of the due process clause (the jurisprudence of "substantive due process"). Lambert's thesis was twofold: 1) by virtue of their social origins, educations, and recruitment, judges were always reactionary, to the point of being dangerous to the proper evolution of society; and, 2) judicial review, because it inevitably leads to judge-made constitutions, must also inevitably give effective governing power to courts. (Lambert introduced the term *gouvernement des juges* into French parlance.)

Lambert, responding directly to what he called "the skillful and perseverant campaign . . . to introduce into our constitutional life [American-style] judicial review," wished to show the likely political outcome if the movement were to succeed.[91] Pointing out that *le droit* in France was dominated by the conservative, individualist notions of classic liberalism and neo-natural law, Lambert's conclusion was unequivocal:

> The day when the French judiciary acquires the power of judicial review, it will discover in our declaration of rights all of the constituent pieces of what I have described as due process of law, and which have provided the means by which the American judiciary to force the legislature to bow to their supremacy. The same patient and surreptitious play of constitutional decision-making, which permitted American jurisprudence . . . to enclose the legislature in a network of constitutional limitations which every day becomes more dense, will probably enable ours to bind the French legislature as quickly and quite as tightly.[92]

French political life would be permanently altered: *laissez-faire* capitalism and its attendant morality would be frozen judicially while society evolved away from both; working-class movements would be frustrated and become dangerously alienated; and political parties would seek to control the recruitment of judges as a necessary means to ensure the success of their programs.[93]

Lambert's book had an incredible impact: it destroyed whatever effective political support existed within parliament, and weakened doctrinal consensus. For politicians, according to Lemasurier: "Judicial review was no longer considered to be only 'a play thing for jurists,' nor even a means of defending individual liberties, but was henceforth a weapon in the hands of Reaction"—palatable only to the far Right and to representatives of monopoly capital.[94] Whereas before 1921, the doctrinal community was all but unanimously in favor of judicial review, once dutiful adherents began to express their reticence, including the editor of the *Revue du droit public*, Gaston Jèze. Having been an advocate of judicial review since at least 1895,[95] he withdrew his support in an influential article, in fact more of an editorial, in 1924.[96] Jèze did not hesitate to confirm—approvingly—that *le droit* had conclusively demonstrated the logical, juridical necessity of judicial review, but he dismissed the movement's demonstrations that the courts had already begun doing it as acts of "pure imagination."[97] Unfortunately, he argued, "*At present*, French public law being what is applied *at present* by the courts, . . . the power to control the constitutionality of legislation does not exist" [emphases in original]; and this would remain the case so long as judges suffered from low prestige, and lacked sufficient independence.[98] In his opinion, following Lambert, judicial review, far from increasing judicial prestige and authority, could very well have the opposite effect:

> Let's suppose, and the hypothesis is not an idle one, that the ordinary courts or even a supreme court showed itself hostile towards democratic, social, or fiscal reforms. Under the pretext of substantive judicial review, these courts would have the formidable power to block, judicially, reform legislation of this kind. We would then have a government of judges . . . We would begin anew the sad history of the *parlements* of the *ancien régime*. And towards what result? Conflict between a democratically elected parliament desirous of social reform, . . . and [judicial authority] . . . would lead to the obliteration of the judges, to the discredit of the courts, and a new diminution of the prestige and of the independence necessary to the judiciary. May the French courts avoid such a catastrophic course![99]

By the end of the Third Republic, the practical side of the debate was put to rest, by the courts themselves. In *Arrighi* (1936), the *Conseil d'Etat*, echoing Jèze, ruled that ". . . *in the present state of French public law*, this ground of appeal [the unconstitutionality of a statute enabling an administrative act] may not be entered before the *Conseil d'Etat*" [emphasis added], a position subsequently adhered to by other courts.[100] The doctrinal debate did not die, but was left hanging pending the outcome of the drafting of the constitution of the Fourth Republic.

Constitutional Review and the Valeur constitutionnel *of the Preamble to the 1946 Constitution*

The Constitutional Committee and the system of "popular review" met first with scorn—because the system of review was wholly dependent on a sovereign parliament and excluded the judiciary. All important treatises continued to support *judicial* review. The strange assertion that the new system constituted a form of "popular review" was not accepted by *le droit*. "If the people are called to intervene, it obviously will not be to say if a law does or does not conform to the constitution," wrote Laferriere. "That would be a question which the people are radically incompetent to resolve."[101] The committee later engendered complete indifference, due to its inactivity. Had it been more active, few doubted that it would serve less as a "judge who sanctions and condemns," than "as a consultative commission which absolves and justifies . . . new water for the mill of power."[102]

The new constitution's preamble, however, proved to be of enormous importance to public law scholars and judges, in spite of the fact that its *valeur constitutionnel*—a term which denotes constitutional status superior to *la loi* and thus binding on all public authorities, including judges and parliament— could only be asserted with great difficulty. Because the Constitutional Council, against the express wishes of the founders of the Fifth Republic, would incorporate the 1946 preamble and raise it to full constitutional status in 1971 (see chapter 3), an account of its origins is crucial to an understanding of present-day constitutional politics. What is remarkable is the extent to which doctrinal authority accepted—virtually unanimously—the *valeur constitutionnel* of the preamble, while a careful reading of the preparatory work and the construction of the text itself overwhelmingly leads to the conclusion that the founders of the Fourth Republic—like their predecessors in 1958—did not intend to bestow such status.

The very existence of a preamble resulted from the founders' failure to unambiguously "constitutionalize" a new declaration of rights. On the opening of the first Constitutional Assembly, all three of the major parties agreed that the 1789 declaration was out of date and would have to be substantially revised to be acceptable; indeed, the assembly voted 429–119 against outright incorporation of the 1789 text.[103] The deputies devoted fully one-quarter of their rancorous often paralyzing debates to the new declaration which, as one commentator put it, exposed the almost "unbridgeable gulf between Marxist materialism and collectivism on the one hand, and Christian democracy and individualism on the other."[104] Upon completion, the declaration was placed in the very first chapter of the constitution of April 1946. Thus, there is every reason to support the view that had the April constitution not been rejected in referendum, the declaration would have possessed clear *valeur constitutionnel*. Moreover, there is a wealth of evidence in the assembly record in support of a conclusion that the framers—even those on the Left, because they were able to, among other things, curtail the right of property in the name of the public good—expected the declaration to be possessed of such status. The *rapporteur* of the drafting committee, Gilbert Zaksas (Socialist), stated, "The preamble is a true judicial text, part of the whole of the constitution"[105]; and Raoul Calas (Communist) even admitted that the "nation's representatives of tomorrow will be obliged to conform to it, and to translate its *spirit* into legislation" [emphasis added].[106] While acknowledging its *valeur constitutionnel*, such statements must not therefore be taken to mean that the founders recognized the declaration to be superior to legislation, or that legislation must conform to the declaration in order to be considered valid. First, no provision was made for the declaration's protection by an autonomous authority; such protection was left to parliament. Second, and in contradiction with doctrinal orthodoxy, the acknowledgment that the declaration was a constitutional text did not necessarily constitute a public renunciation of the ideology of the general will. In a striking example, Edouard Herriot had this to say before the assembly:

> In the solemn hierarchy of texts which guarantee the liberties of the people, there are 3 degrees. There is, first, *la loi*, which determines how principles will be applied. . . . Below *la loi* there is the constitution, which brings together the organic principles [organizing] the life of this state. And below the constitution, there is the declaration of rights and responsibilities, which comes into play where *politics meets or, more precisely, should meet, morality* [emphasis added].[107]

In summary, *had the constitution of April been ratified, France would indeed have seen the birth of a new bill of rights but not therefore the inevitable death of parliamentary sovereignty.*

For the framers of the constitution of October 1946, the *valeur juridique* of the document was hardly a matter of controversy: it simply had none. In order to save time and another embarrassing rejection by the electorate, the drafting committee voted unanimously to withdraw the declaration from the constitutional text and to instead place a general statement of principles in an attached preamble.[108] *Those for and against judicial review, and for and against the establishment of a bill of rights binding on lawmakers, agreed that the preamble would not possess valeur constitutionnel.* Jacques Bardoux, who led the fight both to establish a bill of rights and judicial review in the constitution, argued the following:

> I would rather have an incomplete declaration than none at all. . . . A declaration divided into articles [may] have the force of a legal code, a preamble divided into paragraphs is as weak as an academic preface. . . . The preamble does not have the force of law. Its prescriptions, purely verbal and platonic, bind no one, neither the simple citizen, nor the public authorities, nor this Assembly, which is henceforth free to contradict [it] . . . .[109]

Most understood the preamble to be "verbal and platonic," or, "a polite bow to the general rules of the polity," and certainly not "a juridical expression in a form which a judge could one day apply."[110] I can find no affirmation to the contrary, even by minor figures, in the debates of the second assembly.[111] It is worth recalling in this regard that the Constitutional Committee, which possessed powers of what might have been called constitutional review, was explicitly forbidden by the constitutional text itself from appealing to the provisions of the preamble in any of its decision on the constitutionality of legislative acts.

Last, the structure of the final text of the preamble was not conducive to judicial application. To the general satisfaction of the Right, the preamble stated simply that "the French people solemnly reaffirm the rights and liberties consecrated by the Declaration of Rights of 1789 and the fundamental principles recognized by the laws of the Republic [FPRLR]." The so-called FPRLR were left unenumerated, but everyone understood the inclusion of the phrase to be an attempt to introduce the principle of educational choice as a means of protecting the Catholic school system.[112] As compensation for the Left and collectivist center, the vast bulk of the preamble consecrates a long list of "political, economic, and social principles particularly necessary for our times" [cited throughout this book as "the 1946 principles"] which guarantee, among others, the following: equality of the sexes; the rights to work, to join a union, to strike, and to obtain social security; and the responsibility of the state to nationalize all industries which are either de facto monopolies or which have taken on the character of a public service [the 1946 preamble is reproduced in Appendix A]. The final product therefore constitutes an uncomfortable compromise between radically opposed notions of individual and collective rights, and of the proper relationship between the state and society. It is certain that the preamble would not have been included at all had the framers understood that it would be applied by judges or elevated to constitutional status; it is even more certain that the 1789 declaration would not have been mentioned had they been able to foresee the Council's later incorporation.

With rare exception,[113] doctrinal authorities (including two future Constitutional Council members) saw in the preamble a welcome grounding for a renewal of its objectives. Ignoring the political context which gave it birth,[114] public law energetically and overwhelmingly declared its *valeur constitutionnel*,[115] and old debates were recast, if in wholly recognizable forms. These arguments rested on one or a combination of the following: the permanence of the 1789 declaration had been confirmed and given voice again by the preamble; the preamble, because it, along with the constitutional text, had been submitted to referendum benefited necessarily from the same judicial status (that is, a higher status than that which may be accorded a legislative act); the terms of article 81 of the new constitution constitutionalized the preamble. This last argument, rare in the early years of the Fourth Republic, is of interest because doctrine later became increasingly comfortable invoking it. Article 81 states the following:

> All French nationals, and those . . . of the French Union, are citizens of the French Union, and are assured the enjoyment of the rights and liberties guaranteed by the preamble.[116]

However, nothing in the debates on the drafting of the constitution can lead to the conclusion that the framers wished to constitutionalize the preamble by this article. In fact, debate on article 81 was entirely dominated by considerations of colonial policy: the drafters simply wished to avoid controversies which would surely have been raised had the door been left open to the creation of two classes of French citizens, one for French nationals and the other for colonial subjects.[117] It was both an expression of good faith to the populations of the French Union, and an acknowledgement that any law passed which would deny these populations the same rights enjoyed by French nationals would be unconstitutional on its face. *No discussion on the status of the preamble accompanied the debates on article 81, and the framers certainly did not seek to change that status by the latter's inclusion.*

In any event, the very existence of the preamble reinvigorated legal scholarship. First, the doctrine immediately began the work of adjudicating between the evidently contradictory principles contained in the preamble. Great efforts were made to separate out those which possessed legal force (*valeur juridique*) and those whose content or import must more rightly be called "philosophical."[118] Broad categories emerged—explicit interdictions and prescriptions, affirmations of moral and political objectives, general ideas—and these were ordered into hierarchy. Texts most likely to prove most useful to judges, or put differently, those texts which judges would have least difficulty "constitutionalizing" (by referring to them in their decisions), received the most attention. Much of the 1789 declaration was not in question, probably for two main reasons: first, public lawyers had been preparing for this step for decades; and second, many of the principles enunciated had long formed the bedrock of the private law, and of penal law and procedure. The rest of the text was more problematic, and it is doubtful that, absent the 1789 declaration, the preamble would have exercised public law scholarship to any important degree. Thus, in the purely partisan context of the drafting of the 1946 constitution, the legal community came out overwhelmingly on the side of the Right.

Second, many renewed their efforts to convince judges that the introduction of judicial review into France was necessary to establish and to protect the new hierarchies of legal norms generated by the preamble. Maurice Duverger and others argued that the preamble unambiguously provided judges with a written source of general principles with which to construct a jurisprudence of fundamental rights. The 1789 declaration could finally be judicially incorporated into the constitution by the judiciary; Duverger stated,

> The myth of the "sovereignty of the National Assembly," invoked by the parties on the Left, has made it impossible to establish effective constitutional review. However, we think that judicial review . . . is possible because no express provision of the constitution forbids it, and because the obstacles which opposed it under the 1875 regime have disappeared. . . . We think . . . that judges should have the courage to declare that they will accept pleas based on the unconstitutionality of legislation.[119]

No less than the eminent professor F. Gény agreed, arguing that the preamble "formulates the most important rules of law," constitutes "an insurmountable barrier to the legislature itself," and that "in the present state of our political organization, the sanction can only be judicial."[120]

Judges proved less "courageous" than hoped: to this day, no court has refused to apply a promulgated law on the basis of its unconstitutionality. But in important ways, public law lost the war but won some important battles. Most important, the movement's project to restore the primacy of judges over interpretation largely succeeded. Courts, and particularly the *Conseil d'Etat* began to catalog, and quite explicitly, a vast array of constitutional and extra-constitutional principles which could be invoked in attacking executive acts—but not statute. These "general principles of law," include such discoverable notions as "individual liberty," "equality before the law," "freedom of conscience," and "nonretroactivity," as well as previously existing, if unexplained, principles like "the continuity of public service." Related to this development, the preamble, and especially the 1789 declaration, rapidly became a fertile source for annulments of executive acts,[121] and the *valeur juridique* of the text was explicitly proclaimed in 1956 by the *Conseil d'Etat in Amicales*.[122] As important, the core precepts of the movement animated public law discourse well into the Fifth Republic. And to that extent the discipline maintained a coherent vision of itself as an institution related to, but fundamentally autonomous from, the greater political system.

Conclusion

I have described two ideologies, the salient strains of which have been opposed, one to the other, for centuries, and especially since the advent of the Third Republic. Each provides the basic elements of a state theory. Each speaks to the great systemic issues of state formation and maintenance: the meaning and content of "sovereignty" and representation, the proper relationship between law and politics in society, the capacity of legal norms to structure the interaction between government and governed. What I have called the ideology of the general will quickly became official state ideology, enshrined in constitutions and embedded and defended by the most powerful institutions in successive regimes. What I have called the ideology of constitutionalism exercised no such power or influence at the systemic level. It could not. Denied an institutional base, the ideology was denied social agency. Although elaborated and reproduced faithfully by and within the public law community, these ideas were unable to attach themselves to, and then embed themselves in, an institution capable of defending it against rival ideologies. Nevertheless, as chapters 3 and 4 will show, the ideology of constitutionalism would eventually find a home in the Fifth Republic, in the Constitutional Council.

2

From Watchdog to Policymaker: Structure, Function, Mandate

In both context and detail, the paralysis of politics in the waning years of the Fourth Republic, the forceful coming of a heroic, charismatic leader to establish a new one, even the constitutional niceties of the emergent regime can not but recall past Bonapartist solutions to the problem of the apparent ingovernability of France in crisis.[1] The new constitution, drafted principally by *conseillers d'Etat* under the watchful eyes of de Gaulle, Michel Debré, and their associates, shifted effective power over the legislative process and over the form and content of legislation from parliament to the executive. In a word, the parliamentary system was *rationalized*, that is, placed under the management of a government detached from parliament (if left responsible).[2] A special body, the Constitutional Council, was created to guarantee the viability of this new distribution of powers, and—not wholly unlike the Bonapartist Senates— the institution was expressly denied a judicial role, and its competence was limited entirely to parliamentary space. This chapter, first, examines the creation of the Council—with special attention paid to the intention of the founders—along with attributes of the body's jurisdiction, composition and recruitment.

The Council and Original Intent

After a nearly century-long period of unrivaled supremacy, parliament was mastered by the political settlement that gave birth to the Fifth Republic. The central objective of the founders was to "alter the status of parliament so that it would no longer be at the center of political life . . . and . . . permanently be incapable of obstructing government action. From this point of view, their success was complete." The settlement, as everyone knows, resulted in a "servile" legislature,[3] in the famous words of François Mitterrand, in a "permanent *coup d'état*."[4] Without belaboring an overworked subject, the central features of the rationalized legislative process are worth recalling. First, and most important, the constitution distinguishes between statute—*la loi*—and a certain class of executive acts—*le règlement*.[5] Whereas parliament was free to legislate on any subject during the Third and Fourth Republics, article 34 of the new constitution lists inclusively those legislative subject matters which together constitute what the constitution calls the "domain" of *la loi*. These subject matters include among others the "fixing of rules concerning" civil and fundamental rights of citizens; nationality, marriage, and inheritance; changes in the penal code and the code on penal procedure, amnesties, and the creation of new courts and the status of judges; electoral laws; the rights of the civil and military services; the creation of "public enterprises," the nationalization of industry, and the expropriation of private property; local administration and education; and labor laws and social security. It later, in article 40, forbids any member or group of parliament from proposing bills or amendments which would have the effect of either raising public expenditures or reducing public funds. All subject matters not listed in article 34 are expressly reserved to the executive by article 37. In sum, *la loi* was no longer to be defined by its form, an act of parliament, but by its content, the matter to be regulated. Second, the process itself was "streamlined" in favor of the government. The constitution grants to the executive alone control over the legislative calendar, and the means to control parliamentary discussion, the amending process, and voting procedures.

The function of the Council in this system was made explicit: to facilitate the centralization of executive authority, and to ensure that the system would not somehow revert to traditional parliamentary orthodoxy.[6] Its primary role, as seen by the founders, was to police the frontiers of the domains of *la loi* and *le règlement*, to be a "watchdog on behalf of executive supremacy."[7] As Debré put it, in an speech of August 1958 outlining the general contours of the new constitution to the *Conseil d'Etat*:

> We must . . . suppress . . . parliamentary arbitrariness, which—under the pretext of sovereignty, not of the nation (which is just), but of the Assemblies (which is fallacious)—has subverted without limit the status of the Constitution and of governmental authority. The creation of the Constitutional Council manifests the will to subordinate *la loi*, that is, the decision of the parliament, to the superior rule [*règle*] laid down by the Constitution. It is neither in the spirit of the parliamentary regime, nor in the French tradition, to give to judicial authorities . . . the right to examine the status of *la loi*. The project therefore imagines a special institution to which only four authorities will have access. . . . The Constitution thus creates an arm against deviation from the [new] parliamentary regime.[8]

The most important source on the making of the 1958 Constitution is the discussions of the Constitutional Consultative Committee (CCC), a multipartisan group of parliamentarians, law professors, and others who were asked by the government to debate and to comment on the constitution during final stages of the drafting process. These discussions have been published as the *Travaux préparatoires* for the 1958 constitution.[9] The document tells us much about what the Council was intended *not* to be. First, although its role in reviewing legislation was that of a referee engaged in settling conflicts between the executive and the legislature, *the Council was not meant to be a fair or impartial referee* (any more than the constitution was designed to be fair or impartial). Its field of play was to be exclusively parliamentary space; it was to have jurisdiction only over legislative and *not* executive acts; and a proposal to balance the equation—to allow legislative authorities to refer executive acts to the Council[10]—was not seriously considered. Moreover, the mode of recruitment proposed all but guaranteed that a majority of the Council's members would be active supporters of the government. Indeed, the government's working draft (as well as the final product) strictly limited access to the institution for rulings on constitutionality of proposed legislation to four officials—the president of the Republic, the prime minister, the president of the Senate, and the president of the National Assembly.

Much of the CCC's effort to perfect the Council idea was undertaken in a spirit of reform, indeed a majority worked to extend the power of referral to one-third of either parliamentary assembly. Some supported this expansion as a means of advancing the rights of minority groups within parliament.[11] For supporters of constitutional review, expansion was viewed as essential to the successful development of the institution. One CCC member, Marcel Waline, a distinguished professor of law and editor of the *Revue du droit public*, even argued that to limit referrals as the government wished would risk repeating the failed experience of the Bonapartist Senates "since," as another member put it, "the system would never attack itself." The government opposed the proposal. In a remarkably prescient speech echoing the orthodox doctrinal positions of the Third Republic, Debré argued that giving parliamentary minorities the power to refer legislation to the Council would transform "constitutional review into a veritable public affair." The whole mechanism would be "deformed," and "politicized": parliament would come to debate the constitutionality of legislation and the Council's activities, and might even be lobbied to refer legislation for review. France would establish, argued Debré, "what would in reality be a 'gouvernement des juges,'" a grave problem, since "neither the assemblies nor public opinion would be willing to accept the constant participation of judges in political life." The CCC overrode Debré, adopted the proposal, and integrated the new referral mechanism into the CCC's final draft constitution.[12] Nevertheless, the government later ignored the recommendation, and it was dropped.

Second, *neither the government nor the CCC considered the Council to be a court*, if by that we mean a judicial or courtlike body. The constitution does not provide for any interaction between the Council and the judicial system,[13] and unlike the constitutional provisions governing the recruitment of other constitutional courts on the continent, *no prerequisite of prior judicial service or minimum requirements of legal training was ever contemplated*. The 1958 constitution does not mention the Council in its chapter on "Judicial Authority," but instead sets it apart in its own chapter. Where the Council is mentioned, it is to grant authority over aspects of legislative process.[14] Perhaps even more important, its review powers were restricted to verifying that a statute or statutory provisions had not 1) been passed in violation of the procedures laid down by the constitution or, 2) trespassed on the domain of *le règlement*.[15]

Discussion in the CCC on the *valeur constitutionnel* of the proposed preamble to the 1958 constitution is instructive on these points. As finally promulgated in October, the preamble is a simple two-line statement, the relevant part of which reads as follows:

> The French People solemnly proclaim their attachment to the Rights of Man and to the principles of national sovereignty as defined by the Declaration of 1789, confirmed and completed by the preamble of the Constitution of 1946.

In July, a working group within the CCC had adopted an amendment to article 34 which would have required that legislation, in order to be valid, respect "the general principles of individual rights and liberties defined by the preamble." The government's spokesman (*commissaire du gouvernement*), Raymond Janot, opposed the amendment on the grounds that "jurists would be tempted to invoke the mention of the preamble . . . as a means of bestowing *valeur constitutionnel* to past declarations of the rights of man," and the following discussion ensued:

> DEJEAN: . . . I had asked if the preamble had, juridically, *valeur constitutionnel*.
> JANOT: No, but if you refer to it in the Constitution itself, . . . it will have. Do you really think that the rules laid down in 1789 still possess normative value in the 20th century, that they respond to the present structure of our society?
> DEJEAN: For the authors of the draft, therefore, the preamble does not possess *valeur constitutionnel*.
> JANOT: No, certainly not.

Waline protested, arguing that if the government's position was upheld and the amendment rejected, the *Conseil d'Etat's* jurisprudence of general principles would be undermined. Janot responded that such principles derived their source uniquely from jurisprudence, and not by virtue of their constitutional status: "As a practical matter, they do not limit the legislator."

The significance of the preamble's status for the future activity of the Council was a matter of crucial concern. After a member of the CCC asked if the amendment would require the Council to "determine if statutes conform to the preamble and the declaration of 1789," Janot answered in the affirmative, and warned that the CCC was flirting with instituting "a government of judges." Dejean then withdrew his support, and called successfully for the amendment to be quashed:

> Would it be a good thing to give unquestioned *valeur constitutionnel* to the contents of the preamble . . . ? We would no longer be able to pass legislation without unhappy people referring it to the Council under the pretext that such and such a principle had been violated. We must be very prudent.[16]

A similar move to strengthen the role of principles contained in the 1789 declaration was opposed by the government on the grounds that it might appear to "constitutionalize the capitalist system."[17]

Composition and Recruitment

The constitutional provisions relevant to recruitment and composition are contained in article 56:

> The Constitutional Council is composed of 9 members who serve 9 year, non-renewable terms. The Constitutional Council is renewed in thirds every three years. Three of its members are named by the President of the Republic, three by the President of the National Assembly, three by the President of the Senate.
>
> In addition to the 9 members mentioned above, former Presidents of the Republic are members of the Constitutional Council for life.[18]

Members need only be 18 years of age or older and in possession of their civil rights—there exist no other formal prerequisites for membership, no nomination or confirmation procedures, and no means to block appointments. Alone among former presidents of the Republic, Vincent Auriol and Rény Coty were seated in the 1959–62 period, and it is likely that they will be the last to do so.[19] In July 1960, Auriol walked out in protest of what he called the Council's excessive deference to de Gaulle, which he linked to the institution's mode of recruitment, and referral mechanism.[20]

In practice, the single most important criterion for appointment to the Council is political affiliation, and the Council has been dominated by professional politicians. This is the case for all five of the presidents of the Council, four of whom had also served as government ministers. Statistically, of the forty-one members who have been appointed to the Council from 1958 to 1988, 59 percent (twenty-four) were selected from the ranks of former parliamentarians and/or government ministers. This percentage has increased dramatically in the past two decades: every Council since that of 1968 has been composed of at least six (67 percent) such politicians, increasing to seven (78 percent) in 1983, and to eight (89 percent) in 1986. The second largest category, representing 24 percent (ten) of total membership, is made up of men who had served in staffs or as advisors to either politicians or political parties, but not as parliamentarians. Other categories are less coherent due to overlapping professional and political activities, but several points deserve to be noted. First, only three judges have been appointed (in 1958, 1969, and 1979), the first two of whom were recruited from the *Cour de cassation*; the last, a former deputy and minister, had served on the European Court of Justice. In addition, seven law professors have been named, some of whom had also been, perhaps more importantly, parliamentarians and/or ministers.

Subtle differences in recruitment patterns exist or have existed, some of which are today only of historical interest. Until 1977, for example, presidents of the Republic named only orthodox Gaullists, a group which includes several prominent professors (notably Marcel Waline and François Goguel). De Gaulle's successor, Georges Pompidou, himself the first de Gaulle appointee to the Council (1958), carried on the tradition, naming only Gaullist politicians. Giscard d'Estaing broke the tradition, using his two opportunities to make what now appear to be the most "neutral" of appointments to the Council. These were André Ségalat, a high functionary (the secretary-general of the government from 1946 to 1958, the entire period of the Fourth Republic), and Georges Vedel, an eminent public law professor, and a specialist in administrative law. Relevant in this regard is the fact that Giscard, more than any other president, made bolstering the Council's public image and its political legitimacy a priority of his presidency. Mitterrand has since replaced the premium on personal loyalty. To date, presidents have made fourteen appointments, including eight former parliamentarians and/or ministers.

The naming of the president of the Council (an important position not least because the Council president casts the deciding vote in the case of deadlock, and controls procedures, including the designation of the *rapporteur* for each decision) is also the prerogative of the president of the Republic. There have been five presidents of the Council to date, two named by de Gaulle, one by Pompidou, and two by Mitterrand, and in each case, the appointment decision was treated as a matter of high politics. De Gaulle appointed men who had been members of his entourage during resistance days, and had later been instrumental in establishing the Fifth Republic: Léon Nöel, a member of the CCC, and Gaston Palewski, appointed by de Gaulle in compensation for his work on the 1962 referendum on the direct election of the president, and for organizing the office of the new presidency.[21] Their ascribed role was no less than to ensure the subservience of the Council to the wishes of the general. As discussed later, they fulfilled this role, if on occasion with some regret. Pompidou's appointment in 1974 of Roger Frey, a "Baron of Gaullism," was made for a variety of political reasons: to guarantee continuity of Gaullist principles in the case of possible upcoming electoral defeat, and—it was speculated—to satisfy calls to avenge the president of the Senate's appointment, of the day before, of de Gaulle's and the Council's most powerful and persistent opponent, Gaston Monnerville (a longtime president of the Senate).[22] Pompidou himself was said to have put it to Frey, a minister in every government from 1959 until his appointment to the presidency of the Council in 1974, and then secretary-general of the Gaullist party, in these terms: "I need you in this post because I have no one else to put there. The second reason is personal, very personal: I must fill the post very quickly."[23] Pompidou died barely a month after the appointment, and the Gaullists did subsequently lose the presidency in the 1974 election. Pompidou's appointment was criticized in an article in the *Revue du droit public* as being analogous to the "entrenchment" of federalists in the U.S. Supreme Court at the turn of the eighteenth century, and the Left cited it as an important reason for their opposition to the 1974 amendment.[24] Finally, Mitterrand's choices are of interest, not least because of his professed scorn for the Council—as late as 1978, for example, he had stated that:

it is the institution that I indict, because the Constitutional Council is a political institution, the political instrument of the executive, nothing more, nothing less. We thought it servile, but it is actually only obedient.[25]

His first appointee, Daniel Mayer, a minister in Léon Blum's 1946 government, a human rights activist, and an intimate of Mitterrand's, served only three years of his term as president, while retaining his seat on the Council. His resignation from the presidency, only weeks before the 1986 parliamentary elections, paved the way for Mitterrand to name Robert Badinter. Badinter at the time was minister of justice (1981–86), as well as a respected law professor and human rights advocate; this appointment thus combined formidable legal expertise and political loyalty. The maneuver was treated as a scandal: it was denounced by the future majority,[26] and legal specialists debated its constitutionality, Duverger calling it a "constitutional fraud."[27]

Appointments made by presidents of the National Assembly have been the most unambiguously "political," if political is understood to mean the appointment of full-time professional politicians. Of fifteen members named, ten had held national elected office before their appointment, including former ministers and a former president of the National Assembly; four others had served as chief of staffs or members of the personal staffs of prominent politicians, including those of General de Gaulle and Pierre Mendès France; the remaining appointee and also the most recent (1987), was recruited from the National Council of the present Gaullist party, Jacques Chirac's RPR. François Luchaire, a law professor and a former Council judge (1965–74) appointed by the president of the Senate, wrote in 1980 that traditionally the president of the National Assembly defers to the wishes of the president of the Republic in making these decisions.[28] It can be inferred from appointments made since that the tradition remains a viable one; the one obvious exception to this rule occurred during the period of *cohabitation* period (1987) when the president of the National Assembly was a Chirac Gaullist.

In contrast, presidents of the Senate have manifested great independence vis-à-vis the executive and has, overall, opted for higher standards of legal expertise. Of twelve members appointed, ten had been either professional lawyers (six), law professors (three), or judges (two) or a combination. Still the majority even of these had engaged in substantial political activities. Of the past six appointees—going back to 1968 all had been former parliamentarians, bringing the total to seven of twelve.

The Council's composition has been the subject of intense criticism by politicians and legal scholars, criticism which has been based on the partisan backgrounds of its members, and its oft-expressed corollary—that the Council's "acquaintance with public law is dubious, to say the least."[29] Because of the high political profile of the great majority of Council members, the Council is vulnerable to charges that its function too is inherently "political." Its vulnerability is made more acute by the fact that many appointments are of men in advanced stages in their parliamentary careers. In the CCC debates on the drafting of the constitution, critics had predicted that the Council would be composed of retired politicians, and even warned of a *"gouvernement des retraites* ("retirees").[30] They have not been proved wrong. Although the average age of Council members from 1958 to 1986 is 68 years, it has steadily increased: to 73 years from 1970 to 1986, and to more than 74 years in the 1980s. With very few exceptions (notably Badinter—the lone Council member to be appointed who was under the age of 60 years in the entire 1968–86 period), appointments have increasingly gone to politicians in the twilight of their careers and, it can be presumed, in compensation for long and distinguished service.[31]

Until recently, criticism of the Council's composition has been framed in traditional Left/Right ideological terms. Until at least the early 1970s, the Council's Gaullist character was virtually an axiom, cited by the Left as a footnote, if an important one, to the history of an alleged *coup d'etat*. After the first *alternance* in 1981, the Council's composition became an affair of high politics. The Left appointed its first Council member in 1983, increased its share to four in 1986, and achieved its first majority in 1989. Since at least 1984, criticism of the Council has not centered so much on partisan make-up as on its jurisprudential activism and expanding influence over the legislative process.

Jurisdiction and Activity

In their determination of the Constitutional Council's jurisdiction and interpretive functions, the founders sought to guarantee the emergence and stability of the "rationalized" legislative process. The Council thus polices the domains of *la loi* and *le règlement* (articles 37 and 41). The Council is also responsible for verifying the conformity to the constitution of the following texts: organic laws (generally, legislation establishing or reforming the status or functioning of public authorities)[32] and the permanent standing orders of the National Assembly and of the Senate, both of which are *referred to it automatically* (articles 46 and 61); and international treaties (article 54)[33] and ordinary legislation (article 61), *upon referral* by the proper authority.[34] Although nowhere specifically prohibited, the Council refused, in 1961, to give itself competence to issue advisory opinions.[35] As will be made clear, the impact of all of the Council's jurisprudential activities attends only policymaking processes. Though the remainder of the book focuses exclusively on the constitutional review of ordinary legislation, the Council's jurisprudence with respect to the standing orders of parliament, and to articles 37 and 41, is worth at least brief examination: the former because it stifled the last gasp of parliamentary sovereignty as traditionally understood; the latter because the jurisprudence on articles 37 and 41 constitutes quantitatively the most important part of the institution's early interpretive activity.

Gaullist concern for controlling the standing orders (*règlements*) of parliament is understandable. Given the traditional French doctrine of parliamentary sovereignty, during the Third and Fourth Republics the assemblies' internal regulations and procedures were unquestionably more important than the constitution (due to the fact that the constitution could be amended by legislative acts). For the hierarchy of laws enshrined in the constitution of the Fifth Republic to have any viability, parliamentary custom, as expressed most concretely in its standing orders, could not serve to grant to the legislature authority which the constitution had taken away.[36] Accordingly, the constitution requires the Council to verify the constitutionality of the assemblies' new standing orders as well as any subsequent change in them. De Gaulle confides in his *mémoires* that automatic jurisdiction was conferred so that in the case of transgression "the standing orders would be amended accordingly," that is, by a Council decision.[37]

Debates on the drafting of the standing orders quickly became a power struggle between the government and its supporters on one side, and those who had opposed the constitutional settlement as undemocratic and "Bonapartist" (i.e., the entire Left) on the other. Brocas, debating with Debré, put the significance of the opposition's work in these dramatic terms:

> Parliament must assure the supremacy of political power, and of the representatives of the nation, over that of the administrators. We . . . must give our democracy what is perhaps its last chance—you abuse the confidence of our electors, that is, of the whole nation. You don't have that right! We were not sent here to diminish but to affirm the Republic![38]

The Left and others committed to defending traditional parliamentary prerogatives worked either overtly to revise the constitution or, more subtly, to ensure that the terms of the standing orders would be flexible enough to allow parliament "to prepare for the future an evolution towards a more balanced institutional regime,"[39] by exploiting the constitution's silences. The prime minister and his supporters argued that anything not expressly permitted by the constitution was forbidden to parliament.[40]

The Council's rulings of June 1959 on the parliamentary standing orders[41] served notice that it intended to interpret the letter of the constitution in restrictive terms and its spirit in Gaullist terms.[42] The Council on the whole adopted Debré's position, and removed from the National Assembly's rules all or parts of ten different articles, and ruled that others were to be considered constitutional only if interpreted as the Council did in its decision ("conformity under reserve of interpretation"). An equivalent number were struck from the Senate's rules, and the government's powers to control the legislative agenda and parliament's debates were strengthened.

A representative example is the fate of rules enabling and governing parliamentary resolutions—nonbinding expressions of opinion. The Gaullist-controlled National Assembly accepted the principle of the resolution but forbade those concerning executive privileges in the legislative process. In contrast, the Senate had simply copied its rules on resolutions from the standing orders under which the upper house had lived during the Fourth Republic. While the constitution makes no mention of the resolution, the Council declared that all such acts were unconstitutional in principle, since they could be used to disrupt the executive's authority or to expand parliamentary initiative.

The decision drew protests from the opposition politicians; as one deputy put it,

> We are the first country in the entire world which obliges its parliament to submit its internal rules to an external authority. The fact that a non-elected authority is charged with judging the validity of texts which are not even of a legislative nature and which emanate from authentic representative of the people appears singularly bizarre.[43]

In fact, the effect of the decision—as de Gaulle had hoped—was to rewrite the assembly's rules. The National Assembly immediately acted to revise its orders in strict conformity to the Council's dictates, dutifully copying word-for-word the Council's language into those provisions which the latter had attacked. The Senate protested, delaying its revision for more than a year and a half—to mark "its disagreement with the decision."[44]

If in its early jurisprudence on the standing orders the Council had helped to pronounce the death of parliamentary sovereignty traditionally conceived, its jurisprudence on articles 37 and 41 served to grease the gears of the executive's new policymaking machine. As mentioned earlier, article 37 defines the domain of *le règlement* to be all those matters not expressly reserved to the domain of *la loi*; it also states that the executive may promulgate "texts in a legislative form" upon a ruling by the Council that their subject matter is not located in the domain of *la loi*. In policymaking terms what happens is that the government asks the Council to rule that a given policy initiative need not be submitted to parliament as a bill, that is, the Council is asked to withdraw a legislative subject matter from what otherwise might be considered the domain of *la loi*.

In the early years of the Republic, the Council tended to give an expansive reading of the notion of *règlement*, or expressed differently, a restrictive interpretation of the domain of *la loi*. Two examples will suffice. In its first decision enabled by article 37, the Council was confronted with an attempt by the government to modify certain administrative structures of the RATP—the Parisian public transport system. The RATP had been established in November 1958 by an executive act called a legislative *ordonnance* under the procedures of article 92 of the constitution. (The notion of an executive act having the status of a law is evidently awkward, but such were the terms of article 92. Article 92 enabled the government to legislate provisionally in the domain of *la loi*—by *ordonnance*, a type of decree—during the months before parliament could be elected and convoked under the new constitution. All *ordonnances* enacted during this period are considered to possess legislative status, until rescinded.) According to article 34, parliament alone, by statute, "fixes rules concerning the creation of public establishments." The Council in its decision of 27 November 1959,[45] ruled—simply asserted without argument—that although the RATP was indeed a public establishment, the proposed modification of its administrative authority fell under the purview of the executive. In its decision of 18 July 1961,[46] the Council was asked to rule on a similar case involving a legislative *ordonnance*. This time, the government was seeking to revise the status and functioning of certain penal courts which it had created in 1959 with an article 92 *ordonnance*. Although article 34 provides that rules concerning "the creation of new orders of jurisdiction [i.e., courts] and the status of judges" fall under the domain of *la loi*, the Council allowed the modification by *réglement* of the number of these courts, their physical location, and even the details of their jurisdiction.

Between 1959 and 1974, the Council handed down eighty-two such decisions, to be compared with nine instances of review of ordinary legislation. On only six occasions did it locate the matter in question in the domain of *la loi*, and on sixteen others it ruled that the matter was partially in that domain. The other sixty decisions secured executive privileges. Moreover, of the first forty-two decisions pursuant to article 37 (March 1959–December 1966), thirty-six— or 86 percent—concerned government attempts to modify legislative *ordonnances* enabled by article 92.[47] The significance of this jurisprudence to the institutional balance of power in the policymaking process was enormous. *In consequence of it, the legislature virtually disappears.* In late 1958, before the first parliament was seated, the government legislated extensively in what it openly acknowledged to be the domain of *la loi*; the Council subsequently ruled (on 15 January 1960, a decision discussed briefly later) that the constitutionality of these *ordonnances* could *not* be contested; finally, in its article 37 jurisprudence, the Council ruled in an overwhelming number of cases that the executive possessed the authority to substantially rework the original legislation (again: enacted by the executive, not parliament) without any parliamentary control, in the process removing a further array of subject matters from the domain of *la loi*. While detailed analysis is beyond the scope of this book, it is important to note that the *loi/règlement* distinction has—at least since 1974—become increasingly flexible. The domain of *la loi* is today considered to have vastly expanded—in practice to virtually all politically important policy initiatives and reforms—and the *règlement* is today considered to be a subordinate act. This return to the traditional hierarchy is to the credit and advantage of both the parliament and the Constitutional Council (since the domain of *la loi* is controlled by both), and is evidence of loss of Gaullist control over the State.[48]

Unlike article 37, article 41 implicates the Constitutional Council directly in the legislative *procedures* taking place within parliament: it allows the government to use the Council to "paralyze"[49] parliamentary initiative in the event of irresolvable discord with the president of either parliamentary assembly. The government may declare any bill or amendment proposed by the Senate or the National Assembly *irrecevable*—that is, constitutionally precluded—on the grounds that the subject matter being discussed falls in the domain of *le règlement*. If the president of the National Assembly agrees with the government's declaration, the initiative is immediately quashed; if, however, the President does not agree, the government has the option of referring the matter to the Council, which has the immediate effect of halting further discussion of the bill pending a Council decision on the matter. Only a text proposed by a parliamentarian can be referred, and only the government can ask the Council for a ruling. In the 1959–68 period, the Council ruled according to this article eight times (six of which followed conflicts with the president of the Senate) resulting in six victories for the government and one partial victory. Since then the Council has been asked to rule on only three other occasions, and the procedure has for all practical purposes fallen into desuetude.

Constitutional Review of Legislation

The most important responsibility of the Constitutional Council—and the exclusive subject of the rest of this book—is its power of constitutional review of legislation. This power is spelled out by the constitution in articles 61 and 62, which read as follows:

> *Article 61*: . . . ordinary laws may be referred to the Constitutional Council, before their promulgation, by the President of the Republic, the Prime Minister, the President of the National Assembly, the President of the Senate, or 60 deputies or 60 senators.
>
> In these cases, the Constitutional Council must decide within 1 month. At the demand of the Government, after a declaration of urgency, this time limit is reduced to 8 days.
>
> A referral of any law to the Constitutional Council suspends its promulgation.
>
> *Article 62*: A provision declared unconstitutional may not be promulgation nor may it enter into force.
>
> The decisions of the Constitutional Council may not be appealed. . . .

It may be argued, however, that the Council does not possess a monopoly on constitutional interpretation. Article 5 reads, "the President of the Republic shall ensure the respect of the Constitution," and presidents have appealed to this provision on occasion as a justification for certain decisions, much to the chagrin at times of the legal community.[50] Moreover, under certain conditions parliament too is empowered to render a definitive judgment on the constitutionality of bills before it, when it votes *motions d'irrecevabilité* (discussed at length later). In any event, the Constitutional Council had few opportunities to exercise its review authority until the mid-1970s. The increase in the number of instances of constitutional review since is positively correlated with two events: the 1974 constitutional amendment which expanded the right of referral to any sixty deputies or senators, and the electoral victories of the Left in 1981 which resulted in the use of referrals by the Right for purposes of opposition to Socialist reform. Table 2.1 shows the dramatic impact of the amendment on numbers of referrals in quantitative terms, from less than one referral per year from 1959 to 1974, to eighteen per year since 1981.

Before 1974, review was dependent in practice on referrals by either the prime minister (largely to establish and then ensure executive dominance over policy processes) or the president of the Senate (as leader of the only anti-Gaullist institution in the early years of the Fifth Republic). Since 1974, 97

Table 2.1. Constitutional Review and the Constitutional Council, 1958–1987*

	1959–1973	1974–1980	1981–1987
Number of Referrals	*9*	*66*	*136*
Referring Authority			
Pres. of the Republic	0	0	0
Prime Minister	6	2	0
Pres. of the National Assembly	0	2	0
Pres. of the Senate	3	0	2
Parliamentarians (total)	–	62	134
Deputies	–	49	77
Senators	–	13	57
Result			
Number of Decisions Rendered	9	46	92
Censuring referred text	7	14	49
Favorable to referred text	2	32	43

*This table includes all referral and Constitutional Council activity pursuant to the procedures provided by article 61.2 (see Appendix A). Due to multiple referrals, the number of referrals since 1974 is larger than the number of decisions.

percent of all referrals have been of parliamentary origin,[51] and it is unlikely that this percentage will decrease. Prime ministers have not referred a bill to the Council in this decade, precisely because only bills which the government supports are ever adopted definitively by parliament and are therefore eligible for referral. The presidents of the assemblies are just as unlikely to refer bills regularly today: they can rely on their friends in parliament to draft the petitions (which they too may sign as ordinary members of parliament) without putting the prestige of their offices at risk. During the *cohabitation* period, Mitterrand publicly threatened to refer matters to the Council during 1986 to 1988 but in the end did not.[52]

Finally, it is worth noting that the Constitutional Council's constitutional review authority would have been substantially altered had a constitutional revision, first proposed by the Council's president, Badinter, and then taken up by Mitterrand and the Rocard government, been successfully adopted. Simplifying, the proposal would have allowed litigants in the ordinary and administrative courts systems to challenge the constitutionality of trial-relevant legislation on the grounds that the legislation had violated their fundamental rights. Once requested, the *Conseil d'Etat* and the *Cour de cassation*—the final appellate jurisdictions in the ordinary and administrative court systems respectively—would decide if the challenge was a serious one and, if so, to refer the matter to the Council. The Council then would have had three months to render a decision.

Parliament debated the proposal from late April to late June 1990; however, after substantially differing versions adopted by the National Assembly and the Senate could not be harmonized, deliberations ended, and the government chose not to place the revision on the parliamentary calendar for 1991. Politically, Giscard and his allies in the center-Right parties strongly opposed the measure; Gaullists expressed discomfort with such a fundamental transformation of the general's document; and the entire Right knew well that expanding the power of the Council would play into the hands of Mitterrand's party, since its 1988 electoral victories mean that the Socialists will control a majority of the Council's seats until at least 1998. Last, the majority in the Senate worried about a further dilution of its self-proclaimed role as a protector of fundamental rights. The Right's control of the Senate proved crucial, since revision of the constitution requires that both chambers adopt identical texts.[53]

Had the revision been successful, the Council's role and functioning may well have been transformed. The Council would have possessed a formal link to the judicial system and to individual litigants; and its status as *the* guarantor of rights and liberties would have been consolidated. Last, such a change might have provided the Constitutional Council with a more stable source of legitimacy (see chapter 9).

3

From Watchdog to Policymaker:
The Evolution of Constitutional Review

Since its inception, referrals to the Constitutional Council have been used to draw out the legislative process, a means of opposing and blocking policy choices recently enshrined in pending statutes. Whereas in the first decade of the Fifth Republic the primary function of constitutional review was to ensure that Gaullist constitutional ideas would find their expression in stable practices, since the mid-1970s the politics of review have become a central feature of opposition tactics. This development is intimately linked to the Council's steady incorporation, beginning in 1971, of the 1789 declaration and other provisions contained in the preamble to the 1946 constitution and elsewhere. As the Council cataloged substantive restrictions on policymaking, the importance of constitutional debate in policymaking increased, and the grounds of referral open to parliamentarians expanded.

This chapter consists of an analysis of the evolution of constitutional review, divided into three main periods: 1958–70, 1971–81, and 1981–87. In the first period, the Council succeeded in its assigned tasks to tame parliament, and to facilitate executive control of the legislative process; the second period was dominated by a sudden explosion of political discourse on fundamental rights, and by jurisprudential creativity and activism; the last period proved to be one of intense judicial–political confrontation, and the Council came into its own as a major policymaking actor, independent of executive control.

1959–70: "A Cannon Aimed at Parliament"

Throughout the 1959–70 period, the Constitutional Council lacked even minimal autonomy from the executive, and in particular, from General de Gaulle. Its role—to which its jurisprudence was expected to conform—was a subservient one. Mitterrand's polemical judgment of 1964, that the Council was a "Supreme Court from the *Musée Grévin*, a derisory cap of a derisory democracy" whose "sole utility is to serve as an errand boy for General de Gaulle," was not far from the truth.[1] Léon Nöel, the Council's first president (1959–65) remained the general's personal advisor after he took up his duties at the Council, and regularly suggested strategies and procedures for the implementation of controversial policies, even promising the Council's rubber stamp of approval.[2] The General himself put it this way: "The Constitutional Council . . . is in regular *liaison* with me, notably in the person of its president, Léon Nöel."[3] The Council's second president (1965–74), Gaston Palewski, responded to charges that his Council lacked any independence in this way:

> I must plead guilty. In fact, it seemed to me absurd to explain to the author of the Constitution how that text should be applied. When I tried to do so, expressing the most timid of reservations, the General would simply explain to me the precise reasons that had led him to adopt such and such an article— and I could not turn the Constitution against its own author! Had I tried, his socratic dialectic would have very soon stopped me cold.[4]

The preponderance of power politics as a determinant of Council behavior during this period does not mean that judicial considerations were entirely incidental, but only that these too were stacked in favor of the executive. The founders neither hoped nor expected that article 61 would give the Council influence on policymaking beyond simply facilitating the rationalization of parliament. As Luchaire has written, the *raison d'être* of this article was the same as others—"to block parliament from transcending the powers allocated to it by the constitution."[5] From 1959 to 1970, the Constitutional Council indeed functioned as little more than a transparent "defender of the executive"[6]—"a cannon aimed at parliament."[7] As Table 3.1 shows, the Council was asked to review only seven pieces of legislation during this period, and on each occasion it sided with the executive. On the sole instance of referral from a president of one of the assemblies, it declared the matter to be outside of its jurisdiction and thus technically does not constitute review. In each of these cases, the matter at hand was entirely procedural—a question of institutional competence to legislate—and not a question of the violation of fundamental or constitutional rights by the statutes referred.

All six instances of constitutional review followed referral by the prime minister of acts which the government perceived to be parliamentary attempts to legislate beyond its constitutional authority. These decisions can be separated into two categories: 1) those concerning alleged parliamentary overreach of the domain of *la loi* constituted by the terms of article 34 (four decisions), and 2) those concerning alleged violations of article 40, which provides procedures to oppose parliamentary initiatives which would either raise public expenditure or draw down public funds (two decisions). Brief examination of this early jurisprudence shows the extent to which the Council strained to provide maximum support for the executive against parliament.

In its very first decision pursuant to an article 61.2 referral,[8] the Council was asked to decide a controversy that had erupted between the Senate and the government on debates to revise certain provisions of the 1960 budget. The details of the revision are technical, but very briefly, the government was

Table 3.1. Constitutional Council Decisions, 1959–1970

Decision	Referral Authority	Bill Referred	Result	Basis for Annulment
Nov. 8, 1960	Prime Minister	Revision of finance law (1960)	Partial annulment*	art. 34
Jan. 20, 1961	Prime Minister	Social insurance- Farm workers	Partial Annulment	art. 40
Nov. 6, 1962	Pres. of Senate	Direct election of the president	No jurisdiction	—
Mar. 12, 1963	Prime Minister	Real estate reform	Partial annulment	art. 40
Dec. 18, 1964	Prime Minister	Finance law 1960	Partial annulment	art. 34
Jan. 30, 1968	Prime Minister	Evaluation of local taxation	SROI†	art. 34
Dec. 30, 1970	Prime Minister	Revision of finance law (1970)	Partial annulment	art. 34

* In a case of a partial annulment, the Council "amputates" an offending provision from the bill, allowing what remains to be promulgated.

†A decision of "conformity" with binding (strict) reserves of interpretation (SROI) enunciated by the Council.

seeking authority to raise radio broadcasting licensing fees by decree, while article 34 of the constitution grants to the domain of *la loi* the power to set rules concerning "the modalities of tax collection of all nature." After the Senate had rejected the bill, a joint committee of the two chambers hammered out a compromise which would have allowed the government to modify the tax by decree, while the actual collection of the tax would have depended on prior parliamentary authorization. The government opposed the compromise but, recognizing that it would expedite the passage of the bill, did not block its passage. Once secured, Debré asked the Council to remove the compromise from the law,[9] and the Council, on 11 August complied, censuring parliament for attempting "to interfere with the government's authority to manage" the industry. As in many early article 37 cases, the Council relied not on a constitutional text as the basis of its decision, but on a legislative *ordonnance* enacted by the executive before parliament had come into being! The Council later confirmed this jurisprudence in several other decisions restricting the domain of *la loi* during this period.

The jurisprudence on article 40 proved no less harmful to parliament and no more substantiated by constitutional texts. The leading decision is that of 20 January 1961 (the second review of legislation overall),[10] and again involved a conflict between the Senate and the government. In debates on a proposed revision of public health insurance, a matter clearly in the domain of *la loi*, the Senate voted overwhelmingly, 195–14, to expand certain maternity and disability benefits for farm workers, arguing that the added benefits would be more than compensated for by new payments into the system. The government opposed the amendment on the grounds that it would have the effect of raising public expenditures, therefore violating article 40, and threatening Council referral.[11] After the National Assembly accepted the Senate's proposals, Debré asked the Council to annul the provisions on the basis of their violation of the dictates of article 40.[12] The Council complied, accepting virtually the whole of the prime minister's argument.

The Constitutional Council's acceptance of article 40 jurisdiction to annul legislation already adopted can not be justified by any constitutional grant of authority, or by the intended, or actual, functioning of that article. Article 40 (which reads: "Bills or amendments proposed by members of parliament are not receivable when their adoption would result in either a diminution of public funds or the creation or increase in public charges."), stated in one simple sentence, concerns only the procedure of a bill's elaboration in parliament. In practice, it gives to the government and the presidents of the committees or of the chambers the power to raise a *motion d'irrecevabilité*—a parliamentary motion for a vote to preclude discussion of a bill or an amendment on the basis of its unconstitutionality—against any parliamentary proposal whose effect appears to violate article 40. The motion is then put to a vote and, if passed, discussion of the proposal terminates and may not be revived. Although the CCC had at one point considered granting to the Council jurisdiction over article 40 conflicts (similar to that which it exercises over article 41), the idea was rejected. It was argued, first, that such motions are exclusively matters of procedure, and therefore should be resolved in the traditional manner, by parliamentary votes. Second, such a procedure was viewed as one of dubious practical value to the government, since it would have the upper hand in any controversy anyway.[13]

No one doubts that the Council possessed the power to verify the orderly use of article 40. It would therefore be justified in censuring any authority which actually hindered the exercise of the procedure. However, in this case, the Council—at the government's instigation—appropriated for itself the power to adjudicate the very substance of the motion itself, authority previously understood to be exclusively that of parliament. Once it had asserted jurisdiction, the Council proceeded to a severely restrictive interpretation, prohibiting any new expense authorized by parliamentary initiative, no matter how it was to be met.[14] The Council did *not* rely principally on constitutional texts to obtain this interpretation, but on the terms of a 1956 (executive) *ordonnance*, and the alleged intentions of the founders—as expressed by the *same* CCC debate which had chosen to deny the Council jurisdiction over article 40! The jurisprudence was confirmed two years later in the second case on article 40.

The significance of the Constitutional Council's jurisprudence during this period cannot be adequately measured simply by reference to annulled legislative provisions. Constitutional review had revealed itself to be a powerful tool of structuring *future* legislative processes by transforming the constitutional context of lawmaking, and also by shaping policymaker's attitudes and expectations. The message sent to policymakers during this period was an unambiguous one: the advantages enjoyed by the executive in any interinstitutional conflict did not merely extend to its nearly absolute control over the final outcome of the legislative procedure, but to the terms and conduct of constitutional review itself. It must be stressed that in the four cases concerning transgressions of *loi/règlement* boundaries, the government could have obtained identical *legislative* outcomes by obliging the Council to intervene *during* parliamentary discussions (according to the procedures of article 41). But by choosing to wait until *after* parliament had decided, Debré could achieve his policy objective *and* humiliate parliament. Legal specialists characterized the maneuver as "a low blow" aimed at parliament: one meant "less to assure the respect of the constitution than to win a victory for a governmental position."[15] Far more important, he achieved *constitutional* victory: the decision had the de facto effect of elevating the legislative *ordonnance* to a state of *valeur constitutionnel*,[16] thus altering fundamentally the terms of policymaking for every actor in the system. The politics of early article 40 jurisprudence reveal a similar dynamic. The prime minister was free—even before formal discussion of a proposal began—to seek satisfaction by raising *irrecevabilité*; moreover, he was guaranteed victory given Gaullist control of the National Assembly. (In fact, between 1959 and 1964 more than 250 motions of *irrecevabilité* were raised and voted according to the procedures of article 40.[17]) However, if the government could convince the Council to transfer final jurisdiction over article 40 procedures away from parliamentarians, it might also be able to constitutionalize its interpretation of the meaning of that article's terms. At this it was entirely successful, and prime ministers henceforth possessed the authority to abolish, virtually at will, what remained of parliament's power of initiative after the Council's reworking of parliament's standing orders. In consequence of these decisions, parliament could propose but, without the government's approval, it could no longer legislate. As one law professor put it, ". . . all that remains to the Assemblies are their illusions, their regrets, and their resentment."[18]

Throughout this period, the Constitutional Council was viewed by parliamentarians as simply an extension of executive power, no more and no less. Those opposed to the majority did not expect that the Council's jurisprudence would work in their favor, and they were not anxious to court sure defeat by cajoling the president of the Senate to use his power aggressively. Not that he lacked opportunities: while nearly everyone regarded the constitution as de Gaulle's own, there was little evidence to suggest in the crucial early years of the Republic that the president felt bound by it. General de Gaulle, in fact, had little patience for legal niceties, once stating:

> Three things count in constitutional matters. First, the higher interest of the country . . . and of that I alone am judge. Second, far behind, are the political circumstances, arrangements, tactics. . . . Third, much further behind, there is legalism. . . . I have accomplished nothing in my life except by putting the welfare of the country first and by refusing to be entrapped by legalisms.

(And later he asked of a biographer: "Do you really believe I am bound by the constitution?"[19]). On only one instance during this period was the Council asked to rule *against* the executive, when in 1962 the president of the Senate, Gaston Monnerville, asked the Council to invalidate de Gaulle's attempt to amend the constitution by referendum—a procedure not provided for by the constitution. The subsequent decision put the Council on center stage, for one brief moment, but damaged the institution's public reputation for years thereafter.

In late September 1962, de Gaulle announced to a national television audience his plan to institute direct election to the office of the presidency by universal suffrage. Although such a change would require an amendment to the constitution, de Gaulle was unwilling to follow the only procedures providing for revision, those of article 89, which requires that constitutional amendments be adopted in "identical terms" by both houses of parliament. Instead, the government proposed that the revision be adopted by the people in a national referendum according to article 11, which allows legislating but not constitutional revision by referendum, thus bypassing a hostile parliament completely. The stakes of de Gaulle's gamble were high. If he were to succeed, the last argument for parliamentary sovereignty—namely, that the National Assembly was the sole institution elected by the people—would be silenced.

The proposal caused immediate and shrill protest from politicians,[20] the print-media,[21] and from constitutional scholars, including the editor of the *Revue du droit public*,[22] largely to the effect that the procedure to be used was unconstitutional, and would result in a presidential system of government. The government, as required by the constitution, consulted with both the *Conseil d'Etat* and the Council, and *both* bodies ruled—in nonbinding opinions—that the procedure was unconstitutional.[23] Several days later, the National Assembly brought down the Pompidou government, the first and only censure of a government in the Fifth Republic: "Mr. Prime Minister," Paul Reynaud told Pompidou, "go say to the Elysée . . . that this Assembly is not so degenerate as to renounce the Republic."[24]

The referendum passed on 28 October 62–38 percent, and the law was adopted. Days before it was promulgated, Monnerville appealed to the Council to determine if the referendum procedure, and therefore the law, was constitutional. In his referral,[25] the President of the Senate argued that only article 89 could be employed to amend the constitution properly, and that to admit any other possibility would be to "make nonsense of the essential distinctions" between organic, constitutional, and ordinary laws. The president of the Senate argued further that even power exercised by the voters is "only legitimate if it respects the rules and procedures laid down by the Constitution"; to rule otherwise would be "ruinous for *le droit*, as well as for the stability of our institutions."

On 6 November the Council (by a 6–4 vote[26]) ruled, first, that article 61 only grants the Council jurisdiction over ordinary legislation and not over legislation "adopted by the people following a referendum, which constitute the direct expression of national sovereignty," and second, that since nothing in the constitution gives the Council the competence to examine the constitutionality of referenda, it could not do so.[27] Having been declared beyond the reach of control, the law was promulgated on 8 November.

"The Constitutional Council just committed suicide," Monnerville declared afterwards, and asked, "If the Council does not have the competence to judge a violation so patent and so serious of the constitution, who does in our country?"[28] Monnerville's frustration is understandable: the answer to his question is: no one. For opponents—which included large segments of the parliamentary *majority*—the Council's argumentation leads to an absurdity: while the law is an executive proposal, it can not be legally challenged; after the law is adopted by referendum, it is virtually a superconstitutional law which no institution may contest; in between, no amount of protest could deter the government. Every competent institutional authority had declared itself against the plan, and de Gaulle and his government had simply ignored them all. While there is no shortage of compelling arguments which the Council might have used to claim jurisdiction,[29] in the end it was the lack of political will of a majority of its members to stand up to de Gaulle, and not the power of legal arguments, which was crucial.[30]

One remarkable, if on its face ironic, outcome of this affair was the unprecedented achievement of a consensus among parliamentarians for the principle of constitutional review. Gaullists, naturally enough, rallied behind the Council. *For those opposed to de Gaulle* and the presidentialization of the regime, including those otherwise affiliated with the Right, *the abolition of the Council and the establishment of a supreme court came to be viewed as necessary*. It was argued that a supreme court—replete with "real" judges granted the power to exercise a posteriori review of executive as well as legislative acts—was the indispensable means to ensure a proper balance of power between institutions.[31] Between 1958 and 1970, seven bills to create a supreme court were introduced, although none was proposed by the Left.[32] By 1972, the joint Socialist-Communist Common Program included a plan to abolish the Council and replace it with a supreme court.[33]

1971–80: Raising the Preamble

The 1971–80 period was dominated by two events. First, a 1971 decision[34]—characterized by some as France's *Marbury* v. *Madison*[35]—answered in the affirmative an important question left over from the first period: would the Council ever annul a piece of legislation backed by the executive? Of far greater long-range importance, the 1971 decision affirmed the *valeur constitutionnel* of the texts contained in the 1946 preamble—the 1789 declaration, the FPRLR, and the list of "political, economic, and social principles particularly necessary for our times" [*cited as the 1946 principles*]—opening up an unexplored area of *substantive* constraints on policymaking. Second, the 1974 amendment to the constitution expanding the power of referral to deputies and senators who, inspired by the new politics of the preamble, lead to greatly increased Council activity.

"A Revolution Made in Four Words"

The Constitutional Council's decision of 16 July 1971 capped the first parliamentary legislative process in which ordinary legislation *proposed by the executive* was threatened with referral to the Council. The events leading up to this decision, well documented elsewhere,[36] can be briefly summarized. In May 1970, the government, enabled by 1936 legislation outlawing private militias, banned *La gauche prolétarienne*, a leftist political party. In reaction, a group of concerned citizens including Jean-Paul Sartre and Simone de Beauvoir formed the *Association des amis de la cause du peuple*, taking the name of the group's newspaper. In an effort to establish legal personality, the group sought to register with the Paris prefecture, whereupon the minister of the Interior ordered the *préfet* to refuse to issue the requisite receipt, on the grounds that the two groups were one and the same. This order was reversed by a Paris administrative tribunal, conforming to a long-standing jurisprudence of the *Conseil d'Etat*. In June 1971, attempting to obviate such problems for the future, the government introduced into parliament a bill which would have amended a 1901 law on association, by empowering a *préfet* to withhold recognition from any association which "appeared to have an immoral or illicit purpose or to be trying to reconstitute an illegal association."[37]

The bill generated a heated debate in the National Assembly, where a number of prominent opposition figures on the Left and even a Gaullist denounced the measure as an intolerable infringement on liberties long enshrined by the 1901 legislation, but the majority approved it nonetheless.[38] In the Senate, Pierre Marcilhacy, a prominent independent-centrist and the leading constitutional specialist on that body, raised a *question préalable* in which he argued that the bill abridged rights contained in article 4 of the constitution—which states that political parties and groups may "form and exercise their activities freely"—by allowing for the possibility of a priori suppression of free association. The motion was adopted, and discussion of the bill was aborted before it had begun.[39] After the National Assembly overrode the Senate and passed the bill, the president of the Senate, Alain Poher, "acting dispassionately" and after "numerous hesitations," gave in to pressure exerted by Marcilhacy and others and referred the bill to the Council; "to throw some light on the matter," he declared.[40]

Over the ensuing two weeks, the Council was subjected to an unprecedented and unrelenting lobby campaign for the annulment of the legislation. In addition to agitation by centrist senators and the opposition political parties, unions, small leftist groups, and other social formations publicly expressed their displeasure with the bill. Daniel Mayer, the president of the League of Human Rights (and future Council president) denounced the measure as a sign that French rights were being "eroded and ridiculed," and he was joined by other human rights organizations. Law professors, including Robert Badinter (another future Council president) and Olivier Dupéyroux, argued—in detailed and lengthy "briefs" published in *Le Monde*—that the bill was unconstitutional, was sanctionable by any reading of the Conseil d'Etat's jurisprudence, and constituted a direct challenge to the Council to escape its image of "mediocrity." "A child can see that this bill is unconstitutional," wrote Dupéyroux on the eve of the decision, and one which the Council "must strike down" if it is to fulfill "its historic responsibility" to protect fundamental rights, and thus "determine [its] destiny." *Le Monde*'s cartoonist even got into the act, depicting the minister of the interior poised to crush with a huge rock a tiny fly which had lighted on a sleeping and undisturbed Marianne (the symbol of the Republic). Jean Foyer, a law professor, former Gaullist minister of justice, and the president of the powerful *Commission des lois* in the National Assembly, even felt compelled to protest against what he called "this effort of intoxication"—"the absolutely inadmissible political operation" which claims, "in essence, that if the Council is independent, if it is liberal, it will declare the bill unconstitutional."[41]

On 16 July the Council did just that, amputating the bill's controversial provisions, and prompting *Le Monde*'s banner headline: "The Constitutional Council checks [executive] power and affirms its independence."[42] Far outweighing the importance of the annulment, the Council had, by a vote of 6–3 (dissenting was the Gaullist law professor, François Goguel and two former Gaullist ministers[43]) chosen not only to censure the government, but to base its decision on the preamble generally and on the FPRLR specifically. The "liberty of association," which the Council found to be "recognized" in the same 1901 law which the government had attempted to modify, constituted a FPRLR. Because the freedom of association is not listed as a fundamental right in the 1946 preamble, and because the FPRLR are only mentioned and not enumerated, the Council's ruling constituted unabashed judicial creativity (as *any* ruling based on the FPRLR would have). The result is a curious one: the Council's decision enforces substantive constraints on parliamentary activity, constraints which it found in the work of parliament some seventy years before, when constitutional review did not exist! As disconcerting, because the Council had listed no other principles which might be contained in the corpus of the FPRLR, its discretionary power to discover more of them appeared virtually boundless.

For *le droit*, the decision was cause for general celebration, constituting no less than a judicial "revolution . . . made in 4 words": "In view of the Constitution," the Council had written, "*and notably its preamble*. . . ." "With this single phrase," stated Rivéro, the declaration of 1789, the preamble of 1946, and the fundamental principles recognized by the laws of the Republic were incorporated into the constitution, which was thus "doubled in volume."[44] Council members certainly understood the magnitude of their decision. As then-president Palewski remembered later:

> To justify our decision it was necessary to invoke the preamble of the 1958 Constitution, referring to the 1946 declaration and to that of 1789. We could thus create a veritable judicial bastion for the defense of the rights of citizens.[45]

While the decision is inarguably an audacious one, a conjunction of favorable conditions might have led Palewski to believe that his Council could weather any political storm it might create. Several points deserve emphasis. First, *the Council's move had been well prepared for by doctrinal activity.* As discussed in chapter 1, the *valeur constitutionnel* of much of the preamble had been asserted by doctrinal authority long before ordinary and administrative courts went on to affirm it. It was not altogether surprising then for legal specialists like Badinter and Dupéyroux to direct similar arguments at the Council, which they did in high-profile, public advocacy. By invoking the preamble, the Council was also invoking the legitimacy of legal scholarship and the jurisprudence of the *Conseil d'Etat*. Second, while the FPRLR have the dubious distinction of being the least precise of the sources mentioned by the preamble, the *Conseil d'Etat* had already consecrated "freedom of association" during its Fourth Republic cataloguing of the "general principles of law"; the Council therefore had simply to "constitutionalize" this principle. Third, although Marcilhacy had argued in parliament that the bill violated rights guaranteed by article 4 of the constitution, the referral did *not* raise the article 4 argument, instead relying on the FPRLR via the 1901 legislation. The Council's defenders could therefore readily claim that its "activism" was carefully measured: its jurisprudential choices arose from a decision-making context constructed by "politics." (The president of the Senate was only formally the author of the 1971 referral; in fact, the petition was written by a law professor.[46]) Last, the political environment in which constitutional politics were conducted had fundamentally changed. General de Gaulle's departure had, among other things, made the evolution of the French constitution a much more participatory process. The Council was asserting that a primary constituent element of this process would henceforth be constitutional review.

The decision also signaled to the opposition that constitutional review could be used to enshrine substantive rights important to it and to the detriment of the majority's legislative agenda. Of the Council's next three decisions, two had the effect of rebroadcasting, clarifying, and reinforcing this message. In the first, a decision of 27 December 1973,[47] the Council again gave satisfaction to the president of the Senate in a legislative conflict with the government, consecrating the "general principles of equality before the law" found in the 1789 Declaration of the Rights of Man. Barely a year later, on 15 January 1975,[48] the Council refused to annul any aspect of the government's bill to permit abortion where pregnancy puts a woman in a "situation of distress," ruling that the bill did not violate one of the "political, economic, or social principles particularly necessary to our times." Thus by January 1975, the Constitutional Council had formally spoke to each of the three texts contained in the preamble, thus legitimizing their use as sources of constitutional debate in parliament.

Constitutional Politics as Oppositional Politics

In retrospect, it is clear that one of the important outcomes of Giscard's presidency was the loosening of Gaullist domination of the State generally, and in particular its domination of the Constitutional Council. Giscard seems to have been genuinely committed to restructuring the relationship between majority and opposition within parliament. It was politically in his interest to do so: having defeated the official Gaullist candidate *and* Mitterrand, his partisan base within parliament was hardly a stable one. His move to amend the constitution to allow opposition groups to refer pending legislation to the Council appears to have been a sincere effort to give previously alienated minorities a sense of participation in French constitutional life,[49] as well as to "enlarge the presidential majority towards the left."[50] Although the extraordinary transformative impact of the 1974 amendment on French constitutional politics is quite evident today, when first proposed it engendered little interest.[51] The debates on Giscard's proposal deserve close examination not least because they are the best source of parliamentary attitudes about the Council and constitutional review at this time.

The amendment as initially proposed was characterized in minimalist terms, a revision at once "limited, precise, but positive."[52] It proposed two modifications of article 62: (1) an enlargement of the referral power to one-fifth of either house of parliament, and (2) a clause enabling the Council, on its *own* initiative, to convene itself whenever it thought a pending piece of legislation "might infringe on public liberties." The latter proposal was quickly quashed in both houses, in terms reminiscent of those used during the CCC debates: Etienne Dailly, the *rapporteur* for the relevant Senate committee called it "useless, bizarre, inapplicable, and dangerous," and Jean Foyer, speaking for the assembly's deliberative committee joined in the demand for its suppression—"to keep the Council out of the middle of political debates."[53] Opposition to the proposal came from across the political spectrum, and included Gaullists and other elements of the majority, but the following arguments were heard most often: (1) the Council would have an effective—and therefore unacceptable—veto power over legislation; (2) the Council was too manifestly political to be trusted with such authority; (3) even if the Council worked diligently to behave as a neutral and independent "judicial" body, its role would be "politicized" to the extent that decisions to intervene selectively in the policymaking process would be inherently political; (4) the conflictual and imprecise nature of the texts which the Council had recently incorporated into the constitution could lead the Council down any jurisprudential path it might want to follow. In sum, as Alexander Bolo put it, "The power to convene itself seems exorbitant because we would no longer be able to tell who was the real legislator, parliament or the Council."[54] I will argue in subsequent chapters that to the extent that referrals to the Council are systematic, the suppression of this aspect of the reform is, as a practical matter, superfluous, and that the predictions of politicization and the consequent blurring of legislative and jurisdictional powers have come to pass. Its defeat however is dramatic evidence that suspicion of a *gouvernement des juges* situation remained great.

The proposed expansion of referral authority to ordinary parliamentarians fared better, but only barely. After the terms of the expansion were altered from one-fifth of either chamber to any sixty deputies or senators, the constitutional amendment was finally passed by a vote of 488–273, thirteen votes above the total required for adoption.[55] *The Left, as well as those orthodox Gaullists who resented any change in the document, voted against the amendment.* With respect to the rest of the Right, the lack of outspoken criticism appears to have resulted from a combination of three factors. First, the new president made it clear that this was to be considered a high-priority reform, and that resistance to it would promote divisions within a majority facing an increasingly formidable electoral threat from the Left. Second, the president and his Gaullist prime minister, Jacques Chirac, did not hide the fact that they were prepared to use pressure tactics to produce a positive vote. Opposition might thus be politically costly for members of parliament facing a president just beginning a seven year term in office. Third, as Claude Gerbet, minister of justice acknowledged in a candid manner during the debates, some within the majority were prompted to support the proposal for long-term political gain: "We have been thinking about the means which we would have at our disposal to assure the respect for fundamental liberties" if the Left was ever to come to power.[56] For all of these reasons, the majority rallied behind Giscard's proposal even though "they were scarcely more favorable to the reform than their colleagues of the opposition."[57]

The basis of the Left's opposition had already been consistently expressed: any acceptable system of review had to be built from scratch, after abolition of the Council. Review had also to go much further in order to ensure "real" review, including of executive acts.[58] Positive results could hardly be expected from the expansion of the referral mechanism; in Senator Tailhadès words, "because [the Council] is entirely [under executive] influence," "neutral judgements are impossible."[59] The reform also represented for many an ominous "future danger for a government of the Left," especially in regard to nationalization of industries.[60] Still, as Duverger wrote, it appeared that "the Left had nothing to lose"[61] by the change, and between 1974 and 1981 it was the forces of the Left, and especially the Socialists, who first developed the procedures for parliamentary referral.

Initially, the 1974 amendment did not focus attention on constitutional review as a means of protecting public liberties. *The parliamentary impulse was to codify, and thus to secure the primacy of parliament over rights politics.* In February 1975, the Socialist group, the Communist party, and the Gaullists each proposed a draft bill of rights.[62] As in 1946, the attempt failed without minimal consensus as to first principles; indeed first principles were the source of division. For the Left, the struggle for "liberty" was intimately linked to the struggle for socialism, and their proposals took the form of polemical *critique*.[63] The bills sought to secure more favorable terms for exercising of traditional political and economic rights, and to develop new rights, such as the equality of the sexes, and worker's participation. The Right's conception of liberty was predicated on the preservation of the fundamental separation of the domains of "society" and "politics"; in its view, existing public liberties deserved defense, but the active creation of new rights was to be resisted.

The failure of the project simply relocated the political struggle, if slowly and unevenly, to an existing site: to the realm of the Council, newly-incarnated as the sovereign source of constitutional interpretation. Given the lack of political consensus on rights, the Council's canonizing of the preamble was a potentially dangerous move. Unlike most other constitutional courts, the Council can only enforce respect of fundamental liberties by intervening directly in legislative processes, and by invoking unclear, ideologically charged sources of authority (i.e., the texts of the preamble). It bears repeating that the preamble would never have been attached to the 1946 constitution had its authors known that judges would use it to determine the constitutionality of legislation. In 1946, no group had gained much in practical terms from this outcome but no group had lost much either—and each had won symbolic victories. In 1975, *the default position was no longer parliament, but the Council.*

Duverger had argued during the discussions of the 1974 amendment that Giscard's "gift to the opposition," while meager, was nonetheless a positive one, which "the opposition [had] nothing to lose" by accepting.[64] The argument, of course, ignores that for the Right the gift might have been, if only in part, a trojan horse—and it was construed as such by some. In retrospect, the risks run by the majority in opening up the referral process turned out to be slight when compared to the potential benefits. An examination of the Left's attempts to use the Council to enshrine its vision of the rights contained in the preamble reveals this to have been the case.

Of the sixteen annulments or partial annulments made by the Council during the 1971–81 period, seven were based on the Council's reading of the preamble (Table 3.2); after 1974, each decision resulted from parliamentary referral. Some aspects of the 1789 declaration were popular with *both* the Left and the Council, especially those articles which guaranteed individual rights against abuses by judicial and administrative authorities. However, the Left had enormous difficulty winning approval for those rights which it had fought for in 1946 and which were contained in the main body of the 1946 preamble. On only one occasion, and *this remains the only case to date*, did the Council agree to enshrine restraints on legislative activity based the 1946 principles. What is not shown by Table 3.2 are instances in which the Council was asked to balance apparently conflicting texts within the preamble itself or where principles contained by the preamble conflicted with grants of parliamentary competence in article 34. A consideration of these decisions and their legislative contexts are also crucial to an understanding of the constitutional politics during this period.

The Council's decision of 23 November 1977 is an important example.[65] In the fall of that year, the government agreed to support a proposal, emanating from its own majority, to strengthen state support of the private, that is, Catholic, school system at least in part in order to bolster the electoral fortunes of the Right. Coming on the eve of the 1978 parliamentary elections, opposition politicians virulently attacked the bill as an electoral maneuver; Mitterrand declared himself "scandalized" by this "electoral sham, this abuse of power, abuse of a majority facing transition," and accused the majority of a mercenary revival of "the war over the schools" for votes.[66] In parliament, the

Table 3.2. Council Annulments Based on the Preamble, 1971–1981*

Decision	Referral Authority	Provisions Violated
Jul. 17, 1971	Pres. of the Senate	FPRLR†
Dec. 17, 1973	Pres. of the Senate	Decl. Rts. of Man (art. 6)‡
Jul. 23, 1975	Senators	Decl. Rts. of Man (art. 6)
Jan. 12, 1977	Deputies (PS) Deputies (PC)	FPRLR
Jan. 17, 1979	Deputies (PS) Deputies (PC)	Decl. Rts. of Man (art. 6)
Jul. 25, 1979	Senators Deputies (PS)	1946 preamble§
Jan. 19–20, 1981	Senators Deputies (PS) Deputies (PC)	FPRLR Decl. Rts. of Man (art. 8)

*The table does not include decisions on legislation adopted after the 1981 parliamentary elections.

†1971: freedom of association; 1977: individual liberty; 1980: right to legal defense.

‡Article 6: equality before the law; article 8: nonretroactivity of penal law.

§1946 "social and economic principles necessary for our times": the right to strike. FPRLR = fundamental principles recognized by the laws of the Republic; PC = Communist party; PS = Socialist party.

bill was attacked as unconstitutional,[67] on the basis of its violation of the the 1946 principles, one line of which states:

> The nation guarantees equal access to the child and the adult to instruction, to professional training, and to culture. The organization of free and secular public education at every level is a responsibility of the State.

(In 1946, the constitutional assembly had voted, after a tortuously long debate, to reject a proposal to include in the main body of the preamble the principle of "freedom of education," understood by all to be a vote to forbid state subsidies of Catholic education.[68]) The majority had a difficult time countering this argument, the *rapporteur*, Jean Sauvage, admitting that "one would search in vain in the constitutional texts for any text which might affirm expressly the existence of the principle [of state support of religious institutions]." Still he went on to claim that such a principle "was not therefore contrary to our public law," and went on to argue that the principle might be inferred from a FPRLR which he found in the finance law of 31 March 1931.[69]

Sauvage's mention of the FPRLR reveals the preamble in all of its compromised uncertainty. During the Fourth Republic, doctrinal specialists had argued that the phrase—"the FPRLR"—would be the least likely source for creative jurisprudence: in 1948, Duverger noted that "of all of the obscure elements [*obscurités*] of the constitution, this remains the most obscure." Duverger was only able to find one such FPRLR, significantly, the "freedom of education" which article 91 of the finance law of 31 March 1931 proclaims as a "fundamental principle."[70] The Council's 1971 decision on freedom of association had proved that the number of FPRLR was at least one, but it had not yet had the occasion to discover a second. In its decision, the Council found that article 91 of the 1931 finance law did indeed "constitute a FPRLR, reaffirmed by the preamble of the Constitution of 1946, upon which the Constitution of 1958 had conferred *valeur constitutionnel*"; and the bill was promulgated.

To say that the Left, or any opposition, "has nothing to lose" by referring legislation underestimates the creative power of constitutional review. In this case, *the judgment of the political majority of 1946 was repudiated.* The Council gave the following definitive interpretation of the preamble with respect to the long-running controversy over public versus private education: first, the explicit principles enshrined in the preamble on education do not require only one system, nor do they forbid state funding of Catholic schools; second, the FPRLR contained in article 91 of the 1931 finance law forbids the abolition of either system.

The largest class of referrals involving interpretation of the preamble concerned those rights which the Left held most dear—the rights of workers to strike and to participate in the management of the workplace. In the 1977 legislative year, the opposition unsuccessfully referred three pieces of legislation to the Council which it claimed violated line 8 of the 1946 preamble, which states: "Every worker participates, by the intermediary of his representatives, in the collective determination of the conditions of work as well as the management of the enterprise." The Council rejected the Socialists on each occasion, asserting, with almost no argument, that article 34 delegates to the legislature how the rights enunciated by the preamble were to be enjoyed.[71]

For a number of reasons, the Council's decision of 25 July 1979[72] is by far the most important on the social rights enumerated by the preamble. First, it concerned the right to strike, upon which the decision explicitly conferred *valeur constitutionnel*. Second, it remains the only occasion in which the Council annulled a piece of legislation based on the main body of the preamble—the 1946 principles. Third, although nominally a "victory" for the Left in the narrow legislative sense, the importance of the decision is further reaching: indeed, the decision is an example of how an apparent victory may not translate neatly into interpretive victory.

The legislation at hand was designed to respond to complaints made by the management of the state-run television and radio stations to the effect that employees were violating provisions regulating strike action in the industry. These alleged "abuses" were only part of a general wave of work stoppages that engulfed the public sector through the winter and spring of 1978–79. In the broadcast media sector, management argued that the actions hardly constituted strikes, since they could not be regulated as such by the applicable legislation. Briefly, the legislative provisions then in place required unions to file one day in advance a notice of intent to walk out or suffer financial penalties. Upon receipt of the notice, management was then empowered to require personnel to remain on the job in order to assure "minimum service," which replaced normal broadcasting schedules with temporary programs. The unions, ingeniously exploiting these regulations, began filing *daily* notices—the so-called sliding notice (*préavis glissant*)—informing management that only those personnel required to maintain minimum service were to strike. Management was then led to invoke minimum service procedures, but employees suffered no penalties since virtually all personnel remained on the job. The legislation proposed was designed to forbid the practice of the sliding notice, to define those personnel who are "strictly indispensable" to the "fulfillment of the mission" of the broadcast company, and to grant to management the power to require those personnel necessary to assure *normal* service.[73]

The bill's journey through parliament was a rocky one. The opposition, citing the relevant portions of the 1946 preamble, which state:

> Everyone may defend his rights and his interests by union action, and may belong to the union of his choice.
> The right to strike is exercised according to the laws which regulate it,

attacked the bill's constitutionality from the first reading in a series of procedural maneuvers—including motions of *irrecevabilité*,[74] and *quéstions préalables*,[75] both of which required constitutional debate. The majority argued that the dictates of the preamble were to be understood only as "an invitation to the legislator to achieve a necessary conciliation" between professional interests and the general interest, and did not constitute an "absolute" right, and motions were rejected in these terms.[76]

Debate increasingly focused on constitutionality, with the opposition in both houses and many senators of the majority agreeing that the legislation would in effect prohibit the right to strike in the sector, and demanding that majority make clear the constitutional principle on which it was relying. The majority's response was to proliferate such principles. The right to receive "televised images" and radio broadcasts, the right to information, to be entertained, and even the right "to cultivate oneself" were all proferred, and in the National Assembly a *question préalable* even led to a debate as to whether or not such rights were contained in the FPRLR or were corollaries to the "social and economic principles," and thus had constitutional status![77] In the end, the majority settled on the "principle of the continuity of public service," a position relatively enfeebled by the fact that the principle could be found in no text but bolstered by a long line of *Conseil d'Etat* decisions.[78] "But we are not here to study constitutional law," protested the bill's sponsor. "We are here to state clearly that these strikes without strikers, these strikes without penalties, must stop."[79] Nevertheless, proof of the degree to which legal language had become the medium of debate on the bill, the assembly then changed its title: from "Law relative to the right to strike in the radio-television industry," to "Law relative to the continuity of public service in case of work stoppages in the industry."[80] The threat to petition the Council was made by Henri Caillevet, one of the original *rapporteurs* for the bill in the Senate, in these terms:

> . . . it is necessary that the right to strike of these employees be consecrated. You reject this. You are thus in violation of constitutional law and, I will tell you quite plainly, that if this text is adopted as it is I will refer it to the Constitutional Council, and I dare hope that it will . . . recognize our position.[81]

The bill was referred to the Council by both senators and deputies. The petitioners made two general arguments. First, and most important, they argued that while the bill did not explicitly abolish the right to strike, it nullified the effects of any strike, which amounted to the same thing. The petitioners then argued that no limitation to the right to strike could be found in any constitutional text. Thus if the Council did take it upon itself to balance the right to strike with another norm, its choice would be an easy one, since "it would be difficult to see how a nonconstitutional principle could prevail over a constitutional one."

The Council removed from the legislation phrases which it judged to be in violation of the dictates of the preamble, namely, those which would have enabled management to assure "normal service" and the fulfillment of the broadcaster's "mission" by forcing striking workers to stay on the job. The *ancien régime* was therefore left unchanged, and only "minimum service" could be guaranteed in strike situations. The Council then made the following declaration:

> . . . the recognition of the right to strike may not be understood to have the effect of forbidding the legislature from specifying necessary limitations to this right in order to assure *the continuity of public service*, which, like the right to strike, is a principle possessed of *valeur constitutionnel* [emphasis added].

The Council thus put the two principles on equal footing, in effect "constitutionalizing" a rule of law which was wholly the product of administrative jurisprudence. It must be stressed that the Council could have obtained the same result otherwise: it could have simply stated, as the preamble does, that "the right to strike is exercised according to the laws which regulate it," and left it to parliamentary sovereignty; or it could have relied on article 5 of the constitution, which gives to executive authority the responsibility to "assure the regular functioning of public service" (which would have had the effect, exactly seventy years later, of legitimizing Professor Hauriou's interpretation of the *Conseil d'Etat's* decision in *Winkel*, discussed in chapter 1).

The second right to strike decision handed down by the Council demonstrates again the risks the Left assumed in convening the Council during this period.[82] This time the decision concerned an article of a government bill entitled "The protection and control of nuclear materials." This provision established as a crime "any intentional violation of the laws, regulations, or instructions of the management or its delegates" when such violations may "endanger the security of the nuclear installations or of nuclear material, or when it may endanger "*the security of persons and assets*." The Left attacked this provision on the grounds that nothing in the bill prohibited management from using its authority to issue instructions which would have the effect of limiting union activity, including strike action, and its introduction into parliament set off a series of electrical strikes across France.[83] The Council, convened by two petitions, one Socialist, the other Communist, rejected this argument, and declared instead that the right to strike was subject to a new limitation also not found in any constitutional text: in its words, that which is "necessary to assure *the protection of health and the security of persons and assets*, protection which, like the right to strike, is a principle possessed of *valeur constitutionnel*" [emphasis added].

I have gone into some detail on these decisions and on the debates which proceeded them in order to make the following point: the Council's decision making can never be dissociated from legislative decision-making. Put differently, the Constitutional Council does not preside over a process which conforms to a "judicial" one, whether understood from an American or a French perspective. While I will return to this point in the next chapter, it is important to note that in both American and French legal theory, "judicial" processes are to be distinguished from other governmental processes—at a bare minimum— by the existence of litigants, case, and controversy. In French constitutional review, these aspects are wholly absent. Its decision-making processes are structured by, and are embedded in, a greater process—that of policymaking. Whatever understanding may be achieved of how the Council exercises its own proper discretionary power (primarily that of developing constitutional texts of reference) will be infirmed by failure to relate the production of jurisprudence to legislative processes and outcomes. They may not be separated. The point, which has by now been made implicitly on numerous occasions, is emphasized in an extraordinary manner by the second decision on the right to strike. The Council chose to limit the exercise of a right mentioned explicitly in the preamble by enshrining a principle which is found in no constitutional text; instead, the principle—indeed its exact wording—was generated by a provision contained in pending legislation under review.[84]

Analysis of these decisions and of their legislative contexts also provide evidence of what might be characterized as a kind of *judicial inflation*. By this, I mean both the multiplication of texts, principles, and rights purported to be invested with *valeur constitutionnel*, and also the consequent loss of assured value which the use of such principles may command in the legislative process. Political discourse, the obsessive talk of rights during this period, fueled this inflation. A good example occurred during the discussion of the principle of the right to strike when the Right argued that citizens possessed countervailing rights "to receive televised images" and "to be entertained." In 1977, after the adoption of a government bill to grant police wider powers to stop and search automobiles, the Council received three petitions signed by 239 parliamentarians.[85] Taken together, parliamentarians asked the Council to enshrine, among other references to the 1789 declaration and the main body of the constitution, the following FPRLR: of free movement (*aller et venir*), of privacy of person and of correspondence, of the inviolability of the domicile, of equality, of the right to protest, and that principle which "distinguishes between the administrative and judicial police." None of these however are to be found in the text of the preamble itself. Not insignificantly, the Council, for its part, chose to discover and to enshrine a wholly new FPRLR, which it named—without defining—that of "individual liberty."[86]

With such decisions, the Council, too, then contributed to the inflationary spiral: directly—as the principles generated by the right to strike decisions and the jurisprudence of the FPRLR make clear; and indirectly—to the extent that once the Council ratifies claims made by petitioners, newly-enshrined principles become themselves sources of future claims and counterclaims in legislative debate. Moreover, as both right to strike cases demonstrate, the Council revealed both its capacity and willingness to generate constitutional principles which it had no intention of using to annul the legislation before it. This act of creation does more than simply respond to requests to *dire le droit* ("to declare what the law is"), or "to clarify the problem for the legislature."[87] It also functions creatively, to produce constitutional uncertainty while at the same time potentially structuring future legislative processes. Before 1971, the impact of this function was largely procedural; after 1971, the impact is substantive, on the actual content of legislation.

The problem is not a serious one however if policymakers do not fear constitutional censure. In the 1971–81 period, majorities in control of legislative process generally did *not* fear Council censure, and were not led to constrain or sacrifice policy choices due to worries about unconstitutionality or Council censure. The most celebrated annulments, the Council's 1971 decision on freedom of association and its 1977 annulment of the bill to expand police power to search automobiles, occurred *after* government had been more than usually warned. In both of these cases, the constitutionality of the legislation was extensively debated, and the Senate had overwhelmingly rejected the bills on successive occasions as unconstitutional.[88] The threat of appeal to the Council was moreover made explicit in parliament, but on these as on many other occasions governments and majorities simply refused to take them seriously. One must look long and hard to find much evidence of what I earlier called *autolimitation*—the sacrifice of initial policy objectives in the face of opposition threats of referral—especially in the early years of this period.[89] A general juridicization of the policymaking process did occur, but not until after the 1981 elections.

1981–87: Judicial–Political Confrontation in the Age of Reform

The *alternance* of 1981 brought to power a president, a government, and a parliament committed to far-reaching social and economic reforms. The resulting Socialist "experiment" has been the subject of numerous books, conferences, and articles attempting to assess the degree to which these reforms succeeded in transforming French politics and society.[90] These debates will not be entered into here except to make the following point during this period, policymaking institutions generally exhibited much more continuity than change with respect to their role and functioning; the notable exception is the Constitutional Council.[91] This was so because the Right, which had lost control of every other important institution, focused its energies on constitutional politics as a means of opposing Socialist reforms.[93] At the same time, these reforms gave the opposition unprecedented opportunities to juridicize policymaking processes. By definition, radical reform—and both Left and Right saw the Socialist's program as radical—strains the confines of existing law, constitutional jurisprudence, and established administrative procedures. In the terms of constitutional law, for the first time in the Fifth Republic, a government sought to actualize many of the social and economic principles contained in the 1946 preamble, and to defend liberty largely understood as the rights of workers, women, and the (secular) collective. The Right, on the other hand, sought to maintain the spirit of the 1789 declaration, and to defend liberty understood as rights to property, of individuals, and to due process. In response, the Council ventured into unexplored areas of constitutional law in order to discover principles applicable to the legislative debates which had come before it. The return of the Right to power in 1986 did not reverse this situation, partly because the Right's program was as unabashedly committed to the transformation of French society as was its predecessor's, but in an opposite direction. In summary, as the political stakes of constitutional review were raised, the Council, and constitutional law, were unavoidably implicated in the struggle over radically opposed reform agenda.

The rest of this chapter provides an overview of what turned out to be the formative period in the history of the Council as a major policymaker in France. Because the whole of Part II is devoted to the relationship between policymaking and constitutional politics in the 1981–87 period, the politics of the most important Council decisions are only summarized here. Attention is paid to the evolution of this long judicial–political confrontation and why it died out.

Socialist Reform

As early as the summer of 1981, before parliamentary debates had even begun on the most important of the new government's bills, the Right made clear its intention to use the Council as a kind of "anonymous government," now that it was out of power.[93] Newspapers sympathetic to the new opposition openly discussed the coming confrontation as if it were already a fact. *Le Figaro* stated in August that "the only constitutional weapon henceforth available to the opposition is referral to the Council," noting that "its members were all appointed under the former government, a politically novel situation"; *La Croix* noted a few months later that the Right had begun to hail the Council as "the last rampart against the socialist-communist government."[94] By the end of 1981, the government and its majority, constantly invoking parliamentary sovereignty, seconded by the virtually the entire national press, began to compare the developing situation to the archetype of such confrontations, that of New Deal days in the United States.

Underlying this view, and underlying the majority's critique of the Council's role during the 1981–85 period, was the partisan affiliation of the Council. Not only had the Right appointed all nine members—the Socialist's first opportunity to appoint a member did not arise until 1983—but a majority on the Council had been elected politicians and ministers of the Right. The Left ritually invoked partisanship, political bias, and the illegitimacy of a former majority hindering the policies of a new one in all of their critiques. As Lionel Jospin put it after the first nationalization decision, "Eight among them are former politicians of the Right, former ministers, former party leaders. . . . [T]he Council is not an objective body . . . it is of the Right."[95] Significantly, the Council came to be collectively known as the "dinosaurs of the Palais Royal," referring to the advanced age of the political "retirees," but also implying that remnants of the political past had no claim on the future or a right to thwart progress. Only after this point was made did politicians, as well as many newspapers,[96] turn to the substance of the decisions and to their jurisprudential merit. With respect to jurisprudential tendencies, too, many argued that the Council's political biases were clearly expressed, most notably by its refusal to use that part of the preamble dear to the Left—the so-called social and economic principles of 1946 (cited here as the 1946 principles)—to fend off claims made by the Right in the name of the 1789 declaration. Nor did the tendency for politicians and the press to analyze the Council's role and behavior in terms of brute politics diminish appreciably as time wore on. In 1984, Hughes Portelli, a political science professor writing in *La Croix*, stated bluntly, "Composed of a majority of members close to the present opposition, the Council continues to conduct a subtle, judicial guerrilla war against the government."[97]

What follows are summaries of seven of the most important of the Council's decisions during the 1981–85 period, examined for the most part from the perspective of their political impact, largely as reported in the national press. Many of the legal debates which exercised parliamentarians, their advisors, and doctrinal specialists will be looked at much more closely in Part II.

Perhaps the most important Council decision in history was delivered on 16 January 1982 concerning the centerpiece of the Socialist's program, the bill to enable the nationalization of five industrial groups, thirty-six banks, and two financial companies.[98] As Lionel Jospin remarked, soon after what the Left referred to as the "black weekend" of the ruling, it was "the first time in the history of the fifth republic that the Council had blocked the promulgation of a law . . . at the heart of the program enacted by the President of the Republic and a legitimately elected national assembly." The press universally reported the decision as a defeat for the government, and recorded the vocal "jubilation" of the opposition.[99] Given its traditionally low profile, this decision focused unprecedented national attention on the Council.

The most important aspects of the decision, rendered after a full month of deliberation, were predicated on article 17 of the 1789 declaration which asserts that "property is an inviolable and sacred right" which can only be abridged in case of "public necessity" and on condition that "just and prior compensation" is paid. Article 17 conflicted on its face with the 1946 principle according to which the State was required to nationalize all industries which functioned in the "public interest" or as "de facto monopolies." Refusing to bestow upon the 1946 text constitutional status, the Council first ruled that the nationalizations were acceptable in principle, but then declared that the proposed compensation formula was not "just" and therefore violated article 17 (1789). Since nationalizations could hardly proceed without a means of payment, the law could not be promulgated as written. The government was then forced to revise the compensation formula as well as other parts of the bill according to the criteria suggested by the Council in its decision.

After the decision, the potential for constitutional crisis was high, as daily threats were issued by Socialist officials against a censure of the second, revised bill, the prime ministers office even letting it be known that "Mitterrand would not accept" a second negative ruling.[100] Debate among legal specialists about the possible use of referendum to overturn the Council's decision or to preempt a second one was played out in the press.[101] *Le Monde* portrayed the conflict in these traditional, Rousseauian terms:

> On one side, nine "judges" named by representatives of the former majority; on the other, the 15, 714, 598 French citizens who voted . . . in favor of Francois Mitterrand. . . . Which of these 2 legitimacies is more legitimate? For the Communists, the Socialists, and their deputies, the answer is clear: the Council is wrong because it is blocking the change desired by the country.[102]

The Council approved the revised bill in February, and the situation calmed.[103] Still, the economic and political cost to the government were significant. The recovery program was delayed, the price of compensation was raised by nearly 30 percent, a tax hike was necessitated (at a time of otherwise reflationary policies), and the previously divided opposition had been given an issue around which to rally. After two Council members spoke out against the "dishonest and injurious" attacks leveled against them by the Socialists, *Le Figaro* called on its readers to "defend the Republic," and Gaullists, including Jacques Chirac, proclaimed that the country's political divisions were between "Republicans" and "Marxists" rather than Right and Left.[104] However unintended, the Council's decision thus played an important role in shortening what in fact was a nearly nonexistent "honeymoon period."

In November 1982, the Council overturned a provision in the municipal elections reform law, which stated that no party list in communes of more than 3,500 inhabitants could include "more than 75% candidates of the same sex."[105] The awkward language of the provision, intended to institute a 25 percent quota of women candidates, was a result of worries about constitutionality. In 1979, the law professor Georges Vedel, appointed to the Council in 1980, had written an article explaining that "a text which reserved a certain number of places for women . . . without doing the same for men . . . would be contrary to the principle of equality." Vedel further argued that such a law would probably be not be judged unconstitutional given that a number other restrictions on the rights of candidates and voters had long been accepted.[106] In the face of these legal arguments and the growing electoral importance of women, the bill was favorably received by all parties in parliament and was passed by an overwhelming majority. The bill was referred, but the petitioners did not ask the Council to annul the quota provision.

In annulling the quota, the Council relied again on article 6 (1789), which guarantees French men equality under the law, ignoring the 1946 principle of "equality of the sexes" which might have led them to decide otherwise.[107] The minister of women's rights pointed out that the Council's decision implied that her ministry could not exist if the composition of the government too had to be submitted for the Council's approval. A female deputy observed that less than 9 percent of municipal Councillors were women and concluded that only an "antique reflex of misogyny" could have led to the Council's ruling. Given the near unanimous parliamentary support of the quota (at least in public), a Socialist surmised that there was "a new allocation of roles on the Right—the Council daring to do what parliamentarians of the same ideology would not."[108]

In December 1982, the Council annulled the bill extending decentralization to the overseas departments (DOM) in its entirety.[109] The focus of the dispute was an article which sought to implement 1 of the 110 reform proposals which made up the Socialist's campaign platform. This article provided for a single assembly (combining the regional Council and the general Council) elected by proportional representation. The government had argued that the establishment of a single assembly made economic sense in the DOM where, as in Paris, a separate regional assembly seemed superfluous; it made political sense and was justified by the need to allow for representation of ethnic minorities so as to obviate "situations like Algeria and Indochina." Constitutionally, the government appealed to article 73 which provides for what appeared to be a wide grant of discretionary authority, declaring that "measures of adjustment necessitated by the particular situation of the DOM may be taken with regard to their legislative system and administrative organization." For the opposition, such arguments concealed what in reality was a blatant "political operation," since it was forecasted that the proposed system would result in the ouster of Center-Right majorities in the DOM assemblies. The new law, it argued, would not only shift the balance of power toward the Left, but would also encourage radical independence movements. The Council, basing its decisions, almost word for word, on the text of opposition's referral of the bill, ruled that article 73 disallowed "adjustments" as extensive as parliament had adopted and that the DOM could not possess an electoral system which would result in assemblies "of a different nature" than in regions of metropolitan France.[110]

The decision was hailed as a substantial victory by the opposition, and the press portrayed the ruling as a "severe political defeat" for the government, noting that it was especially embarrassing for the prime minister, who was set to embark on a trip to one of the DOM.[111] Spokesman for the Left protested more vehemently than at any time since the nationalization decision, ridiculing Council members as the nine "geriatrocrats," the "dinosaurs of the Palais

Royal," and decrying again the *gouvernement des juges*.[112] Both François Luchaire, a former Council member, and Pierre Marcilhacy, a long-time expert on constitutional law in the Senate, published what amounted to dissenting opinions—lengthy essays in *Le Monde* taking legal stands in support of the government's position. These articles illustrated vividly that the range of plausible constitutional interpretation was broad indeed and that, as the Socialists had long argued, a change in the Council's composition could well have a profound effect. Three months later, Marcilhacy became the first appointee of a Socialist president to the Council.[113]

In January 1984, the Council annulled the provision of the reform bill on higher education which would have enabled the election of all faculty representatives to university administrative Councils by a single electoral college.[114] In the assembly debates on the bill, the majority had argued that unifying all ranks of teachers from professors to assistants into a single body for the purposes of such elections "would advance the notion of a university community." Everyone recognized that the government's primary motivation was to fulfill a campaign obligation to empower a significant and militant constituency of the Left—the assistants and maître assistants who had long felt exploited by a system which featured rigid status distinctions which operated to the advantage of "mandarin" professors. In an otherwise minor piece of legislation, the single electoral college innovation represented the government's principal response to that pressure. The opposition had hotly contested the new electoral system, arguing that it was an "insult" to the professors and that, since junior faculty outnumbered them by more than two to one, it would "increase the trend in universities toward unionization, politicization, and *mediocrotization*."[115]

In striking down this provision, the Council strayed as far as it has before or since in the serach for relevant constitutional texts to anchor its opinion. Given the "numerical disproportion existing between the corps of professors" and the junior faculty, it ruled, "the independence of the professors would be threatened in a variety of ways," and the "free exercise" of some of their responsibilities—especially discipline—would be impaired; the measure was unconstitutional, the Council concluded, because it violated both article 11 (1789), which consecrates the right to the "free communication of thoughts and opinions", as well as the FPRLR which guarantees professors "independence." The opinion is one of the most heavily criticized by doctrinal authority, precisely because its link to concrete constitutional text or language foundation is so tenuous. In political terms, the decision was judged to be a "serious reverse" for the Socialist's efforts to accomodate the demands of some important teacher's unions, and the minister of education, Alain Savary, discerned "the presence of politics in an *apparently* judicial decision."[116]

In October 1984, the Council was called upon to consider the constitutionality of the mostly hotly contested piece of legislation referred to it since the nationalization bill: the reform to limit the concentration and to assure the financial accountability of the press.[117] The press, also one of Mitterrand's campaign commitments, had been presented by the prime minister as one of the government's most crucial reforms—an antitrust bill for the press industry and a means of penetrating the secrecy which generally cloaks the industry's ownership and management structure. Although prime minister Mauroy and Mitterrand had discreetly avoided acknowledging the principle target of the law, many socialists openly admitted the obvious: the *raison d'être* of the reform was the dismantling of the press empire controlled by the conservative, Robert Hersant. Hersant had been charged, in the 1970s, with using illegal tactics in operating his papers and taking over others, but the judicial process remained bogged down in 1983 and few thought that the trial would ever reach fruition. That Hersant had spearheaded attacks against the Socialist program and its alleged campaign of "liberticide" raised the legislative stakes all the more.

The ten month, legislative process which finally yielded the bill proved to be the most brutal in the history of the Fifth Republic, breaking all records for amendments proposed, hours consumed in debate, and the censuring of unruly deputies.[118] Although substantially revised during the process for fear of Council criticism, the bill as written would have forced Hersant to sell off a substantial portion of his empire. The Council, however, ruled that whereas parliament was free to set upper limits on the percentage of the total press market which a single person or corporation could control, it could not apply these limits to "existing situations" unless such situations had been "illegally acquired," or, in effect, if pluralism could not be achieved any other way. Just as in the nationalization decision of 1982, the Council upheld the government's legislation in principle but not in detail. In the press law case, however, the government was forced to abandon its central objective. In response, a Socialist's spokesman proclaimed that the Council's evolution in the direction of a *gouvernement des juges* had clearly reached a dangerous point, and a former member of the *Conseil d'Etat* wrote in *Le Monde*, that the Council had tarnished its reputation and was beginning to "behave like a third legislative chamber, remaking laws . . . according to options more political than judicial."[119]

The Council was convened in August 1985 to consider another law dealing with a sensitive political issue: reform of the electoral and governmental system in New Caledonia, by far the most troubled and potentially explosive of France's overseas territories (TOM).[120] The Fabius-Pisani law had been designed to replace the traditional system, which, critics complained, had allowed the white (French-origin) majority to monopolize power and was an important factor in the growth of violent protests and calls for independence on the part of the Melanesian minority, the Canaques. Under the proposed system, New Caledonia was to be divided into four regions, each of which would elect a Council to a semiautonomous territorial congress. The boundaries were drawn in such a way as to assure that the indigenous Canaques would enjoy a majority in two of the four regions, and the most heavily populated white-dominant region (Nouméa) was accorded fewer Councillors per capita by a factor of around two than the other regions (1 per 4,700 versus 1 per 2,200–2,600) so as to prevent the whites most staunchly opposed to any alteration of the territories traditional system from obtaining an absolute majority of seats within the Congress. In the debates on the measure, the government's representative, Edgard Pisani, had argued that these provisions would guarantee the rights of both the whites and the Canaques while encouraging the two sides to abandon violence in favor of "a democratic political debate" on their future. For the opposition, the reform deserved condemnation as "a sort of apartheid policy" which would only encourage separatism. Many argued moreover that the proposed electoral system constituted an unconstitutional violation of the right to "equal representation (or suffrage)" guaranteed by article 3 of the constitution. In response, the majority argued that the special conditions existing in New Caledonia justified such a difference in representation; moreover, it noted that *in every parliamentary election held since the advent of the Fifth Republic, the number of deputies per capita varied from district to district by as much as a factor of 10* (1 per 318,000 vs. 1 per 30,000).[121]

The decision of 8 August dealt a surprising political defeat for the government. Whereas the judges confirmed the constitutionality of most aspects of the New Caledonia reform, they struck down the proposed electoral system on the grounds that parliament had "manifestly exceeded" the limited degree to which the terms of article 3 of the constitution, the principle of equal representation, could be compromised in favor of "other considerations of the general interest." While the opposition applauded what it termed the "condemnation of injustice," the Left again harshly criticized "the growing and exorbitant role" played by the *gouvernement des juges.*[122]

The Council's decision forced the government to return to the drawing board and seemed likely to cause a long delay in the New Caledonian elections, a potentially irksome political problem given the coming parliamentary elections. Mitterrand avoided the expected delay (at the very least a month, since the new law would have required approval by the New Caledonian assembly after passing through parliament) through an unprecedented procedural maneuver. Invoking article 10 of the constitution, which allows the president to force parliament to reconsider pieces of legislation and which had never been used before in the wake of Council censure, Mitterrand convened a special session of parliament, thus interrupting the sacrosanct summer vacations of deputies and senators. The opposition pushed for a substantial reworking of the government's proposal; the government gambled that the Council would approve a modest compromise according to which Nouméa would receive twenty-one of forty-six rather than eighteen of forty-three Congress seats. The Council, faced with an impatient, beleaguered government and widespread concern among public lawyers that a second annulment could undermine the legitimacy of the French system of constitutional review, approved the revised electoral law, and the contested procedure used to push it through parliament, on 23 August.[123] In its first decision of 8 August, the Council admitted that the principle of proportionality could be sacrificed to accommodate the "general interest," but did not say how far, and then struck down the government's formula—which contained a maximum of variation of 213 percent—as having violated that principle. On 23 August, the Council approved a maximum variation of 182 percent,[124] but gave no indication of how parliament might have been able to determine constitutionality for itself.

The life of the seventh parliament drew to a close just as it had begun—with controversy centered on the future role of the Council. On 19 February 1986, less than a month before parliamentary elections were to take place, President Mitterrand named his minister of justice, the law professor, Robert Badinter, to the presidency of the Council. Daniel Mayer, a Socialist appointed to the Council and to the presidency in 1983, resigned the presidency but chose to remain an ordinary member of the Council until the completion of his term. The appointment, unlike any which had preceded it, was treated as a matter of high politics by the press, dominating the headlines on the front pages of the national newspapers.[125] Politicians on the Right denounced what François Léotard called "an unacceptable politicization" of the Council, and what Jean-Claude Gaudin, president of the UDF (center-Right), judged to be "a veritable provocation taking account of the time chosen, in the midst of the electoral campaign and of the eminent role which the Council is sure to play between 1986–1988."[126] The maneuver demonstrated the seriousness with which Mitterrand and his advisors viewed that coming role. The appointment would allow the Socialists to extend their control over the Council's presidency another three years, but it also placed in that position a man feared by the Right as much for his legal expertise as his loyalty to Mitterrand.

The Return of a (Radical) Right

The year 1986 proved to be a time of intense legislative activity, but also of intense opposition by the Left. This opposition quickly became constitutionalized as the Socialists referred more than 50 percent of the laws adopted through the summer, and as a result relations between the new majority and the Council worsened as the busy session wore on. What was surprising to many, given the fact that the Council had been so staunchly defended by the Right during the 1981–86 period, and the fact that the Council was still composed of a majority of members named by the former Right majority, was that the judicial–political confrontation begun in 1981 actually worsened. In fact, by far the most vitriolic attacks by politicians on the Council ever recorded occurred during this period, and commentators and journalists in France and abroad sought to explain to a largely ignorant public what the polemics were all about.[127] The underlying bases for these attacks had shifted, however, from the Left's emphasis on the party affiliation of the Council's members, to the Right's focus on the Council's discretionary powers which, it alleged were far too broad and were being exercised without discernable restraint. There was more than a little touch of irony in this spectacle of a Right—which after having praised the Council effusively until 1986, and whose only criticism was that the Council had not gone far enough[128]—noisily attacking the Council for, in effect, behaving largely as it had during Socialist rule. As in the 1981–86 period, the Council, faced with the necessity of passing on a series of creative, audacious reforms, responded creatively: by discovering new ways to interpret the constitution and by developing new jurisprudential techniques of control. Both provided the Council with a greater margin of maneuver, important in a political context, of ever-increasing polarization between Right and Left, where middle ground seemed to be precluded.

The first wave of outbursts, from officials of the highest level, occurred in August, just before and after the Council's annulment of one of the government's legislative priorities, a new press law. In an interview with *Le Monde*, the minister of justice, Albin Chalandon, complained of the Council's "vast discretionary power," and asserted that the body functioned as a "third legislative chamber above parliament"[129]; and later: "if we allow the jurisprudence of the Council to develop as it has recently, . . . future governments will no longer have anything to do."[130] François Léotard, minister of culture, agreed, arguing that such activism had led to "a paralysis of parliament" and to governmental "powerlessness." The specter of a *gouvernement des juges* was regularly invoked. As Jacques Toubon, the secretary-general of Chirac's RPR put it, "the Council is a new kind of legislator," a "parliament of judges, regularly substituting itself for parliament in the making of laws."[131]

By 1986 the phrase, *gouvernement des juges*, was regularly used in France. For Chalandon, the Council constituted, in his words, an "anomaly" because it had developed so far from what the founders of the Republic had intended. The founders, he noted, had given the Council "the extremely precise role of policing the boundaries between the domains of *loi* and *règlement*," a role which had changed when the Council took the "revolutionary" step of incorporating the preamble. Today, he continued, the Council primarily functioned to judge the constitutionality of legislation, which it did "by referring not only to the constitution," but to "very vague texts of our former constitutions" (the texts contained in the 1946 preamble), which it then used to judge "the appropriateness of legislation" more than its "legality." The problem thus plainly posed, Chalandon went on to argue that two solutions were possible. The Council could and should behave with more "discipline," that is, with more prudence; and, in any event, the whole constitutional edifice should be changed, by codifying into one comprehensive text "all of the essential legal elements which it would be the role of the Council to defend." But as he noted, "this solution would be dependent upon a constitutional reform."[132]

These and many other similar criticisms were undoubtedly designed to intimidate or at least to warn the Council, but they were also evidence of mounting frustration as the painful effects of constitutional politics were felt. The majority's complex legislative package—on which Chirac hoped to appeal in his coming campaign for the presidency—had been packed into a very tight parliamentary calendar. The majority knew that it did not have the five years accorded the previous parliament to make its case to the people, and thus every delay in implementing the program cost dearly. Moreover, I would argue that in 1986 *generally the Chirac government faced more serious considerations of constitutionality in the drafting of its program than were any of its predecessors.* There are a number of reasons for such a view. First, the most important pieces of the government's program were designed to reform or to replace legal regimes adopted by the previous parliament, themselves the subject of the most important Council rulings. Denationalization and deregulation, a retreat from proportional representation in legislative elections, and a reform of regimes governing communications were drafted to rescind Socialist policies, but were also themselves structured by the Council's decisions on nationalizations, electoral reform in New Caledonia, and the press law. Thus, the Right inherited a relatively dense web of constitutional restraints which they themselves had helped to construct. Second, after five years in power the Socialists had been able to name four of the Council's nine members, and—causing a good deal of consternation—the Council was now chaired by Badinter. Last, Socialist rule had demonstrated to both parties that a tenacious opposition willing to use its petition power liberally could be a serious obstacle to legislative initiative. When the Socialists returned to opposition, they did so armed with a constitutional specialist, Guy Carcassonne, a law professor whose job it would be to scrutinize legislation, advise the party on constitutional matters, and to draft closely argued petitions to the Council.

Table 3.3 provides an overview of the Chirac government's legislative program adopted during the 1986 legislative sessions; indeed, the only important piece of legislation which is not listed, because it was not referred to the Council, is a bill adopted to make more flexible the law regulating employee lay-offs. In summary, sixteen bills were referred, 36.4 percent of all laws adopted (both record numbers), of which eight were judged by the Council to be in whole or in part unconstitutional. Some of the most important bills are examined briefly.

On 25–26 June and on 1–2 July the Constitutional Council rendered decisions on two of the first pieces of legislation adopted by the new parliament.[133] Both were *habilitation* (or "framework") laws which, according to article 38 of the constitution, are delegations from parliament to the government of authority to legislate by executive *ordonnances* in areas otherwise reserved to parliament by article 34. After receiving these delegations, the government is free to write these *ordonnances* without returning to parliament for final approval; they are then promulgated as law upon the signature of the president. The first *habilitation* law was economic in nature, containing (1) a delegation of authority to denationalize, returning to the private sector virtually the entire group of corporations and banks nationalized by the Socialists, as well as other such companies nationalized just after World War II; and (2) a delegation of authority to reform the labor code by, among other things, relaxing rules on maximum hours which employers could ask employees to work and permitting nighttime work for women—both established "conquests" of the labor movement. The second was a request to parliament for authorization to draft a new electoral law to govern parliamentary elections, abrogating the 1985 law which established proportional representation, and to return the country to the previous, two ballot plurality system. In both cases, the Council approved the bills; but in both cases, the Council also enunciated "strict reserves of interpretation" (SROIs), statements that certain specified

Table 3.3. The Chirac Government and Constitutional Review of the Legislation Adopted during the 1986 Legislative Sessions

Legislation	Date of Decision	App.	Par. Ann.	Tot. Ann.	SROI	NR
1. Privatizations	June 25–26	X			X	
2. Electoral reform	July 1–2	X			X	
3. 1986 finance revision	July 3	X				
4. Press law—*Lois Pasquas.*	July 19		X			X
5. Control of identity	Aug. 26		X			
6. Anticriminality	Sep. 3		X		X	
7. Penal code reforms	Sep. 3		X			
8. Antiterrorism bill	Sep. 3			X		X
9. Border controls	Sep. 3			X		
10. Audiovisual bill	Sep. 18			X		X
11. Electoral reform II	Nov. 18		X			
12. Retirement age	Dec. 22		X			
13. 1987 finance law	Dec. 29			X		
14. 1986 finance revision	Dec. 29			X		
15. Competition court	Jan. 23				X	X
16. Labor code reform	Jan. 23			X		X

App. signifies that the Constitutional Council approved the bill and it was promulgated; Par. Ann signifies a partial annulment; Tot. Ann. signifies the total annulment of a bill; SROI signifies that the bill was approved but strict reserves of interpretation were attached (some partial annulments also contained such SROIs); NR signifies that the annulment required a new reading, i.e., a second legislative process, in order for the bill to be revised and ultimately promulgated.

provisions of the bill may only be adjudged constitutional to the extent that they are read a particular way, as the Council reads them.

The SROIs enunciated by the Council in June and July, the details of which are not important here (see chapter 5), might have been forgotten in the bustle of later legislative activity had not Mitterrand invoked them in his refusals to sign the *ordonnances* into law. Mitterrand justified his refusal on the grounds that "the president is charged with the responsibility to guarantee the respect of the Constitution"—the terms of article 5 of the constitution. His action forced the government to resubmit the *ordonnances* to parliament as ordinary legislation,[134] where the threat of a second referral would hang over the majority's head. Unlike the privatization bill, the electoral reform was referred again, and it was approved by the Council in November.[135] Reform of the labor code, however, took much longer (see later).

The Council proved to be a much greater obstacle to the Right after it annulled parts of the majority's press bill and the audiovisual communications bill.[136] The Chirac government had inherited what its minister of culture,

Léotard, called an *"imbroglio juridique,"*[137] created by the Council's 1984 press decision. The result of that decision was to leave in place bits and pieces of conflicting rules enacted over five decades. The 1986 bill was designed to harmonize these rules by abrogating the old ones and erecting a new minimalist regime in their place. Apart from the administrative necessity for a new press law, the Right had political objectives, namely to minimize restraints on the industry as part of its neo-liberal agenda. This is sought to do by eliminating, as a means of protecting pluralism, reliance on legislatively fixed ceilings establishing a maximum percentage of the market any press group was to be allowed to control. After fear of Council censure led the majority to add such ceilings, it raised the percentage to a higher level as a means of encouraging concentration in the industry. The Socialists, working to save what it could of the antitrust mechanisms contained in the 1984 law, asked the Council to reaffirm that pluralism constituted a constitutional principle the protection of which no government could weaken. On 29 July the Council giving the Socialists satisfaction, annulled the provisions governing antitrust on the grounds that inadequately protected pluralism.

The audiovisual bill was designed to privatize certain television channels and radio frequencies, as well as to substantially deregulate the communications sector as a whole, in order to encourage capital and corporate formation and thus strengthen French ability to compete with the rest of Europe, the United States, and Japan in what was proving to be an increasingly competitive and technologically advanced information industry. The bill was mercilessly reworked by the Senate, much to the consternation of the government, but the latter refused to amend the relatively limited antitrust provisions in the law. The Socialists attacked these provisions on the basis of the Council's recent press decision, arguing that the bill as written would allow unacceptably high degrees of concentration of ownership and control over broadcasting. On 18 September, the Council again agreed and ruled that fourteen different articles were nonpromulgable as a result of the unconstitutionality of the antitrust provisions. The government then decided to revise the vetoed provisions and submit them both into parliament as a single law. The law, as the government protested, was not "wished for," but "a required text" written for the Council. Adopted in October, the Socialists did not choose to refer the bill again to the Council, since the majority had written large portions of the Council's decision directly into the beleaguered legislation.[138]

Mitterrand's refusal to sign legislative *ordonnances* enabling privatizations and the return to the plurality electoral system forced the government to resubmit those *ordonnances* as new legislation. On 10 December the government presented for Mitterrand's signature an *ordonnance* (permitted by the same economic *habilitation* law permitting privatization) establishing new rules for work times which would have, among other things, raised to forty-four the number of weekly hours for which overtime pay would not be required, permitted night work for women, and eased restrictions on maximum numbers of hours employers could ask employees to work in seasonal jobs. These rules were contested by the unions and, one week later, Mitterrand refused to lend his signature to them. Given the late date in the parliamentary session, the government had two choices: to call for a *session extraordinaire*, forcing parliament to remain in session (but it had already renounced such a plan publicly[139]); or to attach, by amendment—or "rider" in American parlance—the terms of the *ordonnance* to a bill in a late stage of elaboration. The government chose the latter solution, and the "Séguin amendment"—named for the minister in charge of its passage through parliament—was adopted over the protests of the opposition in an all-night session in the National Assembly.[140] Socialist deputies immediately referred the bill to the Council.

The Council annulled the Séguin amendment on the grounds that it did not demonstrate a necessary "link" with the legislation to which it had been attached.[141] As discussed in chapter 5, the ruling is of interest because it broke with established precedent by giving to the Council much greater power to control the legislative process, as opposed to limiting itself to the legislative text. But it was perhaps even more important politically, as demonstrated by the fact that the ruling produced what are probably the most virulent attacks on the Council ever recorded. After the decision, the right-wing press called the whole process a case of "Badinter-Mitterrand contrivance,"[142] since the reform would not have been overwhelmed by constitutional politics if Mitterrand had not refused to sign it into law. In an unprecedented action, the presidents of the both the National Assembly and the Senate, encouraged by the prime minister, called a press conference in order to publicly condemn the decision which they did on the grounds that is was without legal precedent, "a veritable attack on national sovereignty," and an "unacceptable amputation of the power of parliamentarians."[143] The political aspects of the decision were more than usually a matter of public discussion. The ruling was adopted, it was widely reported and since confirmed, on a 4–4 vote with all four Socialist appointees voting to annul, and all four appointees of the Right voting to approve[144]; Badinter's vote as president broke the stalemate. The ninth member, Louis Joxe, was ill, and had turned down last minute requests by the majority to move from his sick bed to the Palais Royal in order to cast the deciding vote.[145] The policymaking effects for the government were disastrous: the decision forced the text to undergo a *third* juridicized legislative process, which could not take place until the next spring (1987). At that time, hundreds of amendments were proposed and unions protested, but the government refused to compromise so as "not to prove either the Chief of State or the Constitutional Council correct" in the affair.[146] The bill was then finally promulgated.

The End of the Reform Era

Nearing the end of the 1986 legislative sessions, the Chirac government declared that what remained of its reform agenda was on hold,[147] pending the results of the 1988 presidential election. After the 1988 elections, the Rocard government too eschewed ambitious reforms. In fact, during the first year of the Rocard government, fewer laws were adopted by parliament than in the history of the Fifth Republic (45); none of these could be called a *grande réforme*. As important, the Constitutional Council has been relegated to a marginal role in policy. In the end, if the government does not exercise parliament, parliament does not exercise the Council. The era of reform is now clearly over, and as a result the Constitutional Council has had fewer opportunities to break new ground.

4

Understanding French
Constitutional Politics

The French priest's writings were well enough known in New York for the
press to have turned out to interview him. His steamer slid past the narrows
and up the bay toward the North River. He gazed at the skyline, inhaling
deeply, as so many had done at that moment. . . . He turned back to the
reporters. "It is wonderful," he said, "to breathe the sweet air of legitimacy."   CHARLES T. BLACK, Jr., *The People and the Court*

The American law professor, Charles L. Black, Jr., used this story to dramatize
what he thought to be "one of the chief excellencies of the American polity."[1]
What the priest smelled in the air that day had emanated not from an abstract
New World commitment to liberty, equality, or even the rule of law, but from
something more substantial and utterly foreign to the French political system:
the practice of judicial review. It was, indeed, "the sweet odor of the Supreme
Court."[2] To believe the most published and respected French public lawyers,
French citizens need no longer envy such "legitimacy"—the Constitutional
Council now provides much the same thing. In this chapter, I examine academic discourse on the Council. In the first part, revisiting themes developed in
chapter 1, the evolution of doctrinal attitudes to the Council are traced and the
impact of scholarly activity on the Council's behavior evaluated. In the second,
I assess the literature on the Council's *political* role and impact.

It bears emphasizing in advance that the scholarly enterprise I will be
describing is a highly centralized and homogeneous one and, unlike the American study of courts and law, is virtually closed to alternative perspectives.
Discourse on French constitutional law is entirely dominated by public law
specialists trained in the Continental administrative law tradition. Articles on
the Constitutional Council appear in public law journals like the *Revue du
droit public* or journals devoted to administrative law, such as the *Revue
française du droit administratif* or the *Revue administrative*. French political
scientists do not publish research on the Council, and French political science
journals do not normally publish research on the Council.[3] Those which

sometimes do, like *Pouvoirs*, publish articles written by law professors who are important participants themselves in constitutional politics.[4] This same group—no more than a dozen—also monopolizes serious public comment on the Council's decisions in the daily press and other elite fora. Former members of the Council, like law professors François Luchaire and François Goguel, regularly comment on the Council's decisions in *Le Monde*; Louis Favoreu, who writes referrals for the Right in the Senate, writes commentaries for *Le Figaro* and for *Le Monde*; and Olivier Duhamel, professor and official counselor to the president of the Constitutional Council during the 1983–86 period, wrote during that same period many of the most important general articles on the judicial–political confrontation for both *Le Monde* and for weeklies like *L'Express*. While this group provides the public with a certain range of dissent (increasingly limited, however) on the state and quality of the Council's jurisprudence, its orientation to the issue of the Council's macropolitical impact is a general one.

Doctrine and the Council

1958–71: Hostility and Ambivalence

The extent to which a fundamental continuity in the disciplinary commitments of public law scholarship existed from the Third and Fourth Republics well into the Fifth is best illustrated by the doctrinal community's initial hostility to the Constitutional Council. The Council, because it exercised "political review," because it was detached from court systems, and because it lacked even minimal autonomy from executive authority, did not inspire the community. After the 1962 referendum debacle, Loïc Philip put it in these ominous terms:

> If the Council desires approval of its decisions by opinion, if it desires to survive the future reforms of our institutions, it must provide proof of more independence and authority.[5]

Scholars were highly critical of the Council's early jurisprudence but, because it was so sparse, they could hardly be said to have been exercised by it in any important way.

Leading publicists concentrated on administrative jurisprudence, carrying on traditions developed by scholars decades before (see chapter 1). Maurice Duverger, for example, denounced the Council as a "political" institution," "exercised by . . . political goals." Duverger sought to convince the *judiciary* to exercise powers of *judicial* review. His argument was twofold. First, because the new constitution had stripped parliament of its legislative sovereignty, a new American-style separation of powers doctrine had emerged; the judiciary thus must be considered to possess co-equal status with other branches of government. Second, since the 1946 preamble continued to possess *valeur constitutionnel*, judicial review was positively required. Duverger predicted—just as he had throughout the Fourth Republic—that review would be initiated as soon as judges demonstrated the requisite "political courage."[6]

Contrary to the will of the drafters of the 1958 constitution, the *valeur constitutionnel* of the 1946 preamble was immediately and overwhelmingly reconfirmed by doctrine.[7] In the leading article on the question published in the *Revue du droit public* in 1960, Jacques Georgel acknowledged the difficulties of basing constitutional review on a preamble but concluded that

> . . . under whatever angle one examines the Preamble, one is led to acknowledge that it is possessed of *valeur constitutionnel* and is not simply a sentimental reference. France wants to remain the country of the Rights of Man.

He speculated that the Council might even one day be in a position "to censure legislative violations of the preamble."[8] Georgel had to wait eleven years before that event occurred.

1971–80: Is the Council a Court?

The 1971 "freedom of association" decision was celebrated by legal scholars, and brought forth the first spirited argument in defense of the Constitutional Council.[9] Doctrinal hostility, however, did not meaningfully decline immediately thereafter. Commentary on the 1974 constitutional amendment expanding the right of referral to parliamentarians, is instructive in this regard. In the leading article on the subject, Patrick Juillard expressed widely held criticisms about the Council's structure and mandate. For Juillard, the Council was first and foremost "a political institution" which nonetheless may act "in a judicial way" to the extent that it produces a jurisprudence. The 1974 amendment, characterized as "hardly more than a zero degree of change," could not change this aspect. Juillard concluded that the French system was less satisfactory than "authentic constitutional review," the model of which, again, was provided by the U.S. Supreme Court, because only "authentic review" could truly "reinforce guarantees of fundamental liberties."[10] Duverger, for his part, called the amendment a tiny "gram of democracy," and noted that major structural problems were not addressed: "The *a priori* mechanism and the composition of the Council are 'not satisfactory.'"[11] Thus, until at least the mid-1970s, the most important doctrinal voices echoed those which had sounded for nearly a century.

Nevertheless, the 1971 freedom of association (see chapter 4) decision incorporating the preamble had broadcasted two interrelated messages: (1) that doctrinal advocacy could have impact on decisions; and (2) that the Council, like the administrative courts before, would henceforth be attentive to the exigencies of *le droit*. Put differently, the Council acknowledged that its pronouncements were addressed to two audiences: legislators and the legal community. In consequence, public law professors would gradually emerge as central actors in constitutional politics, precisely because the Council's jurisprudence constituted a potentially separate domain of the law and therefore subject to the same scholarly treatment as other domains.

Not surprisingly, the question, "Is the Council a *juridiction* [a courtlike body]?", became a crucial one. The issue deserves examination, not least, because community's traditional hostility to "political review" was overthrown during this period. Briefly, a *juridiction* in traditional French legal parlance denotes all judicial institutions charged with handling litigation; the ordinary and administrative courts possess such status unambiguously. Judged against traditional standards, the Council was inherently *nonjuridictionnel*, and until the end of the 1970s politicians and public lawyers agreed on this point. The debates on the 1974 amendment are again revealing in this regard. At that time, the minister of justice declared in parliament that the Council was "neither a court nor a supreme court" in plain terms: "This organ is not a *juridiction* because it is not composed of judges." It was rather "an organ for the regulation of legislative power."[12] The conclusion was echoed by the majority's *rapporteur* for the amendment, who argued that the Council "is not a *juridiction* properly understood."[13] The Left invoked doctrinal authority; Alexander Bolo stated,

> It is . . . extremely debatable that the Council is principally of a jurisdictional character. . . . *Moreover [such a character] is contested unanimously by* doctrine. Numerous are those who think, on the other hand, that the Council is principally of a political character [emphasis added].[14]

Such conclusions are readily deduced from the traditional French paradigm of "courtliness." According to this paradigm, all *juridictions* must conform to certain minimal criteria (as easily recognized by common law lawyers). *Juridictions* are (1) composed of judges who are (2) primarily engaged in settling disputes brought by (3) real-life litigants who (4) argue a concrete case or controversy before them according to (5) fixed, contradictory judicial procedures. As chapter 1 shows at length, French academic lawyers had long been extraordinarily hostile to any form of review which deviated from this paradigm. In the Fifth Republic, this deviation was the basis of Duverger's, Juillard's, and virtually all of the early critiques of the Council. Former Council members have also invoked the paradigm in their assessment. One *conseiller d'Etat* appointed by de Gaulle had this to say about his tenure at the Council:

> I never thought for a second that the Council was a judicial organ (*organe juridictionnel*); it is a political body by its recruitment and by its function. . . . . [T]here is no hearing before the Council; there is no trial, no parties, no debates, and, still less, no public arguments.[15]

But by the end of the 1970s, consensus had been reached among public law specialists that the Council ought to be considered a *juridiction*. Influential law professors, including two former Council members, Waline and Luchaire, asserted bluntly that "no one doubts" that conclusion any longer[16]; and Jean Rivéro could claim that "the Council's judicial nature . . . is no longer denied."[17] Those who argued that the Council was a *juridiction* arrived at their conclusion by relaxing the criteria. The judicial paradigm was swept away. *A constitutional juridiction came to specify any institution charged with the power to determine, in a definitive manner, the content and applicability of constitutional law.* The Council is such a *juridiction*—par excellence—because it makes final decisions with respect to constitutionality, and because these decisions are in the form of and constitute a jurisprudence.[18] It makes little difference what process yields the opportunity to build this jurisprudence; the result is the same. The absence of concrete litigation or contradictory—*contentieuse* in French—procedure need not disqualify the Council from status as a *juridiction*. On the contrary, as Luchaire argued, the Council is an example of a *"juridiction noncontentieuse."*[19] By the early 1980s, this view had clearly become the orthodoxy among public lawyers.

In my view, there exists a central difficulty to the claim that the Constitutional Council is a *juridiction* if by that public lawyers mean that the Council's function is *inherently* more judicial than legislative. If the Council is a *juridiction* because it at times determines the constitutionality of legislation, then parliament too must be considered a *juridiction*. In debates of motions of *irrecevabilité* and in juridicized processes, parliament decides constitutionality, and a verdict of unconstitutionality kills further discussion. Public lawyers have sought to distinguish the role of the Council from that of parliament by declaring the former's courtliness. However, they do not rely on the traditional notion of courtliness, and their updated notion does not have the power to separate legislative and judicial functions in the case of French constitutional review. Much more will be said about this issue in chapter 8.

That the public law community came to accept the Council as a courtlike body and then to focus its attention on the Council's growing jurisprudence is relevant to the study of French constitutional politics. Law professors are far more important in civil law systems than are their common law counterparts. This is in part the result of a politicolegal culture which denies that judges—the "great men" of the common law—ever make law creatively. It is in part the result of the decision-writing style of French judges, a style which has been adopted by the Constitutional Council. French decisions are short, elliptic, syllogistic. They contain little argument, as if the applicable law or code or constitutional provision is so self-evident that decisions need no justification; and dissenting opinion is not allowed. The entire text of the famous 1971 decision on freedom of association, for example, contains only 6 "considerations," sentence-length assertions about what the law is. The incorporation of the 1946 preamble by this decision was accomplished in just one consideration:

> Considering that among the number of fundamental principles recognized by the laws of the Republic and solemnly reaffirmed by the Preamble of the Constitution, there must also be listed the principle of liberty of association;

This is the *only* mention, or "discussion," in the entire decision of either the preamble or its spectacular rise to *valeur constitutionnel*. At a minimum, social scientists must recognize that legal scholars perform two crucial roles in constitutional politics: (1) they work to develop, strengthen, and synthesize constitutional law and jurisprudence by exegesis and advocacy; and (2) they have appropriated the responsibility to explain what the Council's decisions mean to those—virtually the entire citizenry and the average parliamentarian—who would not otherwise be able to make any sense of them.

That constitutional law had finally "arrived" in France during this period is illustrated by the fact that in 1975 the *Revue du droit public* announced that it would publish regular doctrinal commentaries on the Council's jurisprudence.[20] Since that time, the Council's work has slowly come to dominate the journal's pages. (In 1990, a new quarterly journal dedicated exclusively to the Council studies was founded, *La revue française du droit constitutionnel.*)

1981–87: Legitimizing the Council

The 1981–87 period saw an explosion not only of constitutional jurisprudence but of doctrinal activity, the latter consisting overwhelmingly of traditional jurisprudential exegesis. I wish to take up three issues of wider importance to the development of French constitutional politics: (1) the relationship between constitutional and other branches of law; (2) the nature of the Council's discretionary powers; and, (3) doctrinal reaction to the drawn-out judicial-political confrontation of the period.

The achievement of doctrinal consensus on the courtliness of the Council posed directly the question of the relationship between constitutional law and other fields of law. A central, organizing focus of French legal consciousness and doctrinal activity has long been a commitment to the elaboration and achievement of what is called an état de droit (Rechtsstaat)—a politicolegal system characterized by effective judicial protection of a judicially constructed hierarchy of norms binding on all public authorities. In the Third and Fourth Republics, the absence of judicial review made achievement of an *état de droit* impossible. In the Fifth, the creation of the Council, the taming of parliament, and the incorporation of the 1946 preamble inspired optimism, but problems remained. Calling the Council "judicial" solved some of these, but not the fundamental one: that the Council has no formal interaction with other courts or with the judicial system. The problem, and its importance for the achievement of the *état de droit*, has become an increasingly salient one for the community.[21]

In the most important early article on this issue, Louis Favoreu argued in 1980 that the Council's jurisprudence could no longer be ignored by judges, courts, non-public lawyers, and law professors.[22] Favoreu argued that the legal system had been radically transformed by the development of constitutional review. Whereas the ultimate source of legal norms had in the past been parliament, that source was now the constitution and, by extension, the Council's jurisprudence and doctrinal authority. A true "constitutional law" was being born, which would look much like present-day American constitutional law to the extent that it is largely case law. (Traditional French constitutional law texts contain no cases, but are commentaries on institutional history and typologies of regimes.) The supremacy of the Council in constitutional interpretation would have to be accepted, he argued, and in consequence the judiciary and law curricula would be "constitutionalized."

Council specialists thereafter began to publish in law journals read by non-public lawyers, attorneys, and judges. The purpose of this activity was and is to inform readers of the relevance of the Council's jurisprudence, in the hope that they will see fit to integrate it into their own work. This project has not yet been successful. As Favoreu complained in 1986, judges remain largely unacquainted with the Council's jurisprudence and do not feel bound by the terms of its jurisprudence.[23] This is relevant particularly with regard to Council decisions which include SROI. Such rulings state that a bill or provision is only constitutional to the extent that it is applied in conformity with the Council's interpretation. The *état de droit* is clearly weakened if these interpretations are ignored by public authorities. Although thorough searches have been undertaken, there is little evidence that ordinary courts have sought to apply or otherwise protect these interpretations in their decisions.[24] The relationship between the Council's jurisprudence and that of the administrative courts is more complicated. By most accounts, the traditional rule according to which the *Conseil d'Etat* is bound by the effects of a Council decision[25] but not by its argumentation, has not broken down. The cases cited in support of the contrary conclusion,[26] however, show (to my reading, at least) only that the *Conseil d'Etat agrees* with the Council's interpretation, *not that it feels obliged to agree* (just as the Council has adopted elements of administrative jurisprudence in a great many of its decisions without mentioning source or authority). Public lawyers have also not yet been successful at "constitutionalizing" the law faculties. In standard law school textbooks on the judiciary, the Council is either not discussed at all or mentioned only in passing.[27] One textbook that does discuss the Council devotes a scant dozen pages to the institution, but declares that it is "difficult to establish that it is recognized by other *juridictions*."[28]

A second issue of doctrinal concern was the Council's seemingly unconstrained discretionary powers. During the 1971–80 period, legislators and the Council both were responsible for what I characterized in chapter 3 as rampant *judicial inflation*, the process by which more and more texts and principles were asserted to be possessed of *valeur constitutionnel*. Judicial inflation is a problem for *le droit* because it is a dynamic, unpredictable process. It undermines what Continental scholars hold most precious: legal certainty. It scrambles or levels what had been carefully constructed hierarchies, cheapens values once dear. For legislators, the problem of judicial inflation is of practical concern. By 1979, for example, policymakers committed to drafting legislation capable of surviving constitutional scrutiny were ostensibly required to have an understanding not only of the 1958 constitution, the 1946 principles, the 1789 declaration, but also of a body of FPRLR yet to be specified, and principles of administrative jurisprudence yet to be enshrined!

As chapter 5 will show, this problem was somewhat mitigated by the growing juridicization of the policymaking process after 1981. As the stakes of constitutional review rose, communication between parliament and the Council became more intense and more meaningful. Policymakers and opposition engaged legal experts to advise them on constitutional matters; politicians developed more fluency in the language of constitutional review; and the Council's jurisprudence, increasingly sensitive to the exigencies of *le droit*, became more dense, explicit about its instructions to lawmakers, and therefore productive of this language. This development is not unrelated to the judicial-political confrontations of the post-1980 period. Being unusually reliant on the active support of the legal community for defense of its expanding role, the Council was led, increasingly, to conform to judicial standards of conduct. There is a range of circumstantial evidence in support of this (but due to the secrecy of the Council's deliberations and the terse style of its jurisprudence, circumstantial evidence is the only evidence available).

First, the Council has clearly been sensitive to criticism of its expanding role. In fact, it has occasionally sought to restructure political attitudes and discourse by informing politicians that its role is a judicial not a legislative one. In the 1975 abortion decision, the Council stated flatly that constitutional review authority "does not confer upon the Council a general power of judgement and of decision-making identical to that possessed by parliament";[29] the Council repeated the phrase in several decisions of the 1980s.[30] In a 1985 decision on reform of the electoral system of New Caledonia, the Council again sought to educate political and public opinion about the general purpose and legislative impact of review. The pronouncement is a pure expression of the ideology of constitutionalism against embedded Rousseauianism (see chapter 1):

> . . . an adopted bill expresses the general will only to the extent that its [provisions] respect the Constitution . . . . The object [of constitutional review] is not to hinder or to delay the exercise of legislative power but to assure its conformity to the Constitution. . . .[31]

In the most dramatic example of such declarations, the Council went out of its way to affirm the new doctrinal view of its "jurisdictional" status, releasing the following press statement in response to the extraordinary attacks made on it by Chirac's ministers during the summer of 1986:

> The Constitutional Council, having taken notice of the recent declarations concerning it, recalls that it possesses according to the constitution the *judicial* mission to verify the constitutionality of laws which have been referred to it. It refuses therefore to participate in the present debate, which is inherently *political* [emphases added].[32]

These statements are evidence that the Council recognized and actively sought the legitimating power of legal discourse and judicial function. At the same time, the Council's work, too, became more attendant to judicial norms: its decisions lengthened, developed into a technical and closely argued jurisprudence, and became much more explicit about the nature of parliament's legal obligations in the face of censure. This phenomenon is better demonstrated by the case studies in Part II, but figure 4.1 shows clearly, if crudely, one aspect of this development. If we exclude the 1980 "security and liberty" decision—a landmark decision in many respects[33]—no year in the 1974–80 period shows an average of more than eight "considerations" (one-line phrases) per decision. A more nuanced look shows that the longest and most detailed decisions have had the greatest impact on future legislation. The decision on

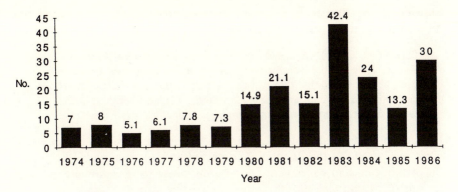

Fig. 4.1. Average number of "considerations" in Council decisions.

the 1980 security and liberty law contained 76 considerations; the 1981 nationalizations law contained 75 considerations; the 1984 press law contained 103; and the 1986 audiovisual reform contained 101. Not surprisingly, in each of these cases the Council member charged with drafting the decision was the lone law professor on the body, Georges Vedel.[34]

Perhaps the most dramatic change in the Council's jurisprudence occurred with respect to its elaboration of a bill of rights. The issue of the Council's discretionary powers was central to criticism of the Council from first the Left and then the Right (see chapter 3). For their part, doctrinal authorities had begun expressing their discomfort as early as 1978. In that year, Louis Favoreu raised the possibility that a growing constitutional jurisprudence might eventually provide *le droit* with an opportunity to codify a charter of rights. At present, he complained, this was impossible, due to the "fluid" (what I would call the "unknowable") nature of the contents and meaning of the principles contained in the 1946 preamble.[35] As discussed in chapter 2, the Council's *preferred* source of annulment for its *most important* decisions rendered during the 1971–80 period was the preamble. By the end of 1980, the Council had used two articles of the 1789 declaration (concerning penal law), the right to strike from the 1946 principles, and 3 FPRLR (freedom of association, the principle of liberty, the right to legal defense) as bases for rulings of unconstitutionality, and had consecrated another FPRLR (the freedom of educational instruction) in its rejection of a Socialists referral. Thus, *of the three texts contained in the 1946 preamble, the Council had found the unwritten, and hence entirely unknowable, one—the FPRLR—to be the most useful "text" to develop.*

Scholars, confronted with a growing and seemingly indeterminate number of superconstitutional principles, engaged in lengthy debates about the status, origin, and relationship of the FPRLR to the constitution proper (the debate rages on today). Favoreu's early attempt at specifying the functional interrelationship of the three texts contained in the preamble is an example of how difficult it was to arrive at a precise conceptualization:

> [The FPRLR] work, apparently, to fill in areas left uncovered by the declaration of rights and the 1946 Preamble, as well as to bridge these 2 texts. But it must also be stated that they work to correct certain principles contained in the texts and sometimes to yield a synthesis. *They are therefore principles with which one can do anything* [emphasis added].[36]

Perhaps most unsatisfactory, the phrase, "the fundamental principles recognized by the laws of the Republic," contained an important ambiguity: was it the principle itself or its recognition in statute which was the ultimate source of its superconstitutional status? Some argued the former, that the principles could be said to have existed previously without reference to a concrete text. As Loïc Philip put it, "The advantage of this solution is to give to the constitutional *juridiction* greater powers of judgement." Others resisted, arguing that the disadvantage in terms of the Council's fragile legitimacy outweighed whatever advantages obtained from increased discretionary power. As former Council member and law professor François Luchaire argued in 1980, ". . . *such a conception would lead straight to a gouvernement des juges. . . .* [O]nly a text, and not the philosophy of the judges, can limit the powers of the representatives of the nation" [emphasis added].[37] But, as Luchaire must have known (he was then sitting on the Council), *when the Council consecrated individual liberty and the right to self-defense as FPRLR it did not refer to any existing legislative text, however dated.* Perhaps the Council meant that the spirit of these principles had so permeated the work of the legislature that its consecration actually aided the legislature in its efforts to protect them in legislation. Or, following Luchaire, we might accept that the Constitutional Council does at times behave as a *gouvernement des juges.*

Discomfort flowed from the native Continental resistance to the idea that judicial lawmaking inheres in the process of judicial decision making. As long as doctrinal activity was confined to commentary on the activities of French judges applying written legal codes in the ordinary and administrative courts, the fiction that French judges never legislate could be maintained. Scholars could always claim that the codes so constrained judicial decision making that lawmaking as such was impossible. But today, doctrinal activity is not confined to the activities of judges and their encounter with written codes. It is also engaged in the active *construction* of constitutional law—a radically different enterprise. Nevertheless, French constitutional lawyers still write about the Council's decision making as other French scholars write about the decision making of the *Conseil d'Etat* or any other court. Doctrine recognizes that constitutional review sometimes requires the Council to interpret both legislative and constitutional texts, but it does not easily accept the fact that the Council *itself* is (and is necessarily) the original source of *all* superconstitutional principles.

In one of the few major articles to address the political aspects of this problem in a sustained way,[38] Loïc Philip complained in the *Revue du droit public* in 1983 that "*the constitutional judge no longer limits himself to ensuring the respect of the constitution, but is more and more led to say what the constitution is*" [emphasis added].[39] The fact that "the number of rules of *valeur constitutionnel* grows ever larger and their impact extends ever wider" had created what Philip called "a quite dangerous situation," because the Council's vast discretionary powers directly "challenge the parliament's powers of judgement" (i.e., its power to legislate).

Although much more could be said about this problem and about doctrinal attitudes to it, what is important here is that the Council responded to this criticism by relegating the FPRLR to a marginal role. Of the forty-eight partial or total annulments of laws adopted during the 1981–87 period, the Council based only two on the FPRLR. The best evidence that the decline of the FPRLR was a matter of conscious Council policy is provided by Georges Vedel, who in 1984 (while a sitting member of the Council) declared at a conference,

> The surest guarantee of the stability and permanence of constitutional juris-
> prudence is to be found in the fact that the Council, after having been warned
> of the danger of a *gouvernement des juges* does not consider itself to be the
> master of the sources of constitutional law. One can hardly cite any decision
> which does not refer with precision to a constitutional text. All the constitu-
> tion, only the constitution—such appears to be the body of rules applicable
> by the French constitutional judge.[40]

The development provides further evidence that the Council is increasingly attendant to norms of behavior generated by the doctrinal community. *The Council is not only aware that legal scholars will judge its behavior according to those norms, but strives to satisfy this community as much as possible.*

But even if the FPRLR had disappeared altogether and the Council had come to rely exclusively on written texts in the 1981–87 period, the problem which Philip identified remains. As Philip put it, the problem is that the Council has asserted the right to "say what the constitution is." Put differently, because even written constitutions are not self-evident, constitutional politics are the politics of constitutional interpretation. Vedel's pronouncement, "all the constitution, only the constitution," can not remove the Council from constitutional politics. The greatest evidence that it did not do so was furnished during the long summer of 1986, when some of the highest officials of the State engaged in unprecedented attacks on the Council—precisely because they believed that the Council's rulings served to make what was clearly written in the constitution seem suddenly obscure.

The anxieties expressed by Chalandon, Toubon, and Léotard in 1986 were identical in substance to those expressed by Philip in 1983 and Luchaire before him. Attacks by politicians, however, yielded a coherent response from the legal community, rallying legal scholars to the defense of constitutional review and all but silencing scholarly criticism of the Council's role vis-à-vis other institutions. Political and doctrinal discourse diverged dramatically by the end of the period. In 1986, although leading constitutional scholars wrote dozens of commentaries on the confrontation for the general public in newspapers and magazines, none proclaimed anything less than the strongest support for the Council. I can find no important exception. So earnestly did these scholars labor in defense of the institution that it is nearly impossible for a general reader, without access to other information, to understand why any confrontation had flared at all in 1986—or 1982.[41]

Legal scholars simply rewrote the history of constitutional review so as to put the Council in the most favorable light. The most striking examples concern the issue of the Council's interpretive powers. Here, for example, is the response, published in a daily newspaper, of Jacques Robert (University of Paris law professor, then editor of the *Revue du droit public*, and since 1989 a Constitutional Council member) to the charges made by the Chirac government that the Council had developed far from the limited role which the founders had given to it:

> The terms of the preamble state that the constitutional judge was, *from the Council's creation*, invested with the responsibility [*la mission*] to declare if a law voted by parliament, and referred to it, conforms or not to a given article of the constitution, *or to the liberties, rights, and principles contained in the texts explicitly and solemnly recalled by the preamble* [emphasis added].[42]

The preamble, of course, states no such thing, and the word of the founders is exactly contrary (see chapter 2).

By the end of this period, the constitution was treated over and over as if it contained no ambiguity, interpretation was characterized as a neutral exercise, and the confrontation was treated as if it either did not exist or was only imagined by bad-tempered politicians. Favoreu even claimed, on the basis of a statistical study of the Council's annulments,[43] that the "tenacious legend" propagated by less-than-competent "observers" according to which the Council "bases its judgments on vague principles" was just that—a legend.[44] And Georges Vedel, assessing his tenure on the Council in *Le Débat* (a general affairs journal widely read by nonlawyer elites and academics), had this to say:

> Constitutional review rests, in . . . France, on texts—not only the Constitution, but on the Declaration of the Rights of Man and of the Citizen and the 1946 Preamble—which possess *objective and permanent status*. I would add that . . . we never acted as a *gouvernement des juges*. We refused, contrary to what the U.S. Supreme Court did before or what sometimes the German Constitutional Court does, to invoke principles not contained in the texts but instead come from the political or moral philosophy of the judges [emphasis added].[45]

As the case studies in chapter 6 and 7 will show, this statement, like Robert's earlier, is extremely misleading.

Finally, public law scholars labored to alter the terms of political debate about constitutional review by reconstructing understanding of the Council's political role and functioning during the crucial 1981–87 period. This activity and the problem it poses for social scientists are the principal subjects of the rest of this chapter.

Understanding the Political Behavior
of the Constitutional Council

At first glance, the case of the Constitutional Council appears to be fertile ground for political scientists. The Council is an example of a courtlike institution enmeshed, quite literally, in the policymaking process. Its members are appointed by and more often than not are themselves politicians. Most important, the French mechanism of abstract, a priori review coupled with a legal history and parliamentary culture extraordinarily hostile to encroachment on legislative prerogatives has led to periodic explosions of judicial-political confrontation.

The Council, however, is largely insulated from the perspectives and methods developed and employed by modern political scientists in the study of courts and their impact on political systems elsewhere. This is partly due to structural characteristics. The body deliberates in official secrecy, votes may not be made public, and dissenting and concurring opinions are not permitted. Thus, although Council judges vote and have differences of opinion, their behavior can not be analyzed in the same way as that of their counterparts in other political systems; although the recruitment of Council members is partisan, and calculations of advantage to be obtained by appointments are made by public authorities, this advantage is almost impossible to measure. To add to these difficulties, the Council's jurisprudence is often cryptic and syllogistic, reinforcing the illusion of impersonality and unanimity.[46]

At least as important, academic specialists only rarely stray from the text of Council decisions. Indeed, the points of reference for the examination of Council behavior are fixed almost entirely by the institution itself, a state of affairs which would clearly be unacceptable in the study of other political actors. This is due to the active interest French scholars have long taken in reinforcing the ideology of judicial independence in France, which has now—for reasons examined earlier—been extended to the Council. But because the Council operates in an unusually unstable environment, this ideology is in constant risk of breaking down. In general, there is fierce resistance on the part of analysts to the notion that the Council is a political actor at all. The "traditional judicial myth"—that of the "impersonal, non-political, law-finding judge whose decisions are the result of the inexorable logic of the law"[47]—much eroded elsewhere, remains remarkably intact in France.

The Cult of the Robe à la Française

In the process of commenting on Constitutional Council decisions and presenting it to nonspecialists, scholars have embraced and propagated what has been called a typically French "illusion . . . of a radical dissociation of things legal and things political."[48] The distinction can be crucial, but it does not flow from theoretical or even doctrinal necessity. It is, rather, part of a coherent agenda to bulwark the Council—and courts in general—against a wide range of criticism. Scholars overwhelmingly embrace the view that the Council's jurisprudential production constitutes its only meaningful behavior and, in consequence of this, that doctrinal exegesis provides the sole means for assessing the body's role and functioning. In a common form of the argument, the very conceptualization of the Council as an actor in the political world is tantamount to an attack on constitutional justice writ large, entailing unacceptable negative consequences for Council legitimacy. Thus, ascribing to the Council the role of "counter-power,"[49] or showing, more neutrally, that the Council has at times functioned as "an obstacle to the reforms of the majority,"[50] is "wrong," "inexact," and "obviously the best way to destroy the authority of the constitutional judge because, as a 'political power,' he has no legitimacy."[51] The point is at times made in extravagant terms; Favoreu states,

> To accuse the Constitutional Council of exercising, by its jurisprudence, an *influence* on the political game, . . . is to call into questions *all* systems of constitutional justice [emphases added].[52]

Dogmatic and party-centric, politics is for French academic jurists an evil which must not be allowed to contaminate discourse on law. The analyst's sole legitimate function is to explain Council pronouncements, and in doing so, to protect the Council from irresponsible charges that it produces partisan decisions and a capricious, arbitrary jurisprudence. "Only after analyzing the Council's decisions are pronouncements [by observers] on the behavior of its members permitted," Favoreu declares, a position affirmed by virtually all leading authorities.[53] Arguments about the Council policymaking powers are settled by appealing to the Council's *own* pronouncement (reiterated in its most controversial opinions) that its review authority "does not confer upon it a general power of judgement and decision-making identical to that possessed by parliament."[54] Of course, scholars and politicians elsewhere have accepted that courts—and especially appellate and constitutional courts—make policy constantly. In France, however, two ideal, polarized positions appear to be the only ones possible: either the Council legislates *exactly* as does parliament, or it makes no law at all.

Separating the respective domains of law and politics also functions as an effective opening defense against charges that the political recruitment or affiliation of Council members makes a difference in how they decide cases. As Favoreu characterizes the charge, the institution's detractors claim that Council members—being political appointees—are *incapable* of independent action and "behave . . . necessarily as partisans and not as judges." This view, he asserts, is "formulated *a priori* without even the slightest attempt at justification."[55] The terms of this debate allow the Council member no space to occupy between, again, two polarized opposites: the partisan-ideologue and the neutral judge. This opposition all but guarantees that any ensuing discussion will be polemical and mystifying.

The very structure of the debate on the politics of the Council reveals a remarkable lack of familiarity with the greater, comparative literature of judicial politics and decision making. Students of judicial politics do *not* argue that judges always decide in their party's interest, or even that they vote "consistently" along an ideological line across issue areas. Evidence, however, does indicate that personal politics is of more than passing significance to a judge's voting performance. In sum, according to Shapiro, the literature shows

> a high correlation between judges' political attitudes and their decisions for and against certain categories of litigants. This literature further suggests that these judicial attitudes fall into the same relatively coherent ideological patterns found in the national political culture. . . . [M]any judges are not entirely neutral, but instead [possess] . . . distinct public policy preferences which they seek to implement through their decisions.[56]

A comparativist has good reason to believe that a Socialist politician appointed to the Council does not cease to be a Socialist upon moving across the river to the Palais Royal. One might point to the German case, where analyses of votes and dissents confirm the conclusions of the general literature. One might quote Professor Bobbitt, when writing on the U.S. Supreme Court, that "justices are far more likely to be committed on the issues of the day than are the rest of us,"[57] and argue that they are likely even more so in France. But one can not adequately study the extent to which such views are true or false in the French context. Such research is unfortunately impossible.

If the internal dynamics of how and why the French constitutional court decides must remain a mystery, arguments to the contrary will not likely convince those not already predisposed to them. Council specialists seek to close debate by first disengaging the institution from its political environment, and then declaring that the only solution to the mystery is to be found in legal language and the exegetical enterprise—what Favoreu calls "judicial revelation."[58] Thus prepared for, the ultimate "proof" of judicial independence—that the Council's decisions are jurisprudentially coherent and virtually always predictable,[59] to those who "regularly study its jurisprudence"[60]—comes without surprise.

Other interested observers—analysts employing other methodologies, and jurists who arrive at doctrinal conclusions unfavorable to the Council—are ridiculed. Politicians, who on the whole criticize the Council when they lose and celebrate when they win, are chastised for propagating "quarrels and combats based of false ideas."[61] Political scientists are accused of actively promoting the "myth of the government of judges," not least—or necessarily?—because "without mythology, political life would lose its charm, and everyone knows that a good jurist is not a good political scientist."[62] Although it is highly revealing that the functional discursive equivalent in France of the American expression, "judicial activism," is "government of judges" (today never used in the United States), the latter is much more highly charged than is the former. Its use here and elsewhere has unproductive consequences, again eliminating any space between two polarized, unrealistic positions: if we do not accept the Council as a neutral body of judges interpreting a benevolent constitution, we necessarily condemn it as an illegitimate incarnation of a government of judges.[63]

Doctrinal specialists whose support of the Council's role and decisions is considered less than wholehearted are criticized, as if the support and protection of the Council were more important than empirical research and open debate. In recent years, scholars regularly apologize before criticizing even the Council's jurisprudence. Carcassonne put it this way:

> . . . rare are those, for fear of being considered adversaries of the Council, who dare to challenge [its] decisions, shrouded [as they are] with a reverence which is almost sacred.[64]

The religious allusions became more and more apt as the 1980s wore on. Indeed, the Council became the focus of a new, increasingly militant version of the "cult of the robe."[65] Favoreu himself complained that Council idolatry has gone too far, noting that defending the Council's honor is the object of nothing short of a holy crusade:

> Not very long ago, those who took up the defense of the Constitutional Council felt very alone; but . . . many have since found their way to Damascus and now their numbers are legion. The zeal and the faith of these new converts is such that they will tolerate no false note in their concerts of praise, and they recall to order, sometimes firmly, those who raise any objection or criticism against the constitutional judge.[66]

Professor Black's French priest can go home.

An Infirm Political Science

A social scientist interested in French constitutional politics faces a challenging problem. On the one hand, the dynamics of the body's decision making are immune to scrutiny; on the other hand, an overwhelming share of academic discourse on the Constitutional Council is allotted to jurisprudential commentary and polemical debate. Understanding how the Council actually functions in the political system is less important than efforts to synthesize doctrine and to defend the Council from political attacks. While these activities have monopolized the resources of Council scholarship, there is no compelling reason why they ought to preclude serious study of the institution's behavior as a political institution. On the contrary, whether one likes or dislikes the Constitutional Council, or constitutional review, is entirely irrelevant. Constitutional control of legislation is exercised by the Council, for better or worse, and that is enough to support a political science of the Council's behavior and impact.

Focus on the a priori review mechanism and its impact on parliamentary life are reliable starting points. First, both in timing and impact, *every* Council decision objectively constitutes the final stage of one legislative process and, at times, the opening stage of another. Second, because every case which the Council receives is a result of enough political controversy to induce at least sixty parliamentarians to pursue the Council's intervention, every decision is more than an addition to the jurisprudential corpus. It is also an important *political* event. It is my central thesis that, as a *description of function*, the Council can be fruitfully conceptualized as a kind of third legislative chamber.

This is not to imply that the Council exercises "identical powers of apprecia-
tion" possessed by the National Assembly or the Senate. The Council is
obviously not the assembly: it is a kind of constitutional court which exercises a
priori control over pending legislation. At the same time, it is an undeniably
powerful policymaker, operates entirely within parliamentary space, and its
decisions are authoritative and final. A less provocative analogy might be that
of an official legal advisory body whose decisions on legislation are final and
binding on policymakers; but the result is the same.

French public lawyers would presumably protest that I confuse the *impact* of
constitutional jurisprudence on lawmaking for Council behavior. If this is a
confusion, it is willful and necessary. It focuses empirical attention on how the
Council actually interacts with other institutional actors, and raises issues important to students of French politics generally (perhaps especially to those whose
primary interests lie *beyond* the study of public law, courts, and judicial processes). The position that the Council is *political*, that its decisions are *political*
events, need not imply that Council members behave as card-carrying members
of political parties. Since at least 1981, the Council has been systematically
implicated in the day-to-day struggles of parliament. Constitutional judges—
however neutral—may find this position uncomfortable, but they can not extri-
cate themselves from it. A simple but hard fact deserves to be underlined:
constitutional review, as it has developed and presently functions in France, is
dependent on the "politicization" of the Council's offices for its very existence. If
politicians ceased to petition the Council, constitutional review would no longer
exist. And the Council would no longer suffer from politicization.

My position—an "unorthodox" one in France[67]—underscores some fundamental differences in the respective disciplinary commitments of political
science and French public law. French public lawyers tend to regard judicial
decision making as a neutral exercise in reason, wherein all legitimate arguments reduce to one—that which is enshrined in the decision. The "politics" of
the law—the socioeconomic importance of a decision or constitutional controversy to public and private constituencies of parliament, for example—are
rarely central to French jurists. They opt instead for more abstract commentaries and active participation in a supposed progressive revelation of logical or
ideological ethical systems—the constitution, the *état de droit*, or an emerging
charter of rights. Students of judicial politics often arrive at very different
conclusions about the Council—or about any other body which has both legal
and political dimensions—because they adopt *exterior* perspectives toward
law. Law is treated as one of many institutional factors that play upon the
subject matter being studied. Many students of law, on the other hand, adopt
an *interior* perspective: law is something that they are in the process of
constructing by their scholarly activity. There are today many earnest and
dedicated builders of the constitutional law in France. My own interest is to
observe, describe, and even evaluate this building process, but not to participate in it.[68]

Conflict within the law and within courts is anathema to doctrine; but
conflict is the very stuff of political science. Reasonable men—even judges—

differ reasonably, and politics, to paraphrase a classic definition, is precisely how these differences are worked out. Council judges, men of differing political persuasions and social backgrounds, assemble regularly to settle controversies about legislation not of their making. In doing so, they produce more than legal language: they produce winners and losers, and they endorse or establish hierarchies of values and norms. Their decisions, enshrined in law, may bear upon judges and legislators, other political actors, and the greater society for perhaps generations to come. These are compelling reasons to take seriously the study of the Constitutional Council as a political actor.

As discussed earlier, the judicial–political confrontations of the 1981–87 period provoked the doctrinal community to defense of the Council. It also provoked the leading Council specialist, Louis Favoreu, to publish the first full-length work devoted to examining the role and *impact* of the Council on French politics, *La politique saisie par le droit* (lit., "Politics Seized by Law"). The work deserves special consideration because: (1) it focuses on the the crucial 1981–87 period, the subject of the rest of this book; and (2) it elaborates and proposes a number of specific hypotheses about what Favoreu calls the Council's political "functions." Two of these functions will be considered later.

The Certificate of Constitutionality: Legitimating the Government . . . or the Council?

Forced to rule on a complex series of controversial reforms beginning in 1981, the long-obscure Constitutional Council suddenly found itself on center stage and the object of harsh attacks by disgruntled politicians. The cry of "government of judges" rose with regularity, and comparisons of the confrontation with one between the U.S. Supreme Court and President Roosevelt were debated in parliament and the press. Professor Favoreu, a specialist on the Council since its birth, entered this debate at a crucial point in the evolution of public perceptions about the institution's role. Downplaying the seriousness of the confrontation, he argued that constitutional review during this period, even when resulting in partial censure, was not wholly a negative power. On the contrary, each time the Council decides not to annul entirely any piece of legislation, it in effect "delivered a certificate of constitutional conformity, of regularity, to the initiatives made by the new government."[69] Once beleaguered legislation was then "legitimized," or "authenticated," since it henceforth enjoyed the benediction of "a supplementary authority."[70] Thus, far from being an obstacle to reforms, the Council had actually benefited the government, and acted as a necessary "guarantor of *alternance*" (alternations of political power between Left and Right in France) for a fragile, uncertain Fifth Republic.[71]

The notion that the Council bestows on the government a "certificate of authenticity," and that in doing so it legitimates legislation and changes of government deserves to be examined closely, not least because Favoreu asserts that it is a universal function of constitutional courts: "in all countries where it exists, constitutional justice assures the regulation of political *alternances* and change," an idea claimed to be "generally accepted."[72]

The idea is not novel. In 1959, Black argued that a legitimating power constituted an essential component of American judicial review:

> Judicial review has two functions—that of imprinting governmental action with the stamp of legitimacy, and that of checking the political branches of government when these encroach on ground forbidden to them by the constitution as interpreted by the court.[73]

This formulation was Black's response to critical accounts of the Supreme Court's role during New Deal days, accounts which he thought impaired the court's public standing, obscured the legal issues, and focused too exclusively on crude "politics"—invariably ending by describing how the court was saved by switched votes and new Roosevelt appointees. Objecting to this "canonical version," Black wanted to "to show how the whole story could be told from an entirely different perspective." In his version, after two years of "balking," the court "placed the definitive stamp of legitimacy on the New Deal, and on the whole conception of government in America." A good thing, too, since Americans "had no other means, other than the Supreme Court, for imparting legitimacy to the New Deal."[74]

Professor Favoreu and Black found almost identical solutions to similar problems. In both cases, constitutional courts found themselves under attack by critics who believed that popular mandates to effect reform were being flouted by nonrepresentative, judicial bodies. In rising to their defense, both professors based their arguments on the belief that constitutional justice offered the only solution to patently political crises, that only a constitutional court could legitimate the New Deal or guarantee the survival of the Fifth Republic.

The existence of such a legitimating function has been disputed and is certainly not "generally accepted," at least not in political science literature. In West Germany, for example, Landfried has criticized the concept on normative grounds, and has argued that "the function of a constitutional court is to legitimate processes, not outcomes."[75] In an exhaustive review of the U.S. literature on the concept,[76] Adamany has noted that none of the proponents of a legitimacy function "offer the slightest empirical basis for its reality."[77] After reviewing the historical examples of those judicial–political confrontations positively correlated with critical electoral alternations, Adamany concludes that "the legitimizing function of the Supreme Court cannot summon adequate empirical support from public opinion studies, does not square with the history of relations between the justices and the popular branches, and will not withstand a searching analysis of its assumptions."[78]

Still, *accepting certain restrictive assumptions*, the notion may be on firmer ground in France. Because the Council's deliberations take place immediately after a piece of legislation has been definitively adopted, they are viewed with the same partisan fervor that attended the controlled bill's elaboration. A decision which permits legislation to be promulgated as adopted will be celebrated by a vindicated government, and the opposition can do little more than protest or move quietly on to the next battle. This will remain the case as long as the Council is used for public policy purposes by politicians. In this light, Favoreu's "certificate" analogy is not wholly false. But it is incomplete and distorts the dynamics of constitutional politics in France. Most important, the advantage for the government of a declaration that it did not behave unconstitutionally is far less than the damage it suffers in practical and public relations terms from censure. This is true of judicial review situations elsewhere, but in France the asymmetry is especially acute. The opposition has little if anything to lose in initiating Council proceedings. Government participation in the process, however, is entirely coerced. The government can never "win," but can only be exonerated[79]—at best "rewarded" with what it had already.

The analogy also leads to narrow readings of the policymaking impact of Council decisions. According to Professor Favoreu, the Council does not function as a legislator, an "obstacle" or a "barrier" to legislative programs. It instead "redirects" (*un aiguillage*) them. Reforms are not "prevented," but "shaped," "corrected," and "authenticated."[80] This view—the orthodox one in France—is reiterated constantly by doctrinal supporters of the Council, and has recently received the approval of then Council member and law professor, Georges Vedel:

> The constitutional judge . . . is not a censor [of legislative activity] but a switchman [*un aiguilleur*] on a train. He does not forbid the moving of the train: he limits himself, by virtue of the rules which he is charged with applying, to directing it on the "good route."[81]

As a matter of legislative process, the Council was indeed an obstacle and a formidable one to Socialist reforms. In the context of the Fifth Republic, that of the "rationalized Assembly" and the impotent Senate, if the Council can not be considered to have been an obstacle to Socialist reforms, then no institution can! Perhaps this is merely a semantic dispute, but the language used—insisted upon as an important part of the analysis—does not explain and can only obscure why the Council's policymaking role regularly engenders controversy. In working to insulate the Council from criticism, public lawyers reinvoke the law-politics distinction: judges "correct" reforms by simply assuring that the legislator has not violated constitutional requirements, but only politicians can "obstruct" and make politically relevant decisions about matters of policy.

But the view that the legitimation thesis might be on firmer ground in France than elsewhere—due to the timing and politics of Council intervention in the legislative process—would certainly *not* be accepted by French advocates. This is because the legitimacy allegedly conferred is symbolic, that is, it operates independent of "content legitimation," or "the merits of the policy" being examined.[82] Neither Black nor Favoreu claim that when courts legitimate they are expressing agreement with the details or the expediency of particular reforms. To do so would be to acknowledge that not only do judges help to make public policy, but that they are sometimes more qualified to make some policy judgments than are politicians. The source of symbolic legitimacy is the reverence accorded by the polity to the constitution and, in consequence, to those judges which interpret and defend it. Indeed, at bottom, this judicial power can exist only to the extent that "adoration for the constitution becomes adoration of its guardians."[83]

Once it is asserted that electoral mandates alone do not and cannot confer the legitimacy necessary for elected officials to carry out their programs, it is a relatively short step to argue that these same officials need the approval of judges, who alone possess the power to bestow the favor of the constitution upon successful politicians or ruling coalitions. Thus, the advocacy of a "legitimating function" is an elaborate attempt to settle the interminable controversy over the democratic nature of constitutional review. Its supporters seek to "justify judicial review as a robust exercise, rather than a denial of the democratic principle."[84]

Professor Favoreu's argument fits squarely within this tradition, but stands French political history on its head. In France, where effective review of governmental initiatives has existed only since 1971, it is unclear why a government would need such legitimation at all. How and when did governments and legislators lose their legitimacy? How did they do without the constitutional court until 1981? More to the point, to what extent did Mitterrand's winning coalition need the benediction of the Council's "supplementary authority" to proceed with its program after the 1981 elections?

I would argue not at all. Even if we accept at face value the power of the U.S. Supreme Court to perform a legitimizing function based on the prestige and adoration accorded by elites and the general public to the constitution, to judges, and to the regime, the argument for such a power in France is far less compelling. First, both the Socialists and the Communists came to power in 1981 pledged to revise the constitution, to abolish the Constitutional Council, and to establish a "real Supreme Court." Second, in 1981 the average citizen's knowledge of the role and functioning of the Council (as in the United States for that matter[85]) was certainly no more than rudimentary, and it is unlikely that a majority even knew of the Council's existence as late as 1986.[86] With respect to *elite* opinion, the same appears to be true. In all standard political science and constitutional law textbooks of the 1980s and before, the Council received less than a dozen pages, often critical of its role in the regime. A class devoted to the Council and its jurisprudence did not appear on the curricula of the *Institut d'études politiques* in Paris until 1986. Favoreu himself has complained that the Council's jurisprudence is not taught at all in a number of *grandes écoles*—including the national schools of administration (ENA) and of the *magistrature* (which trains judges).[87] One wonders how and from where a nearly unknown institution, enjoying uneven support among elites within the political system, obtained the power necessary to legitimate a government which had just been given confidence by the greatest parliamentary majority in the Fifth Republic's history.

In any case, French legislative majorities have not appreciated the supposed benefits of the certificate of constitutional legitimacy bestowed on their programs by the Council. After the Council struck down parts of the Socialist's nationalization law, one parliamentarian put it in this way:

> When the Council behaves like a political tribunal opposed to national representatives, as it does today, it condemns itself and its political nature and composition become obvious. This fact has not escaped the French people. They interpret the decision of the Council as censoring the policies chosen by the sovereign people. There is no room for another interpretation.[88]

Moreover, as Carcassonne puts it, "Decisions of non-conformity [with the constitution] are big events, while those of conformity are non-events which pass practically unnoticed beyond a small circle of specialists."[89] We therefore might turn Professor Favoreu's proposition on its head: given the historical lack of elite consensus around the constitution of the Fifth Republic and its institutions, the long-standing tension between democratic theory and judicial power in France, and the general lack of public knowledge about the role of the Council, *it is much more evident that constitutional review and the Constitutional Council had greater need of legitimation than had any French government after the elections of 1981.* This is in no manner a critique of the Council. The 1981–87 period is remarkable because the institution not only survived the intense pressures generated by two reform regimes coming to power successively, but strengthened its position vis-à-vis other public authorities in the legislative process. In the end, elected officials did not abolish the Council, and they obeyed its decisions. But by doing so, one might argue, these same officials conferred legitimacy on the Council and on the constitution, not the other way around.

Of course, to accept the legitimation thesis is also to admit that the Council possesses *political* power of enormous consequence. Bickel put it in these modest terms: "The rule that the Court must always legitimate whatever it is not justified in striking down fails to attain its intended purpose of removing the Court from the political arena," it instead only "shifts the direction" of the court's "intervention" into politics.[90] As Bickel recognized,[91] the power to legitimize is only meaningful because courts also possess the power to block legislative initiative, that is, to the extent that courts can *delegitimize* the governing coalition and its program. But neither Black nor Favoreu admit this possibility. I will return to the legitimation thesis in the case study of the Council's 1982 nationalization decision in chapter 6.

The Juridicized Parliament Is Not a Pacified Parliament

I use the phrase, *juridicization* of parliament, in this book to describe the totality of the influence of Council decisions, past constitutional jurisprudence, and the threat of future censure on the legislative process. Professor Favoreu, in contrast or in addition to this use, employs the phrase to describe a tangential "pacification of parliament" brought about, "in a decisive manner," by the "control exercised by the Constitutional Council."[92] His argument is the following. As constitutional review became a matter of daily importance in the making of legislation, French politicians developed a reverence for constitutionality and for constitutional principles that had been absent before. Gradually, the Council came to exercise a new kind of *tutelle* (tutelage) over parliament, which politicians generally accept and even rejoice in. In this "pacified" parliament, "quarrels," which before would before have been fought in partisan terms, are "appeased," and worked out more reasonably—in constitutional terms.[93] Indeed, Professor Favoreu declares that the Constitutional Council's role as an moderator of conflict is "obvious" and constitutes another "function" of the institution.[94]

The idea that juridicization and pacification are synonymous fails as a description of political reality. In Part II of the book, I will demonstrate at length and in great detail why and how this notion fails, the analysis of the media pluralism decisions in chapter 7 constituting a crucial case study of the pacification thesis.

Conclusion

During the course of the Fifth Republic doctrinal attitudes toward "political review," and thus to the Constitutional Council itself, radically changed—from unmitigated hostility to virtually unanimous support. Two elements were crucial to this evolution. First, the Council incorporated and then undertook to actively develop a bill of rights. Second, the Council's work became increasingly attendant to judicial norms of behavior (norms generated by doctrinal activity) in a host of other ways. In doing so, the Council sought to legitimize an expanded role for constitutional review by tapping into institutionalized discursive structures that had been in place for nearly a century (see chapter 1). At this, the Council was remarkably successful. The public law community, for its part, found in the Council what it had been searching for since at least the 1880s: a stable basis for the building of constitutional law. By the mid-1970s, doctrine had come to accept the Council's status as a courtlike institution, in large part because it had clearly signaled that its jurisprudence would be open and sensitive to doctrinal advocacy. Scholarly support quickly became overt and militant. In short, a symbiotic, mutually legitimizing relationship was formed between institution and discourse, between concrete structure and cognitive structure.

The emergence of an intimate relationship between the Council and *le droit* is a crucial, perhaps requisite, condition of the Council's development as a relatively autonomous political actor. The autonomy issue is important on its own terms, as an element in the potential evolution of the French legal order, in the consolidation of a stable constitutional framework, and so on, however, it is also significant to institutional interaction and policymaking processes. Judicial bodies possess relatively few resources with which to defend their institutional positions once attacked. Their powers of self-defense are infirmed by the relatively more passive nature of office, the constraining terms of jurisdiction, and the lack of formal authority to implement policy. In the United States, the existence of a vertically integrated court system provides some compensation. A policy made by the Supreme Court may be implemented throughout the land by hundreds of lower courts; it may also stimulate demand for more of the same policy by structuring lawyerly activity and litigation. The American court has also greatly benefited from a second source of legitimation—that of academic discourse; and law professors constitute a stable and powerful constituency, providing crucial defense in times of crisis. Bereft of direct contact with the greater judiciary, the French Council is all the more reliant on the scholarly community for defense of its legitimacy. And to the extent that public lawyers can convince other lawyers and the ordinary and administrative courts that the Council is indeed a kind of high *juridiction*, then its position will be that much more secure.

These points accepted, academic discourse on the Constitutional Council is woefully inadequate to the task of building a social science of Council behavior and impact. Indeed, it is positively hostile to such activity: there is a fierce resistance to the notion that the Council is a political actor at all; a radical dissociation between legal and policymaking processes is propagated and actively defended; the impact of constitutional review on macropolitics is obscured or altogether ignored; and doctrinal analysis is privileged as the only true and "revelatory" method. In contrast, I have argued that conceptualizing the Council as a policymaker is a necessary first step toward building a political science of Council behavior. This step and many others are taken in Part II.

II

POLICYMAKING IN
THE SHADOW OF THE
CONSTITUTIONAL COUNCIL

5

The Juridicized
Policymaking Process

"The legislator legislates in the shadow cast by the Constitutional Council."
FRANÇOIS LÉOTARD, minister of culture,
La Libération, 11 August 1986

I have argued that to limit our understanding of the Constitutional Council's political behavior and impact to the terms of its jurisprudence obscures its political role and functioning, and leads to a narrow reading of the impact of constitutional review on policymaking. Focus on the application of the Council's decisions by legislators is a necessary but only partial corrective. Given the Council's potential to exercise indirect, deterrent power over policy decisions, the full picture is only visible to the extent that the analyst attends to each stage of the legislative process, and is able to evaluate, as systematically as possible, the full range of Council impact. This indirect impact too constitutes the Council's policymaking behavior.

This chapter provides a schematic overview of what I have called the juridicized legislative process. The constitutional and political bases of juridicization are recalled and summarized; the legislative process is broken up into stages; and each of these is examined from the perspective of constitutional politics and Council impact. Subsequent chapters will serve to illustrate many of the general points made in this chapter, and in much greater detail.

Lawmaking and the Constitutional Council

As described in the introductory chapter, the legislative process is juridicized to the extent that Council decisions, the pedagogical authority of past Council jurisprudence, and the threat of future Council censure alter legislative outcomes. The increased importance of constitutional debate in the elaboration of legislation can be explained by two factors, one specific: the constitutional mandate of the Council; and one more general: an amalgam of political

119

traditions, practices, and psychologies that characterize French politics. In consequence, the Constitutional Council is permanently politicized to the extent that it is systematically implicated in the day-to-day partisan struggles of parliament. Politicians use and think of the Council as a tool of obstruction and its decisions, whatever their jurisprudential import, are viewed as legislative victories or defeats.

Because the Council's decisions may not be appealed, referrals to it are extraordinarily efficacious weapons in the hands of the opposition. This is due to the immediate impact which every decision exercises on legislative texts, an impact which deserves to be recalled. While Council *approbation*—a decision in which no part of a referred bill is judged to be unconstitutional—allows the promulgation of the referred text, the mere referral to the Council of a bill will suspend its promulgation until a decision has been reached; a bill once judged unconstitutional is *annulled* and may not be promulgated, and a provision once judged unconstitutional may not appear in subsequent legislation. The Council may also declare that a bill contains unconstitutional provisions that are "inseparable" from the whole—that is the bill is judged to be so "contaminated"[1] by the offending provisions that the whole can have no separate constitutional integrity—and in this case the bill also may not be promulgated. And finally, although the president can decide to promulgate a bill "*amputated*" of those provisions deemed unconstitutional—but separable from the whole—he may also decide that such an amputation unacceptably thwarts the original intent of the legislation, and order a new reading; such an amputation is tantamount to an annulment, and the legislative process must then be retraced from the beginning with the possibility of a second referral looming at the end. Thus, in timing and impact *every Council decision objectively constitutes the final stage of one process and, at times, the opening stage of another*.

Table 5.1 shows the Council's direct impact on legislation outcomes in statistical form, and in the terms already used. In the 1974–81 period—the Giscard presidency—the Council approved 73 percent of all bills referred to it, and censured the remaining 27.2 percent (twelve of forty-four). Of those bill censured, one-third were annulled. After 1981, the period of *alternance* and reform politics, the percentage of referred bills judged to be constitutional falls dramatically—to 52.7 percent (forty-eight of ninety-one). The number of total annulments as a proportion of all negative decisions also decreased—to one in seven; the Council, as will be discussed, has sought to control the legislative process more flexibly, without relying on simple, outright annulment, understandable given the recurrent controversy surrounding review in France.

The attractiveness for politicians of petition to the Council must be understood in the context of the revitalization of parliamentary institutions in the legislative process generally,[2] revitalization which is itself linked to some important macropolitical factors. First, the development of the presidential election as the essential political prize in France had the effect of concentrating partisan formations; as a result parliament gradually bifurcated into a relatively stable majority and a tenacious opposition. The Gaullist rhetoric that the president was "above politics," although still ritually proffered by Left and

Table 5.1. Council Activity and Legislative Outcomes*

Year	No. of Laws Referred	Approbation	Amputation	Annulation
1974	2	1	1	0
1975	4	3	1	0
1976	6	3	2	1
1977	8	7	0	1
1978	9	6	3	0
1979	7	4	2	1
1980	10	8	1	1
1981 (Right)	0	0	0	0
Total (1974–81)	46	32	10	4
1981 (Left)	8	4	3	1
1982	19	11	7	1
1983	9	5	4	0
1984	15	5	10	0
1985	15	7	6	2
1986 (Right)	16	7	7	2
1987	10	4	6	0
Total (1981–87)	92	43	43	6

*Only referrals by sixty senators or sixty deputies are considered here. As the 1974 constitutional amendment enabling did not enter into force until late 1974, the figures for 1974 are not comparable. Instances are listed according to the date of their referral, and not by the date of the Council decision. *Approbation* results in promulgation; *amputation* results in promulgation of the law less those provisions judged unconstitutional; *annulation* includes all bills judged nonpromulgable by either the Council or the competent legislative authorities.

Right, lost whatever practical meaning it might have had, by the Giscard era at the latest: it is by virtue of the strength of their majorities or coalitions in parliament that presidents are able to ratify their policy choices. In the period of *cohabitation*, Matignon's relations with parliament were central—Chirac's claim to legitimacy was his parliamentary majority, itself a "family" of party formations. As important, two experiences of *alternance*—electorally sanctioned alternations of power between these two groups—have made the legislature much more than a simple *chambre d'enregistrement*, or voting machine, rubber-stamping executive initiatives. In the age of reform mania, parliament also became a testing ground for future ministers and a battleground for radically different social agenda. In consequence, the French penchant for polarized legislative debate and unrelenting obstruction was accentuated, because the stakes of legislative outcomes were raised. Finally, although the government retains its stranglehold on legislative *initiative*,[3] parliamentary deliberations do make a difference: among other indexes, the number of hours spent working on legislation in public sessions has increased from 639 hours in the fifth parliament (1973–77), and 712 in the sixth (1978–80), to 942 and 930 hours in the seventh (Socialist rule, 1981–85) and eighth (*cohabitation*, 1986–87), respectively.[4] Perhaps more important, parliamentarians—and this has been true since the mid-1970s—are three times as likely to be at the origin of *successful* amendments than are ministers. In sum, parliament is today much more central to the policymaking process than it had been in the the first decade of the Fifth Republic.

The development and reinvigoration of parliamentary techniques of obstruction are linked to the juridicization of this process. This is due to one simple reality: for all of its mastery over parliament, governments and their majorities can not avoid having their bills judged if any sixty deputies or sixty senators believe that such bills may be unconstitutional. Since 1981, every fifth bill adopted by parliament has been referred to the Constitutional Council, including virtually every major piece of legislation and especially those giving rise to intense partisan debate. The systematicity with which the Council is called upon to intervene in the legislative process impacts upon policymaking in two important ways. First, governments and their parliamentary majorities are obliged to work to avoid constitutional defeats, albeit within subjectively defined limits. To save time and embarrassment, successive governments have engaged in substantial exercises of what will be called *autolimitation*, in which they strive, by self-restraint, to insulate a bill from possible future Council censure. Second, a petition to the Council acts as a kind of jurisprudential transmission belt: the more petitions the Council receives, the more opportunity it has to elaborate jurisprudential techniques of control. This elaboration, in turn, expands the grounds of judicial debate in future legislative processes, a potentially crucial consideration in those cases where lawmakers are forced to rewrite legislation after a negative decision—what I term the *corrective revision* process. At these times, indirect and direct effects are not easily separable, since legislators are, in essence, working to "apply" the Council's decisions. Put somewhat differently, corrective revision processes reveal the Council unambiguously as a lawmaker, and parliament functions in this process as the *Council's chambre d'enregistrement.*

Autolimitation and *Corrective Revision*

As early as 1977, Pezant foresaw the potential for a "deterrent" effect, when he hypothesized that "even the simple threat of a petition to the Constitutional Council might henceforth be enough to reorient" legislative procedures.[5] This effect is here called *autolimitation*, by which I mean the *government's exercise of legislative self-restraint resulting from anticipation of a referral to, and an eventual negative decision of, the Constitutional Council.* He did not mention that the substantive content of actual legislation might also be "reoriented." The omission is understandable: before 1981, majorities in control of legislative processes generally did not fear Council censure, and were not led to sacrifice policy choices due to worries about unconstitutionality. In what was one of its most important decisions of the pre-1981 period, the Council annulled a government bill to expand police power to search automobiles.[6] The government was more than usually warned. In the Senate, the bill received a hostile reception: the committee concerned, citing the Senate's responsibility to "set an example for the defense of liberties," asked the upper chamber to reject the bill, which it did overwhelmingly.[7] In the National Assembly, *exceptions d'irrece-vabilité* were moved and declarations of opposition made by the major associations of lawyers and magistrates were read and cited.[8] After the Council annulled the bill, called "one of the essential pieces" of the government's program to better assure the security of French citizens,[9] no efforts were made to revive it in another guise. Another celebrated annulment, the Council's 1971 decision on freedom of association (see chapter 3), was also preceded by Senate rejections, long debates about constitutionality, and the public protests of concerned social groups. The threat of appeal to the Council was made explicitly in parliament, but on these as on many other occasions governments and majorities simply refused to take them seriously.

Government refusals to compromise—or at least the appearance of refusal—are rare in the post-1981 period, which sees a scramble to perfect the use of constitutional law as a means to oppose legislation, to cajole or enforce changes, and to justify delays entailed by recourse to the Council. *Auto-limitation* is today built into the legislative process. Still, a glance at Figure 5.1 shows that the Council is not therefore petitioned less often: the average annual percentage of laws referred to it has more than doubled since the 1974–81 period. In fact, *once debates become juridicized, petition can be said to be inevitable*. Neither have *autolimitation* processes sufficiently protected legislation from annulment, especially true of the most important and controversial reforms enacted during the 1981–88 period. On the contrary, statistically, *autolimitation* has a miserable success rate: more than 50 percent of all bills referred to the Council since 1981 were judged to be in whole or in part unconstitutional as adopted (Figure 5.2); research shows however that in virtually every important case the offending provisions were attacked on constitutional grounds during the elaboration process, and amendments which in hindsight would have passed constitutional muster were proposed by the opposition.

In theory, *autolimitation* effects may be studied and evaluated at every stage of the policymaking process—in the individual ministries, in the advice of

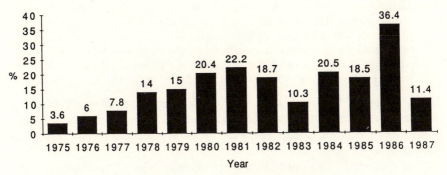

Fig. 5.1. Percentage of laws referred to the Council.

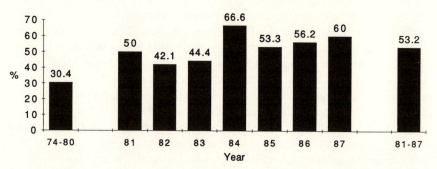

Fig. 5.2. Percentage of referred laws declared in whole or in part unconstitutional by the Council.

the *Conseil d'Etat*, in the Council of Ministers (cabinet), in parliamentary committees, and on the parliamentary floor. The most important stage—the governmental stage, where most important bills are conceived and given shape—is, however, the one we know least about, since government proceedings are cloaked in official secrecy. In general, the first crucial juridicizing role is played by the *Conseil d'Etat*, as the government's official legal advisor. Article 39 of the constitution *requires* that all government bills must be referred to the *Conseil d'Etat* for an *avis*—a nonbinding, formally secret, advisory opinion—*before* they may be discussed in cabinet or communicated to parliament. Prior to 1981, the overriding motivation for these *avis* was a concern to harmonize government initiatives with existing legal regimes by, in effect, verifying that the terms of a new bill would not conflict with existing statutes, or lead to incoherence in their application.[10] After 1981, discussions of constitutionality became the central priority. In December 1982, after more than a year of intense legislative and constitutional activity, the body's annual report (the reports, which are not publicly circulated, are the only available evidence of the *Conseil d'Etat's* own view of the process) admitted as much:

> When the *Conseil d'Etat* examines government bills . . . , its first concern is to verify their conformity to the Constitution. It proceeds in this examination in order to assure the government a maximum of judicial security, not unaware of the fact that this security is all the more necessary since the expansion of the petitioning procedure to the Constitutional Council has multiplied the risks that a new law will be referred to the latter.[11]

The government thus begins its own deliberations and later moves on to parliament apprised of the constitutional issues which may come into play and, in the *Conseil d'Etat's* words, "of the risks it takes of its bills being censured by the Council."[12]

The *Conseil d'Etat's* position in this enterprise is hardly a secure one, and some general remarks on this point are warranted. First, its deliberations often take place under conditions of extraordinary political pressure, not least, to render *avis* as quickly as possible; indeed, every annual report of the body's advisory activities, at least since 1982, complains of the "excessive haste" which the government forces upon its work, at the cost of quality.[13] Second, the *Conseil d'Etat* can not impose its policy choices on politicians. While the increased efficacy of constitutional review has undoubtedly added more weight to its *avis*, the government is free to disregard it. Third, while secret, the government may at its own initiative make public the opinion, invoking the authority of the *Conseil d'Etat* in order to reinforce its position in juridicized debates, and especially in battles over controversial provisions. The *Conseil d'Etat* is thus in the position of having its prestige put on the line, but with little control over how or in what context; furthermore, it may not comment on these debates in public. With this in mind, it is important to note that the *Conseil d'Etat* only considers the *initial* version of a bill, and is not consulted on amendments made in Parliament. Thus, a bill's overall economy may be changed by the process, and initial considerations of constitutionality may no longer be valid at the time of the bill's adoption. Nonetheless, the Council annulments of provisions proposed or approved by the *Conseil d'Etat*—and which the government agreed to and supported throughout the process as a means of ensuring constitutionality—risk appearing as repudiations of the former's authority. Not surprisingly, the rivalry between the two Councils has at times flared into a public affair.

Like their legal advisor, governments must assume that important bills will be referred to the Constitutional Council, and prepare for the possibility of juridicized debates accordingly. However, it is important to emphasize that legislative debates are not juridicized evenly or in the same way: the opposition is more likely to be successful juridicizing debates to its advantage in those legislative areas over which the Council has developed substantial control; the government, on the other hand, possesses relatively more power to resist effective juridicization when working in legislative areas on which the Council has either not yet been asked to rule, or, if it has, where rulings favor the government. In cases where there is a jurisprudential history, governments often make their constitutional "frames of reference" explicit—ritualistic bows to Council jurisprudence upon the introduction of a bill in parliament. These are statements to the legislature, and especially to the opposition, that the government had already been through a significant, if private, *autolimitation* process, often accompanied by surveys of the relevant jurisprudence. Sometimes the government goes out of its way to include in proposed bills word-for-word formulations approved by the Council in past decisions. Though difficult to document, governments may, due to obsessive constitutional anxiety, have problems even getting their legislation out of the blocks. In the first year of the Chirac government (1986) for example, key legislative priorities—including privatization of the prison system and a long-promised reform of the nationality code— were delayed: both were subjected to unusually strong attacks on constitutional grounds, and had elicited President Mitterrand's public disapproval. *Le Monde* reported that the government had been "very worried about the attitude that the Council will adopt" on the issue of private prisons, and had commissioned "diverse studies seeking to avoid the wrath of Badinter and his colleagues."[14] We also know that the government was retreating from its commitment on the strictly private status of prison employees.[15] The tightening of the nationality code was kept under wraps all year, but it was widely reported that the government had watered it down after the *Conseil d'Etat* had expressed its displeasure.[16] In the end, neither bill ever made it onto the floor in 1986, and both were later unceremoniously dropped. Finally, certain aspects of government proposals to alter the status of New Caledonia were watered down or abandoned as a result of threats, made by Mitterrand in cabinet meetings, to refer the matters to the Constitutional Council.[17]

Once legislation becomes the subject of discussion in parliament, *autolimitation* effects are more easily traced. Many important bills during the 1981–87 period were sent to the legislature by governments expecting not only that they would be attacked for being unconstitutional, but that they would be substantially amended. There were two main reasons for this. First, because many of the important reforms of the 1980s were not only controversial but complex and technical, their passage was expected to take much longer than more simple, incremental initiatives. In both 1981 and 1986, governments were obliged to squeeze into tight legislative calendars a large number of these reforms. To the extent that a race against time took precedence over elegance in lawmaking, some bills sent to the legislature were only roughly sketched out; they were then reworked as they made their way through parliament. Second, and this is generally the case, governments are largely unsure of the requirements or applicability of Council precedent, or of the temper of opposition with respect to a particular piece of legislation. Governments may decide to send to parliament bills which reflect first choices unaltered by constitutional compromises, and use the parliamentary process as a partisan airing for a wide range of constitutional arguments. The majority then has the choice of responding or not.

In parliament, a bill, and especially an important one, may become the focus of systematic, unrelenting obstruction by opposition groups. The full panoply of procedural maneuvers are employed, and hundreds, sometimes thousands, of opposition amendments are discussed and debated, clogging up the process and disrupting the parliamentary calendar. Constitutional considerations are part and parcel to this obstruction. The *règlements* of the two chambers of parliament allow the opposition three types of procedural maneuvers: the *exception d'irrecevabilité*, the *question préalable*—both of which can be raised in deliberations in either the relevant committee or on the floor of parliament, or both—and a motion to return a bill back to committee for further discussion. Constitutional debate may precede votes on each of these motions, which are often raised in succession. *Motions d'irrecevabilité* are uniquely and specifically designed for debates on the constitutionality of pending legislation. As article 91.4 of the standing orders of the National Assembly has it, deputies raise and then debate these motions—which are presented in the form of a judicial decision—"in order to determine if the text proposed is contrary to one or more constitutional provisions." Once raised, parliamentarians *must* debate and vote on the motion; if the motion passes, the bill is killed.[18] During these debates, sophisticated arguments may be made by the legislators who cite past Council decisions, rumors or leaks concerning the *Conseil d'Etat's* opinion, and the work of respected law professors. These motions, invariably moved by the opposition, are routinely rejected by the assembly on party-line votes,[19] but not before the majority's own legal specialists or spokesmen have responded to the charges leveled against the bill. During the 1981–86 period, the Senate, claiming a role of protector of public liberties, adopted a number of such motions. In general, *motions of irrecevabilité, which occur as systematically as Council referrals, are employed as part of the process of developing constitutional arguments to be submitted for Council approval.* As Autin wrote in 1983, the subsequent debate "is a serious warning to the government," as well as a "simple prelude . . . to the real debate" which will be pursued in the appeals to and the deliberations of the Council.[20] Moreover, just as grounds for referral to the Council expand with constitutional jurisprudence, so do grounds for raising motions of *irrecevabilité.* Table 5.2 shows the remarkable increase in the popularity of these motions in the National Assembly (the table excludes motions raised in committees). Until 1974, only 4 such motions were raised and voted, to be compared with 42 between 1981 and 1985, and 51 in 1986–87—more than 100 more were raised but did not come to a vote in 1986–87!

During the amendment process, the arguments begin all over again, often in minute detail, as the opposition works to force the majority to compromise by threatening referral and proposing changes which will allegedly insulate

Table 5.2. The Use of the Motion of *Irrecevabilité* in the National Assembly*

Year	Motions Raised	Motions Voted On	Motions Passed
1968–80	47	29	1
Avg./year	*3.9*	*2.4*	*0.08*
1981	8	6	0
1982	6	6	0
1983	9	9	0
1984	12	11	0
1985	14	10	0
Avg./year	*9.8*	*8.4*	*0*
1986	67	25	0
1987	87	26	0
Avg./year	*77*	*25.5*	*0*

*Motions of *irrecevabilité* require debate and then votes on the allegation that a bill is unconstitutional; if a majority supports such a motion, the bill in question is rejected; motions are virtually always raised by the opposition, and the vote is virtually always along party lines.

SOURCE: *Statistiques, Bulletin de l'Assemblée nationale, numero spéciale* for each of the years cited. The 1968–80 figures do not include figures for 1969: the 1969 edition of the statistical bulletin omits these figures. Statistics were not available for the pre-1968 period.

beleaguered provisions from negative rulings. Not surprisingly, it is precisely those bills which raise the greatest constitutional controversy that elicit the greatest numbers of amendment proposals: during the first reading in of the 1982 nationalization bill, for example, more than 1,400 amendments were considered, then a record; 2,491 amendments were tabled during the first reading of the 1984 bill on press pluralism—more than the total registered during entire legislative years in the 1960s; moreover, the Senate rejected both bills on several occasions. The Council's decisions on both of these bills— complex partial annulments—are, moreover, recognized as among its most important by both politicians and law professors, not least, because they went on to structure subsequent reform efforts, and because they settled long-standing legal controversies. Intensely juridicized debates like these reveal the significant resistance of governments in the 1980–87 period to the *autolimitation* process. There appear to be certain boundaries beyond which ministers are unwilling to go in the *autolimitation* process, and these tend to be fixed politically and not "constitutionally," accounting, one might argue, for the poor success rate of *autolimitation*. It is important to note, however, that in many cases of audacious, creative reform, attacks by the opposition are not limited to those provisions ultimately amputated by the Council. They instead range over the whole of the law, beginning with basic principles—the right of any government to nationalize banks, or to privatize the broadcast media, for example. However impassioned and sophisticated, most of these arguments were *not* later accepted by the Council. Had the government accepted them and amended accordingly, the legislation would have been needlessly compromised.

The resistance to *autolimitation* occurs, predictably, where basic political objectives are jeopardized. Majorities believe that the legitimacy of their legislative agenda derives not from their understanding of Council precedent but from their electoral victories. The opposition has only one means of challenging this view: a threat of Council censure, or, more precisely, the invocation of the legitimacy of the constitution. A government can be penalized for misunderstanding constitutional principles; the opposition, however, can proliferate arguments and interpretations with impunity. The resulting decision-making problem constitutes a form of "brinksmanship," or game of chicken, in which the government must decide how far it is willing to compromise its objectives in order to ensure a bill's constitutionality.

Brinksmanship contrasts sharply with wholesale exercises of *autolimitation*. Governments may simply decide that compromise with some opposition positions may be less painful than suffering the damage of Council censure. Dozens, sometimes hundreds, of amendments might be adopted during a bill's run through the constitutional gauntlet. The classic case is the 1982 decentralization law when, in the course of its passage over 500 amendments were accepted by the government, and many of its most important elements were successively removed.[21] By the time the bill was actually promulgated, Favoreu reports, "the state of the new law [was] not very different from the situation . . . which existed previously."[22] In cases such as these, as Carcassonne has pointed out, it is almost impossible to ascertain whether "prudence"—real fear of Council censure—or good "diplomacy"—part of a quid pro quo—is the motivating factor for compromise.[23] In addition, governments may use constitutional arguments as convenient pretexts for abandoning radical measures once promised to party activists but later viewed with misgiving, blaming the Council's negative "attitude" for the change of heart.

Because *autolimitation* processes did not, or could not, protect many of the most important reforms during the 1981–87 period from annulment or serious amputation, successive governments were often forced to repeat the legislative process after a negative Council decision in the hope of salvaging what they could of bills or certain key provisions judged to be nonpromulgable. This process, which I term corrective revision—the reelaboration of a censured text in strict conformity with Council prescriptions in order to avoid a second censure—implicates the Council most directly as a policymaker *during* the governmental and parliamentary stages of the legislative process. As Etien characterizes it, the process is begun with the Council "indicating . . . with precise recommendations . . . what the attitude of the [legislative] powers should have been had they wanted to avoid the invalidation" in the first instance.[24]

The Council Decides: Inside the Black Box

The Constitutional Council is housed in a small wing of the east, rue Montpensier, side of the Palais Royal, a building complex otherwise dominated by the *Conseil d'Etat* and the Comedie Francaise.[25] Its offices are contained on part of one floor of this wing. Each member has a private office as does the secretary-general, the chief administrator of the institution. There is a meeting room, which principally contains an oval table around which members sit when the Council meets in plenary session, and there is also a small library containing legal materials.

Compared to their German, Italian, or American counterparts, Council members are aided by a relatively small group of supporting staff. As of June 1989, the total number of legal specialists working full time at the Council in support of its constitutional review role was three,[26] all *conseillers d'Etat*. One of these is attached to the president of the Council, Robert Badinter, and a second is the current secretary-general, Bruno Genevois. The secretary-general's position is one of enormous importance. His responsibilities include overall supervision of the day-to-day operation of the Council and of its finances. More important for our purposes, he oversees the Council's legal offices (*service juridique*), which exist in order to aid members in legal research and to assemble dossiers on individual cases, and he helps in the writing of the decisions.

Genevois has filled this position since March 1986, having been recruited by Badinter upon his appointment to the presidency by Mitterrand. Genevois, a former student of Council member Georges Vedel, graduate of the prestigious

Ecole nationale d'administration and a *maître de requêtes* at the *Conseil d'Etat*, was described by the press at that time as the country's "brightest, most competent, and knowledgeable expert on jurisprudence—not only that of the *Conseil d'Etat* but also of the *Cour de cassation*, the European Court of Justice, and the Constitutional Council."[27] In addition to his duties at the Palais Royal, the secretary-general has played an unprecedented, active role in presenting the Council to legal specialists and political elites alike in public fora. In 1988 he published the first full-length synthesis of the Council's jurisprudence,[28] and regularly publishes articles on the Council in journals devoted to both law and political science; he teaches the only course offered on the Council at the elite *Institut d'études politiques* in Paris, and he regularly attends and presents papers at symposia and other academic meetings devoted to the Council or to other aspects of constitutional and administrative law.

The constitutional review process formally begins only after a bill has been definitively adopted by parliament and a referral signed by sixty deputies or sixty senators has been delivered to the Council. In practice, however, referrals are prepared and even signed before final adoption of the bill in question. Both chambers have engaged public law professors to write referrals. In the 1981–85 period, for example, the most widely published of all Council experts, Professor Favoreu, regularly wrote the Senate's petitions. When the Socialists returned to opposition in 1986, the law professor, Guy Carcassonne, formally attached to the Socialist group in the National Assembly, wrote the assembly's petitions and aided that group in its attempts to juridicize debates during the legislative process itself. Since 1983, the texts of referrals have been published in the volume of the *Journal officiel* (the French state's official record, equivalent to the Federal Register in the United States) devoted to *legislative* texts, immediately following the text of the Council's decision. Before 1983, referrals were published only irregularly in the *Revue du droit public*, and in a well-known compilation of constitutional documents edited by a constitutional specialist.[29] Because of the terse nature of the Council's jurisprudence, particularly in the years before 1980, it was extremely difficult for any interested outsider lacking access to the referral text to understand the context and import of any Council decision. The publication of these texts in the *Journal officiel*, probably a result of doctrinal pressure finally acceded to, provides access to political as well as legal context, since petitioners regularly refer to partisan issues involved and to the policymaking impact of the legal arguments invoked. With respect to the relationship between the arguments submitted to the Council in referrals and the final decision, it is important to note that *the Council has asserted its power to annul any part of a bill—including provisions which have not been expressly attacked by petitioners*. In fact, it does so increasingly: in the 1959–81 period, this occurred only twice; in the 1981–87 period, the Council, on ten instances, annulled provisions which had not been the subject of the petitioner's referral.[30]

Surprisingly, there has never been a systematic study of referrals, even from a legalistic perspective, although such a study would yield important data about parliamentary-Council interaction and the evolution of juridicization. It is clear, however, that as Council jurisprudence has become more dense and argumentive, so have referrals (undoubtedly also a result of the fact that the writing of referrals is left to full-time Council specialists).

In the Constitutional Council, too, work begins on a case before final adoption and referral of a bill. The secretariat provides each Council member with parliamentary debates as well as compilations of press clippings (*dossiers de presse*), updated weekly, on bills which the staff thinks *might* be referred upon their adoption. The task of identifying such bills is a relatively easy one since motions of *irrecevabilité* regularly contain explicit threats of future referral. The secretariat also regularly circulates doctrinal commentaries on the Council's past decisions as well as articles which appear on the Council in general newspapers and in academic journals.

Once a referral is registered with the Council, the formal process begins with the designation by the president of the Council of one member as *rapporteur* for the case. There are a number of criteria used by the president in this designation. First, the president is excluded from consideration, unless a *rapport* is abandoned before completion. Second, the president seeks to spread responsibility among the remaining eight members as evenly as possible, so that all members are actively engaged in the institution's work, but also so that a single member's role and influence will not become preponderate. Third, the president seeks to encourage specialization and to favor preexisting competence. Thus, Georges Vedel, a professor of administrative law who was charged with writing a report on the state of economic concentration in the press industry in 1979, was assigned to the 1984 and 1986 legislation which sought to regulate media pluralism; a senator or deputy might be assigned disputes which involve parliamentary procedures. Finally, the president may take into consideration the tastes and proclivities of members in these decisions.

The *rapporteur* has three main responsibilities. First, he compiles a dossier on the legislation in question with the help of the secretariat. This dossier is composed of (1) *travaux préparatoires*, the record of legislative debates in committee and in the full chamber on the bill, (2) a *dossier de presse* on the bill and its journey through parliament, (3) the text of referrals, a reply from the government and other communications in legal brief form, (4) texts of relevant past Council decisions, (5) doctrinal commentary, and (6) administrative reports when necessary. Although not required or foreseen in any constitutional text, the government has, since at least 1974, regularly responded in written briefs to petitioner's referrals. This practice is proof of the recognition that in most cases, unlike in the 1959–71 period, the government will be the "defendant."

To the extent that the government is encouraged and expected to reply there thus exist a kind of contradictory, or adversial, process; however, both the government and the assemblies have consistently denied that this process is judicial. Badinter as president of the Council sought to strengthen and to institutionalize the adversery nature of the process, proposing that the *rapporteurs* for the bill within parliament as well as the government respond formally to issues raised by the referrals as well as by the Council itself. Before 1986, such communication did occur, but only on an informal, ad hoc basis. The presidents of the National Assembly and of the Senate rebuffed the proposal: the president of the assembly stated that the role of the *rapporteur* in the legislative process ceased with the adoption of the bill; the president of the Senate, echoing what his counterpart in the assembly had implied, in effect argued that the Senate's work was to pass legislation not to aid the Council in undoing it (but he did express the view that informal contacts between the Council and the parliamentary majority were at times useful).[31] The Chirac government also refused to be drawn in to a more formalized, adversarial, and therefore more courtlike process. In a letter to the Council of 30 June 1986, the secretary-general of the government made its views known:

> When a law is referred to the Council by 60 deputies or 60 senators, the secretary-general of the government furnishes the Council with all of the elements of law and of fact relevant to the Council's work. To this end, it directs questions at the ministers concerned and assembles, in the form of written observations, their responses. The secretariat can make precise in these observations its own legal position.
>
> *The written observations presented by the secretary-general of the government in no way constitutes a brief in defense.* More often, they are limited to responses to questions asked . . . by the member of the Council designated as the *rapporteur*.
>
> The progressive development of this procedure began in the mid-1970s.
>
> *The procedure does not constitute, I insist on this point, a contradictory procedure in the judicial [juridictionnel] sense of the term.* The debate which takes place between the Council, the secretary-general of the government, and the ministers concerned is not in effect a "trial of a law" . . . [emphases added].[32]

Other interested parties, including groups within the parliamentary majority and even private individuals, have at times submitted briefs to the Council. There is evidence that Council members and the secretariat consult with outside legal specialists on an ad hoc basis during the decision-making process. In its decisions, however, the Council mentions and responds *only* to arguments contained in the official parliamentary referrals of the bill. Once completed, the dossier is distributed to every Council member.

The second task of the *rapporteur* is to draft a decision. The *rapporteur* is assisted in this process by staff, and mostly notably the secretary-general. One crucial role of the latter is to remind members when necessary that although the conflict may be of political origin, it must be resolved in legal terms. The secretary-general thus ensures that the *rapporteur* is sufficiently apprised of the potential impact existing law and precedent might exert on the Council's present work and on the process of coming to a decision. This role would appear to be all the more important given the fact that a majority of the members on the Council are not jurists by training. After a number of ad hoc meetings with other members, the *rapporteur* proceeds to draft one or more decisions as well as a report, which seeks to justify the solution arrived at with respect to the materials contained in the dossier.

The third task of the *rapporteur* occurs in the plenary sessions devoted to discussion and voting of the decision. In principle, seven members constitute a quorum, unless time constraints make delays impossible. These sessions begin with the presentation of the *rapporteur*'s report. The members then discuss the report and and vote on the outcome; all ties are broken by the president. After determining constitutionality, the arguments contained in the text of the draft decision are debated point-by-point, and voting may be used to determine final language.

According to the organic law which established the Council, votes and deliberations of the Council may not be made public. Favoreu explains the rationale for the rule as follows: "the anxiousness to preserve anonymity is the tradition of French legal procedure and serves . . . to permit the judge to decide in total independence." Moreover, members are forbidden from discussing either even after they have left the body. As discussed briefly in previous chapters, the Council's decision writing also follows French tradition, a tradition whose stylistic exemplar is the administrative jurisprudence of the *Conseil d'Etat*. André Tunc has identified two ideal types of styles commonly employed by what he calls "the constitutional judge": either he "seeks to explain his decision, to make understood its exact justification and significance, or, obliged by the law to make some justification for it, the constitutional judge does so as briefly as possible." The French Council, in contrast to the American and German courts, is an example of the latter type. Still, the Council's jurisprudence has evolved away from that of the traditional model in certain important respects, undoubtedly a result of the Council's enhanced political role. As the *conseiller d'Etat*, Labetoulle, put it, in a comparing the style of the two *conseils*:

> The *Conseil d'Etat* traditionally wrote for Dean Hauriou or for Professor Waline [both of whom wrote administrative law commentaries for the *Revue du droit public*]; the Council must write [as well] for the political world and for the media.[33]

As discussed in chapter 3, since at least 1980 Council decisions have become much longer and contain more argumentation than they had before. This is partly the result of the increased sophistication of referral writing, partly a result of the influence of Georges Vedel, and partly a response to what I called *judicial inflation*. From 1975 to 1981 particularly, petitioners, to some extent encouraged by the Council, worked hard to convince the judges to expand the *bloc de constitutionnalité*—a term which denotes the corpus of principles possessed of *valeur constitutionnel* to which all legislation must conform in order to be valid. Since at least 1980, the Council has felt obliged to address the referrals point-by-point, especially with respect to the status and meaning of the constitutional principles invoked. This it did, I believe, in part to reduce levels of uncertainty about the contents of the *bloc de constitutionalité*, as well as to fend off doctrinal criticism that it was creating principles of *valeur constitutionnel* in an unnecessarily promiscuous fashion. The lengthening of constitutional jurisprudence is also good evidence of the self-conscious, pedagogical role which the Council plays, pedagogy which is aimed at facilitating the penetration of constitutional discourse into legislative discourse. Finally, the development probably functions as a self-defense mechanism for the Council. In theory at least, a more dense jurisprudence can lessen the uncertainty of policymakers engaged in future legislative processes, and may provide better doctrinal standards for the judging of jurisprudential coherence. To the extent that the Council succeeds at both, it can preempt, better control, and/or be in a better position to enlist the support of legal specialists in efforts to fend off criticism of its expanded role as a policymaker.

Legislating Under Constitutional Surveillance

After the Council hands down a decision, lawmakers are concerned with two questions: who won or who lost and how badly? At issue is the fate of a piece of legislation; jurisprudential or doctrinal coherence is far less salient. A bill approved by the Council poses no problem and is promulgated immediately; but any other decision forces the government to make tough decisions. Often, partially annulled bills are promulgated as amputated, and the offending provisions—although duly adopted by parliament—pass into the oblivion reserved for all rejected bills or amendments. Equally important, Council jurisprudence structures future legislative processes.

Corrective revision processes are highly structured: in essence, the legislative application of constitutional jurisprudence under duress. In cases where laws have been annulled for procedural violations of the constitution, revision is a relatively simple matter of adopting the legislation according to standard parliamentary practices.[34] In 1979, for example, after a significant part of the majority (the RPR) refused to support the government's budget, the prime minister, Raymond Barre, was forced to use strong arm tactics to regain control of parliament for his ministers, ruthlessly controlling the National Assembly's agenda, limiting debate and considerations of amendments, and on four occasions resorting to article 49, which links a vote against the budget to a vote of confidence. The opposition filed ten motions of censure, and the Gaullist group, short of supporting censure, behaved as if in opposition.[35] On 24 December 1979, the 1980 budget was annulled in its entirety by the Council —because of violations in legislative procedure, the details of which are not important here. One week later, after the budget had been voted on a second time according to normal procedures, the Council approved its promulgation.[36]

Total invalidation is rare, and politically extremely dangerous for the Council. In consequence, a host of techniques have been developed to allow the Council to avoid striking down legislation while at the same time placing it on hold pending a new reading. Corrective revision is the result of one such technique: Council acceptance of the *principle* of a reform but not of the *means* chosen by lawmakers. The latter are then required to "complete" a censured bill in order to give effect to the legislative package. Of course, we can not know for sure if a law so revised would have been acceptable to the government and adopted by the parliament in the absence of the initial Council intervention. In most cases the answer is almost certainly no. Still, the control is extraordinarily efficacious: as will be confirmed in the case studies which this chapter, *governments eschew imaginative reworkings of once-censured legislation in corrective revision processes, often choosing instead to mechanically copy the exact terms of Council decisions into beleaguered legislation.*

A second technique is to approve the constitutionality of a bill or provision in principle, but on the strict condition that certain provisions be read as though they were written as the Council interprets them. As the stakes of constitutional review have increased so has the popularity of this technique— likely because it allows both sides to claim partial victory. Table 5.3 shows this evolution clearly: during Socialist years, nearly one in five texts *approved* by the Council were, at least formally, subject to interpretive control; during the cohabitation period the Council attached SROIs to an extraordinary 56 percent of all laws or provisions which it otherwise approved.

Although SROIs may produce *autolimitation* effects in future legislative processes, they can not normally be policed by the Council since a promulgated law is immune to control.[37] The context for this latter point was altered in 1986 when President Mitterrand refused to promulgate three *ordonnances* enabled by two *habilitation* laws—one on the electoral system, the other on macroeconomic policy—passed at the beginning of the Chirac government's tenure. (*Habilitation* laws are umbrella statements of purpose which, according to article 38 of the constitution, grant the executive authority to make rules by *ordonnance* in areas otherwise reserved to *la loi*; they require the president's signature to enter into force.) The Council approved the bills, but attached SROIs to both, giving all sides reason to celebrate; as *Le Monde* put it,

> . . . the Constitutional Council has found a way to satisfy everyone, Right and Left. This third choice [after approval or censure] . . . has the advantage of silencing its detractors, at least publicly. The Right can congratulate itself on the high marks given to the government. The Left feels vindicated because the Constitutional Council has limited the action of the government. And, most important, the Council arms the president for an eventual control, by himself, of the constitutionality of *ordonnances*, when they are submitted to him for his signature.[38]

Table 5.3. Council Decisions of Conformity Under Reserve of Interpretation

Year	No. of Decisions Containing SROIs	% of Total by Period
1959–October 1974	1	11.0
October 1974–May 1981	7	14.5
May 1981–March 1986	13	19.5
March 1986–March 1987	9	56.0

The new electoral system and the redrawing of electoral boundaries survived unscathed a second Council decision,[39] but aspects of the economic reform did not. The subsequent legislative processes for the latter deserve close attention because they illustrate: (1) the power for SROIs to make their way into law, a result which confirms a general tendency for corrective revision processes to be entirely controlled by the Council; and, (2) aspects of problems of institutional "learning," given constitutional surveillance of procedural contexts.

Barely two weeks after the Council's 26 June 1986 decision on the economic *habilitation* law,[40] President Mitterrand, invoking his responsibility under article 5 to protect the constitution, refused to sign the *ordonnance* which would have allowed the government to proceed with its privatization program.[41] Although this affair engendered much controversy and doctrinal discussion, it is important for our purposes because the government was forced to reintroduce the reform into parliament as a piece of ordinary legislation, where it was then subjected a second time to juridicized debate. As Mitterrand had wished, debate on the rules governing the denationalization program—originally, the second part of the *habilitation* law—focused on the government's compliance with the Council's SROIs. These interpretations, which made specific what the original formulations had left vague, established a handful of basic rules governing the evaluation of the worth of companies to privatize and their subsequent sale. The government, under the watchful eyes of a vigilant opposition, scrupulously followed the Council's dictates, to the point of copying the SROIs—line-for-line, comma-for-comma—directly into the law. While Mitterrand's ploy restricted the government's discretionary authority and delayed the program by seventeen days, the reform went ahead, and without being referred a second time to the Council.[42]

The "Séguin amendment," originally the first part of the economic *habilitation* law, fared much worse. As discussed in chapter 3, Mitterrand's decision not to sign the government's *ordonnance* reforming the labor code, coming late in the parliamentary session, forced the majority to attach the reform to a bill then in a late stage in the legislative process. On 23 January 1987, the Council voted 4–4, with all Socialist appointees voting censure and Badinter's vote as president preponderate, to amputate the text of the *ordonnance* from the bill on the grounds that the subject matter of the amendment and the subject matter of the bill were not sufficiently "linked."[43] This affair illustrates how Council control over parliamentary *procedure* has at times been crucial with respect to legislative outcome, and it raises some interesting problems concerning constitutional surveillance. While I am convinced that this decision can not be understood without reference to crude partisan politics, many commentators ignored these aspects, instead focusing on what they saw as a progressive development of control over the legislative procedure seemingly exhibited by recent Council decisions. A brief review of the relevant 1986 rulings will make the structure of the argument clear.

On 22 December 1986, the Constitutional Council ruled in its decision on the bill entitled "Age Limits of Certain Bureaucrats" that an amendment suppressing the third avenue of admission into the *Ecole nationale d'adminis-*

tration (which the Socialists had opened to members of unions and other civic organizations) was not made in violation of the constitution.[44] The original purpose of the bill was simply to raise the retirement age of bureaucrats at the *Conseil d'Etat*, the *Cour des comptes*, and *Corps d'inspection et de contrôle*. The Socialists petitioned the Council, not least, on the basis that the amendment "had no link with the other provisions of the bill,"[45] and a reading of the commission debates shows that the majority made no attempt to argue that there was such a linkage upon proposing the amendment.[46] The Council disagreed, arguing that the bill's broad objective was to modify a "particular mode of recruitment." One week later, the Council rejected a Socialist petition which, among other things, protested against certain amendments made to the 1987 budget.[47] These amendments were introduced *after* the National Assembly and the Senate had adopted different versions, and *after* a meeting of a joint committee had ironed out the divergences. As Carcassonne—who wrote the referral for the Socialists—argued later in the journal *Pouvoirs*, the effect of such a maneuver was to reduce parliament to a "simple . . . voting machine," because, "when confronted with entirely new provisions, it can neither vote on these amendments, nor discuss them, nor drop them."[48] In both of these cases, the Council gave the benefit of doubt to the legislature, the only limitation being that late amendments must have a link, however obscure, with the subject matter of the bill.

The case of the Séguin amendment combines these structural settings: the government introduced additional articles, seemingly without a link to the bill in question, at such a late date that normal procedures for discussion and amendment could not have been observed. Furthermore, the Socialist's referral essentially reiterated the arguments it had made in its referral of the budget a few days before. The contextual similarities were not lost on politicians, the press, or on constitutional scholars—the most well known of whom, Professor Favoreu, argued on the eve of the decision that the amendment procedure was constitutional, that the Council would refuse to become embroiled in such a patently "political question," and that jurisprudential precedent shows a long line of Council reticence to rule on the internal functioning of parliament in these sorts of matters.[49] After the decision proved Favoreu wrong, Olivier Duhamel, a professor of constitutional law, counsel to the president of the Council, and a frequent public commentator on Constitutional Council issues, argued a different line.[50] For Duhamel, the *political* controversy over the decision (and particularly the reactions of aggrieved legislators) revealed little of value for Council watchers. Rather, it served to confuse the public and obscure the real lesson: that of a successive unfolding of Council jurisprudence which seeks to protect the rights of parliament from a potentially abusive executive. Even if such a view can be sustained—a difficult task since, inarguably, the censure would not have occurred had those members appointed by the Right been present to vote—the pedagogical authority of such a development is, in this case, virtually nil. The two decisions discussed earlier (of 22 December and 29 December) which might have served as warnings (of a kind), were rendered *after* the Séguin amendment was adopted (the night of 19–20 December).

The affair of the Séguin amendment holds little interest for legal scholars, and will, in the words of one legal specialist, "fast be forgotten" by *le droit*[51]: its impact was procedural and not substantive; it revealed, in an unprecedented manner, the "politics" of constitutional review, with votes made public and along party lines; and it gives lie, by yielding an unpredictable decision, to the claim that politicians need only understand constitutional law to behave constitutionally. The impulse of public law specialists to synthesize doctrine and to champion coherence does not always provide a convincing solution to the legislator's dilemma; and the result reinforces criticisms that Council decisions, however "coherent" in hindsight, can not adequately and consistently be predicted by lawmakers. It seems fair to say, given the imprecise nature of the texts involved, that constitutional control over the *substantive* terms of legislation is even less certain from the legislature's perspective—especially true in cases of radical reforms. In these cases, both the legislator and the Council must balance complex considerations of political values and social interests against constitutional texts which are often unclear or are undeveloped as sources of constraints on policymaking. Where constitutional jurisprudence is sparse or nonexistent, uncertainty is heightened. Pézant, a constitutional specialist and former chief administrator in the National Assembly's powerful *Commission des lois* assessed the Council's impact on policymaking in these terms: ". . . the legislative function is no longer simply a limited function; it is also an unsure function, . . . dependent upon an organ whose decisions forge the conditions of its practice."[52]

Looking Ahead

In the case studies which follow, the juridicization phenomenon is examined more concretely, and in minute detail, by tracing the development of the influence of constitutional considerations on several policy "sectors," or clusters of policymaking on similar legislative matters. The research method is largely archival. Each piece of legislation is followed, step-by-step, from its initial elaboration to its final promulgation. At the governmental stage, the analyst is largely dependent on press reports, leaks, postpromulgation interviews, and published remarks of participants. Once a bill is introduced into parliament, however, *autolimitation* effects can be traced empirically by following the development of constitutional debate in parliament, on threats of referral, and on the majority's efforts to anticipate the terms of constitutional jurisprudence as recorded in parliamentary records and other primary sources. Most successful amendments originate in committee, and are later ratified on the floor: in 1985, for example, deputies in committees were at the origin of 44.9 percent of all amendments proposed, but accounted for 72.9 percent of all of those adopted; that same year, the government's rate was 12.9 percent of all amendments proposed, and 19.9 percent of those adopted.[53] The researcher looking for evidence of juridicization is therefore obliged to sift through committee debates before moving on to the final amending process in each chamber.

The chapters which follow examine two policy sectors: (1) the nationalization and privatization of industry, and (2) press and audiovisual law. These sectors were chosen because each was a site of a succession of high-profile reforms sought by two successive reform-minded governments, because they provide examples of lengthy, complex *autolimitation* and subsequent corrective revision processes, and because the Council's decision in these areas are recognized by politicians and constitutional scholars alike as among its most important. Each chapter also contains an assessment of the importance and meaning of the cases examined for French constitutional politics generally. Several issues raised in Part I concerning the Council's role and function will be addressed at that time. In chapter 6, for example, the case study of the 1982 nationalizations provides the context for a discussion of Professor Favoreu's legitimation thesis. This is especially appropriate because he formulated the notion on the basis of his reading of the Council's decision on that reform. Chapter 7 provides what might be called a crucial case study of Favoreu's thesis that juridicization leads, or is equivalent, to pacification.

A central organizing thesis of the studies which follow is that the Constitutional Council acts as a third chamber of parliament whenever it engages in constitutional review of pending legislation. The logic for such a view derives in part from my concern for macropolitical impact, a concern which may at times override the more narrowly conceived foci of many French academic lawyers. I do not mean to imply that more legalistic concerns are necessarily less interesting or less important. They are simply not my concerns. From a policymaking perspective, the Council's role and impact is entirely legislative in nature. A bill is introduced by the government into the National Assembly; it then moves on to the Senate; and, then, especially if it is an important bill, it moves on to the Constitutional Council. Moreover, any total or partial amendment by the Council is a legislative act, whose impact is *exactly* equivalent to a successful amendment voted by the assembly or the senate. Furthermore, that act has no greater, nor any less, impact on the judicial system than does any other legislative provision. This view deserves much greater discussion than is appropriate at this point. In chapter 8, I will lay out the third chamber thesis more explicitly and respond to the most common objections made to it.

6

The Council Legislates:
Nationalization and Privatization Policy

In the late spring of 1981, under the euphoric spell of electoral victory, the newly constituted Mauroy government began work to concretize in detail what had been the central priority of the Left for most of the century: the extensive nationalization of industry and commerce. The move was unprecedented. As Ross and Jenson write, this was "the first time in modern Europe that any government had moved to extend public ownership to the core of the profitable oligopoly sector"—an extension, by any standard, "far beyond the established boundaries set for European mixed economies."[1] By the spring of 1982, the task largely completed, the State enjoyed a virtual monopoly over France's finance and investment sectors. It owned every major bank, controlled more than 90 percent of all deposits, and more than 85 percent of all outstanding credit; it had purchased a dying iron and steel industry, but also leading giants in the modernized, strategic industries of the international economy. Of France's largest twenty corporations, thirteen were now in public hands. Taken together, the public sector would henceforth account for or control three-fifths of all investment, one-half of all production in big industry, one-half of all exports, one-fifth of the domestic retail market, and one out of every three jobs.[2]

Though past instances of nationalization in France had proceeded amid a remarkably high level of political consensus, the Socialist plan enjoyed no such general support. Indeed, while the bill was still in its gestation stage, the lines had already been drawn for what was expected to be a new version of a "classic French war of religion." For the former majority and for a large segment of "*le grand patronat*" ("big business"), the plan was viewed, and publicly characterized, as nothing less than a "first step toward totalitarianism." For the government's supporters, nationalizations represented the key "to smashing the domination of *grand capital*," "to limiting and circumscribing the monopolistic base of society," and "to bringing about a new social and economic politics."[3] To this polarized political situation one must add the existence of another obstacle which had not impeded past nationalizations: that of constitutional review.

In 1981–82, constitutional politics in France became high politics. That is, the fundamental political debate about general principles, appropriateness, fairness, and even the minute technical details of the 1981 nationalization bill—by far the most far reaching, legally complex, and politically significant reform legislation passed in the history of the Fifth Republic—was quickly transformed into a dense and technical constitutional debate aimed at, and ultimately channeled toward, the Constitutional Council. Not surprisingly, the doctrinal community—particularly that centered at the University of Paris— was exercised in a remarkable and unprecedented manner. The government for its part commissioned a report on the constitutionality of the legislation from a team comprised of two such professors—one a former Council member, and the other an editor of the *Revue du droit public* (named to the Council by Mitterrand in 1989)—even *before* the bill was sent to the *Conseil d'Etat*. Once introduced into parliament, a newly formed association of angry stock- holders—urged on by executives of banks and corporations to be nationalized and by leaders of opposition parties—engaged three more Paris professors to prepare the ground for referral to the Council. The bill's journey through parliament was a stormy one, with the opposition employing every means of obstruction at its disposal. The Council's decision—a complex, partial annul- ment of key provisions—required a corrective revision process. A second Coun- cil decision, this time, positive for the government, enabled promulgation.

The 1982 nationalizations, in all of their staggering political, economic, legal, and administrative complexity, can not be adequately studied here, or for that matter in any brief treatment. This chapter, instead, seeks to describe and to evaluate the role and function of debate about the presumed or preferred attitude of the Constitutional Council on the policymaking processes, as well as the impact of the Council's decision on the ultimate outcome. Doctrinal disputes are noted along the way because they are inseparable from the process. In a concluding section, the undoing of the great reform—the 1986 *Privatisations*—is briefly examined.

Table 6.1 summarizes the legislative history of the 1982 legislation from the perspective of juridicization. It should be noted that the process was fully juridicized—no reading, in either chamber of parliament, proceeded without obligatory constitutional debate, and the Senate rejected the bill, on consecu- tive occasions, on constitutional grounds.

Stage 1: The Government's Draft

From the beginning, the nationalization project engendered intense legal de- bate, precisely because constitutional considerations were inseparable from political considerations; indeed, they extended to the legitimacy of the princi- ple of nationalization itself. While the new majority argued that the single most specific legislative mandate it possessed was to expand the public sector, it also realized that appealing to popular support alone might not be enough. For one thing, the language of the constitution on this issue seemed to require the

Table 6.1. Legislative History of the 1982 Nationalization Law

Sep. 18, 1981: The *Conseil d'Etat* renders its *avis*, criticizing, among other things, the compensation formula, and criteria for exclusion of certain categories of banks from nationalization.

Sep. 23: The bill is adopted by the Council of Ministers, which accepts the *Conseil d'Etat's* recommendation on compensation, but rejects the nationalization of foreign banks. The bill is sent to parliament.

Oct. 13: First reading begins in the National Assembly, after lengthy examination and some revision in Special Committee. Procedural motions are raised, including an *exception d'irrecevabilité*, a *quéstion préalable*, and *motion de renvoi en commission* (to return bill to committee for further debate) which are then debated and rejected.

Oct. 26: After 13 successive days of debate, the bill is adopted by the National Assembly in first reading.

Nov. 20, 21, 23: The bill is sent to the Senate for first reading. Objections are raised as to the bill's constitutionality in debate on a *quéstion préalable*; the motion passes, and the bill is therefore rejected.

Nov. 25: A joint committee of the National Assembly and the Senate fails to arrive at a compromise text.

Dec. 1, 2, 3: The National Assembly adopts the bill in second reading, after a motion of *irrecevabilité* is defeated.

Dec. 16: The Senate adopts a motion of *irrecevabilité*, and the bill is rejected.

Dec. 18: The National Assembly definitively adopts the nationalization bill, after rejecting a third motion of *irrecevabilité*. One hundred seventy-four senators refer the legislation to the Constitutional Council.

Dec. 19: One hundred twenty-two deputies refer the bill to the Constitutional Council.

Jan. 16: After 9 days of deliberation, the Council annuls 6 articles in their entirety, and a provision of another, declares the law inseparable from the annulled compensation formula, and the law cannot therefore be promulgated.

Jan. 20: The Council of Ministers, after consultation with the *Conseil d'Etat*, adopts a reworked bill.

Jan. 26, 28: The National Assembly adopts the bill in first reading.

February 3, 4: The Senate adopts a *quéstion préalable*, and the bill is rejected.

Feb. 4: The National Assembly adopts the bill in second reading.

Feb. 5: The Senate adopts a *quéstion préalable*, and the bill is rejected.

Feb. 5: The National Assembly definitively adopts the revised nationalization bill, overriding the Senate. Eighty deputies refer the bill to the Constitutional Council.

Feb. 11: The Constitutional Council approves the bill, and it is promulgated.

government to justify the project in terms of "obvious public necessity," or, less restrictively, "public utility." The government, aware that opposition groups were already arming for a long judicial battle, felt compelled to form its political argument as to the desirability of nationalization into a legal argument as to its necessity. That argument congealed around an expansive vision of the importance of the State in bringing about a fundamental transformation in political, social, and economic life. Extensive, targeted nationalization would give the State control over what Mauroy—and the constitution—called "*de facto* monopolies" whose output and economic impact was viewed as "essential to the nation." Nationalization would equip the State for a more creative—as opposed to Keynesian, reactive—macroeconomic role in a time of crisis and change in the international economic environment. Taking a page from the Gaullists, another justification was noted—to neglect nationalization today is to risk internationalization and loss of national independence tomorrow. Finally, nationalization was cited as the necessary first stage of a greater "social experiment."[4] The second stage was to be effected by the "Auroux laws," which sought to restructure the French system of collective bargaining, and to expand workers' participation in economic decision making and management.[5]

Given these stated objectives, the scope of the nationalizations would have to be extensive indeed. If the experiment was to work, new policies undertaken in the public sector would have to be made as irresistible as possible—so that they could not be sabotaged by a hostile private sector on the one hand, and so that new and positive social practices would find favorable ground for their reproduction through the whole of national economic life on the other. If the determination of scope was intimately linked to the determination of necessity, the former raised a number of delicate judicial problems.

The acts of creating and then filling categories, and justifying exceptions to general rules of treatment in cases of expropriation, are obligations in virtually every Western legal system. In this case, the government selected twelve large industrial groups, two financial societies, and thirty-six banks to nationalize, but the criteria used to make this selection differed within and among these categories. For the industrial corporations, five were to be included in the nationalization bill (the others were to be acquired according to different procedures, and in those cases of foreign ownership, because of concerns about extraterritoriality[6]). In each case, the parent company was a dominant force in a wide range of strategic sectors: Compagnie générale d'électricité (CGE), which controlled more than one-third of all French sales of electrical materials and equipment, and one-fifth of all sales of telecommunication products, and whose biggest customer was the public sector; Saint-Gobain, France's biggest manufacture of glass, insulation, and paper products; Péchiney-Ugine-Kuhlmann, a world leader in the production of aluminium, chemicals, pharmaceuticals, and nuclear materials; Thomson-Brandt, the most competitive French firm in the international computer market, and enjoying a virtual stranglehold over the domestic market of household and business appliances; and Rhone-Poulenc, a chemical concern ranking ninth in the world in total sales. These corporate conglomerates also owned, operated, or held stock in thousands of more companies: CGE, for example, had a stake in more than 1,100 other companies, Saint-Gobain in more than 110, and Péchiney had investments and subsidiaries on nearly every continent. While their economic importance could not be questioned, it was difficult if not impossible to define in a judicially convincing manner why these specific groups were to be nationalized and not others. The same situation existed with respect to the decision to include two finance giants, Paribas and Suez, the unrivaled forces of capital intervention in the economy. Cutting through the rhetoric and the statistics, the government's ultimate justification was anchored to legislative sovereignty: the necessity to nationalize these concerns and not others was demonstrated sufficiently by the very decision to nationalize.

The rationale for nationalizing what remained of the private banking sector was also more easily demonstrated in politico-ideological than in legal terms. For the government, control over the money supply was a "national function," and thus must be placed under public management, in order to better serve the "general interest."[7] The argument was not on its face persuasive, not least because the public sector in 1981 was already greater than the private banking sector, and because the Bank of France and the Treasury had no rivals in the creation and restriction of the money supply.[8] The problem of equal treatment might have seemed more manageable. The government decided to make its selection criteria explicit, and it chose size as measured by levels of deposit. The bill therefore listed all of those banks whose deposits exceeded 1 billion francs, and targeted them for nationalization. Exceptions were made for those banks that were foreign-controlled (because of international legal and political concerns), and for mutual and cooperative institutions (because their impact was almost exclusively local, and Mitterrand had promised the exemption during the campaign).[9] The government argued that in both cases difference in treatment was justified by prior acknowledgement of difference in situation.

Another decision related to scope, how much control over these companies was necessary or desirable, resulted in the most intractable legal problems. Rocardiens in the cabinet argued that the government could both save money, and cut the ground out from under reactionary forces, if the bill proposed to acquire only a majority stake. The proposal was opposed by a solid majority and by Mitterrand himself, and the government went ahead with its plan to nationalize at 100 percent.[10] Undoubtedly, the most important factors in this decision were ideological. But legal considerations did play a role: the government believed that they would have more difficulty defending public necessity if only majority control was asserted, for example.

Compensation for expropriation was recognized as the thorniest judicial problem. The problem has bedeviled courts and legal scholars around the world; as an eminent international lawyer, Oscar Schacter, has put it, "Apart from the use of force, no subject of international law has aroused as much debate and strong feelings as standards for payment of compensation."[11] Past national experience could provide few relevant lessons for the Left in 1982. Not only had nationalizations been effected outside of the domain of *la loi*, but a wide variety of compensatory formula had been employed, ranging from virtual outright expropriation without compensation for those punished for Nazi collaboration (certain shareholders of Renault), to using quoted stock market prices.

The government wrestled with two main formulas. The first proposed payment according to the average share price quoted on the market from January 1978 to December 1980, plus a sum representing a dividend for 1981. A three-year period had the advantage of smoothing over conjunctural anomalies, while the exclusion of 1981 would remove from the formula the negative impact on the market of the Right's defeat. Critics complained that buyers seeking majority control must in normal circumstances pay a higher than market price, not least because stockholders can not be obliged to sell. One study published at the time showed that the average price paid in takeover bids from 1978 to 1981 was 50 percent higher than the market price.[12] The second option became known as the *multicriteria* solution. It would base compensation on a more complicated and more costly formula taking into account stock prices, profits, and net assets. A large majority supported the first option—a standard solution which had also been the choice of policymakers in recent nationalizations in Britain, Italy, and Spain. But the government was fearful enough of constitutional censure (or mindful enough of the potential virtue of paying more in exchange for social peace), that it raised the possibility of a multicriteria solution pending consultations with legal advisors and the *Conseil d'Etat*.[13] For those companies not publicly traded, the formula arrived at was based on average profits for the last three accounting periods, multiplied by twenty.[14] In all cases, conforming to French and European precedent,[15] payment was to be made in publicly tradeable, interest-carrying government bonds redeemable at fifteen years, or earlier by lot.

At this point, the government asked the law professors, François Luchaire and Jacques Robert, to examine the bill with respect to its conformity to constitutional texts and jurisprudence. The choice of these jurists could not have been incidental. Luchaire combined three important qualities. In 1981, he was the *only* former Constitutional Council member who was both a law professor *and* a non-Gaullist. His political sympathies were with the left of Center, and he had shown himself less inclined to allow his judicial training to blind him to the importance of political context. Robert was a well-known human rights advocate, a frequent contributor to *Le Monde*, and an editor of the *Revue du droit public*. Robert would be used as a formal and informal consultant to the Socialists in the 1981–86 period, and in 1989 he would be plucked from his professorship at the University of Paris to sit on the Constitutional Council. The government could thus expect a reasoned, but not-unfriendly exposition of the relevant texts and jurisprudence, and a capable prognosis of future Council behavior.

The brief provides the best evidence[16] of what the government might have viewed as its "constitutional frames of reference" at this time. The Luchaire/Robert report (hereafter cited as LR) provides answers to the two most important constitutional questions facing the government: does the nationalization program violate a constitutional right to property?; does the compensation formula adopted violate the principle of equality? For LR, the answer in both cases was a resounding no. In the first instance, the legal problem flowed from the basic and historically intractable contradiction between two constitutional texts: article 17 of the 1789 declaration, and line 9 of the 1946 preamble. It is worth recalling, because LR do not, the political context of 1946, and examining how and why these texts came to coexist in the same document.

During debates on the first draft of the 1946 constitution, a majority of the constitutional assembly rejected enshrining the 1789 declaration, or even constitutional mention of it, by a vote of 429–119.[17] They instead determined to draft a new bill of rights, to be included in the body of the new constitution. *The impulse for the rejection of the 1789 text was hostility toward article 17, and other articles relevant to property rights, which were taken by the majority to be dangerous and reactionary expressions of classic liberal dogma.*[18] There was consensus among the three big parties—the Communists, the Socialist group, and the MRP—that "the right to property must move aside when confronted with the needs of the general interest."[19] Constitutional limitation of this right was considered necessary both to clear the way for the consecration of new social rights, and to enable future nationalizations. For the far Right, private property was revered as "divine,"[20] and it remained steadfastly attached to article 17 (1789), which states:

> Property being inviolable and sacred, no one can be deprived of it in the absence of public necessity, legally declared, obviously warranted, and without just and prior compensation.

The drafters worked to desanctify and to update article 17 (1789), adopting, as a working principle, a fundamental distinction between two kinds of property: (1) that which any individual can normally possess, by work and by savings; and, (2) that which is constituted by big corporations—*les grandes industries concentrées*—which no private individual owns anymore, but whose impact weighs heavily on the economic life of the nation. In article 35, the power of the state to expropriate was explicitly affirmed, but only after parliament had declared the property to constitute a "public utility," and on the payment of "just compensation." Article 36 proclaimed that the right to property was a limited one: it could not be "exercised contrary to social utility," or in a way which might "prejudice" the rights of others. That article then went on to impose an *obligation* on public authorities to nationalize property given certain requisite conditions, namely, when property functioned as either a "public service," or as a "*de facto* monopoly." When the constitutional draft was rejected in a national referendum in April 1986, the second Constitutional Assembly was faced with the prospect of returning to ground zero. This they refused to do.

The second Constitutional Assembly removed the declaration of rights from the body of the constitution, placed various parts of it in a preamble, and then denied the preamble's legal status. The 1946 preamble, as adopted with the constitution in the referendum of October 1946, is made up of two parts. The first, one short sentence, states that the French people

> reaffirm solemnly the rights and the liberties of man and of the citizen consecrated by the Declaration of Rights of 1789 and the fundamental principles recognized by the laws of the Republic.

The second enumerates the 1946 principles, line 9 of which reproduces the language of the recently rejected article 36, stating:

> Every asset, every enterprise, whose exploitation is or has acquired the character of a national public service or of *de facto* monopoly, must become the property of the collective.

The contradiction was evident to everyone, but it was a harmless one, since the preamble was considered to be without *valeur constitutionnel.*

Moreover, the second Constitutional Assembly took great pains to stress that the notion of the right to property contained in article 17 (1789) had been superceded by the 1946 principles. André Philip, the president of the Constitutional Committee, explained to the assembly the committee's attitude during the debates:

> We proclaim the character, I will not say "sacred" because I do not believe that any material thing is sacred, but the character profoundly respectful of the right to personal property—when it is the fruit of work and of savings.
>
> We recognize personal property, and all forms of its transmission, any time when it is possible for the worker to accede by some means to it.
>
> But when private property, due to the concentration of enterprises and of the development of modern technology, becomes monopolistic, that is, essentially a way to deprive others of their property, we believe that transfer to the collectivity of the means of production is the only technical means to give to workers of these industries management of these means.
>
> [Speaking to the Right] I know that the difference between you and us is that you are still attached to a conception of economic liberalism, [but] the great majority of this Assembly has condemned [that conception].[21]

In 1981, it was entirely unclear as a matter of interpretation and of constitutional law what significance if any the terms of article 17 (1789) or of line 9 (1946) should have for the government's nationalization project. The Council's jurisprudence during the 1971–80 period had incorporated the whole of the preamble into the constitution of the Fifth Republic. Nevertheless, from a policymaking perspective, incorporation of the preamble looked much more patchwork and incremental. The Council's post-1971 jurisprudence was certainly important to the 1982 nationalizations, but not because constitutional norms governing such initiatives were any more clear than they had been in 1946. In 1981 no Council decision had ever made mention of article 17 (1789) or of line 9 (1946)—while incorporation and explication of other texts by the Council had been steady and even audacious. The situation could inspire hope on opposition *bancs*, dread on the government's, and a huge amount of speculation everywhere else.

LR argued that in 1981 property rights were neither "sacred" nor "inviolable," by virtue of the fact that article 17 (1789) could no longer be said to possess *valeur constitutionnel.* This view, probably a minority one among legal scholars, nevertheless accorded with that of certain leading commentators, including Loïc Philip.[22] The "men of 1789," LR argued, had a different, now outmoded, conception of property. Proof could be found in texts adopted subsequently, like line 9 (1946), surely, but also article 34 of the 1958 constitution, which states: "*la loi* fixes rules concerning . . . the nationalization of enterprises and the transfers of property from the public to the private sector." Moreover, they claimed that numerous statutes on the books explicitly granted to the state the power to expropriate for public purposes. The civil code, for example, states that property may be taken for "public utility" (as opposed to the "public necessity" language of article 17); and the code of public expropriation confers generous power to invoke imminent domain. Because these provisions had long been embedded in the codes, LR argued that they must be accepted as evidence of a FRPLR to the effect that legislators are free to nationalize after the determination of "a certain necessity or public utility." Nor did this FPRLR require a standard of "necessity":

> . . . what justifies, and legitimates the nationalizations, is not the utility (or the necessity) for the collectivity to take these assets, but its desire to replace capitalist direction of a given enterprise with public direction.

The LR viewpoint, in its entirety, generally accords with that of the first and second Constitutional Assemblies.

How the Council would judge the determination of utility or necessity could be predicted, according to LR, to the extent that its important 1980 decision on the bill, "Security and Liberty" was analogous. In the referral of that legislation, the Socialists had attacked one provision on the basis of an alleged violation of the terms of article 8 of the 1789 declaration, which states that "*la loi* may only establish those punishments which are strictly and obviously necessary." The Council responded by pronouncing that its power of constitutional review "does not confer upon the Constitutional Council a general power of judgement and of decision-making identical to that of parliament," and thus, according to LR, the Council would again refuse to "substitute its own judgement for that of the legislator's with respect to necessity." "It does not appears to us," the professors concluded, "that the government's nationalization bill will be censured on grounds of unconstitutionality" with respect to the right of property.

Examination of the principle of equality of treatment under the law required LR to confront the bill in much more detail. The professors argued that the difference of treatment accorded foreign-owned and mutual and cooperative banks (i.e., the government's decision not to nationalize these concerns) was constitutional. In the first case, LR noted, the right of equal treatment applies only to "citizens"—no provision is made for foreigners; moreover, while there exists no principle forbidding better treatment of foreigners than French citizens, much legislation—tax codes, for example—requires such unequal treatment. In the case of mutual and coop banks, LR appealed to a long line of administrative jurisprudence (later taken up by the Council in its decision of 12 July 1979), according to which public authorities may justify differences of treatment where differences in situation are both present and relevant to legislative intent. In consequence of this principle, equal treatment is required only of those banks to be nationalized, that is within categories, since "if one really wanted absolute equality, . . . every company would have to be nationalized." Finally, payment for expropriated property must also proceed in a unified manner by category. As for compensation, "prompt, adequate, and effective" payment was required (the international legal standard, which dates from the nineteenth century and was in part based on the terms of article 17).[23] LR—citing past precedent and "the French legal tradition with respect to nationalizations"—then approved the government's method of evaluating the value of companies to be nationalized, and payment in bonds rather than cash.

The unprecedented consultation—a formal, legal opinion about the constitutionality of draft legislation solicited *before* obligatory consultations with the *Conseil d'Etat*—demonstrated, if not an implicit vote of no-confidence in its official legal advisor, the government's desire to enter into the deliberations prepared and armed to defend its project. The government apparently expected the deliberations to be conflictual, one institution against another. The system, of course, is designed to worked very differently: the *Conseil d'Etat*'s opinion on the legality of a bill is solicited as a means of securing constitutionality.

The drafting of the bill did not take place in a vacuum. In June, opposition politicians, interest groups, and leaders of private industry began campaigns to influence the government's deliberations, and to subvert their ultimate effect. In the ministries, a "guerilla war" developed between "certain high functionaries who had served in proceeding governments" and those in the new secretariat for nationalizations: the former being accused by the latter of working more to protect industry than to further the government's legislative objectives. Presidents and corporate administrators of companies to be nationalized[24] published tracts and purchased publicity against the nationalization plan, and even made trips abroad to ask other European governments to put pressure on Paris to abandon it. In the fall, a public scandal developed after it was revealed that the president of the finance company, Paribas, had begun making arrangements to spin off assets of his and other companies to foreign-based subsidiaries as a means of avoiding their nationalization.[25] The Socialist party even published a *communiqué*, protesting what it characterized as a coherent program of sabotage, as banks restricted credit, industrial output slowed down, and negative propaganda proliferated.[26]

The government's deliberations were followed closely, with attention focused primarily on the details of the compensation plan. In July, the president of the newly formed *Association des actionnaires de France* (French Stockholder's Association), stock market officials, and other leaders of finance came out in favor of the multicriteria option, but had little realistic hope that the plan would be adopted. As some experts had it, according to *Le nouvel économiste*, the prospect was "too wonderful even to be envisaged."[27] Foreign banks agitated for either exclusion from the bill or immediate payment in cash for their assets.[28] In September, a *Financial Times* editorial judgment—to the effect that the proposed compensation plan was surprisingly "generous," and that stockholders would be compensated as well as they could hope to be even by a "pro-business government"—was widely reported and discussed.[29] The government's judicial occupations were also followed closely, and legal analyses proliferated. Long debates on constitutionality appeared in the press, undertaken by and among editorialists, politicians, threatening referral, and readying for juridicized parliamentary debates,[30] and law professors, including

Luchaire, who published what was in effect an abridged version of the LR report in *Le Monde*.[31] Notwithstanding abandonment of the reform, referral was known to be inevitable. The deputy, Michel Aurillac (RPR), in an article in *Le Monde*, gave a point-by-point analysis of the bill's alleged unconstitutionality:

> The nationalizations are going to provide the occasion to put to the test once more the mechanism for the protection of rights and liberties which the 1958 constitution has created. . . . The debate will be all the more interesting because it will allow review of the entire body of constitutional principles from 1789 to our days.[32]

What is extraordinary is that this public debate about the Constitutional Council's future decision began *before* the bill had even been examined by the *Conseil d'Etat*, adopted in cabinet, or introduced in parliament.

On 18 September after two long days of deliberation, the *Conseil d'Etat* rendered its *avis*. The process was followed closely by the press, and the details of the formally secret *avis* were leaked and made headlines.[33] By what was reported to be "a weak majority," the body voted to accept the "necessity" or "utility" of the plan, that is, it upheld the nationalizations in principle. The government's plan to exclude foreign banks from the list of those to be nationalized, however, was criticized as a violation of the principle of equality before the law. The *Conseil d'Etat* judged the compensation formulas to be constitutional, but suggested that judicial security might be enhance if profits and assets of the companies to be nationalized were also taken into account in the evaluation of their worth. Thus, the multicriteria option was dramatically revived.

On 23 September after evaluating the *avis*, the government adopted the bill.[34] It accepted the *Conseil d'Etat*'s recommendation on the compensation formula, "in order to create the best psychological climate,"[35] and agreed to evaluate the worth of nationalized industries according to the following formula: 50 percent of "total value" to be calculated by average share prices for the 1 January 1978–31 December 1980 period, 25 percent by the average net profits for the same period multiplied by ten, and the remaining 25 percent by net accounting assets as of 31 December 1981.[36] The change raised the cost of project by 25 percent, but the government believed that satisfying the *Conseil d'Etat* placating shareholders was worth the added expense. On the question of foreign banks, the government examined three options; it could: (1) maintain the 1 billion deposit criterion and treat all banks above this level equally (that is, by nationalizing them), an option quickly rejected as simply "out of the question"[37]; (2) raise the floor to a level of say 3 billion francs in deposits, which would have the advantage of allowing the largest foreign bank to escape, but which would also reduce the number of French banks to be nationalized from thirty-six to twelve; or, (3) ignore the *avis*. It chose the latter solution, Mauroy told the special commission, because "a French law, desired by the French, must not have consequences for foreign nationals."[38]

Stage 2: Parliamentary "Combat"

Discussion and adoption of the nationalization bill by parliament occasioned the most detailed constitutional debates as well as some of the ugliest incidents seen on the assembly floor in the history of the Fifth Republic. At issue seemingly was the very legitimacy of Socialist rule, and therefore of *alternance*. André Laignel noted, "In contesting this program, the Right cries very loudly that the consequences of universal suffrage are insufferable to it."[39] Mitterrrand's assessment at the time—that the Right had yet to psychologically accept its electoral defeats, and that its militant opposition to the nationalization program was part of that process—is compelling.[40] The opposition did indeed wage what it called "a long parliamentary combat,"[41] but, within parliament, it was a wholly ineffectual one. The government steadfastly refused, with one important exception, to compromise the basic structure and economy of its bill. Once definitively adopted by the National Assembly, one week before Christmas, all eyes turned toward the Palais Royal, to the Constitutional Council—the site in all but name of the bill's final reading.

Because of the complexity of the project, and in order to facilitate efficient discussion, special committees were established in both houses to examine the bill, thus eliminating what would have been discrete but concurrent discussions in six different committees. The committees heard testimony from ministers and certain representatives from business, including most notably the president of the COB—the official operating committee of the stock exchange. In the Senate committee,[42] the president of the COB, Bernard Tricot, called the new multicriteria formulas "excellent" and "based on valid, legal principles"—a view seconded by a leading specialist in business law[43]; and "in no case could they be called ruinous." That said, Tricot iterated three basic criticisms. First, the 1978–81 period chosen for averaging stock prices, profits, and dividends was one of high inflation, and thus the plan should compensate for monetary depreciation. Second, since many of the companies to be nationalized possessed in varying amounts participation in other companies, provision should be made to evaluate "consolidated accounts"—the total value of the company, its subsidiaries, and other participations. The practical problem, as Tricot admitted, was that due to the arcane provisions of French tax laws, companies were not legally required to consolidate these accounts in their own declarations, in spite of the efforts of the COB to cajole them to do so. Last, the president argued that stockholders should not be deprived of a 1981 dividend.[44] The attitude of the COB is important for a number of reasons. First, it was not incidental to the drafting: as the government admitted during these hearings,[45] the compensation formula suggested by the *Conseil d'Etat* had been adopted, not least, because it had been advocated and approved beforehand by the COB, and after the the body had strongly criticized the government's original formula, that based on quoted stock prices. Second, Tricot's criticisms immediately became basic elements of the Right's opposition[46]—which all but ignored his statements of basic approval—and, later, found their way into the referral to the Constitutional Council.

Debate in the special committee of the National Assembly was juridicized from the outset, prefiguring the parliamentary discussion to follow: *irrecevabilité* was moved by Jean Foyer and rejected[47]; and Michel Noir stated flatly that the Council would be petitioned.[48] The government, however, proved steadfast in its support of the bill, and accepted only those amendments which would improve it from a technical standpoint. The single significant case of *autolimitation* during the whole of the parliamentary stage occurred after this committee voted to remove outright article 33. This article was a vague provision which the government had sought to enable the future administrations of the two finance conglomerates, Paribas and Suez, to sell off assets not associated with banking, insurance, or the expanding public industrial and commercial sectors. The Socialist *rapporteur* for the committee moved to suppress the article after bipartisan opposition developed on the grounds that article 34 of the constitution grants to the legislature alone the right to authorize transfers from the public to the private sector; this decision was ultimately ratified by parliament.[49] That achieved, the opposition made the same criticism with respect to articles 4, 16, and 30 of the bill, which sought to enable similar spin-offs of assets held abroad in order to avoid problems of extraterritoriality, but with no success. In parliament the provisions were heavily criticized on the Right and Left, and dozens of amendments to remove them were debated and defeated. The Council would later do the work for them, amputating the three articles from the bill for their violation of the separation of powers flowing from article 34 of the constitution, and the government decided not to rework them in the corrective revision process.[50]

Discussion before the full National Assembly opened on 13 October with the *rapporteur* for the bill stating: ". . . we affirm with vigor that the right for parliament to proceed with nationalizations is not contestable. The bill . . . conforms to constitutional texts and principles."[51] Not convinced, Foyer's motion of *irrecevabilité* immediately followed. The motion, which puts to debate and to a vote the proposition that a bill is unconstitutional and should be rejected before it may be read, was charged with a historic significance which none before or after has equaled.[52] The Right's claim, that the centerpiece of the new majority's electoral program was patently unconstitutional, took on great symbolic import in light of the history of the Fifth Republic. The constitution had been custom-made for the Right, and François Mitterrand and his party had opposed it, voted against it, and railed at it for institutionalizing a "permanent *coup d'état.*" And now, the Right hoped to use it to gut the Left's program. The debate on this motion, which remains the most detailed and complex in history, set the tone—of a series of professorial lectures continuously being interrupted by scenes of noisy unrest—for the long months to follow; and the arguments first stated here were to be reiterated literally hundreds of times during the amending process. The discussion was led by Jean Foyer, a Gaullist, and a former professor of law, long-time president of the assembly's *Commission des lois*, and minister of justice. André Laignel, a Socialist representing the parliamentary majority, and Robert Badinter, a former law professor and current minister of justice, represented the government.

The text of Foyer's motion, written in the form of a judicial decision, stated that the bill was unconstitutional in principle and in detail, and focused debate on the following points: (1) the nationalizations constitute an unjustifiable violation of the right to property; (2) the determination of which companies were to be nationalized violate the principle of equality; and, (3) the compensation would neither be just nor prior. In the following summary and analysis, the main elements of this argument will be discussed along with the private opinion commissioned by the Union for the Defense and Development of Private Stockholding, an association created to lobby against the nationalizations, who made it available to the Right as a means of juridicizing debate. This brief, written by the Paris law professors, Yvon Loussouarn, Roland Drago, and Pierre Delvolve (hereafter cited as LDD), complements Foyer's remarks and offers a more closely argued doctrinal analysis than that contained in the government's own LR report.[53]

For both Foyer and LDD, the power to nationalize and to denationalize granted by article 34 to parliament could in no sense be considered a general grant. On the contrary, as Foyer put it, due to the development of Council jurisprudence, legislative discretion is "now tightly constrained by a variety of constitutional . . . provisions" contained in the preamble. These provisions are superior to general legislation delegation in a hierarchy vigorously defended by the Council. Moreover, the 1789 declaration not only is possessed of *valeur constitutionnel* in its *entirety*, but it constitutes what LDD called "the foundation, of general—even universal—scope and significance," which the 1946 principles only supplement and bring up to date. The 1946 principles, they asserted, "may only have effect within the context of the provisions [of 1789] which established them," and they "may not reach beyond the prescriptions" fixed by 1789. Thus the property rights contained in article 17 (1789), being no less "sacred and inviolable" than they were in 1789, possess what Foyer called "supra-legality," since these rights may be abridged *only* under circumstances specifically provided for in other constitutional provisions. The obligation for the legislature to nationalize that which has acquired the characteristics of either de facto monopoly or of a public service contained in line 9 (1946) must therefore be read restrictively: if these attributes have been acquired, "the nationalization must take place"; "but," LDD continued,

> if these conditions are not fulfilled, the fundamental principles of the right to property are fully restored, and must be respected. Just as nationalizations are necessary and constitutional when the conditions of a national public service or of monopoly are met, they are equally excluded when these conditions have not been. . . . Any nationalization outside of these conditions would be a violation of the right to property proclaimed by the declaration of 1789. It would thus be unconstitutional.

Reading the preamble in this way shifts the focus of the debate to a verification of these requisite conditions. The government had argued that nationalizations were desirable because expanding the role of the State in the economy was desirable; nowhere had it attempted to demonstrate that the companies targeted were either monopolies or public services. For Foyer, the lack of a legally based criteria for nationalization led to discrimination, incoherence, and to an arbitrarily constituted list of companies to be nationalized:

> What you propose to nationalize . . . are conglomerates of all kinds. One of these makes a considerable part of its profits by selling washing machines and dishwashers, electric stoves, televisions and refrigerators. . . . What public service does it perform in any material sense? With this logic, you might as well go ahead and nationalize the manufacturing of coffee grinders.

LDD, for their part, made a "detailed analysis" of the nationalizations according to criteria developed in administrative and private law, and concluded that

> no monopoly exists; no national public service exists; no public national service is constituted by the law; the nationalization of the industrial groups is therefore unconstitutional.

The same criticism applied equally to the nationalization of the finance companies, and to the banks (but again the government had not pretended to make such a demonstration).

The point carried even greater weight in the case of the banks. While distinctions in treatment, according to established administrative law, could be justified for reasons of "general interest"—mostly economic—or by virtue of differences in situation, these conditions were not met in a legal sense. The argument for general interest was subverted, reasoned LDD, in the same way as that for public necessity:

> Either the activity of banking is an activity of a general interest and all of the banks must be nationalized; or if certain banks alone are nationalized it is because the activity of banking does not constitute a general interest and the nationalizations may not occur.

Differences in levels of deposits or situation could not be said to justify exclusion since, and the law admitted as much, the banks exempted performed the same functions as those to be nationalized, and possessed identical legal personality. Differences, instead, were purely "geographic" (in the case of the foreign-owned banks) or a matter of management or political "correctness" in the case of the coops,[54] but in neither case a matter of judicial status.

Foyer and LDD labored under a serious jurisdictional problem. While the the translation of legal principles and reasoning from administrative to constitutional law had been successful on important occasions in the past, the Constitutional Council, as discussed earlier, had refused in the Giscard years to stand in judgment of parliament in its determination of "necessity." Its stance constituted a French equivalent of the American "political question" doctrine. In the Council's jurisprudence, *the very adoption of legislation by parliament confirmed the determination of necessity*, since necessity can *only* be politically determined. Foyer was inviting reversal of precedence. To allow the determination of necessity to be made entirely according to what he characterized as "ideology and mythology" would not only make a mockery of legal norms, but subvert the very basis of French society. "This republic," Foyer averred, "is not a socialist republic, and the . . . extension of nationalization beyond the limits inscribed by the preamble would be of the nature to transform its character."

Less politically provocative, and presumably more judicially fruitful, were attacks on the compensation formula. *While the opposition entertained little hope that the government could be persuaded to abandon the bill or to limit its scope, they knew that their chances of raising the payment to expropriated stockholders were much better.* After all, everyone agreed that compensation was a constitutional obligation governed by explicit constitutional provisions. It was also expected that Council "audacity" would assert itself here, since the Council would likely balk at confronting the program head on.[55] Foyer echoed the COB's concerns: while the multicriteria solution was considered a better method of evaluation than quoted share prices, it should also include an assessment of the value of "consolidated accounts," take into account monetary depreciation, and include a dividend for 1981. Moreover, he argued for payment in cash, prior to formal transfer from private to the public sector. As Foyer concluded, he invited the government to engage in a massive *autolimitation* effort, and abandon its project altogether:

> The fear of Council censure has been for you [in the case of the acceptance of the *Conseil d'Etat's avis* on compensation] . . . the first step toward wisdom, but only the beginning and you still have more steps to take. . . . Instead of risking censure, which would not increase your standing, admit this *exception d'irrecevabilité* . . . kneel down now, spontaneously, before *le droit*.

Laignel rose to respond, in a speech rooted in the terms of traditional, Rousseauian notions of parliamentary sovereignty. For Laignel, the essential problem of the nationalizations—their principle and legitimacy—was entirely a political one, to be resolved by politics, and not by appeal to "legalisms." By working to separate law from politics, Foyer had sought to "obscure" the real issue, but had only succeeded in revealing the opposition's true interest: the defense of "private interests" and "privileges." In what was by far the most oft-quoted passage of the entire parliamentary debate, a statement which Foyer later predicted would "make him immortal,"[56] Laignel summed up the majority's argument on the public necessity of nationalizations:

> I know that this affirmation may sound provocative, but *Mr. Foyer is judicially wrong because he is politically in the minority,* just as we were judicially wrong when we were politically in the minority [emphasis added].
>   (HAMEL: What an idea of law, my dear colleague, it's incredible!
>   FOYER: It's the negation of law.)
>   What is "public necessity"? What are its contours and criteria? The answer is simple. Public necessity is what the sovereign people say it is. . . . Can a court tell us? Certainly not. None has the power, and the Constitutional Council . . . has . . . renounced it in advance, stating that . . . the

constitution does not confers upon it "the general power of judgement and of decision identical to that of parliament." All that remains is parliament, and it alone. . . . Wasn't it General de Gaulle . . . who said: "In France, the Supreme Court is the people?"

A point-by-point rebuttal of Foyer's motion was left to the Minister of Justice, Badinter, who affirmed that constitutional questions had been "minutely studied and explored at great length" by the government. There is no need for detailed analysis, since Badinter followed the main lines developed in the LR report, which he cited and referred to in order to bolster his position. In summary, Badinter argued that property rights were no longer "inviolable and sacred," that nationalizations were wholly within the purview of legislative discretion and authority, limited only by the obligation to make provision for just compensation and for equal treatment. On the issue of compensation, Badinter reasoned that payment need only be made for the stock, and not for the assets of a company, since no stockholder may possess assets; the fact that the government had chosen to accept asset-based criteria recommended by the *Conseil d'Etat* was simply a gift. Finally, on the problem of equal treatment, Badinter noted that he considered the exclusion of foreign-owned banks to be the only serious question of constitutionality for the bill, but one necessary for good foreign relations.

The motion was rejected, 330–154, with voting along strict party lines, and the bill's first reading began. The majority was immediately faced with a severe problem. On the one hand, it wanted to move as quickly as possible to pass the bill which was, after all, only a first step. On the other hand, it wanted to allow parliament full opportunity to debate the measure, to allow its own rank and file its triumphant day in the sun, and to show that the government's promise not to use draconian measures against parliament was a good one. On the first day of debate, more than 800 amendments to the bill were registered—more than 600 by the opposition—smashing all records for entire bills. At the same time, the Paribas scandal erupted into the open (when it was revealed that the president of the finance company had purposely lost control over a key foreign subsidiary to a once-tiny Swiss finance company suddenly flush with new resources). Fears mounted that if the nationalizations did not proceed in haste, the dismantling would spread, and there was evidence—later confirmed—that other companies and banks were following Paribas's lead.[57] On 14 and 15 October the prime minister made an official declaration of urgency—which essentially limits detailed discussion to one reading in each chamber—and threatened more drastic measures.[58] In the end, a poll published by the right-wing newspaper, *Le Figaro*, showed that the public supported nationalizations by a majority, with only 29 percent opposing them. The opposition, fearing backlash, withdrew over 100 amendments (which sought to exclude from nationalization, one-by-one, the subsidiaries of the affected companies), thus saving the assembly at least eight hours of debate under normal but *minimal* circumstances.[59]

Once discussion of the bill began in earnest, the debate turned ugly. The Right used every artifice of procedure at its disposal: an "avalanche of amendments," many of which were without any reasonable object, seemingly endlessly repetitive "questions" in the form of constitutional lectures, suspensions of meetings for strategy sessions, and other miscellaneous motions. The rhetoric became increasingly heated. Jacques Toubon (RPR) called the program "the beginning of dictatorship," equating the tone of the debates with that of the revolutionary terror, and at one point even threatening Socialist deputies with physical violence. Gilbert Gautier accused Socialists of willfully instituting "the political model of Khomeini's Iran," and equated the majority leaders with mollahs and ayatollahs. Certain Socialists were called "Stalinists," another "a new Goebbels." The Socialists answered: Laignel labeled Michel Noir a "fascist," and another, in what turned out to be one of the great "affairs" of the debate, denounced the Right's "defense of private groups," producing a long, detailed list of the "financial, personal, and family links" which leading politicians—including Giscard d'Estaing, Couve de Murville, Michel Debré, and the president of the Constitutional Council, Roger Frey—were said to have with the management of the industries to be nationalized.[60] On the final day, before adoption, Jean-Paul Planchou, a deputy elected for the first time in June who had won wide respect during the debates for his intelligence and moderation, summed up his impressions: "I am beginning to understand the violent statement which Léon Blum made to you, Messieurs of the Right: 'I hate you.'"[61]

Given this backdrop, debate over some of the more controversial of articles proved tortuously long. One example, that of article 13, which defined the field of application for the nationalizations of banks, will suffice to illustrate. Debates on this article took up more space in the *Journal officiel* minutes than most whole bills had in previous years. Here as elsewhere, the opposition, working on the assumption that nationalization was, by definition, a punitive measure, sought first to remove the entire sector from nationalization and, failing that, to exploit the exceptions so as to allow the greatest number of banks to escape. Charles Millon, for whom the article was "philosophically unacceptable, politically insupportable, and judicially indefensible,"[62] proposed amendments to suppress the entire list of banks from the law. When they were rejected, Millon had thirty-seven amendments ready to remove each bank from the list one-by-one, engendering a series of redundant discussions which lasted several hours.[63] François d'Aubert offered an amendment which would have raised the 1 billion franc deposit floor to 5 billion francs, and then, appealing for "compromise," another raising the floor to 3.3 billion: "That would render your project constitutional; you would no longer be courting the wrath of the Constitutional Council for violation of equality between French and foreign banks."[64] Finally, after failing to remove the allegedly unconstitutional exception for mutuals and coops, the Right disingenuously offered amendments which would have given every bank six months to change their status to a mutual, and thus avoid nationalization.[65]

The assembly adopted the bill on 26 October after thirty-six meetings on thirteen straight days, and after handling 1,438 amendments,[66] many of which were alleged to have been proposed in order to offer the government the means to ensure constitutionality. Given the bill's complexity, it is remarkable how few changes were made. The few "compromises" which were agreed to were hardly cause for anything but cynical celebration on opposition *bancs*.[67] In December, the bill passed subsequent readings also without major changes to the legislation. Debate focused alomost exclusively on constitutionality, after Foyer raised virtually identical motions of *irrecevabilité*, an "obsession" the Socialists diagnosed as "the Foyer syndrome"—"the attainment of the summits of repetitive capacity."[68] The bill's fate, everyone knew, would be settled "elsewhere" (i.e., in the Council). As Foyer quipped, "He who laughs last, laughs best."[69] After invoking the specter of constitutional censorship, Millon defended the opposition's vote, in second reading, in these terms:

> This text is fundamentally unconstitutional. If our assembly adopts it, it will be deliberately violating constitutional law. . . . To sum up, articles 1, 2, 3, 4, 5, 6, 12, 13, 14, 15, 16, 17, 18, 24, 27, 28, 30, 31, 32 are contrary to the Constitution.
> GUY BECHE: The Constitutional Council has nothing to do with it!
> MILLON: Mr. Beche, I know that bourgeois law is horrifying to you. But we, on the *bancs* of the opposition, think that the *état de droit* is the guaranty of our liberties!"
> BECHE: I prefer the people's law! [*le droit du peuple!*].[70]

In the Senate, as expected, the bill was rejected on consecutive occasions, on constitutional grounds. On 23 November the Senate adopted a *quéstion préalable*, argued by Etienne Dailly, who alleged that fourteen articles of the bill were unconstitutional,[71] with, he stated, "special mention reserved for article 13, which is unconstitutional for 7 different reasons."[72] On 16 December the Senate quashed the bill by adopting an *exception d'irrecevabilité*, the first in its history.[73]

Stage 3: The First Decision

The bill was referred to the Constitutional Council by the two longest petitions in history,[74] and the Socialist group in the assembly addressed its own *mémoire* to the Council defending the bill.[75] Speculation about the possibility and consequences of outright annulment mounted as the day of the decision approached, and a series of articles by legal specialists appeared in the general press, notably in *Le Monde*.[76] Consensus among academics congealed around recourse to referendum—even in the case of a partial annulment. Roger Pinto argued, for example, that it was "obvious" that even if the Council only annulled the compensation formula, the government would be "required" to appeal directly to the people. Nevertheless, by all accounts, the government was sanguine: on the eve of the decision, *Le Monde* reported that government officials expected that the Council would decline to rule on the "public necessity" issue, was confident that the *Conseil d'Etat*'s compensation formula would hold up, but expected trouble to come, if any, from the lack of provision for a 1981 dividend payment, and from the exclusion of foreign banks.[77] The latter concern was a result of the *Conseil d'Etat*'s negative *avis*, and the subsequent refusal of the government to abandon the exception. The lack of provision for a 1981 dividend appears at first glance to be more puzzling, given that the government had agreed to wholesale compromises in order to satisfy its legal advisor and the COB. Parliamentary staff who worked on the legislation at that time suspected that the government did not provide for the 1981 dividend in order to give the Council the opportunity to amputate it—and thus the opportunity to placate the Right and angry stockholders—without directly challenging either the principle or the overall economy of the bill. Such gamesmanship is said to have been carried on by the Right after returning to power in 1986 as well.[78]

The Constitutional Council rendered its decision on 16 January,[79] after having met more times and deliberated longer than for any decision in its history.[80] We know little of the Council's discussions, but the Council released, for the first time ever, the name of the *rapporteur* for the decision in advance, that of Georges Vedel, undoubtedly to bolster its image as a "jurisprudential" body. In brief, the decision struck down all or parts of seven different articles in the bill, and notably the compensation formula. Furthermore, since a law nationalizing industries could not be aplied without provision for purchase, the compensation formula was declared to be "inseparable" from the bill's whole, and the legislation could not be promulgated at all. Leaving aside other doctrinal issues for the moment, and focusing on the significance of the decision for the fate of nationalizations, the Council provided a detailed discussion of the constitutionality of: (1) the legislative authority to nationalize, and the relative weight of constitutional provisions governing this authority; (2) the definition of scope and field of application; and (3) the compensation formula. The decision also outlined the contours of a future corrective revision process necessary to obtain promulgation.

First and foremost, the Council ruled that article 34 of the constitution granted to the legislature the authority to nationalize, but stated that this authority could only be exercised "in the respect of the principles and rules possessed of *valeur constitutionnel*." The effect of this declaration was not only to shift attention to the relevant constitutional texts contained in the preamble, but also to reinforce the Council's control over interpretation, since appeals to article 34 are—by their very nature—appeals to legislative sovereignty and discretion. If a victory of sorts for the majority, it was only a slight one, for the Council's most spectacular pronouncement was the affirmation that the right of property contained in article 17 (1789) possessed "full *valeur constitutionnel*." Reasoning that the rejection of the work of the *first* Constitutional Assembly in referendum invalidates any discussion of legislative intent at that time, the Council imposed an interpretation wholly antithetical to the intent of the *second* assembly. While recognizing that the context for the enjoyment of property rights had evolved since 1789, it reasoned that these rights had been expanded in some cases, probably with reference to the notion of stockholding restricted in others, for the advancement of the "general interest," for example. The Council then declared that article 17 (1789) not only consecrated "a fundamental right" whose "preservation constitutes one of the objectives of public society," but that it "occupies the same [constitutional] rank as liberty, security, and the resistance to oppression." Going further, the Council generated a new, if related, general principle of *valeur constitutionnel*, which it called the *liberté d'entreprendre* (roughly, the right to engage in commerce, or capitalism), which it stated could not be restricted in an "arbitrary or abusive" manner. The Council then composed a binding hierarchy of texts, ruling that *other principles mentioned in the preamble, most notably the 1946 principles can only "complement" (completer) the 1789 declaration, and can never contradict or limit the enjoyment of the rights which that text contains.* Line 9 (1946), which the Council mentions in only one sentence, was judged to have no legal effect on the question at hand, and thus debate about public utility and de facto monopolies was made irrelevant.

For policymakers, the rules laid down on these points were clear. Nationalizations are governed principally by article 17 (1789), can take place only after their "public necessity" has been "legally declared," after "just compensation" has been provided for, and to the extent that they do not restrict the *liberté d'entreprendre*. The Council, as expected, ruled that legislative motives—"to give to public authorities the means to confront the economic crisis, [and] to promote growth and employment"—constituted a determination of necessity, which was not, in the absence of "manifest error," reviewable. ("Manifest error" is, in Jean Rivero's words, "that which can not escape a man of good sense"[81]—a French version of the "reasonable man test." It is a notion which the Council found in administrative law, where it is used by the *Conseil d'Etat* to annul executive acts.) While it is not obvious how a decision made by an entire parliament could be in manifest error, the Council's likely intent was to assert that no aspect of legislation is a priori immune to constitutional scrutiny, even if here the Council gave the legislature the benefit of the doubt.[82] The Council thus repudiated the majority's view that, on this point at least, parliament did not just "possess discretionary power but sovereign power."[83]

Second, on the issue of scope, the Council distinguished between the industrial and finance sectors on one hand, and the banking sector on the other. For the former, it ruled in effect that the legislature was free to determine which companies were or were not to be nationalized, since the problem of equal treatment could not be raised or resolved in legal terms: the diversity of the companies affected made "useful comparison" among and between categories virtually impossible. For the banking sector, comparison was facilitated by the fact that the law affected a homogeneous class of entities in the same way, with specified exceptions. The Council approved the 1 billion franc limit, stating that the power to exclude small banks was "a function of the public necessity declared by the legislature" "not unrelated" to legislative intent. Likewise, it ruled that parliament could exclude foreign banks for the general interest—in order to "avoid the difficulties which their nationalization . . . might occasion on the international scene." The Council, however, declared that the exception made for coops violated the principle of equality, since difference in treatment could be "justified neither by their specific character, nor by their status, nor by the nature of their activities, nor by potential difficulties in the application of the law." Article 13 was thus amputated of this exception, and the three banks affected were restored to the list of those to be nationalized.

Third, the Council annulled in their entirety the three articles governing compensation, but it did so in enough detail to indicate how the government and the *Conseil d'Etat* should have handled the problem in the first place. As Badinter would later complain: "Constitutional truth on one side of the Palais Royal, constitutional error on the other."[84] The basic standard for just compensation owed to expropriated stockholders was declared to be "compensation for their losses, evaluated on the day of the property transfer, taking into account the influence which the prospect of the nationalization might have had on the value of their shares." Stated differently, *the way to proceed is to correctly imagine what the price of any given stock would have been on 1 January 1982,*[85] *had the Socialists not won the election*! The multicriteria formula was criticized on several levels. Generally, in addition to stock prices only constituting 50 percent of the total evaluation, the formula was judged to have "unequal" effects on the evaluation of the worth of a company. More specifically, the Council disliked the "uniform usage" of average stock prices during a three-year period (1978–80). It led to "considerable distortions," and thwarted the attempt to determine the "real value" of each company in 1982 because the short-term trajectories of share prices go through different cycles, beginning and ending at different times. Third, it criticized the asset-based criteria for not taking into account "consolidated accounts." Finally, it censured the lack of provisions for the payment of a 1981 dividend, and for counteracting monetary depreciation.

Reaction to the decision was predictable. The Right celebrated—but complained that the Council had itself engaged in *autolimitation*, having been intimidated by the Socialists. As a result of these "pressures," it had reached an incorrect decision on the principle of nationalizations.[86] The Left reacted on two fronts, with the government working to salvage what it could of the affair,[87] and leaving it to journalists and parliamentarians to carry out the protests. These were made in shrill, ideological terms. The left-wing *La Libération* entitled their front page headline: "Le *hold up* de l'année" ("the hold up of the year"), and, drawing out the wild-west analogy, called the Council, "the Palais Royal gang." The Communist daily, *l'Humanité*, contrasted the electoral legitimacy of the Left government with the Council, which it averred was "representative of nothing but *le grand capital* and the desire for revenge."[88] The president of the assembly, Louis Mermaz, impugned the Council's neutrality, and Lionel Jospin, the secretary-general of the Socialist party asserted that the decision should be understood as a political one:

> . . . especially when one notes that 8 of them [Council members] are in fact either former politicians of the Right, former ministers, or former high

officials of Rightist parties. . . . As long as the Constitution is what it is, the decisions of the Council may not be appealed. The Government must respect the Constitution. But being a [parliamentarian] . . . , I am not subject to the same constraints, and my feeling is that the Council is neither an objective body nor [legally] correct . . . , it is on the Right.[89]

The government had few choices: the Council had made it crystal clear that the nationalizations could go forward only after the compensation formula had been corrected, and if the coops were included. The government could have appealed directly to the people, but the referendum option was rejected, likely due to considerations of the delay involved, but also because the government knew that organizing such a referendum would fire up the constitutional debate all over again, and this time it would rage in the country at large. The Left could have moved to abolish the Council and to institute a supreme court, as promised by the Common Program of 1972 and by the 1981 electoral platform; however, a constitutional amendment would have been required, which the Senate would never have supported, thus obliging again recourse to referendum. In any event, the government, after consulting with the *Conseil d'Etat*,[90] chose to undergo a corrective revision process, at the same time threatening escalation if the nationalizations were thwarted a second time. As Mauroy explained to parliament,

> Certainly the Constitution . . . does not only have [positive] qualities. We have often emphasized its faults, including some concerning the Constitutional Council. These analyses, which figure in the letter of all of the programs that we have submitted to the country, remain [viable]. We could have . . . , we can still, pose the institutional question. We have chosen not to . . . for the stability of the country and therefore the continuity of [our] policies.[91]

After cautioning against a "test of force" between the Council and the government, a counselor at Matignon warned, "One time, yes, two times, no, Mr. Mitterrand would never accept it."[92]

Stage 4: The Corrective Revision Process

The second nationalization bill, as it was put in committee, was a result of the government "mechanically" accepting the consequences of the Constitutional Council's decision. Those articles which had escaped censure were reproduced without change; article 13 was disabused of the exemption accorded the three cooperative banks; and, last, the government rewrote the compensation formula based on what it described as the "outline of a solution indicated" by the Council.[93] As Mauroy declared on several occasions before the assembly, "We are aware that popular sovereignty has expressed itself clearly, but the government has decided to risk a second censure."[94] This scrupulousness, and the fact that parliamentary debates were cut short by the government's invocation of article 49(3)—which ties adoption of a bill to a vote of confidence—made it virtually impossible for the opposition to exact additional concessions by further juridicizing the process. Still, the Right stubbornly refused to accept that "public necessity" had been adequately demonstrated, or that the nationalizations were constitutional.[95] The Senate rejected the bill twice more, after adopting *quéstions préalables.*

The government had difficulties only with its own majority, who hoped to avoid nationalizing the three cooperative banks by specifying in the law why their exemption was justified. "We reject," declared the *rapporteur* for the assembly's Special Committee,

> *the suggested nationalization* of the three cooperative banks. We have thus refused to give in to the perverse consequences of a bizarre judgement, and I am persuaded that in this affair like all others, *political rigor must take precedent over constitutional rigor* [emphases added].[96]

Although the prime minister agreed with Charzat that it was "absurd to have to nationalize these establishments," Mauroy argued that the Council's decisions was "of such precision" that to do anything else would be to risk a second censure. An article was added to the bill which stated simply that future legislation would be proposed which would denationalize the banks, after "their specific character" had been defined.[97] Although denationalization of the cooperatives was proposed in April and subsequently became law, the obligation for the government to nationalize them in the first place raises some interesting points. First, the opposition's attempt to block the nationalization of banks had boomeranged, succeeding only in *extending* the bill's application, an unintended result of focusing arguments on the principle of equality before the law. Second, as Luchaire implies in an unusually critical commentary on the decision,[98] the Council, after having declared that a declaration of "public necessity" alone could justify the abridgment of the right to property, then required nationalizations which parliament had specifically judged unnecessary.

As for the compensation formula, the government wrestled with two basic options[99]: (1) to maintain the multicriteria formula, but add provisions requiring the evaluation of "consolidated accounts"; or, (2) return to the original plan of the past summer, basing evaluation on quoted stock prices. The second option was selected, probably for its simplicity. In the final bill, the new formula addressed all of the Council's criticisms. Compensation was based on the *highest* monthly average registered between October 1980 and March 1981 (as compared to the average monthly price from 1978 to 1980 foreseen in the first draft), thus shortening the time frame and discounting for the effect of the Left's victory on prices; 14 percent of this sum was added to make up for monetary depreciation, determined by the 1981 rate of inflation; and a sum equivalent to the dividend earned by stockholders in 1980 was added, also increased by 14 percent.

The bill was definitively adopted by the assembly on 5 February, referred to the Council on the same day by the opposition in the assembly, and promulgated on 11 February, hours after receiving the Council's approbation.[100]

An Assessment

One simple, but important and enduring, lesson of political jurisprudence is that courts are, and should be studied as, governmental and governing agencies—in deciding cases judges necessarily make public policy. This is no less true when judges seek to "balance" social interests, even when these interests appear before them dressed up in the clothing of legal argument. Quite the contrary.[101] As is the case for both the American Congress and the Supreme Court, the Constitutional Council is a site of intense lobby activity by social interests who want something from government. But unlike the situation for the U.S. Supreme Court, the Council's official litigants are exclusively official policymakers, lobbying to have their policy choices ratified and then enshrined in law. Particular, too, the Council can not depend on lower courts to implement its policies, nor does it need to. Implementation is instead structured by the complex relationship between legislative text, Council jurisprudence, and the extent of the majority's commitment to salvage promulgation.

A referral of a bill to the Constitutional Council constitutes a direct and overt form of official lobby activity, but in the case of the nationalizations, lobbying of the Council can be said to have begun long before. Certainly, solicitation and subsequent discussion within parliament of outside legal opinions was an implicit form of pressure, augmented by the government's choice of a former Council member—who was also the most respected and subsequently productive of legal specialists to have served. Likewise, in the *avis* provided to the Right, LDD quoted long passages of doctrinal work published by Georges Vedel—hardly insignificant given the fact that Vedel was, in 1981–82, the only law professor sitting on the Council, and considered by most insiders to be the body's dominant personality. Moreover, Pierre Delvolve, one of that *avis'* authors, was both a colleague of Vedel's and his co-author on what is recognized as the most weighty text on French administrative law, also quoted at length in LDD to bring authority to bear on crucial issues. In one passage, LDD reminded readers that Vedel and Rivéro, in a seminal commentary on the 1946 preamble, had paid particular attention to the status of article 17 (1789) and had concluded that

> ... private property, in the 1946 Constitution, remains, in spite of the new legislation on farm leases, in spite of the legislation on rent control, and in spite many other examples, an "inviolable and sacred right." The fundamental institution remains individual property understood in the most traditional sense.[102]

Politicians regularly and explicitly treated the Council as if it were a permanently captive audience (*Le Monde* noted early on that the Council was being treated as a kind of "anonymous government"[103]), which in a sense it is. Laignel's celebrated, parsimonious response to the excursive and detailed constitutional argument that nationalizations were unconstitutional in principle was iterated as much for the Council's as for Jean Foyer's benefit: "You are judicially wrong, because you are politically in the minority." The Council, on this point, agreed with Laignel. Lionel Jospin, first secretary of the Socialist party, compared the developing situation to the judicial–political confrontations of American New Deal days. "Never have the great currents of reform been allowed to be obstructed by a Supreme Court, of whatever kind," he declared, adding that he hoped that the members of the Council would "reason as judges of the constitution and . . . not as . . . political men."[104] At that time, the Council had not yet rendered a decision on *any* Mauroy government bill! The opposition in the National Assembly, for their part, began their referral with a statement designed to counteract what was alleged to be a "carefully undertaken" leftist campaign to impugn the integrity of the Council and of constitutional review. Quoting previous writings of Luchaire at length, the deputies wished to show that an annulment would not necessarily constitute "censure of the popular will."[105]

Rhetoric aside, virtually none of the participants believed that the Council would disallow the bill altogether—not the government, nor the *Conseil d'Etat*, nor the opposition. Had constitutional review been neither existent nor efficacious in 1982, the debate on "public necessity" would likely have been just as salient, passionate, and unruly a spectacle, and would have covered much the same substantive ground. But the language of the debate would not have been the language, however forced at times, of constitutional law. *The real issue was price.* Interests organized, stockholders formed associations and commissioned and circulated legal advice, and right-wing politicians waged their "combat" in order to increase compensation to stockholders. In this enterprise, they were successful: by accepting the changes proposed by the COB and advocated by the *Conseil d'Etat* in September, the government raised the cost of its bill more than 20 percent; by incorporating the Council's prescriptions into the bill, the cost was raised an additional 30 percent—*an increase of nearly 50 percent overall.* The corrective revision alone raised the compensation costs—measured against the bill adopted in December—for the five industrial giants by an average of 22 percent, for the finance companies by an average of 36.6 percent, and for the banks by an average of 31.5 percent.[106] The economy of the nationalizations bill was destroyed, and that destruction can only be attributed to constitutional politics.

No stockholder who has ever been bought out by a modern, industrial state, in any major nationalization, has ever enjoyed terms as good as those in France in 1982. As European comparative legal specialists noted, the Council seemed to go out of its way to allow "the market and its economic laws," rather than "the general interest" determined by the legislature, to decide price. The Italian constitutional court, for instance, has consistently ruled that compensation need not be based on "real value," but, in that court's terms, only on "the maximum . . . which the public administration can guarantee" in its pursuance of "the general interest."[107] After the Council's second decision, not even the slightest grumble was heard from expropriated stockholders in France[108]— surely a first. As Luchaire pointed out, it was those stockholders who were *not* bought out (and the taxpayers who provided the funds) who suffered inequality before the law financially.[109] In 1981, stocks dropped on the Bourse, and virtually across the board, on the average of 17.4 percent, due to general trends but also in reaction to the Socialist's electoral victories. The Council's decision had the effect of sheltering nationalized stocks from decline - because value was based on the *highest* monthly average beginning in 1980. Moreover, since the State compensated for monetary depreciation, based on the rate of inflation for 1980, stocks were sheltered from a similar fall in the value of money for 1981. *In short, stockholders of nationalized companies received, on average, 31.4 percent more than stockholders who sold their holdings in companies left off of the lists in 1981.* For the government and its majority, this was the central point of the Council's decision. "I believe that I have understood," said the prime minister the day after the first decision, "that what the Council wanted was us to have given more money to the stockholders. In any event, it is the taxpayers who are going to pay."[110] Pierre Joxe, president of the Socialist party in the National Assembly, complained that "the Council only intervenes when it's a question of increasing the amounts to be paid to the capitalists"; the executive office of the Socialist party stated that the decision "took account more of the financial interests at stake than the national interest"; and Michel Rocard quipped, "Instead of stating the law, [the Council] is stating the price."[111] *Of course, in this instance, a statement of law is a statement of price.*

Speaking in the National Assembly during the corrective revision process, the prime minister had lamented the fact that opposition politicians had behaved like "active, effective lawyers" for the stockholders.[112] The characterization is apt. Indeed, to believe some of these stockholders, lobbying went much further than was ever reported at the time. Jean-Maxime Leveque, for example, the director-general and then president of the bank, *Crédit commercial de France* (CCF), before it was nationalized, singled out rightist parliamentarians in his *mémoires* of the period as his "collaborators" in the "combat" against the bill, and confides that "the majority of the amendments that they decided to propose were studied first at the CCF."[113] Leveque also claims that his arguments against the compensation formula "played a decisive role in the Council's annulment," as did a private audience with the *rapporteur*, Georges Vedel, to explain his position (which, he tells us, took place after the referral had been made, but before the decision had been rendered!). Although he boasted that compensation for CCF stock rose by 56 percent in consequence, he added magnanimously, "It is not only to [CCF stockholders] that the Council that day rendered a service: it was to France."[114]

Rhetoric like this reached new heights, even for France, during the debates on this bill. The fate of the nationalizations and the fate of civilization itself were treated by right-wing politicians as if they were somehow organically linked. On the Left, two ideologies were said to be in open conflict: that of popular sovereignty and of the general will on one side, and that of a narrow constitutionalism—in the service of reaction—on the other. This rhetorical discourse, evidence certainly of growing pains for a Republic entering a new phase, can nevertheless be taken too far. The Right won this battle, that much is clear, and the government lost. But it can not be said that there was real danger that the Republic would fall: escalation simply would have meant referendum and, probably at worst, a repudiation of a single Constitutional Council decision. Nonetheless, it is from his reading of this decision, that Professor Favoreu developed his version of Black's "legitimacy function," a thesis according to which the Council provides a "certificate of constitutional conformity" on any piece of legislation it decides not to entirely annul to the government. Favoreu further argued that the legitimation of governments is one of the Council's political "functions." Last, the analysis goes, the Council's decision in effect saved the Republic, and the Council adopted a new role— that of "guarantor of *alternance.*"[115]

What evidence is there to support the claim that the Constitutional Council legitimated the Socialist's decision to nationalize in 1982? What I have found is very slight, a few low-key governmental declarations to the effect that the censure was not total, that at least the reform could go ahead once modified, made of course to deflect the overwhelming attention from what everyone understood to be a defeat. "The Council," declared the prime minister before parliament, as the second nationalization bill was being introduced, "has legitimated the nationalization policy."[116] This is the *only* time where language similar to Black's and Favoreu's was used. In context, however, Mauroy's declaration loses much if not all of its force. It was made only after he himself had threatened to "pose the institutional question"—that is, to abolish the Council!—and only after the terms of the decision had been strongly criticized by the prime minister and others in the majority during the same debate. The opposition, not insignificantly, responded to the declaration with howls of derision. Mauroy's comment, in fact, came *in response* to this part of a speech made by François d'Aubert immediately before the prime minister was recognized to speak:

> Make no mistake . . . about the meaning of the Council's decision, and do not see in it a justification for your economic choices with respect to the nationalizations. Certainly, the Council has admitted, although only after establishing as a fundamental principle the *liberté d'entreprendre*, the public necessity of the the the nationalizations. Why? Simply because, having the choice between an extensive and a more restrictive conception of its role as a judge of the constitution, it clearly preferred the latter. But it would be particularly dishonest to present before public opinion this decision of the Council, as you have tried to do, as a sort of . . . absolution for your ideological and dogmatic errors.[117]

The extent of the defeat was much more profound than may be measured by legislative outcome alone. In chapter 3, I discussed how ambiguous is ultimate legislative victory when the battle over interpretation is lost. This is because the Council, in stating *le droit*, works not only to settle legislative conflicts, but also to construct constitutional law. It may at times seek to clarify the relationship between two principles—such as the right to strike, which is written into the preamble, and the continuity of public service which, although unwritten, turns out to modify substantially the former. In doing so, the Council seeks to reconcile what appear to be contradictory principles, and to mitigate tensions in the law which have evidently become unbearable both to it and to the legal community. In this enterprise, the Council is led to develop the law far beyond what is necessary to decide the issue at hand. Not only might it seek to provide definitive interpretations, or guidelines, for future legislative processes, but it may also create new principles of *valeur constitutionnel*— although neither may be necessary or even intended for use at the moment.

As in the United States, the moment chosen by judges to engage in expansive and creative interpretation is not incidental to the case at hand. Stated differently, some cases are determined by courts to be more conducive for effective, judge-led constitution-building than are others. Obviously the Council considered the nationalization affair to be such a moment, and such a case, par excellence. The decision was the first in history on the right to property. But far more significant, *the decision fixed—that is, created—a general hierarchy of legal norms, contained in the preamble, to be protected by constitutional jurisprudence.* The discordant terms of the 1789 Declaration of the Rights of Man and the rest of the preamble were fully harmonized by this decision, in favor of the former. As a legal text, the 1789 declaration must, in all instances, take precedent over the 1946 text, which henceforth may serve only a complementary, and never a contradictory, jurisprudential function.

The Constitutional Council's discussion of the texts governing the principle of the bill did not alter the legislative result: nationalizations proceeded. However, the discussion of property rights served to ground the Council's elaboration of a constitutional hierarchy of texts, texts which now constitute, incontestably, a bill of rights. *The Council could have arrived at exactly the same legislative result,* by: (1) simply ignoring the opportunity to settle the issue of hierarchy; or (2) declaring that the language of line 9 (1946), "public utility," had superceded that of article 17 (1789), "public necessity"—*effecting a more ideologically "balanced reconciliation."*[118] Now, however, the public utility language of expropriation—which is enshrined everywhere in the civil, urban, and expropriation codes and, by extension, in many other legal regimes—is unconstitutional (more precisely, these codes enable the unconstitutional taking of property), if beyond the Council's reach.

In conclusion, not only the legislative result but the Council's constructive interpretation of the preamble in this case is central to the question: did the Council legitimize Socialist rule by allowing promulgation of an amputated and deformed nationalization bill? I would argue that the answer is unequivocal: absolutely not. Indeed, the destructive effects of the Council's interpretation—in terms of legitimation—go far beyond legislative impact. They strike a blow at the very identity of the French, and for that matter, the European, Left. For the Council, ideological commitment—to expansion of the state's role in the economy, to public ownership, to collectivism—is never enough to make nationalizations constitutional. Parliament, under the constitution of the Fifth Republic, cannot destroy capitalism, or even substantially weaken it. The decision in Luchaire's words, "is a condemnation of the whole of socialist doctrine"; in Favoreu's, "[the French] republic . . . can never be a socialist republic."[119] This aspect of the decision was not lost on politicians. Charles Millon, recounting the attacks he led on the bill in the National Assembly, rejoiced that

> . . . above all else, the decision irreversibly consecrates 2 fundamental principles of our society: the right to property and the liberty to engage in commerce, of which no serious abridgement may occur. Thus, our Constitution is not socialist, and parliament must always respect the principles of liberty. Who could dare say now that our combat had been ineffective?[120]

Professor Bickel, who accepted and incorporated Black's legitimation thesis into his own work, called the function, significantly, the "mystic function."[121] This power to legitimate, if power it is, operates in the concrete, or legislative world, only formally. It finds its true agency, its creative impact, in the world of political symbols and belief. In essence, the power to legitimate is the power to reconstitute ideological meaning and context. In this, such a power can never be neutral. I would dispute even the existence of this "function" in France, not least, because the French constitution (as interpreted by the Constitutional Council) hardly performs the same function that Black and Bickel claim the American constitution (as interpreted by the Supreme Court) does—namely, as the symbolic equivalent of the queen in Great Britain, the ultimate source of national legitimacy. That the legal community would like us to believe that the French constitution is developing in this direction is evidence of an essential continuity in its own professional needs and aspirations, namely for a stable, judicially guaranteed *état de droit*. Understanding the meaning of this continuity may be important to our understanding of how the legal community in France behaves politically, and how it justifies that behavior; it may even help us (in fact, it certainly does help us) understand better how and why the Council decides as it does. But doctrinal advocacy of a legitimation function provides no evidence in itself of legitimation. At the same time there is a wealth of evidence that the Council's decision had the opposite effect, that is contributed to delegitimation. *If the Council did legitimate the nationalization reform, the fact remains that it did so in terms wholly unacceptable to the Left—indeed, in terms manifestly antithetical to the Left's political commitments, and in terms inimical, indifferent, and callous to more than a century's worth of political commitment and struggle.* We should remember that the constitution of 1946 would never have been adopted by the second assembly—in fact its rejection would have been by an enormous majority—had the Council's 1982 interpretation of the preamble been attached to either the property rights there enshrined, or to the textual hierarchy.[122] I fail to see how these realities can be reconciled with the argument according to which the Council performed a "legitimation function."

The Privatizations of 1986

On 16 December 1982, two days before the National Assembly overrode the Senate's veto and formally adopted the nationalization bill, the leader of the

RPR, Jacques Chirac announced that he would undo the reform upon regaining the prime minister's office.[123] In fact, the very first law adopted by the eighth parliament (1986–88) contained provisions which enabled the Chirac government to privatize sixty-five companies, including the entire public sector expansion of 1982, three banks nationalized in 1945, the insurance groups nationalized in 1946, the national oil company Elf-Aquitaine, and the Havas agency.[124] Constitutional politics played a role in the 1986 privatizations, but this role cannot be said to have been a significant one: Mitterrand's refusal to sign the enabling ordonnance merely delayed and did not substantially alter the reform. As a matter of public policy process and as a matter of constitutional law, it proved to be much less difficult for a government to virtually eliminate the public component of the industrial, finance, and banking sectors in 1986, than it had been to expand those same sectors in 1982. Why was this the case?

In the first place, the Chirac government chose to proceed not by legislation, but by legislative delegation—that is, by virtue of a *habilitation* law (a power granted to governments by article 38). (*Habilitation* laws are umbrella statements of purpose which in effect transfer authority to the government to legislate in the domain of *la loi,* by *ordonnance*.) In doing so, the government knew that it could be much less precise than would otherwise be possible, and that the upcoming debate would therefore proceed on a high level of abstraction. The Left would be able to attack the reform only in general terms, on the desirability of the political determination to denationalize, an issue largely insulated from constitutional censure. The bill, incidentally, included much more than reference to privatization: it also enabled the deregulation of much of the wage and price system in France, and contained the outlines of an ambitious reform of the labor codes. While one of the most far-reaching economic reforms in the history of the Fifth Republic, it contained only eight short articles, and did not take up even one page in the *Journal officiel* when promulgated. As a site for juridicized debate, it was, much to the Socialist's chagrin, wholly inadequate.

Still, the new opposition warned the government, even before discussions began in parliament, of its intention to refer the bill to the Council,[125] and it was able to exact some concessions, one of which was due to the nature of the Council's control over *habilitation* laws. The government claimed that the bill was drafted with respect to the leading decision which requires a government to be precise as possible as to the nature of the legislative authority it is requesting—and it conceded in committee that such precision was "indispensable," since "vagueness" would be "susceptible to censure by the constitutional judge."[126] The Socialists immediately raised a motion of *irrecevabilité* in committee, and once defeated,[127] the majority's own *rapporteur* counseled that the law as written was "too general," and made way for sweeping amendments "to respond to the obligation for precision formulated by the Council."[128] These ultimately resulted in a longer law, a slightly less vague description of the administrative procedures to be followed in the denationalization process, and an appendix listing the sixty-five companies to be affected.[129] To recall how tortuous were the deliberations and the debates on the scope and application of the nationalization bill, and notably on article 13, is to be struck at the sparseness of the Chirac government's original bill. Not only had the government not felt obliged to list those companies to be privatized, but it did not fix any explicit mechanism or procedures for evaluating the worth of the public's interest before selling it off.

Second, the Council's decision on the 1981 nationalization bill provided little in the way of constitutional ammunition to the Socialists. On the contrary, its ruling on property rights and the sanctity of the private sector made it extremely unlikely, notwithstanding a dramatic and unprecedented reversal, that it would invalidate the initiative on the basis of a reading of the preamble. After going out of its way to affirm a conservative reading of private property rights and to create a constitutional principle, the *liberté d'entreprendre*, the Council could not be expected to now forbid transfers from the public to the private sector. In addition, the Council's refusal to rule on the legislature's determination of "necessity" seemed to be equally as applicable in this case. In any event, after long, rancorous debates, the Socialists argued, in their referral, that the reform was unconstitutional in principle to the extent that it violated line 9 (1946), since many of these companies could be shown to be objectively, in fact, monopolies.[130] Saint-Gobain was the only manufacturer of a range of glass products; Havas was the only manufacturer of telephone books; Rhone-Poulenc had a monopoly on the manufacture of numerous vaccines whose administration was required by law (thus the company also functioned as a "national public service"). The second important line of argument concerned the vagueness of the financial mechanism: the Socialists reasoned that if just compensation was good for stockholders, it was just as good for the State, and invited the Council to annul the bill until explicit mechanisms to determine fair price were included.

In its decision of 25–26 June 1986,[131] the Council rejected these arguments, ruling that it was for the legislator to decide on the transfer of companies from the public to the private sector, and for the legislator to determine if these constituted a monopoly or not. The *habilitation* was however ruled to be constitutional only on the condition that certain SROIs were respected and applied. Each of these was to structure, by making more precise, the selling procedure to be followed: (1) the evaluation of the worth of a company must be made only by "competent experts totally independent from the eventual buyers"; (2) these experts must use "objective methods currently practiced in [such] matters" by "taking account, according to the appropriateness in each case, of the market value of the shares, the value of the assets, dividends, and the existence . . . of subsidiaries"; (3) the *ordonnance* must forbid sales when the proposed price is less than the evaluated worth; and (4) sales must not endanger "national independence," presumably by restricting acquisition by foreigners. Mitterrand appealed both to the Council's decision and to his role as the defender of the national interest and "arbiter" of the constitution in his refusal to sign the *ordonnances* into law.[132]

Mitterrand's refusal forced the government to turn the text of the *ordonnance* into legislative bill and resubmit it to the parliament. The bill incorporated all of the SROIs enunciated by the Council, often word-for-word: thus consideration number 63 of the Council's decision is contained in article 3 of the bill, and considerations number 79 and 61 are copied, or "integrated" in the president's language, into article 20. Although the government admitted that the Council's ruling had "clarified" the bill, it was careful to warn the Council that it would not be divested of its powers of interpretation, stating in committee that:

> With all due respect to the . . . Constitutional Council, the legal analysis of such reserves brings up 2 observations. On the one hand, to take up the remarks of the Prime Minister, the practice of [generating] such reserves must not lead to "a system called the government of judges." On the other hand, we must . . . interpret the adjective "strict" . . . in the sense of . . . *linked* or *close* meanings . . . and not . . . in the sense of *precise.*[133]

Only one reserve, the vague statement requiring the government "to respect national independence," was ignored.[134] Indeed, article 10 was ultimately amended to allow foreigners to purchase up to 20 percent of the companies after European Community officials warned the government that the first rule was inadequate with respect to Community laws on free capital flow.[135] Mitterrand's ploy thus resulted in a weakening of the bill, from his perspective, in this one respect.

The Senate rejected the bill in first reading, to protest the president's decision, by adopting a *quéstion préalable.* One week later, the bill was adopted by both houses and the Socialists decided not to refer the bill a second time because, as their legal advisor stated, Mitterrand's prestige would have been unacceptably at risk.[136]

7

The Council Legislates:
In Search of Media Pluralism

The search for coherent, stable, and pluralistic regimes to govern the French press and broadcast industries has been an extraordinarily active one this past decade. It has occupied vast amounts of the time and legislative resources of governments, parliamentarians, and bureaucrats, led to the creation of numerous regulatory commissions, and opened up new areas of law and administration. Media politics dominated the political agenda and front-page headlines in the 1980s; only the politics of nationalizations and privatizations were more salient or controversial. This chapter examines attempts by successive governments, in 1984 and 1986, to reform legislative regimes governing the media. These reforms led to the most rancorous legislative debates in the history of the Fifth Republic, as measured by standard indices of obstruction,[1] and to the two longest decisions ever handed down by the Constitutional Council.[2]

The impact of constitutional politics on the reform of communications policy is too extensive and complex to be comprehensively examined here. This chapter will mainly focus on the problem of *media pluralism*—the possibility for French citizens to exercise meaningful choice from among a range of information sources representing diverse ideological views. What follows is divided into three parts. The first part is a case study of the Socialist's 1984 press law. The second part examines that law's abrogation and its replacement by the 1986 press law, and the 1986 audiovisual reform. Finally, I assess these cases from the general perspective of the evolution of constitutional politics and policymaking in France.

Reforming the Press Regime: The 1984 Press Law

One lesson of recent French attempts to reform communications law is that the print and audiovisual media can be treated separately only with great difficulty. Publishers and broadcasters provide essentially the same product—information—and can be expected to compete in the same markets for consumers and advertisers. Nevertheless, the two media historically have operated under radically different legal regimes in most European countries. Stated simply, whereas the private sector provided print information and services, the public sector possessed a monopoly on radio and television broadcasting. In the 1980s, Western Europe underwent a "communications revolution."[3] Governments, partly in response to the growing importance of the telecommunications industry to the international economy, sought to decentralize and to privatize the airwaves, and to encourage national firms in efforts to compete with the United States and Japan. Many recognized that in telecommunications big can be better, and encouraged the formation of large multimedia groups. The Chirac government was no exception, however, the French government was thwarted by the Council's jurisprudence on media pluralism. The Council's antitrust policies, originally designed for the press sector in 1984, were in 1986 applied to the whole of the communications sector. The Chirac government's audiovisual communication reform cannot be adequately understood without extensive attention paid to the previous government's press law.

Background

Perhaps in no other Western democracy are individual politicians, political parties, and the advocacy or opposition to party programs as intimately associated with the press as they are in France. Individual newspapers are vital elements of national political identity, but also of the machinery by which regional notables have ruled their fiefdoms. Noteworthy examples include the national daily, *l'Humanité*, the official organ of the Communist party, and the *Provençale* empire radiating out of Marseille, controlled for decades by the late Socialist mayor of Marseille, Gaston Deferre. In general terms, the ethics and ideologies of journalistic objectivity have never found firm roots in France. They are even actively resisted, and this resistance constitutes an accepted "rule of the game" governing the interplay of French journalism and politics.

For much of the nineteenth century, the relationship between public politics and the print medium was openly conflictual, and the right to print free from government interference was by no means secure. Free expression, enshrined in article 11 of the 1789 Declaration of the Rights of Man, was not recognized by governing authorities. Even if it had been, the same text also foresaw its regulation. Article 11 (1789) bears reproducing in full not least because the Council would use it to construct a complex constitutional edifice to govern communications policy:

> The free communication of thoughts and of opinions is one of the most precious rights of man; every citizen may therefore speak, write, and print freely, but is responsible for the abuse of this liberty in circumstances determined by *la loi*.

In the 1815–81 period, the right to publish was largely dependent on "prior state authorization" (*autorisation préalable*) and approval of the censor. The "long struggle" between government and press ended in the Third Republic, with the adoption of the press law of 29 July 1881.[4] Article 5 of the law, which has never been abrogated, virtually interdicts state regulation of the press: "every newspaper or periodical may be published without prior state authorization."

Encouraged by what was perhaps the most liberal license to print in the world, newspapers proliferated. But after World War I a dramatic concentration process began,[5] and by the 1930s major titles were controlled by monopolistic concerns, whose bases were industrial (coal and steel, for example) but tied to political formations. The industry as a whole polarized between Left and Right, and fierce struggles were waged in the press over social politics. Under the occupation, major newspapers published as organs of Nazi propaganda but, upon liberation, many established press groups were dismantled, their property confiscated along with their right to publish. These were distributed among resistance groups and to others who had closed down their newspapers rather than print under Nazi tutelage and censorship.[6]

To ensure the long-term success of this restructuring, a legislative *ordonnance* had been passed by the National Council of the Resistance in Algiers in 1944. The 1944 text sought to regulate the industry in two ways. First, it established the principle of *financial accountability (transparence)*: the right of readers to know who owns and manages the publications they read, and from where their financial resources come. The use, extensive before the war, of fronts—bogus names and organizations—to disguise true ownership was made a criminal offense. Second, as a means of guaranteeing "press pluralism," the *ordonnance* forbade any one person from owning more than one publication—the so-called one-man/one-newspaper rule.

Until 1986, the 1881 and 1944 texts constituted the main apparatus of a press regime. (Constitution-makers in 1946 and 1958 neither contributed to nor detracted from this state of affairs, since neither makes mention of freedom of speech.) Nevertheless, the 1881 and the 1944 texts were in contradiction: the latter sought to regulate what the former had consecrated as free from state intervention. How they might have coexisted might have been revealed had the 1944 text been applied by judges and administrators. But it was not. No government adopted administrative guidelines which might have assured effectiveness, and none made efforts to pursue violators. Politicians, public opinion, and the press industry were more comfortable not applying the provisions than enforcing them.[7] In any case, the policies pursued after liberation had halted the concentration process, and for much of the 1945–70 period the French press industry was among Europe's most vital and diverse. Events of the 1970s, however, put the politics of press ownership and concentration back on the front pages.

The Hersant "Problem" and the Vedel Report

By 1975, concentration of the French press industry had reached the previous high level obtained in the 1930s, and showed no signs of slowing. This dramatic development was due to the activities of one man: Robert Hersant. The building of Hersant's press empire violated not only the letter of the 1944 legislation but the spirit of the postwar settlement. During the war, Hersant had led a German-sponsored, collaborationist and anti-Semitic youth corps, was accused of extorting the property of Parisian Jews, and managing an extensive black market ring. When the war ended he was convicted of collaboration and sent to prison, but was released in the general amnesty of 1952. In 1956 he was elected deputy from the l'Oise; the election was invalidated by the National Assembly on the basis of his wartime activities, but his constituency refused to turn him out, and he retook the seat in the subsequent election. Hersant has remained in the National Assembly, except for brief periods, ever since.[8]

Hersant amassed a fortune publishing automobile and leisure magazines and managing his own advertising agencies. Beginning in the early 1970s and aided by right-wing Gaullists, he turned his sights on general interest news weeklies and dailies. From 1971 to 1978, his holding company acquired a number of important regional papers, including *Paris-Normandie*, and the Parisian (national) dailies, *Le Figaro, l'Aurora*, and the paper with the largest circulation in France, *France-Soir*.[9] The *Paris-Normandie* takeover established a general pattern. *Paris-Normandie* had been, since its founding after the liberation, "openly socialist."[10] Its purchase provoked a strike by journalists and printers anxious about potential editorial redirection, worries which turned out to be founded. Hersant moved in his own editorial team, transferred the paper's advertising business to his group's firm, and within months the paper was running headlines such as this one on the military coup against Allende in Chile: "The Army Did Its Job."[11] Hersant was able to purchase *Le Figaro* in 1976, it was widely reported, with help from then prime minister, Jacques Chirac, and other conservative business leaders who helped his group secure the necessary loans from state-controlled banks.[12] Within one year of the purchase of *Le Figaro*, the oldest of all Parisian dailies and a venerable bastion of the moderate Right, the majority of the writers had resigned and the entire editorial staff had been replaced. From that point on, the paper served as the quasi-official organ of the right-wing of the RPR—railing almost as much against Giscardiens and Barristes on the center-Right as against the Left. The paper's quality, and respect for it in elite circles, seriously declined thereafter.[13] Aided again by Chirac and by former banking associates of Georges Pomipdou,[14] Hersant next took control of *France-Soir* and *l'Aurora*. In 1976, *France-Soir* was sold to an individual buyer acting as a front; two months later he took Hersant on as a partner, the paper's staff was purged, and in 1981 the paper was transferred officially to the Hersant group. *L'Aurora* was purchased in 1978 by an anonymous holding company; from 1979 the paper was being printed in the same building and under the same editorial direction as *Le Figaro*; and the two papers' contents were soon virtually identical. By 1979, the Hersant group controlled 47.2 percent of the Parisian market, possessed the largest share of any group in the total regional market, had launched a general news service to rival the state-controlled press service, and had consolidated a string of printing and advertising corporations enjoying monopolistic agree-ments with leading papers across France.

General alarm at these developments led to mass demonstrations (100,000 marched in Paris in 1976), to legal actions brought against Hersant by unions as diverse as the Confédération générale de travail (CGT) and the Confédéra-tion française démocratique de travail (CFDT) on the Left and the Force ouvrière (FO) on the Right, and to promises by the united Left that it would quickly move to dismantle the group should it prevail in the 1978 legislative elections. The ineffectiveness of the 1944 legislation was evident to all. Hersant was clearly in violation of the provisions regulating press pluralism, and financial accountability simply did not exist in the industry. It was (and still is) almost impossible to find out details concerning the ownership structure of many French newspapers. As one analysis has it:

> The world of the press remains, with a few notable exceptions [presumably *Le Monde* and *La Libération*], very opaque as viewed from the outside, and too often completely closed to students of the press. The management of newspapers remains enveloped in secrecy and it is extremely difficult to separate financial interests from the political interests which control individ-ual companies and the press groups.[15]

The intractability of the problem is illustrated by the fate of the legal actions against Hersant. In 1978 Hersant was indicted, and a year later the plaintiffs succeeded in convincing a court that their suit was justiciable. By 1986 the court still had not rendered a judgment, thwarted by the fluidity and complex-ity of the ownership and management structure which Hersant had purpose-fully erected to disguise his ownership and control. (It took the court several years simply to determine that Hersant was the legal owner of three papers in Lyon and Grenoble.)[16]

After intense political pressure from the center-Right and the Left, Prime Minister Raymond Barre asked the Economic and Social Council to study the problem. The task was conferred on the law professor, Georges Vedel. The Vedel report evaluated the state of concentration in the press industry and made specific policy recommendations believed necessary to ensure against further concentration. Vedel's conclusions[17] are worth summary mention be-cause they became constituent elements of the legislative debates of 1984 and 1986.[18]

Vedel identified an industry in the midst of a crisis brought on by rising printing costs and a declining readership, and noted "a strong evolution in the direction of concentration." The number of newspaper titles had declined from 175 in 1946, to 100 in 1960, to 72 in 1975, and many more were ripe for takeover. However, Vedel wrote,

> With regard to pluralism, the phenomenon of the press group is ambiguous: for any given case, the press group might allow a title to survive whereas alone it could not, or, on the contrary, a means of concentrating and monopolizing power over public opinion.

Acquisitions and concentrations should be allowed to occur, according to Vedel, when it is in the "public interest," that is, when it may actually enable some papers to continue to be published. But "pluralism must be protected" when a "homogeneous ideological group" may attempt to build an "ideological monopoly." The Hersant group alone was singled out by Vedel as an example.

The law professor proposed that the 1944 *ordonnance* be updated and enforced by a "quasi-judicial" administrative body, the Commission of Press Operations. This commission was to be composed either of professional judges chaired by a *conseiller d'Etat*, Vedel's preferred solution, or by a mixture of judges, political appointees, and representatives of labor and management. The members were to be given vast powers to enforce the following provision:

> All purchases [*concentrations*] which would weaken the pluralism of expres-
> sion and of opinion, or which would lead to a change in the political
> orientation of the publications concerned, are forbidden.

If the commission found that a violation of the text had occurred, it would possess the power "to force the reestablishment of the former state of affairs." Vedel considered but rejected reliance on legislatively determined maximum percentages of the market a group could control—hereafter referred to as *fixed-ceilings*—preferring to leave it up to the commission to decide on a case-by-case basis.

Initially, Vedel's recommendations went nowhere. In November 1979, the Minister of Culture convinced deputies to withdraw a broadly supported bill to revise the 1944 legislation, after promising to introduce an equivalent government bill. In May 1980, the National Assembly was informed that the government wanted more time to study the problem,[19] and the proposal was never heard from again. After the 1981 elections, Hersant's decision to use his papers to oppose Socialist government—opposition which *Le Monde* characterized as "systematic obstruction"—no doubt emboldened the Socialists to seek ways to curtail the press baron's influence.[20]

The "Loi Fillioud"

Proposition 95 of the Socialist's electoral manifesto, *110 propositions pour la France*, promised that "the ordonnances of 1944 will be applied." However, it was not until June 1983 that Matignon informed the Elysée that it was ready to move forward on legislation.[21] Mitterrand received the idea coolly and reportedly expressed his "very strong reservations." Fearing that such a reform would likely provoke a "new and hot battle" comparable to that waged over nationalizations, the president counseled caution and informed the government that he would not allow the bill to be heralded as an Elysée "priority."[22]

The *loi Fillioud* (named after the minister of culture, Georges Fillioud) was unveiled by the prime minister on 11 November.[23] Mauroy identified four guiding principles: (1) no person or group would be allowed to possess more than three national titles, defined primarily as daily newspapers with national scope and distribution and weekly news magazines, *of which only one could be a daily newspaper*; (2) no person or group would be allowed to possess both a national and a regional title; (3) no person or group would be allowed to control more than a certain percentage—later fixed at 15 percent—of the total regional market as measured by total number of copies distributed; and (4) each title would be required to have its own autonomous editorial and publishing staff (aimed at forbidding future *Figaro-Aurora* situations), and to conform to a number of other obligation as a means to guarantee financial accountability.[24] Following Vedel, a *Commission pour la transparence et pluralisme de la presse* (CTPP) was to be created and given powers to dismantling existing groups and forbid takeovers. The body was to be composed of six members: three to be appointed by the president of the Republic, of the Senate, and of the National Assembly, respectively, and three "active judges," one each from the *Conseil d'Etat*, the *Cour des comptes*, and the *Cour de cassation*, to be appointed by officials of the courts themselves. The bill was adopted in cabinet on 23 November, after having been revised in private consultations with the *Conseil d'Etat*.

Intense partisan maneuvering began even before the details of the bill were made public. As early as October, opposition leaders pledged to use "every constitutional tactic at [its] disposal" to oppose the bill, "not in defense of the freedom of Mr. Hersant, but in defense of all liberties."[25] For the Right, the expressed motivation of the law, the protection of pluralism, was little more than a transparent smoke screen. "They want to pass a law against M. Hersant because they have not been able to convict him [in the courts]," accused Madelin, while, in truth, "the papers of M. Hersant contribute to pluralism."[26] Although both sides couched their positions in the language of rights, the issue was Hersant. The proposed law, it turned out, would touch immediately *only* the Hersant group, forcing its owner to either sell off *all* of his regional publications *and* parts of his national group or retain only his regional empire with limitations on future acquisitions. Left-leaning groups like the *Provençale* group controlled by the minister of the interior, Deferre, were protected because the bill abandoned the one-man/one-newspaper standard for regional papers—but not for national papers—in favor of a fixed ceiling solution.

From November onward, political positions rapidly polarized. Even before the bill's first reading in the National Assembly, concerned political observers and legal specialists had all but given up hope that constructive debate about the public liberties involved and the state of the industry would be forthcoming.[27] Their despair turned out to be well-founded. The government, expecting the worst, felt obliged to convene an extraordinary session of parliament in order to focus exclusively on the press bill. Once debate had begun, the opposition employed every means of obstruction—from motions of censure,[28] of *irrecevabilité*, and literally hundreds of others, to the flooding of debate with amendments with no hope of being accepted.[29] As *Le Monde* noted in late January, "the affair has become political in the largest sense of the term." For the majority, enmity for Hersant enhanced determination to pass the law, while the opposition, "deprived of the control which it had exercised over the audiovisual media, believes itself obliged to defend tooth and nail certain news-papers which [function as] veritable organs of their parties." By all objective standards, the legislation encountered the most virulent, unrelenting obstruction of any bill in the history of the Fifth Republic. In committee, before first reading, 1,753 amendments were proposed, 95 percent of opposition origin, and more than 112 hours were required to debate the opposition's amendments alone. The committee (Cultural Affairs) reached only article 6 (of 42) before the process broke down entirely, and the bill was summarily sent to the whole assembly.[30] In the National Assembly, every record was shattered: longest assembly debate in first reading (166 hours), most amendments proposed (2,598, breaking the pre-vious record number, 1,438 for the 1981 nationalization bill, and higher than the *total* amendments proposed for every legislative *year* from 1959 to 1974), and most procedural suspensions of meeting (70).[31] The president of the National Assembly regularly lost control of discussion, which periodically turned violent. On the first day of discussion, Fillioud, introducing the law, was unable to utter more than one sentence at a time without being interrupted by calls of "liar!," "*provocateur*!," "idiot-fool," and Jacques Toubon's constantly reiterated: "He's drunk!"[32] Before the bill was finally adopted on 13 February 1984, three promi-nent opposition deputies were censured—the first time in the history of the Fifth Republic that censure had been voted.[33]

The parliamentary battle over the *loi Fillioud* was waged primarily in the language of constitution law, but arguments were no less recognizable as pro-or anti-Hersant. For the Left, the collective had a responsibility to restrict the rights of private enterprise when its exercise weakened or endangered the rights of others. This was especially true of the imperative to protect freedom of expression. As the sponsors of the bill to the National Assembly put it,

> Liberty, conceived simply as an absence of interdiction, opens the way to its confiscation by those who have the material means to exercise it, and to the negation of the rights of others. . . . The press participates in an dispensable manner to the democratic debate of ideas. . . . Regulating concentration appears therefore to be more necessary in this sector than in any other, because beyond the production line there is democracy and liberty.[34]

Freedom of the press was conceived entirely in terms of the rights of readers to be informed as to ownership and control, and to have the possibility to choose from among a variety of papers representing the diversity of opinion in so-ciety.[35] These rights could no longer be guaranteed, claimed Fillioud in his opening presentation, because certain men had engaged in "fraud," "cheating," and "embezzlement."[36] The opposition argued that talk of rights only obscured the government's true motives:

> No, this text does not favor pluralism against monopoly. On the contrary, it's a Socialist law targeted at one man. Everyone knows it, it's obvious—this text's object is Robert Hersant.[37]

For the Right, freedom of the press was conceived entirely in terms of property rights, of what Jacques Chirac called the "inseparable principles of the freedom of expression, the right of private enterprise, and the rights to property":

> Yes or no, may press groups operate freely? Are they free to establish a new paper? Are they free to buy new titles, to increase their standing and their incomes by their own success? Are they free, in case of failure, to sell, if that is viewed as necessary to save a paper in difficulty? Yes or no, is the press free from the control of the state . . . ?[38]

Fillioud worked just as diligently as the opposition to reveal true motive behind rhetoric:

> [Y]ou want to protect certain interests . . . and the privileges, advantages, and dominant position of monopoly capital. It is only by allusion that you cite the freedom of expression.[39]

On specific details too, no compromise was possible. Whereas for the majority, the protection of pluralism positively *"require[d]* limits on concentration,"[40] the opposition opposed *any* legislatively-mandated limitation on concentration. In the Right's view, concentration worked to *enhance* pluralism. Moreover, it argued that the bill's provisions disallowing a national publisher from creating a separate regional daily would encourage regional monopolization.[41] The recruitment, composition, and future role of the CTPP also drew controversy. The majority claimed that in structure and mandate the CTPP had been inspired by the Constitutional Council, but with more independence from politicians and more reliance on judicial authority. Unconvinced, the Right charged that the body would function as an "inquisitorial commission,"[42] under political tutelage, and argued that jurisdiction should be conferred on the ordinary courts.[43] (Administrative lawyers, too, worried that the body would be more "political" than judicial and would lack independence.[44]) The debate turned into a public polemic after Hersant published a front page attack on the proposed body—which he branded a "revolutionary committee"—in *Le Figaro*. Hersant alleged that even the judges appointed by judicial authorities would be little more than Socialist puppets, leading high officials of the *Conseil d'Etat*, the *Cour des comptes*, and the *Cour de cassation* to publish rebuttals in major newspapers in defense of their honor.[45]

Autolimitation: *The (Un-)Making of the 1984 Press Law*

Once sent to parliament, the legislation suffered one of the most extensive *autolimitation* processes in history. The government immediately lost control over the amendment process to the committees, and particularly to the *Commission des lois*. A group of Socialists in that committee, believing the most important provisions of the legislation to be constitutionally vulnerable,[46] prepared dozens of amendments to the legislation before official discussion had even begun. They then worked to convince the Cultural Affairs to ratify their proposals. While conflict between the two committees, and between the government and its majority, could not be concealed,[47] the Law Committee

Table 7.1. The Making of the 1984 Press Law: *Autolimitation* and the "Protection of Pluralism"

Government Bill (Nov. 1983)	Committee Amendments (Dec.–Jan. 1984)	Final Assembly Version (Fixed in Feb. 1984)
	Antitrust Provisions (title II):	
No person or group may control more than 3 national news dailies or weeklies, nor more than 1 daily. Any person or group may control up to 3 dailies if its combined share of the national market does not exceed 15%.	Any person or group may control *"more than 1 daily,"* to a maximum of 3, if its combined share of the market does not exceed 15% (weeklies removed from the purview of the law).	Any person or group may control *"several dailies"* if its combined share does not exceed 15%.
Any person or group may control *"more than 1"* regional daily only if its combined share of the total regional market does not exceed 15%.	Any person or group may control *"several regional dailies"* if its combined share of the total regional market does not exceed 15%.	No change.
No person or group may control a national daily and a regional daily.	Any person or group may control *up to 3* national dailies and "several" regional dailies if: (1) its combined share of the national market does not exceed 10%; (2) if its combined share of the total regional market does not exceed 10%.	Any person or group may control *"several"* national dailies and "several" regional dailies if:(1) its combined share national market does not exceed 10%. (2) if its combined share of the total regional market does not ex-cede 15%.
Antitrust provisions apply to "existing situations."	Antitrust provisions apply to "existing situations."	Antitrust provisions apply to "existing situations."
Intent to buy or sell an existing publication must be declared to the CTPP 1 month in advance of expected closing date; this declaration *suspends* the sale for a maximum of 3 months pending CTPP verification that it will not violate the above provisions. *If the CTPP rules that the sale would constitute a violation, the sale is nullified* [the control is thus a priori].	Declaration requirement retained; *suspension of sale removed.* If the CTPP rules that the sale would constitute a violation of above provisions, it "may oppose the sale, request the parties to respect the provisions, *and take the* [unspecified] *necessary measures.*"	Declaration requirement retained; if the CTPP rules that the sale would constitute a violation of the above provisions, it "informs the interested parties." If the sale goes forward in spite of the such a ruling, the CTPP may proceed to title III sanctions [the control is thus made explicitly a posteriori].
	On the Powers of the CTPP (title III):	
Art. 18: The government, the permanent parliamentary committees, press enterprises, and professional associations may request the CTPP to	No changes.	Changes made: referral authority of parliamentary committees removed; referral authority bestowed on the management of press groups.

182

Table 7.1. (continued)

Government Bill (Nov. 1983)	Committee Amendments (Dec.–Jan. 1984)	Final Assembly Version (Fixed in Feb. 1984)

On the Powers of the CTPP (title III):

rule on *existing* violations ofthe above antitrust provisions; the CTPP may also convene itself (*autosaisiner*).		
Art. 19: If the CTPP finds that a violation has occurred, "it prescribes all measures necessary to assure their respect," including, "notably, the separation of companies, or the cessation of common control." [*Power to dismantle recognized explicitly.*]	If CTPP finds that a violation has occurred, "it asks the interested parties to respect the provisions" before "prescribing necessary measures." [*Dismantling language retained.*]	If CTPP finds that a violation has occurred, it asks the interested parties to respect the provisions" before "prescribing necessary measures." [*Dismantling language removed.*]
Art. 20: In the event of noncompliance, the CTPP suspends the "effects of the *certificat d'inscription* [which provides certain postal and fiscal advantages to press enterprises] until the conditions of pluralism have been restored."	No substantive changes. [The precise nature of tax and fiscal advantages to be suppressed specified.]	In the event of noncompliance, the CTPP "deprives" the violating party of certain postal and fiscal advantages "until the conditions of pluralism have been restored. [*Mention of the certificat removed.*]

Commission pour la transparence et le pluralisme de la presse (Commission on Financial Accountability and Press Pluralism).

NOTE: In its decision of 10–11 October 1984, the Constitutional Council placed strict controls (SROIs) on how title II was to be interpreted, *annulled* application of antitrust provisions to existing situations, and *annulled* articles 18, 19, and 20 of title III as unconstitutional.

SOURCES. Text of government draft: *Le Monde*, 25 November 1983, p. 10; texts of National Assembly committee amendments at *Rapport #1963 (Annex)*, pp. 51–53, and *Rapport #1963 (supplementaire)* of the National Assembly. Final Bill: *Débats*, National Assembly (*Constituante*), 12 September 1984, pp. 4431–433.

and the National Assembly prevailed. As *Le Monde* put it: "Aided by fear of the Constitutional Council, the Socialist deputies . . . endeavored to improve the bill, and succeeded—but not without difficulty—in convincing the government of the necessity to compromise."[48]

Of the bill's forty-two original articles, twenty-six were rewritten in committee. Of these, every article of title II, on press pluralism, and much of title III, on the powers of the commission, underwent substantial revision. Table 7.1 depicts, from left to right, the evolution of changes to these provisions. Most dramatic, revisions to title II repudiated the two guidelines established by Mauroy—that no person or group control more than one national daily (mention of weeklies was simply suppressed together[49]), or control both a national and a regional daily.[50] The committees, after long rancorous discussions of Council jurisprudence on "equality under the law," sought to harmonize the regimes for regional and national papers.[51] A number of provisions advocated by the *Conseil d'Etat* but rejected by the government were revealed and then restored.[52] Most important of these, *fixed market ceilings were extended to all categories of ownership as the essential means of ensuring pluralism.* As Jean-Pierre Michel, *rapporteur* for the Law Committee put it, "The criteria of fixed ceilings . . . has the merit of providing an objective standard, and thus eliminates all risks of arbitrariness."[53] Finally, the legal definition of *national* was rewritten and clarified in the direction suggested by the *Conseil d'Etat.*[54]

Changes affecting the powers of the CTPP were no less dramatic. Debate was dominated by the Council's decision of 16 July 1971 (see chapter 3). In that ruling, the Council, following a long line of administrative jurisprudence, had declared unconstitutional an attempt by the government to require groups to register with an administrative authority *before* being granted certain rights accorded civic associations. The Council ruled that the right to enjoy certain liberties could neither be suspended nor made subject to *prior authorization* (*autorisation préalable*). The constitutional argument about the press bill's anti-trust provisions focused on the extent to which its enforcement mechanisms would or would not institute an unconstitutional requirement of *prior authorization* (*régime d'autorisation préalable*). According to the original terms of title II, a declaration to the CTPP of intentions to either sell or acquire a newspaper was obligatory; the effect of this declaration was to *suspend* automatically the sale, pending CTPP verification that it would not lead to a violation of the antitrust provisions; a negative decision of the CTPP would automatically *nullify* the transaction. Opponents of the bill argued that the provisions constituted prior abridgment of freedom of the press and of expression enshrined in article 5 of the 1881 legislation, as well as of the rights of property, enterprise, and of expression guaranteed by articles 11 and 17 of the 1789 declaration.[55] The government responded that it was not seeking the power to suspend freedom of expression or the right to publish, but rather to authorize or to forbid the fulfillment of a contract—just as the right to acquire or to use property may depend on the prior granting of a building permit. Thus, the argument went, the Council's 1971 decision was not relevant to this case.[56] Socialists in the *Commission des lois* disagreed with the government and amendments removed the suspensory effect of the declaration, and denied the CTPP the power to forbid the transaction before it was to occur.[57] In the final version of the provision, the CTPP possessed the power only to inform the parties concerned of the possibility of future litigation in the event of a negative ruling. This only partially satisfied the Right, since the obligation of owners and buyers to declare to the CTPP proposed sales was retained.

Title III too was significantly altered. In the original version, the CTPP could be asked to rule on the state of compliance to the antitrust provisions of *existing situations.* In the event of a finding of noncompliance, the CTPP would possess two important powers: (1) to force the dismantling of press groups; and (2) to suspend certain tax advantages and state subsidies otherwise due publishers. The Right, relying on the Council's decision on the 1981 nationalization bill, argued that these provisions would allow the CTPP to take property without a prior guarantee of fair compensation,[58] and that, to the extent that the power to deny fiscal advantages would give the CTPP "a veritable power of life and death over press groups," such powers would constitute again "a totally unconstitutional system of prior authorization."[59] As Table 7.1 shows, these provisions were significantly watered down by the National Assembly, but the CTPP retained the power "to prescribe the necessary measures" to force compliance, and to deprive publishers of subsidies. Finally, not shown in Table 7.1, extensive changes reinforced due process and contradictory procedure, granted defendants the right to appeal decisions to the *Conseil d'Etat*, and watered down the CTPP's powers to investigate in an attempt to disarm criticism of the body's political nature. These changes too were encouraged by readings of Council jurisprudence, particularly of the 1980 "security and liberty decision."

The *autolimitation* effort worked to expand political and institutional support for the bill. The *Conseil d'Etat* and the Law Committee could celebrate the fact that the former's suggestions had been successfully implemented. The government, having shown its capacity for compromise, could still be satisfied since the effort had presumably enhanced the bill's constitutional security. Although less onerous than its initial bill, Hersant would still be obliged to make tough choices. He would be required either to: (1) choose to keep either *Le Figaro* or *France-Soir*, likely creating regional editions of the chosen title; or, (2) keep up to fourteen regional papers, while abandoning his national empire; or, (3) keep *Aurora* and with it several regional papers. Not surprisingly, the *autolimitation* effort did not satisfy the opposition. The Right continued to argue that the bill was "liberticidal,"[60] and threats to refer the bill to the Council became as banal as the constitutional debate.[61] Dozens of unsuccessful final amendments to revise the bill's title—"law on the financial accountability and pluralism of the press"—expressed the Right's *constitutional* position succinctly, anticipating the grounds for referral. Examples include: the "law to assure political discrimination between press groups"; the "law to destroy the right to property"; the "law to reestablish a regime of prior authorization and to create a Court of State Security for press groups"; the "law to violate the Declaration of the Rights of Man"; and the "law to destroy press pluralism."[62]

The Senate, after declaring the bill unconstitutional, chose not to vote *irrecevabilité* in order to allow a special committee headed by Charles Pasqua to elaborate alternative legislation.[63] The Senate removed nineteen of the forty-three articles contained in the National Assembly's bill, introduced twenty-five more, and left only three untouched.[64] Pasqua, declaring that the 1881 law constituted for the Senate "the principal reference text and the best guarantee of press freedoms," argued that "concentration is a natural evolution . . . which permits certain titles to survive," and denounced the establishment of fixed ceilings as "anti-economic, anti-social, and anti-constitutional."[65] The Senate's rendition, accordingly, abrogated entirely the 1944 *ordonnance*, abolished all mention of press groups, and removed any limitation on concentration. It also altered the mandate and composition of the CTPP, refusing it any power to force sell-offs and giving press owners what amounted to veto authority over its decisions.[66] The National Assembly, on successive occasions, simply restored its version. Finally, on 12 September 1984 the Senate rejected the bill on a motion of *irrecevabilité* in third reading.[67] Fillioud responded to this rejection for the government as follows:

> Neither of us is naive. . . . Permit me to say . . . that you have used up all of your political arguments and that you are forced now to return to legal ones. In any event, the judges in the Constitutional Council will ultimately decide between us.[68]

The Senate's veto was overridden by the assembly, and the law was definitively adopted and referred to the Council that same day.

Senators and deputies referred the matter to the Council, invoking fourteen different grounds of unconstitutionality.[69] In addition, a lawyer for Hersant and the press baron himself sent letters to the Council in Hersant's defense.[70]

The 1984 Decision on Press Pluralism

In one of its most complex decisions in its history,[71] the Council, under the direction of the *rapporteur*, Georges Vedel, annulled ten of the bill's forty-five articles and pronounced several SROIs. First and most important, the decision saved the Hersant press empire by interdicting the CTPP or any other authority from applying antitrust provisions to *existing* situations. Second, the Council annulled several parts of title III, gutting the CTPP's powers to force compliance in the event of future violations. Third, the Council articulated a number of general constitutional rules governing legislative competence to reform regimes affecting fundamental liberties. While the decision addressed a host of other issues, the discussion will focus on these aspects.

As a matter of interpretation, the Constitutional Council agreed with the government that at issue was the protection of the rights of readers to choose from among diverse publications, and not the rights of publishers or of property. Reasoning from article 11 (1789) and ignoring petitioners' appeals to consecrate the 1881 legislation as a FPRLR, the Council declared that "pluralism in the market for daily newspapers . . . is in itself an objective possessed of constitutional status." Pluralism constituted a "necessary corollary"[72] of article 11 (1789), since freedom of expression may be effectively enjoyed only if pluralism is assured. It then went on to rule that financial accountability, because it enhances readers' abilities to make "clear judgements" about the origin of the information at their disposal, "tends to reinforce" pluralism, and therefore constitutes a legitimate legislative (presumably not a constitutional) "objective." Translated into policymaking terms, the decision *requires* lawmakers to guarantee pluralism in the press industry, in the interest of ensuring the "constitutional principle" of freedom of expression, and *allows* measures to guarantee financial accountability, in the interest of ensuring the "constitutional objective" of pluralism.

As a matter of concrete impact, the decision destroyed the bill, a total annulment in all but name. Though the Council affirmed lawmakers' competence to fix ceilings for market shares, it also ruled that title II's provisions governing pluralism were "obviously unconstitutional," in that they violated article 11 (1789). Title II was allowed to stand, but only after the Council had pronounced strict reserves and a partial annulment. First, the Council ruled that the fixed ceilings could only be considered constitutional to the extent that they did not prohibit press groups from surpassing them as a result of expanding readership for *existing* publications, or as a result of the creation of *new* publications. Thus, the ceilings could *only* apply to future acquisitions. Technically, this SROI did not thwart legislative intent, but merely clarified potentially ambiguous terminology, however, its prominence and language prepared the way for what constituted an effective veto of the legislation. Second, *the Council annulled that part of title II which would have allowed fixed ceilings to apply to "existing situations," that is, to "groups built under prior legislative regimes."* Although some commentators saw reliance on the principle of nonretroactivity,[73] the Council does not refer to it. In fact, *no general principle of law or line of administrative or constitutional jurisprudence provided a source for this annulment.*

Before examining this part of the decision, it is important to note that established legislation and administrative law governing antitrust matters had consecrated clear precedents for the government's initiative. Furthermore, in his 1979 report Vedel himself had advocated giving his version of the CTPP immense discretionary authority to force compliance, including the power to dismantle press groups formed in the past. That the Council may have settled first on a desired legislative outcome and only then worked to get the jurisprudence right should at least be entertained.[74] Taken at face value, however, the jurisprudential logic of the decision—complex and anything but evident[75]— flows from the Council's general desire to expand its control over all legislative processes affecting fundamental liberties.

The Constitutional Council arrived at its decision in the following way. In its discussion of title II, the Council declared that legislative competence extended to "fixing the rules concerning the exercise of the rights to free communication and to the liberty of speaking, writing, and printing," but that this power was not absolute. It chose to clarify legislative sovereignty in these, wholly general, terms:

> In cases of fundamental liberties [like freedom of expression], which are all the more precious since their exercise is one of the essential guarantees of the respect of other rights and liberties and of national sovereignty, *la loi can only regulate their exercise in order to make it more effective or to balance it with the exercise of other rules or principles of valeur constitutionnel* [emphases added].

For the first time (if extending recent jurisprudence[76]), the Council ruled that lawmakers could never weaken legislative protection of a public liberty, but *could only legislate to strengthen that protection.* This has since become known as the *ratchet effect* (there can be no turning back). This general admonition did not shed much light on the constitutional acceptability of the bill's antitrust provisions. One could argue that the objective of pluralism required, or at the very least would allow, legislators to provide for the dismantling of press groups in violation of the law as a means to strengthen and reinforce freedom of expression. But at this point, the Council shifted ground, away from an interpretation of article 11 (1789) privileging readers to one privileging publishers:

> In cases where existing situations touch upon a public liberty, lawmakers may only limit its exercise when one of the following conditions are met: when these situations have been illegally acquired; and when limitations are truly necessary in order to assure the realization of the constitutional objective pursued.

The Council ruled that neither condition had been met. With respect to the former, the Council declared that because the annulled provision did not make mention of such illicit situations, legislative intent on that score could not be assumed. In so ruling, the Council willfully ignored the lengthy discussions in the *travaux préparatoires* and in parliament on the illegality of Hersant's situation. (But the Council did appeal to the authority of the *travaux préparatoires* in attaching the SROI which restricted application of fixed ceilings to acquisitions!)[77] As to the latter condition, *the Council unambiguously substituted its judgment for that of the government and parliament*:

> With respect to national daily newspapers, it can not be validly argued that the number, the variety, . . . and the conditions of their distribution presently weaken pluralism in a manner so serious that it would be necessary to apply [antitrust provisions] to existing situations.

(The Council provided no analysis of why this was so; its ruling is pure assertion.) This declaration—not to mention its spectacular legislative effect— is impossible to reconcile with the oft-repeated claim, reiterated continually by doctrine and by the Council itself, that the Council does not exercise discretionary power comparable to that of parliament. In sum, the Council's decision froze existing situations, making it legally impossible for any other group to rival Hersant.

The Council then moved on to the powers of the CTPP. Admitting that the system of enforcement provided for in title III—namely, the power to deprive publishers of state subsidies—was not in itself "a regime of prior authorization," the Council ruled that it nonetheless would "function" as one, and was therefore "equivalent" to such a regime in a constitutional sense. This bit of reasoning was necessary because *the CTPP's powers to force compliance clearly did not constitute a system of prior authorization as traditionally understood in law*. In situations which the Council's decision of 16 July 1971 had interdicted and the 1881 text had abolished, the state possessed the power to suspend one's public liberties prior to legal determination that one's situation was illicit. No one disputes that such a power violates French administrative and constitutional law. In this case, however, the CTPP would have possessed powers only to *encourage* press groups to conform to the law, only *after* a violation of law had occurred, and only *after* an official ruling to that effect had been ignored. Under *no* set of circumstances envisioned by the law could the CTPP force a newspaper to cease publication; it could only suspend certain administrative privileges (state subsidies). And in *all* circumstances, the CTPP would be operating solely to protect a public liberty (pluralism) which the Council itself had elevated to constitutional status. The Council's application of the notion of prior authorization did not convince those versed in established administrative procedures and law,[78] but it did destroy the CTPP as an enforcement mechanism.

These and other annulments so distorted the bill that the Council was faced with the problem of determining if what remained of it could fulfill intended legal functions. Because the legislation had been designed to update and to replace portions of the 1944 *ordonnance*, the bill had made provision for the abrogation of thirteen articles of that text. The Council felt obliged to annul this provision, declaring,

> It is not up to the Council to determine how the legislature would have meant
> to make such abrogations if the latter had known in advance of these
> declarations of unconstitutionality.

Le Monde's headline the next day was to the point: "The Hersant group is saved."[79] The government downplayed the significance of the defeat and elected to promulgate the law as amputated. It may be strongly inferred that Mitterrand, whose initial opposition to go after Hersant had proved well-founded, made it clear that he did want the fight drawn out by a corrective revision process.[80] Parliamentary leaders, as is usual, were more publicly hostile: the *rapporteur* for the bill in Cultural Affairs, Jean-Jack Quéyranne, complained that a movement towards a "government of judges" regime in France, begun with the 1982 decision of nationalizations, was now unmistakable.[81] Pasqua, joined by other opposition leaders, claimed victory for the Senate and called for Fillioud's resignation from the government.[82] Other supporters of the bill put the best face they could on the decision. *Le Monde* editorialized that since the law would forbid Hersant from buying up papers in the future, "perhaps his arrogant activities have found their limits." Furthermore, it noted that because the 1944 *ordonnance* remained in force, the judicial proceedings against Hersant begun in 1977 could move forward (they had stalled in early 1984 pending the outcome of the legislative battle).[83]

The most critical reaction to the decision came from the eminent *Conseiller d'Etat*, Georges Maleville, appearing as a signed article in *Le Monde*.[84] Maleville claimed that the Council's reasoning had proved contradictory and confusing to those "disconcerted jurists" who had "taken the time" to try to understand it. Most important, the decision positively created a violation of the principle of equality:

The Council has admitted the constitutionality of this law, but for the future only, thus preserving the totality of the Hersant group. It has ruled that this group, with 18 dailies and several magazines, does not threaten the freedom of the press, while the creation after the law of a group less important would threaten this liberty. The Council has given no precise reasons for this distinction. . . . The decision thus puts the Hersant group in a privileged situation, . . . and no other person can ever possess as many papers as does he.

Even more astonishing than this unprecedented public voicing of the *Conseil d'Etat*'s displeasure, the *conseiller* then declared that the Council's decision revealed the extent to which that body functioned more as a group of legislators than as a group of judges:

[T]he general assembly of the *Conseil d'Etat, composed in its majority of professional jurists*, had admitted the constitutionality of these [annulled] provisions when the bill was submitted to it. The Constitutional Council decided otherwise. Hersant can shout victory, but his shout sounds a defeat for *le droit* and for democracy. The decision tarnishes the reputation of the Constitutional Council as well. Since June 1981, *that body has exhibited a tendency to behave more like a third legislative assembly*, remaking legislation, after the National Assembly and the Senate, and according to rationales more political than judicial [emphases added].

Aftermath: A Thwarted Reform

Bereft of an effective mechanism of enforcement, the 1984 legislation proved inadequate. In an all night session on 17–18 December 1985, days before adjournment of the eighth parliament, the Senate adopted Pasqua's counter-legislation as a new bill.[85] The Right, expecting victory in the coming legislative elections, sought to give the new government a running start in the coming legislative sessions. Not coincidentally, Hersant purchased *l'Union de Reims* within days of the adoption. Then, on 3 January 1986, three days after the CTPP had ruled the acquisition of *l'Union* illegal, Hersant bought *Le Progrès* of Lyon, the nation's fifth largest paper by circulation.[86] In addition to violating the antitrust provisions of the 1984 law, Hersant chose not to inform the CTPP of the purchase, thus violating the obligation of prior declaration. In identical, front page editorials printed in *Le Progrès* and in *Le Figaro*, Hersant explained that he considered the 1984 press law to be without force and would very soon be formally abrogated. "Sometimes," he wrote, "in order not to be late for a war, it is better to be in advance of a law."[87]

By March 1986, the Hersant press group controlled more than 38 percent of the national market for daily newspapers, and more than 26 percent of the total market for regional dailies,[88] including an absolute monopoly in the nation's largest multipaper regional market, the Rhône valley. In fact, the percentage of the total French market controlled by Hersant is greater than that controlled by any press group in any Western democracy. Furthermore, by March 1986 there was virtually no likelihood that his dominance would be challenged. After the Right won the March elections, judicial proceedings against Hersant were again suspended—this time pending the proposed abrogation of both the 1944 and 1984 texts by the Pasqua bill.[89]

The Chirac Government and Media Pluralism

Most of the summer of 1986 was devoted to Right's emerging communications policy. The Chirac government accepted the Pasqua bill as its own, inscribed it on the parliamentary calendar, and gave it immediate priority. It would be one of the first bills adopted by the new parliament. The audiovisual law, entitled the "Liberty of Communication," too, was a platform promise. Its main objectives were to fix the rules by which radio frequencies would be allocated, television channels denationalized (TF1) and ownership rights reallocated (channels 5 and 6), and to create an administrative body to replace the CTPP.[90] Both bills went through extensive autolimitation processes; both were struck down by the Constitutional Council on the grounds that they would inadequately protect pluralism; and both would require a second legislative process to integrate the Council's criticisms into the legislation. These corrective revision processes were carried out in one bill, which finally became law in November 1986.

Reforming the Press Regime: The 1986 Press Law

The Senate presented its press bill as one forced on lawmakers by an ill-conceived and unconstitutional law which the Constitutional Council had happily "amputated . . . of its most unacceptable provisions."[91] The new bill was short and consonant with the Chirac government's neoliberal orientation. The minister of culture, François Léotard, told the National Assembly, "The text is more important for the provisions it abrogates than for those it proposes."[92] In its original rendition,[93] the bill was to: (1) replace the 1944 and 1984 texts in their entirety; (2) abolish fixed ceilings, with no other antitrust mechanism foreseen to replace them; (3) loosen rules of financial accountability; and, (4) abolish the CTPP, leaving enforcement of the law to the regular judiciary.

Although discussion of the bill raised other constitutional issues, and led to several low-level compromises,[94] the most important debates centered on the legislative obligation to assure pluralism. In the first meeting of the Assembly's Cultural Affairs Committee, the Socialists raised *irrecevabilité* on the grounds that *the new law would not protect the constitutional objective of pluralism at least as much as the regime to be abrogated* (the jurisprudence of the ratchet effect). The majority responded that

> recent examples demonstrate that concentration does not weaken pluralism, but has permitted the survival of certain publications. In these conditions, the absence of antitrust provisions in no way implies that the bill is unconstitutional[95];

and the motion was rejected. Later in the same meeting, the law was reluctantly amended.

The crucial amendment was proposed by the *rapporteur* for the bill, Michel Pericard, after a long, tortuous exposition of the relevant Council jurisprudence.[96] Pericard agreed that the Council had seemingly forbidden any legislative act which would weaken legislative protection for pluralism. But, he continued, the Council did not therefore mean to declare antitrust provisions "necessary guarantees," or positively required since it had ruled that pluralism was not threatened in present circumstances. Pericard noted that the abolition of the fixed ceilings would have the effect of placing press groups under the general French antitrust regime established by the law of 19 July 1977. The committee then adopted what later became article 11, the terms of which "interdicted"

> . . . the acquisition of any general daily newspaper . . . when this acquisition would have for effect to permit the buyer to detain more than 30% of the total national market. . . .

A subsequent amendment specified prison sentences and fines for violations, to be imposed by the ordinary courts (article 12.5).

Péricard claimed that the figure of 30 percent was selected with respect to the Council's jurisprudence, in order to provide a ceiling "sufficiently high to permit powerful press groups to develop in order to contribute . . . to the maintenance of pluralism."[97] A closer look at this amendment, however, reveals recognition of a constitutional imperative reconciled with less lofty motives. As the Left put it, the majority had reluctantly come to accept that had the "majority of the Assembly followed the terms of the Senate's bill, it would have been censured by the Council."[98] Simply stated, *fear of Council censure had restored the linkage, if not identity, between fixed ceilings and the requirement to protect press pluralism,* an interpretation confirmed by interviews with committee staff.[99] The ceiling of 30 percent was not chosen at random.[100] Calculated in terms of the total national market for all categories of daily newspapers, the Hersant group's control at the time fell somewhere between 28 percent and 29 percent. Without this ceiling or one higher, Hersant would have found himself in violation of the 1977 general antitrust law, which fixed market share ceilings at 25 percent. The Left characterized the bill flatly as an "amnesty law" for Hersant,[101] a sentiment echoed by the non-Hersant press and journalist unions.[102]

The rest of the debate replayed that of 1984: "Same arguments, same disagreements, but the roles have been reversed," opined *Le Monde.*[103] The Left worked to restore the terms of the 1984 bill, threatening referral on dozens of occasions. One Socialist counseled the government that only the autolimitation process, and not the Right's majority sitting on the Council, could save the bill from censure:

> We do not forget . . . that the majority of those sitting at the Palais Royal have been there for a long time, notably since before May 1981. But when

> violations are so obvious, even if you do not see them, jurists do. We know
> the value of having a majority in the Council, but . . . it is not possible that
> they could [fail] to respond to this question if you yourselves do not do so in a
> satisfactory manner.[104]

Péricard's amendments stood up. No substantive changes were made to these provisions until the Council annulled them in July.

Petitioners appealed to the Council's consecration of the ratchet effect.[105] They invited the Council to annul the bill on the grounds that its promulgation would lead to a weakening of protection for press pluralism relative to the regime the legislation sought to abrogate. Furthermore, both argued that article 11 in combination with looser rules governing financial accountability, could not guarantee its object. Nothing in the law would forbid bogus front organizations from buying up titles for a press group, and nothing would forbid a group from buying up titles and then subsequently liquidating them, thus increasing their own market share to the detriment of pluralism. Moreover, the deputies argued, failure to distinguish between national and regional papers would open the door to regional monopolies. Finally, they pointed out that the bill would only apply to groups whose acquisitions would surpass the 30 percent limit. Those which might be above the ceiling at promulgation would be free to buy up titles to 100 percent of market share.

The Constitutional Council, in a short decision which broke no new ground, reaffirmed that pluralism was an objective of constitutional status, and then annulled article 11 (and 12.5, which fixed penalties for the former's violation). However, the Council chose not to rely on its own 1984 jurisprudence on the ratchet effect. The raising of fixed ceilings from 15 to 30 percent and the abolition of the distinction between regional and national dailies by the legislature did not, presumably, weaken legislative protection of pluralism. On the other hand, the Council accepted more specific criticisms made by the parliamentarians, namely, that article 11 was poorly worded and therefore could not provide an effective guarantee of pluralism. As in 1984, the judges chose not to declare inseparability, but did the next best thing: they annulled the provision abrogating the 1944 and 1984 texts. Thus, the press industry was now governed by three contradictory texts, and the CTPP was unexpectedly revived. Given these conditions, *the partial annulment constituted a Council command to engage in a corrective revision process.*

The 1986 Audiovisual Law

By 1986, trust building in the electronic media had never materialized for the simple reason that the French state tightly restricted or forbade outright private broadcasting.[106] Moreover, there was political consensus on the necessity of maintaining state monopoly of the airwaves. In Kuhn's terms, this monopoly was viewed by the Right as an instrument of "nation-building . . . in a traditionally divided and fragmented . . . society"; Socialists and Communists feared that privatization would inevitably lead to the domination of the

industry by big capital.[107] Broadcast policy was nevertheless intensely politicized, due to the influence which the government exerted over news content
and editorial decisions, particularly during electoral campaigns. By the 1980s,
however, this consensus broke down, and one of the benefits of deregulation
emerged. In 1982, the Mauroy government received parliamentary approval to
gradually open up radio broadcasting to the private sector, and in 1985,
France's first two private television stations appeared. The Chirac government's bill of 1986 would accelerate the commercialization of radio broadcasting and by privatizing TF1, France's most popular channel, leave the state
sector with only two (A2 and FR3) of six television channels.

Debates on the audiovisual bill began in the Senate as the press law was
being definitively adopted by parliament. The government sought to establish
a regulatory regime flexible enough to adapt to rapid and unforeseeable
developments in the audiovisual industry. The government proposed that a
regulatory body—the National Commission of Communication and Liberties
(CNCL, after the French)—be created to allocate rights to broadcast in accordance with "the public interest." The public interest was defined by a number
of criteria, including the prospective broadcaster's prior experience and financial stability, but by little which might constrain the CNCL's exercise of wide
discretionary authority. In addition to criticizing the CNCL's composition and
future independence from political authorities,[108] the opposition worked to
limit the body's discretion and to give to it the responsibility to protect media
pluralism. Amendments seeking to fix more detailed rules governing the future
responsibilities of the CNCL proliferated into the hundreds. One government
official, speaking before the Senate, characterized this part of the debate in this
way:

> One can choose between two methods of attacking the problem of multi-
> media concentration. The first is the one we have chosen: to leave the details
> of the rules and principles to the judgement of the CNCL, that is, to an
> independent regulatory authority which will judge on a case by case basis
> according to the evolution [of the sector] and to a certain number of criteria.
>   The second method is that which you [the Socialists] are advocating: the
> bureaucratic method, with precise quotas that would be determined once and
> for all time, and which would confine the sector. . . .[109]

The opposition's arguments were identical to those proffered during the press
debates, namely, that the power of capital and the rights of ownership must be
limited in matters of access to information. It is crucial to note that the
government could reasonably respond that the audiovisual sector was unlike
the press sector in at least one crucial respect: in 1986 private capital did not,
could not, pose an existing challenge to pluralism, since remnants of the state's
former monopoly constituted the *sole* measurable concentration in the sector.
Moreover, because the bill would create wider access to broadcasting rights (by
further dismantling state control, and by extending a greater number of
authorizations to broadcast to a greater number of operators) its legislative

effect—at least at this stage in the development of the industry—could only favor pluralism. That said, the government sought to encourage not discourage the formation of media groups. The French telecommunications industry, it was stated repeatedly, was far less concentrated and therefore less competitive internationally than the German, Dutch, or even the British industries.

The bill was introduced in the Senate, where the government immediately lost control of the amending process to the special committee established to debate the bill. Aided by unprecedented obstruction on the part of the Socialists[110] as well as by the Council's decision of 25–26 June on the privatization bill,[111] the committee extensively rewrote the bill. In the end, it adopted 136 amendments,[112] often to the consternation of the government. In the National Assembly, the government restricted debate (by declaring article 49.3), but only after the Assembly's Cultural Affairs Committee had adopted another 70 amendments.[113]

Changes made in the bill's provisions on pluralism and antitrust are summarized in Table 7.2. The amending of article 3 was largely symbolic—affirmations by parliament that it recognized its duty to protect pluralism—and the result of political compromise. Amending article 29 was of greater importance since this article enumerated guidelines to be followed by the CNCL in its awarding of broadcast frequencies. In the government's bill, the protection of pluralism was listed as the third criterion (of four) to be taken into account in allocating such rights. But the bill did not specify that the protection of pluralism would take precedence over others. Parliament added two other considerations: (1) the CNCL was to oppose excessive concentration; and (2) the CNCL was to take into account limited advertising resources in any region, and strive to maintain a viable balance between the press and audiovisual sectors. Against a background of similar amendments sponsored by the opposition, the committees expressly appealed to the authority of the Constitutional Council in support of these changes.[114]

Two sets of antitrust provisions were established. The first forbade any one person from owning more than a 25 percent interest in any television channel, the violation of which would entail penal sanctions and heavy fines, to be imposed by judicial authorities. "In such a small market [as the present one], it is incontestable that the control by one person of one of these channels would confer, *ipso facto*, a 'dominant position,'"[115] explained the government. Such a ceiling also recognized the brutal economic reality that even the largest of French companies presently operating in press, publishing, or broadcasting would have difficulty raising the necessary capital to purchase a greater share (a fact later confirmed). The law would therefore have the effect of encouraging the formation of new multimedia groups and cooperative efforts among a wide range of industry heavyweights. The Senate, quoting the Council's 1984 press decision on the immunity to be afforded "existing situations," rewrote the article so that only *acquisition* of more than 25 percent could be controlled by the courts: "The will of the Council is extremely clear," stated the *rapporteur* for the bill in the Senate, "and we are looking to take that into account in our version."[116]

Table 7.2. The Making of the 1986 Audiovisual Bill: Provisions Concerning Media Pluralism

Government Bill	Senate Version	Assembly Version
*Art. 3: On the Mission of the CNCL**		
No mention of pluralism or antitrust.	The CNCL "assures free competition" and "encourages the pluralist expression of currents of opinion."	No change.
Art. 29: On Criteria for CNCL Authorization of Broadcasting Rights in a Geographical Zone which the CNCL Shall Determine; The CNCL Must Take into Account		
"The necessity to diversify ownership and to assure the pluralism of opinions."	"The necessity to diversify ownership and to assure the pluralism of *ideas* and opinions."	No change.
	"The necessity to avoid the abuses of dominant positions" [in the market, enjoyed by any operator].	The necessity to avoid the abuses of dominant positions "notably" in how advertising resources are divided, and with respect to both press and audiovisual communication.
Art. 39 and 41: Antitrust Provisions		
No one may "possess" more than 25% of the capital of a group in possession of TV broadcasting rights.	No one may "*acquire*" participation so as to raise their share to more than 25%" of the capital of a group in possession of TV broadcasting rights.	No change.
	(On radio broadcasting rights)	
A person already in possession of radio broadcasting rights may not obtain further rights if such authorization would lead to their serving a "potential audience" of more than 15 million inhabitants.	No change.	Clarified, no substantive changes.

The second set of antitrust provisions proved to be much less stable, enduring substantial change at every stage of the process. The notion of control provided in this part of the original bill was by now a familiar one—fixed market ceilings for audience. According to the original version, an operator of a radio station could only obtain subsequent licenses to broadcast if this new license would not expand the operator's potential audience above 15 million; if the station already served an audience greater than 15 million (the case for the quasi-national Europe 1 and Radio-Monte Carlo), its operators also could not obtain subsequent licenses. The same rules applied to operators of television channels. The opposition argued that since licenses were tied to regions (to be predetermined by the CNCL) and since no region contained more than 15 million inhabitants (the Paris region contains only 10 million), "the bill recognizes explicitly and overtly the possibility for one person to control a multi-media chain covering one or more regions," as well as the possibility of total monopoly *within* a region. The special committee in the

Table 7.2. (Continued)

Government Bill	Senate Version	Assembly Version
	(On TV broadcasting rights)	
A person already in possession of TV broadcasting rights may not obtain further rights if such authorization would lead to their serving a "potential audience" of more than 15 million inhabitants.	No substantive change.	Removed.
"The total potential audience is the sum of the population served by at least one station."	The total potential audience of one station is equal to the population which can receive its signals. The total potential audience of several stations is the sum total of the potential audience for each individual station (*committee version*).	Removed.
		Replaced by: A person possessing broadcasting rights in one region may not obtain further rights in the same region.

Commission nationale de la communication et des libertés (National Commission on Communication and Liberties).

NOTE: In its decision of 18 September 1986 *the Constitutional Council annulled articles 39 and 41* as unconstitutional and declared articles 28 to 31, which fix the mandate and functioning of the CNCL, nonpromulgable due to their inseparability from articles 39 and 41.

SOURCES: Text of government bill: *Rapport #402*, Senate, 1985–86. Senate changes: *Rapport #415*, Special Committee, Senate, 2 (19 June 1986): 68–69, 75–81; *Débats*, Senate, 1 July 1986, pp. 2140, 2155–157. Assembly changes: *Rapport #339*, Cultural Affairs, National Assembly, 1 (4 August 1986): 283–84, 297–300. The final text is at *Recueil des lois*, National Assembly, 1 (1986): 355–433.

Senate largely agreed, and rewrote the bill in order to ensure that a "potential audience" did not stop at the boundary of any geographical zone, but would instead be understood to comprise the entire population which could receive any given broadcast signals.[117] The National Assembly and the government objected, and removed this new definition of "potential audience," and with it a similar one governing television market shares. In the final version, operators licensed to broadcast in one "determined geographical zone" would not be able to obtain a second license within the same zone, but groups would not be discouraged from expanding horizontally into other zones as the broadcasting system expanded.

Given that the Council later agreed with the opposition's and the Senate's criticisms of these provisions, it is important to stress that their debate revealed a stubborn refusal on the part of the majority to add more detailed and complex rules. This was not due to lack of opportunity. The Council's amputation of the press bill came just as the audiovisual bill was being discussed in the National Assembly for the first time, and the debates became more heated as a result. This was so for a number of reasons. First, after the press decision, the government had decided to wage a scarcely veiled campaign of intimidation against the Council. As discussed in chapter 3, it was during this period that the minister of justice, Albin Chalandon, and the minister of culture, Léotard, began to complain that the Council possessed too much discretionary authority, and Chirac himself warned that a potential "government of judges" situation was developing.[118] Ministers let it be known that unspecified "institutional changes" might be initiated to deal with the problem.[119] Second, the Council had annulled article 11 of the press law in the following terms:

> The provisions of article 11—far from adjusting, as the legislature could have done, the modalities of protecting press pluralism, *and more generally, the means of communication which the press is one component*—do not protect its effective character [emphasis added].

Everyone took this pronouncement to be *an expression of the Council's wish that parliament elaborate a more comprehensive regime for the whole of the communications sector*.[120] One of the effects of this part of the decision was to arm the opposition in its attempts to juridicize the proceedings toward that end. Third, the Council's decision emboldened important elements within the majority, notably supporters allied with Raymond Barre (Barristes), to go on the offensive for stricter and more comprehensive antitrust provisions.[121] Both Barre and his associate, François d'Aubert (the Right's most outspoken advocate of tougher rules), hailed from Lyon, a region in which Hersant enjoyed a total press monopoly. Hersant, a undisguised anti-Barriste whose *Le Figaro* had been unmerciful in its attacks on Barre's anticohabitation stance, had already announced his candidacy for ownership of one of the three television channels to be made available (his group was eventaully awarded the channel[122]). The elaboration of the audiovisual law gave the center-Right an occasion to work concretely to limit Hersant's influence, but under the guise of constitutional politics.[123]

Debate in the National Assembly became increasingly dominated by considerations of the Constitutional Council's influence over the legislative process. The Socialist's leading spokesman, Jean-Jack Quéyranne, labeled by the majority "the *petit rapporteur* for the Constitutional Council," relied almost exclusively on elaborate discussions of what the Right characterized as the Socialists' "bible"—a "litany of Council jurisprudence."[124] The majority argued both that the bill was constitutional and that the legislature should not "curtail its own liberty to legislate" by excessive preoccupations with constitutionality.[125] The most remarkable protest against the Council's growing influence was voiced by the *rapporteur* for the bill, Péricard:

> As far as the Council is concerned, it is my duty as *rapporteur* to call attention to an evolution which appears worrisome to our institutional life. In several of its recent decisions—notably on the privatization bill and the reform of the press bill—the Council has tended to create, *ex nihilo*, constitutional principles which it then legitimizes by reference to "guaranteed public liberties." But its definition of the source of these liberties is made according to means which escape all rationality.

Queyranne's response to these remarks is worth recording:

> Since March 16 [the date of the 1986 legislative elections], the supreme judges
> have been visited by fantasy? I think that you are denouncing too fast what
> you have adored for the past 5 years.[126]

Because of the government's imposition of 49.3 during the bill's first reading
in the National Assembly, only those amendments emanating from the government could be debated or considered for adoption. In a last ditch attempt to
amend the bill, D'Aubert (As he put it, "inspired by prudence—we know what
the Council has imposed on us in matters concerning pluralism.") offered a series
of amendments which he asked the government to sponsor as its own.[127] Had
they been adopted, the bill might have been saved, since they would have had the
effect of treating the press sector, the audiovisual sector, advertising shares, and
fixed market ceilings as general problems requiring general solutions. The government refused, however, observers suggested, because variously it did not fully
understand its constitutional obligations, was committed to facilitating the acquisition of a television channel by Hersant, or because it felt that it had already
conceded too much. In any event, *Le Point* reported, Barristes were left mutter-
ing that the law was "too vague and too imprecise to make it past the Council."[128]

Deputies referred the bill to the Council on 18 August,[129] and asked the
Council to annul articles 39 and 41 on the grounds that nothing in them would
prohibit, first, any person from buying 25 percent of *each* private television
channel or, second, one broadcasting company from enjoying a monopoly in
one region while at the same time obtaining licenses which would allow it
national coverage. Thus, it would be possible for a company not only to obtain
national television coverage and to enjoy local monopolies, but also to control
interests—even pluralities of interest—in every other television channel.

After deliberating the full thirty days, the Council accepted these criticisms
as stated and annulled both articles. It also added a number of other criticisms
not mentioned by the referral, including the fact that the bill excluded long
wave radio frequencies from control, and did not attempt to limit a company's
possession of both television and radio licenses. Clearly, the Council had
hoped that parliament would construct a regime of broader scope, to regulate
in much more precise detail the *future* development of the industry. It then
made that point clearly: it appealed to article 34 of the Constitution (which
enumerates those legislative matters *exclusively* within the competence of
parliament and, thus, constitutes the most detailed expression of parliamentary sovereignty in the document) and turned that article on its head:

> Considering that in the terms of article 34 of the Constitution—"*La loi* fixes
> the rules concerning: . . . fundamental guarantees accorded to citizens in the
> exercise of their public liberties"; that due to the insufficiency of the rules laid
> down by articles 39 and 41 of the bill . . . the legislature has misused
> [*méconnu*, lit. "misunderstood"] its own competence with respect to article
> 34 of the Constitution; that because of this, and because of the the gaps in the
> bill, *there is a risk that situations of concentration will develop*, in particular
> in a given geographical region, *not only with respect to audiovisual commu-*

*nications, but likewise with respect to the whole of the communications
sector of which the audiovisual is an essential component* [emphasis added].

It then ruled that fourteen other articles were nonpromulgable on the basis of
their "inseparability" from articles 39 and 41. The most important of these were
four articles which fixed the mandate and functioning of the CNCL. These could
not be promulgated, according to the Council, because the CNCL, as presently
empowered "would not be in a position to adequately perform its constitutional
responsibility to limit concentrations in order to assure the respect for pluralism."
The Council then declared that the CNCL must "as a priority," be concerned
with "preserving the pluralistic expression of currents of opinion." Finally, with
respect to the abrogations or former law in the bill (necessary, for example to
create the CNCL, to abolish the High Authority, and to establish new rules) the
judges declared—for the third time since 1984—that it was not in their power "to
determine how the legislature would have meant to make such abrogations if the
latter had known in advance of these declarations of unconstitutionality." The
abrogations were therefore annulled, leaving the government with no choice but
to open a new legislative process to achieve its reform.

Implementing the Council's Media Policies: The Corrective Revision of the 1986 Press and Audiovisual Laws

The government chose to complete the amputated press and audiovisual laws
at the same time, in one bill. The corrective revision process which followed is
probably the most virulent and sustained exercise of Constitutional Council
bashing by politicians to date. Tempers were raised not least because the
Council's decision had thwarted a basic objective. "The legislature," the majority recalled,

> had not [desired] to regulate in advance a sector which was still only in an
> embryonic stage, preferring to leave it to the CNCL the care of first forging a
> pragmatic jurisprudence.[130]

But this, the Council had ruled, it could not do. If one accepts the government's
logic that a flexible regime was necessary "to encourage the emergence of
French communication groups capable of competing with foreign giants,"[131] the
decision might indeed "condemn France to an archaic position."[132] A second
reason for discontent was that the extensive rulings of inseparability had left
dormant crucial articles—those abolishing the CTPP and creating the CNCL,
for example—which could only be revived after the government had undergone
a successful revision process. The majority characterized this technique (in what
was an apt and popular phrase) as "more of *a taking of constitutional hostages*"
by "suspending the application of the law until the legislator has agreed to vote
new provisions which have in fact been dictated to it by the Council itself" than
"sound judicial argument."[133]

The government presented the bill to parliament as an "unwished for,"
"required text."[134] The government admitted that it felt obliged to allow the

Council "to take over the *a priori* elaboration of the law," and incorporated, often word-for-word, the express terms of the decisions.[135] While the opposition cheered this result, the parliamentary majority pressed the government to search for creative solutions to restore the orientations of the original law. The president of cultural affairs in the National Assembly, agreed with the deputies that simply "respecting the letter of the decisions" would constitute a "sterile solution" to the problem, but explained that the committee's work had been constrained in advance by the government:

> Confronted with the alternative of either following scrupulously the prescriptions of the Council, or preparing for the future and assuring a certain permanence to the rule of the law, the government preferred to protect itself against any future censure. But the other solution might have warranted exploration.[136]

Léotard responded in this way:

> The government has refused to consider any proposals which might exacerbate the conflict between the legislature and the Council. . . . It is indeed regrettable that parliament is now led to legislate under the injunction of the Council, and that the incessant speculations about the Council's decisions can only succeed in paralyzing our lawmaking bodies.[137]

"Henceforth, Léotard told the Senate later, "the legislature legislates in the shadow of the Council."[138]

The Senate, protesting what it called an "affront" to the "rights of parliament," voted 222–91 to reject the bill by *quéstion préalable.*[139] The move was explained in committee in this way:

> Might the adoption of such a motion be taken as a repudiation of the government? In no way, since this bill is only formally of governmental origin. Its true author is not the government but the Council. If one must see repudiation in this motion, it is directed at the decision of the Council.
>
> Let us be understood. Your committee is not declaring that the Council has shown [partisan] partiality. . . . We state simply that, since 1971, and continually thereafter, the Council has developed its powers, irrespective of who has constituted parliamentary majorities and governments.
>
> Where are we today? The Council no longer is content with judging the conformity of a bill with a written constitutional norm known to all; it elaborates as it goes along, according to its needs, the constitutional bases from which it will block the promulgation of bills. To do so, it needs only create . . . "constitutional principles."
>
> Are we moving toward a Government of Judges, as we hear said and see written sometimes? After having believed that it would be impossible until recently to validly employ this expression, . . . your committee is, alas, obliged to state that the decision of September 18 [on the audiovisual law] shows how the Council can itself become the legislator.
>
> It does so, first, in interpreting the bill which has been submitted to it and finding within it the "intention of the legislature" which nothing in the *travaux préparatoires* would suggest. But second, and especially, it does so in

suspending the application of the law until the legislature has agreed to adopt new provisions dictate by the Council itself.

These considerations have led your committee to propose to the Senate to move a *quéstion préalable* whose adoption would be more rich in significance than the pursuit of debate limited by this sword of Damocles suspended above our heads.[140]

The new law contained eight articles, each designed to reinsert provisions amputated by the Council. In some cases the rewriting of these provisions was substantial. The most dramatic example is that of article 41 of the audiovisual law (antitrust): in the initial rendition, the article contained barely 200 words; revised, it contained more than 2,200. Only the most important changes are listed in Table 7.3.

An Assessment

Legislative reform of the press and audiovisual regimes from 1984 to 1986 confirm the general points made about French constitutional politics in my assessment of the 1982 nationalization decision (see chapter 6). The particular

Table 7.3. Corrective Revision of the 1986 Press and Audiovisual Laws

---

For the Audiovisual Bill:

*The future functioning of the CNCL was recast by a series of insertions into the law specifying that the commission would operate with "an imperative priority to safeguard the pluralism of currents of sociocultural expression, and the necessity to avoid the abuses of dominant positions."

*Article 39 was rewritten so that any person already in possession of a 15 to 25 percent interest in a television channel could not legally acquire more than 15 percent of any other channel; any person already in possession of less than 5 to 15 percent in two or more channels could not acquire more than 5 percent in another.

*Article 41 was transformed into a general anticoncentration regime governing the whole of multimedia communications. Elaborate and technical, highlights include: the inclusion of detailed provisions treating long wave radio, and satellite and cable broadcasting; the tightening of the meaning of ownership (in the direction of the 1984 press law) notably with explicit reference to the notion of corporate (group) ownership; the redefinition of national and regional broadcast zones in such a way as make it impossible for television or radio companies to acquire new licenses once they had exceeded certain audience levels. Finally, *the technique of using fixed ceilings to regulate concentration was expanded to all of communications with respect to the creation and expansion of multimedia groups.* According to this part of article 41, a group could not possess more than two of the following four operations, defined as national: (1) of a television channel serving more than 4 million; (2) of a radio frequency serving more than 30 million; (3) of a cable station serving more than 6 million; or, (4) of the publishing of daily newspapers accounting for 20 percent of the total national distribution of all newspapers. Similar such rules are fixed for regional groups.

For the Press Bill:

*Article 11 was rewritten to forbid the use of front organizations and other legal personalities from making acquisitions for existing press groups. The language adopted was essentially that used by the Socialists in the 1984 press bill (which the Right had vehemently opposed).

SOURCE: The final bill is at *Journal officiel* (*Lois . . .*) 28 November 1986, pp. 14297–4300.

interest inherent in the media pluralism decisions, however, derives from the unprecedented intensity of legislative–Council interaction concentrated in a short period of time. The Constitutional Council was asked to intervene on the issue of pluralism on three occasions in less than two years. It thus had the opportunity to structure successive legislative processes, rare until very recently. The cases provide the analyst with an opportunity to observe and evaluate the *cumulative* impact of constitutional review on reform politics. Most important, these case studies demonstrate that the Council's impact on policy outcomes is far greater than that of the "negative legislator" of French doctrinal authority. The Council not only exercised its veto authority over important legislative priorities, but it also demonstrated its capacity to recast the policymaking environment, to encourage certain legislative solutions while undermining others, and to have the precise terms of its jurisprudence written into legislative provisions. The Council's policymaking powers can be creative and transformative.

Two generalizations can be made concerning the Council's impact. First, *lines of jurisprudence*—that is, multiple decisions on a given cluster of related pieces of legislation—*result in ongoing restrictions of legislative discretion and the emergence of concrete Council policy*. One curious effect of this restriction is that legislative outcomes may have little relationship to initial policy objectives. The virtual *constitutionalization* of antitrust mechanisms based on fixed market ceilings is a dramatic example. The Socialists settled on fixed ceilings because it viewed them as an effective tool with which to dismantle the Hersant press group. The Council's decision not only thwarted legislative intent, but had the perverse effect of freezing Hersant's dominance. Once in power, the Chirac government and much of the Right, virulently opposed to fixed ceilings in principle, were then unsuccessful in eradicating them in their reform of the press regime. That government was then obliged to extend much more complex and multidimensional ceilings to the whole of communications, in spite of the fact that one central priority of its programmatic agenda was to allow the emerging audiovisual sector to develop free from such shackles. *The antitrust formulas now prevalent in this area*—certainly not the only ones imaginable, nor the only means of protecting pluralism imaginable—*have acquired a kind of indirect constitutional value of their own*. This result can only be understood by taking into account constitutional politics, by taking into account the Council's positive policymaking powers.

Second, *complex rulings of inseparability, as in the nationalization case, lead to Council-written legislation*. That is, governments would rather secure constitutionality by mechanically copying the terms of Council decisions into new, revised bills than to search for more imaginative solutions. (Governments *could* decide to explore alternative means, but they do not. Doctrine and probably the Council itself has underestimated the extent to which governments are willing to go to avoid the risk of a second censure. The Council has sought to force legislators to legislate again by handing down rulings of inseparability in conjunction with the annulment of legislative abrogations. The result, peculiar on its face, has been that its pronouncements have simply generated new law.) In a colorful phrase, the majority characterized the decision on the audiovisual law as a "taking of constitutional hostages," since the decision suspended effective functioning of the CNCL and stayed the abolition of the *Haute autorité*. The same could have been said of the decisions on the 1982 nationalization and the 1986 press laws, since the Council made policy implementation impossible until its policy choices had been written into legislation.

These points focus attention on the nature of the Constitutional Council's pedagogical role in the legislative process. As discussed in chapter 4, the analytical separation of jurisprudential from legislative outcomes often serves the disciplinary needs of academic lawyers, and probably of the Council itself. But such a separation also serves to distort—unacceptably in my view—French constitutional politics. Since 1971, all "great decisions" have been annulments of legislation. Leading decisions have another common trait: they extend the Council's control over legislative activity by bestowing constitutional status upon principles whose status had until then been ambiguous or controversial.

From a lawmaker's perspective, *jurisprudence attaches to the 1958 constitution as an unfolding, extraconstitutional modification of article 34 of that document.* Lawmakers have an interest in taking seriously these modifications in order to avoid future annulments. The capacity for the Council's jurisprudence to perform a pedagogical function is thus potentially great, but it is largely contingent on the quality of the flow of communication from legislature to Council, and vice-versa. Leading decisions are unpredictable by their very nature. Such decisions destabilize beliefs about legislative competence; they also arm the opposition in its efforts to juridicize future reform processes. As a result, the legislative dilemma—how best to achieve a policy objective while avoiding constitutional censure—may be deepened by a leading decision. However, jurisprudence building on earlier leading decisions would presumably be more predictable if lawmakers received the right signals and knew how to interpret them.

In the case of media pluralism the Council had to strain a great deal to extend its authority. The notions of press and media pluralism are mentioned in no constitutional text—not in article 11 (1789) or in the press law of 1881 (if considered a FPRLR and therefore replete with *valeur constitutionnel*), or in the constitutional proper. Politicians had appealed to a number of texts and general principles of law in order to ground, in what they hoped would be constitutionally compelling manner, their discussion of "press pluralism." The Left had sought to justify antitrust regulation as a means of protecting freedom of expression, understood as the rights of the public to access information; the Right had asserted that the same freedom could tolerate no state regulation of any kind. The Council's solution was to create an entirely new category of constitutional principle binding on legislators—the specific "constitutional objective" deduced from a more general, written principle.

Legal specialists have emphasized, as a means of legitimizing the Council's expanding control in this area and of defending the Council from the criticisms recounted, the essential "coherence" and predictability of the jurisprudence. Favoreu and Philip, in their commentary on the 1984 decision in the leading case book on the Council's most important rulings, devote only one short line to the decision on the 1986 press law (and none to the audiovisual decision), declaring that the Council "confirmed its jurisprudence."[141] Georges Vedel, in a recent assessment of his nine years on the Council (1980–89), had this to say:

> All that the Council had formulated in its decision on the freedom of the press with respect to the *loi Fillioud* in 1984 was literally reaffirmed with respect to the *loi Léotard* after the 1986 alternance. Censure and approval applied in the first case with the Left's bill, and in the second case with the Right's bill, but we held the same course. ... I therefore truly felt the comforting sentiment, as a jurist, that the construction of constitutional review is not a work of fantasy. It rests, in France, upon certain texts (not only the constitution but also the 1789 declaration and the 1946 preamble) which have an objective and permanent value. Moreover, during this same period, we did not fall into a "government of judges" situation. Contrary to what at times the U.S. Surpreme Court and the German constitutional court have done, we refused to invoke principles flowing from the political or moral philosophy held by the judges and not found in the text.[142]

If we accept for argument's sake that media pluralism has always possessed an objective constitutional value binding on lawmakers, that is, is not merely a confection of the Council, these declarations of coherence certainly have the merit of making an obvious point: namely, that the Council on three occasions has ruled that the principle of media pluralism is possessed of constitutional status. Stated differently, the Council did not reverse itself by stripping pluralism of its status.

However, the Vedel and Favoreu and Philip assertions of coherence beg an important question. If the jurisprudence is coherent, why were lawmakers, not to mention their legal advisors, unable to adopt laws conforming to it? One could argue, as many doctrinal commentators do, that politicians will regularly act on their always latent "liberticidal" tendencies unless constrained by *le droit*. But one might also argue that the source of the problem is the Council's tendency to extend boldly its field of reference, and thus its future control, without at the same time communicating precisely enough the legislative consequences of that extension. *The affirmation and reaffirmation that pluralism is a constitutional objective which legislation must protect can not of itself communicate something of practical value to politicians.* Coherence at this level of abstraction—far from the *details* of proposed attempts to enhance and defend the objective—is crude at best. Such coherence had an impact: each decision made the problem of pluralism increasingly more salient and controversial politically, and each guaranteed that the incessant talk about the problem begun in late 1983 would not diminish. But it did not provide legislators with solutions to their dilemma.

Let us look at the examples contained in this chapter. In the 1984 decision, the Council ruled that press pluralism was not then threatened and then forbade application of the law's antitrust provisions to "existing situations." It apparently arrived at this conclusion without reference to any objective criteria. In fact, the crucial questions of how much concentration in the industry would constitute a threat to pluralism, or how such a determination could be made, were never addressed. We know only that at least five members of the Constitutional Council had agreed that this point had not yet been reached, and that they voted to overrule the contrary opinion expressed by the government and parliament. Nevertheless, the 1984 decision seemingly contained a number of rules which might have aided future governments in future efforts to reform communications regimes. Doctrinal commentators on the 1984 decision were exercised, *above all else*, by the Council's seeming consecration of the ratchet effect, to the extent of seeing in it the beginnings of a "construction of a general theory of fundamental rights" binding on legislators.[143]

In 1986, the Constitutional Council was asked by the Socialists to strike down the Right's press reform on the grounds that the Right had forced the ratchet back. This request could hardly have surprised the Council. Given that the ratchet effect was generated by the Council's own examination of the fixed ceilings contained in the 1984 press law, it might be hard to imagine a case where its application would be more appropriate than the 1986 undoing of those same ceilings. The Council did rule that the antitrust provisions in the 1986 law were inadequate, but it did not rely on this jurisprudential precedent. Indeed, the judges again articulated no preexisting, knowable, guiding principle to justify their ruling; and they did not inform us as to why one such rule— the ratchet effect—did not, could not, or should not apply to the case at hand. As with that part of the 1984 decision assessing the existing state of press pluralism, the judges apparently did not arrive at their conclusion by a process any more inherently "judicial"—if understood as decisions bound by legal reasoning and precedent—than processes which other policymakers and interested observers had gone through to reach *their* opinion on the matter. The Council's opinion is just one of many contending assessments of media pluralism and of how best to protect it.

Commentators have not clarified the matter. Pépy, one of the few to take the issue head on, has argued that "the ratchet effect is not applicable to the regime governing the liberty of the press," because the Council was forced to "reconcile the principles of press pluralism . . . with the *liberté d'entreprendre* guaranteed to publishers."[144] This argument is not compelling. First, it was the Council which applied the ratchet effect rule to the press sector in the first place. And it did so freely—petitioners did not request it. Second, *the Council*, in its discussion of why the antitrust provisions contained in the 1986 law were unconstitutional, *makes no mention of the right to free enterprise or to any other property right*. Pépy's assertion is guesswork; but it is not confirmed by the terms of the Council's decision.

In the end, the Right was censured and forced to revise its press law. But this was perhaps a small price to pay: by refusing to be bound by the opposition's reliance on the ratchet effect, the majority was able to abolish the distinction between national and regional papers, and to raise the fixed ceilings in such a way as to legalize the situation of the Hersant press group. If the legal experts employed by the opposition to juridicize the process and to write referrals get the applicable constitutional law wrong, how can it be expected that the government would somehow get it right? In the end, no pedagogical authority over legislative processes issued from the 1984 reading or inheres in this line of cases. And in the end, the Council was led to impose, by the constitutional equivalent of brute force, solutions to legislative problems it had itself created.

The media pluralism cases reveal the extent to which the "pacification" thesis proffered by the Council's supporters misses the mark. According to Professor Favoreu's identification of the "juridicized parliament" as the "pacified parliament" (discussed in chapter 4), partisan "fevers," which had mounted during the parliamentary process, fall after the Council renders its decision; there is then no further constitutional conflict about the bill examined.[145] This is especially true, he argues, after a decision on a controversial bill. One would expect, according to the dictates of Favoreu's thesis, that a succession of Council interventions on a sensitive and highly visible political issue would lead to gradual if not total pacification of that issue. This certainly did not occur. The 1986 corrective revision processes examined here shows the extent to which the Council's decisions can create new controversy, not only about the bill in question, but about the role of the Council itself. Indeed, I would argue that the case studies presented here and elsewhere constitute a crucial case study test and lead to a number of opposite conclusions. The null hypotheses, that: (1) partisan "passions" fall naturally both after a bill is promulgated and *especially* when the Council is *not* petitioned for a ruling; and (2) the Council may at times raise new "partisan fevers," are much more compelling than is the pacification thesis. The Council's jurisprudence served to juridicize debates after the 1986 *alternance*, but it also served to implicate the Council in the growing politicization of the issue. The juridicization–politicization dichotomy is a fiction. Empirical study shows, again and again, that juridicized legislative battles are not, other things being equal, more "passive," less political, or less "partisan" for being waged in constitutional terms. *What is new—* and this is the essence of juridicization—*is that the constitutional text is now often a site of partisan conflict.* Parliament can be said to be juridicized, but not therefore pacified.

Finally, these studies shed some light on another important macropolitical aspect of the evolution of French constitutional politics. By the end of 1985, the Constitutional Council's role in the legislative process had expanded, matured, even become banal, as a result of five years of intense activity following the first *alternance*. The first few months of the second *alternance* obliterated what little remained of what was once an axiom of French political life—that the Council, created and staffed by the Right, could therefore only serve the interests of the Right. Attacks on the Council during the *cohabitation* period were unprecedented, by virtue of their extraordinary intensity and by the fact that they emanated from the highest officials in the Chirac government. Péricard expressed the general opinion held by the Right:

> The decisions [on the 1986 press and audiovisual laws] have led to a phenomenon without precedent: legislators are forced to legislate by taking into account the warnings dispensed by the Constitutional Council. . . .[146]

Of course, the phenomenon was not without precedent: the Socialists had struggled with exactly the same problem for the previous five years. Had the Right suddenly developed collective amnesia? Perhaps. More likely, such protests are best understood as symptomatic of a painful process of adjustment. In 1986, the policymaking environment to which the Right returned was not the same one it had given up in 1981. The Constitutional Council had transformed it.

8

The Third Chamber Model: A Review and Defense

The study and understanding of the political behavior and impact of the Constitutional Council is infirmed by the fact that the body's deliberations and votes are formally secret, and by a scholarly tradition which is formalist, restrictive in scope, and ideologically committed. Consequently, perspectives and methods developed and employed by political scientists in studies of courts and their impact on political systems elsewhere cannot be or have not been applied to the French case. Study of the Council's behavior instead overwhelmingly consists of traditional doctrinal work and in efforts at institutional legitimation. Part II of this book shows that one fruitful alternative to legalism and to polemics is to focus on the Council's role in the legislative process. By doing so, the institution's concrete impact can be observed and measured. Indeed, political scientists can and ought to conceive of the Council as a third legislative chamber. I do not mean by this that constitutional judges necessarily desire lawmaking powers or that they make law according to the same criteria as do parliamentarians. It is to assert, at the very least, that abstract, a priori constitutional review and the evolution of French constitutional politics have combined to bestow upon the Council legislative powers. These powers it uses all of the time.

When the Constitutional Council annuls a bill entirely or amputates sections from legislation which it otherwise allows to be promulgated, this authority is clearly a veto power. The annulment of the provisions governing press pluralism in the 1984 press law is a clear example of such veto authority; yet, it is no less legislative for being negative. Moreover, constitutional judges can create new law, that is, they can *produce* policy outputs. This occurs most often when, in resignation, governments and parliamentarians feel obliged to copy the exact terms of Council jurisprudence into "revised" or "corrected" bills after an annulment. Examples are the 1982 revision of the compensation formula of the Socialist's nationalization law, and the 1986 revisions of the press and audiovisual bills. It also occurs when the Council enunciates binding SROI, as it did in the 1986 privatization affair. As important, I have shown that the Council's *indirect* impact on the policy process yields outcomes which meaningfully differ from those which would have resulted absent constitutional review.

Chapters 6 and 7 examined what were arguably the most high profile and controversial "grand reforms" of the 1980s, focusing attention on the Council's role as a salient policymaker. By extending such research, we would be able to further disaggregate Council impact. Theoretically, each policy area manifests its own dynamic of constitutional possibility and constraint conforming to the development and extension of constitutional control. Debate is more or less juridicized as a function of this variation. Moreover, initial research shows that the perceived legitimacy of constitutional review also appears to vary across issue area, but for different reasons. This point deserves to be explored further given the polemics which have accompanied the expansion of the Council's legislative role.

In August and September 1986, the Council rendered five decisions on a series of bills (the *lois Pasquas*) which together constituted one of the central planks of the Right's platform: the tightening of the penal codes.[1] The government's sought to restrict the rights of accused, lengthen sentencing requirements for certain crimes, and to relax regulations restricting the discretion and powers of the police and security forces. The process by which these bills became law illustrates again the extent to which anticipatory reactions triggered by fear of future censure—can alter legislative process and outcome (the *autolimitation* effect). Crucial to this result was the fact that by 1986 the Council had largely "constitutionalized" penal law: that is, its pre-1986 rulings on legislative amendments of the penal codes added up to a relatively coherent and knowable jurisprudence.[2]

At first resistant to compromise, the Chirac government allowed the reforms to be gradually but substantially rewritten. Left to a small group within parliament, each bill was discussed with regard to its constitutionality and to relevant Council decisions. Deputies involved possessed advanced legal training, and tended to see the exercise as a technical one, relatively, but not completely, divorced from partisan concerns. One deputy aptly characterized the *autolimitation* process which developed as an exercise in "judicial pointillism"[3]: the deliberate, almost bipartisan effort to rewrite and improve the texts line-by-line, point-by-point with respect to constitutional jurisprudence. Changes made were important, such as those which extended to the accused rights to counsel, or to the convicted certain rights of appeal. The most partisan wrangling occurred over which side would be able to claim credit for these changes: the Socialists regularly charged that the Right was stealing its amendments, and undaunted, the majority "rejoiced" that there was "such a convergence of views."[4] In a striking example, Michel Sapin (Socialist) congratulated the majority on its good sense after the 1986 law expanding police powers to demand personal identification cards was amended to the Socialist's—and later to the Council's—satisfaction. This led to the following revealing but not uncommon exchange:

SAPIN: From the first examination of the bill in committee, we emphasized . . . that if you had refused to modify your position [by accepting a
Socialist amendment] on this point, your text would be unconstitutional.

JEAN-LOUIS DEBRÉ: Mr. Sapin claims authorship a little too easily. Let's
just say that there is a confusion about paternity.

BERNARD DÉROSIER: We would need a blood test. . . .[5]

In the end, the bills came out far less draconian than the ones promised. The
Council even expressed its appreciation of the effort: in the text of its decision
of 26 August 1986, it cited with approval "the role conferred on judicial
authority [i.e., judges] contained in an amendment adopted requiring the
police to obtain judicial approval before photographing and fingerprinting
subjects."[6] The legislation was referred to the Council, and the latter did annul
provisions contained in two of the bills. But the annulments were minor
matters, and there was *no* reported political reaction to them.

Politicians largely accept that constitutional control over penal law, at
least, is legitimate, even healthy. This appears the case even for highly politicized and controversial legislation. The leading decision—on the Barre government's security and liberty bill for example—was the very first Council ruling
on what was, unquestionably, a "*grande réforme*."[7] Although the bill was the
subject of violent debate within parliament, within doctrinal circles, and in the
press, and although a large number of provisions were annulled on the grounds
that they violated constitutional principles of due process and judicial procedure, neither the government nor its parliamentary supporters protested the
decision. In fact, in striking contrast to many of the decisions reviewed here,
none of the Council's dozen decisions on revisions of penal law have provoked
protests or charges of usurpation.

I believe that this is so because the penal codes have long been inspired by
principles already enshrined in parliamentary work, that is, in code law. Many
of these principles, such as nonretroactivity of laws, equality under the law,
and elements of due process, are contained in the 1789 Declaration of the
Rights of Man. *But unlike other principles contained in that document, such as
the "inalienable right to property," the 1789 principles relating to penal law
had long been enshrined and extended in the codes.* As important, they have
long been accepted by both the Right and the Left. Neither side views them as
partisan possessions or contaminated by ideological bias. Thus, *when the
Council "constitutionalized" these principles (by asserting their superlegislative
status), it also constitutionalized a consensus, one which had existed before the
Council was born, and one which had largely inspired, in concrete ways, the
work of the legislature.* This is one area then where it may even be said that
Council control of penal matters is viewed by politicians as functioning to aid—
and not to subvert—the legislature's desire to strike a proper balance between
the rights of the accused and the State's interest in assuring "law and order."

In any event, disputes which arise during legislative attempts to revise these
codes are "legal" disputes relatively narrowly defined (which is not to deny that

they are politically significant). This must be contrasted with the sorts of disputes which have given rise to attacks on the Council. When the Council reviews legislation enabling nationalizations, establishing antitrust regulations, redrawing electoral boundaries, and so on, it is on very different ground, one less amenable to "constitutionalization." In these areas, the Council is forced to pass judgment on what are for politicians first and foremost disputes not about constitutional law but about policy and ideology. As former Council member, Luchaire, wrote in *Le Monde* as the country awaited the Council's decision on nationalizations:

> Apart from the legal debate, it is true that the nationalization pose a problem of societal choice; [the Council] must choose between the individualist and property-oriented philosophy of the 18th century and the economic and social principles which according to the preamble of 1946 are particularly necessary for our times. It is a political choice. The judge must make it; he cannot make it less political.[8]

In French constitutional politics, policy disputes are transformed into constitutional disputes, by oppositions who wish to see the majority's policies vetoed or watered down.

The Council Conceptualized as a Third Chamber

Whether politically controversial or not, the Council's concrete impact is entirely legislative in nature. Its review authority is limited exclusively to *parliamentary* space; the effects of its decision attend *only* legislation and the legislative process. In this formal sense, statutory sovereignty was not overthrown by the introduction of constitutional review into France in 1958. In the Third and Fourth Republics, all legislation duly passed by parliament was promulgated without obstacle. The founders of the Fifth Republic, however, added another step to the legislative process, requiring some bills to be approved by the Council before they acceded to sovereign status. Put somewhat differently, every Council decision forms part of, attaches itself to, controlled legislation. Constitutional jurisprudence is nothing more or less than the lasting, written record of a third reading by a third institution required to give its assent on a bill before promulgation. What impact the Council does have outside of legislative space is informal, indirect, and derived from the fact that the Council is a partner of parliament in lawmaking, and from the fact that ordinary and administrative courts are bound by *la loi*. It should not surprise, therefore, that the administrative courts of the *Conseil d'Etat* accept the *effects* of a Council decision—as they must accept all legislative outcomes—but *not* the Council's argumentation or interpretive authority. The Council's jurisprudence is, at least until now, part and parcel of the legislative process, and no part of that process, save the result as enshrined in statute, binds the courts.

In a recent paper entitled "The Myth of the Government of Judges," the leading French specialist on the Council, Louis Favoreu, presented five reasons "why the Constitutional Council is not a third chamber."[9] It should be noted that Professor Favoreu defines a "third chamber" as a "political organ": that which possesses "a power of judgment and decision-making identical to that possessed by parliament." The phrase was first iterated by the Council in its 1975 abortion decision, and was repeated word-for-word in several important decisions rendered in the 1980s, when it declared that its review authority

> does not confer upon the Constitutional Council a general power of judgment and of decision-making identical to that possessed by parliament.[10]

Favoreu therefore appeals to the Council's own language to clinch the argument.[11] This claim notwithstanding, Favoreu's argument invites debate because it successively introduces additional criteria for comparing the Council to a legislative chamber. These five reasons are listed as follows along with my response:

1. "The Constitutional Council does not examine . . . all of the laws adopted by parliament."

   —A comparison of the total number of laws adopted with the number of laws referred to the Constitutional Council is irrelevant in the context of this discussion. A majority of laws are only of narrow technical interest, take up practically none of the time and resources of the average parliamentarian, and/or involve no substantial debate or the exercising of "powers of judgment." In qualitative terms, however, nearly all major pieces of legislation since 1981, and every budget since 1974, has been referred to the Council, a fact which Professor Favoreu otherwise celebrates as evidence of juridicization. If referrals had not become systematic in the 1981–87 period, then Favoreu would not have been able to argue that the Council was able to legitimate new governments, or that juridicization led to a pacification of parliament (chapters 4, 6, 7).

2. "The Constitutional Council can not convene itself."

   —If all third chambers must be self-activating, then the Council is not a third chamber by the sole virtue of restrictive definition. However, if such a definition were to be accepted, we might not be able to include the House of Commons or the National Assembly in a list of parliamentary chambers. Neither is self-activating, and for the same reasons. Both are nearly archetypal examples of what Polsby calls "arena legislatures," to be contrasted with "transformative legislatures": the former does not legislate, but instead formally enacts and thus legitimates policy choices made by the executive; the latter (the U.S. Congress) legislates free from formal outside control.[12] In both the British and French cases, governments dictate legislative agendas: parliament cannot determine for itself what it may debate or when. Although members of Parliament and deputies may initiate bills, actual discussion on them is dependent on prior government agreement or approval. In normal circumstances, neither chamber has the power to pass laws or to adopt amendments over the government's objection, and governments have wide-ranging, constitutionally derived powers to turn lower houses into mere voting machines, ratifying its policy choices. Finally, governments can get by without upper house approval because the latter's veto authority is merely suspensive, that is, a veto may be overturned by a simple majority vote in the lower house. The Council, on the other hand, is the *only* institution having impact on legislation whose policy preferences the government can neither ignore, nor reverse, nor quash (which, of course, accounts for its popularity with the opposition).

3. "The Constitutional Council does not have the liberty of choice of a political assembly, because its decisions are motivated and rest on a jurisprudence: the accumulation of precedent, and the following of a path known to all, limit considerably the margin of manoeuvre of the constitutional judge."

   —Again, while no one claims that the Constitutional Council is "identical" to the National Assembly, it does possess and exercise *discretionary* powers which can be called legislative. As the decisions on the Socialists' nationalization and press bills show, when the Council is ruling for the first time on a given legislative issue area or where the accumulated jurisprudence is thin, the Council enjoys a huge "margin of maneuver." At these times, the Council's "path," as the preceding case studies sufficiently demonstrate, is certainly not "known to all," if anyone. As important, parliament does not make law in total liberty either. In the context of the juridicization phenomenon, legislators too must make "motivated" decisions, are limited by rules and precedents, and make decisions on the constitutionality of legislation. Furthermore, many of these rules and precedents have been created and are policed by the Council.

   In policymaking terms, the statement that parliament has greater "liberty of choice" than does the Council does not stand up to empirical scrutiny. Exceptions are easily found: one need only measure the concrete impact of the respective institutions on any given legislative process. It is an empirically verifiable fact, for example, that the Council's impact on the 1982 nationalization law, the 1984 press law, and on many other reforms, far outweighed that of the National Assembly or the Senate; that is, the Council amendments to these government bills were more extensive and significant than were parliament's amendments. This should not shock. In the context of the "rationalized" parliament, the Council's role will at times be far greater than that of the two chambers of parliament. The primary function of an arena legislature is to legitimize, not to legislate.

4. "There is not really, within the Constitutional Council, a majority and a minority which corresponds to political cleavages and votes together in most of the decisions."

   —While containing a piece of potentially interesting, privileged, but impossible to verify information on the political dynamics of the Council, the argument can easily be pushed to absurd results. If the House of Commons one day ceased to contain a fixed opposition, if the Bundestag no longer reflected German political cleavages, or if the National Assembly adopted a law in quasi-unanimity, would each institution be less than a legislative chamber? There are, in fact, many laws which pass through the National Assembly without dissent. Some 80 percent of Italian laws are adopted in legislative committees unanimously, and *90 percent of all German laws are passed unanimously upon final reading*.[13] Even if we agreed, for argument's sake, that the Council behaved more as a court than as a legislator, *why should we presume that the Council is different from every other collegial judicial body in the world?* From non-French experience, we know that judges do agree to rule unanimously, especially on minor matters, and that sometimes they achieve greater consensus by intrachamber bargaining and compromise before rendering their decision. But we also know that patterns of voting are identifiable, and that in certain issue areas majority and minority factions do develop and do regularly vote together.

5. "The Constitutional Council does not have the last word: the political powers can bypass its decisions . . . by amending the constitution in the Constitutional Congress or by referendum."

—This is certainly true, but the same applies *equally* to all legislative powers. Any law may be abrogated or amended at some point, by some method. Such changes in law are really not "last words" at all, but are formally and conceptually wholly separate acts, with their own legislative histories. They should not be confused with what had been decided before. *The Council's word in any legislative process in which it is asked to intervene is sovereign*, and that is why Professor Favoreu celebrates the fact that "*a priori* constitutional control such as it is practiced in France" is possessed of "complete efficacy."[14]

In many countries, students of judicial politics—and even judges—have largely accepted that courts can at times behave as third chambers, and that the boundaries between judicial decision making and lawmaking are not absolute. The American judge, Learned Hand, once noted (in his 1958 Holmes lectures at Harvard University) that the distinction is almost an impossibly blurred one:

> I cannot frame any definition that will explain when the Court will assume the role of a third chamber and when it will limit its authority to keeping Congress and the states within their accredited authority. Nevertheless, I am quite certain that it has not abrogated the former function.[15]

As is the case with all constitutional courts in the world, the Council too can function as a third legislative chamber. I believe it does so continually.

Few if any doctrinal authorities in France are willing to admit publicly that the Council makes law. In fact, the question is either not directly posed or simply swept away in a flurry of unsubstantiated assertions. This is, again, the result of a scholarly community which almost instinctively labors to insulate law from politics, and has great difficulty recognizing that judicial interpretation exists, or if it does, that is in part a creative act. As Merryman writes of the civil law tradition generally:

> . . . the mass of scholarship on interpretation in civil law countries . . . is in part an uneasiness over the fact that courts are interpreting statutes, in part an expression of anxiety that they will abuse their power of interpretation; only a small proportion of it focuses on the actual process of interpretation. Many writers have sought to prove that judicial interpretation is not really in conflict with legislative supremacy and a strict separation of powers.[16]

These tendencies may be more understandable in scholarship on the work of ordinary and administrative courts, because judges sitting on these courts are formally bound to the terms of the legal codes. Legal scholars specializing on constitutional law continue to be trained in the administrative law tradition, and thus bring to their doctrinal activity these same attitudes. This orthodoxy, which may yield doctrinal benefits narrowly conceived, is inadequate to the task of examining and assessing judicial politics broadly conceived. The French constitution is not like the civil or penal codes, and cannot be said to constrain judges or to bound interpretation in the same way; after all, the constitution, as it has developed since 1971, is almost entirely the creation of the jurisprudence of the Constitutional Council. As important, the Council's activity, unlike those of other courts, may never be separated from the activity of primary policymakers.[17]

Guy Carcassonne, a law professor who wrote all of the referrals for the Socialist party during the 1986–88 period, wrote in 1988 that the Council "has *never crossed the line which would make it a third chamber*, imposing its will on the other two chambers" [emphasis added].[18] What is of interest in Carcassonne's claim is the implicit recognition that the Council *could* cross this line, although neither Carcassonne nor any other legal scholar ever tells us where this line is drawn or how we might know when the Council has crossed it. Several points should be made in response. First, there is nothing in the Council's constitutional mandate to stop it from crossing that line. The constitution has proved to be quite elastic, and to contain a great number of unwritten provisions which were only known after the Council rendered a decision. Second, Carcassonne's statement is untrue on its face. Exceptions to it include every total annulment handed down by the Council, as well as Council "amputations" of important provisions constituting legislative intent (as when it removed and rewrote the anti-Hersant provisions contained in the 1984 press law). For constitutional review to be effective, anywhere, the institution which exercises it must be able to impose its will on other institutions; and if total annulments do not constitute such an imposition, no act of the Council or any supreme court could. Finally, the statement flies in the face of political reality. The Socialists hired Carcassonne in 1986–87, and the Senate majority has long engaged Favoreu, to write referrals precisely because they hope that these law professors can convince the Council to "impose its will on the other two chambers."

Politicians—and not only those frustrated with constitutional politics— think of the Council as a third chamber and employ variations on the metaphor constantly. One parliamentary supporter of constitutional review and of the Council, Pierre Pascallon, writing in the influential *Revue politique et parlementaire* in 1986, described the Council's evolution as a gradual transformation "into a *3rd chamber of 'appeal'* [for parliamentarians] . . . , or better, a kind of *second parliament* adding, on its own, to the content of legislation, and dictating the conduct of the first parliament" [emphases added].[19] Later that same year, Jacques Toubon called the Council "a new kind of legislator" and "a parliament of judges."[20] The very notion of a parliament of judges underlines how ambiguous is the Council's place in classic separation of powers schemes. A classically trained public lawyer—in France as much as in America—might rail at such characterizations, at such a "confusion of powers," but the confusion is a genetic one—the Council was born that way. French politicians have primarily conceptualized the Council as "political," and use it as an adjunct policymaking body precisely because it is a powerful policymaker.

French legal scholars, on the other hand—but only since the late 1970s— have conceptualized the Council as a courtlike institution whose principle function is to produce a constitutional jurisprudence; this jurisprudence in turn encourages and structures doctrinal activity, primarily the building of constitutional law. As discussed at length in chapter 4, the heart of the refusal to recognize the Council's legislative function derives from a now deeply held doctrinal belief that the Council is a *juridiction*, that is, that it is more like a court than it is like a "political" body. This conclusion is arrived at by stretching the concept of *juridiction* beyond the traditional French one. In its traditional French sense, the word *juridiction* denotes any institution—virtually always understood to be a court staffed by professionally trained judges— which decides concrete legal conflicts according to established law and adversarial, judicial procedures. Present-day constitutional scholars have altered the necessary criterion (rather, they have created an exception to exclusionary criteria) in order to include the Council in that class of things denoted by the word *juridiction*. According to this formulation, an institution which determines "what the applicable law is," and whose determination is final and binding, is a *juridiction. Thus, the Council qualifies as a special "constitutional juridiction," because it determines what the constitutional law is, and is therefore to be treated by the legal community exactly as any other court or court system would be treated.* French academic lawyers do not ignore the fact that the process in which the Council has authority to intervene is legislative and not judicial (since neither litigation nor lower court decisions are ever involved). Unlike the overwhelming majority of legal scholars from the 1890s until at least 1971, French doctrinal authority today simply refuses to grant that the fact makes any difference. As Michel de Villiers, commentator on the Council's decisions for the *Revue administrative*, puts it, "Although the [Council's] intervention is one stage of legislature procedure, it constitutes a *juridictionnel* stage."[21]

The argument is employed to depoliticize the Council and thus bolster the legitimacy of French constitutional review. In essence, the argument goes like this: because the Council is a *juridiction* and therefore like a court, and because other courts in the world exercises review legitimately, the Council's exercise of review is legitimate. (That the legitimacy of judicial review is regularly challenged even in countries where constitutional courts enjoy far greater prestige than does the Council in France, e.g., the U.S. Supreme Court, seems not to have been noticed.) As I have pointed out before, in the effort to prove that the Council is more courtlike than not, French public lawyers have blurred what is meant by "judicial" to the point of irrelevance. It also artificially separates what the Council does from what parliament does. Doctrinal consensus now has it that because the Council is a *juridiction*, its role and function is *intrinsically* judicial and therefore differs from the role and functions performed by political bodies. But by stretching the concept of *juridiction* to allow the Council to come in by the front door, parliament slips in easily through the back. This point deserves to be explored in light of the phenomenon of the juridicized parliament described in chapters 5, 6, and 7.

In an article published in the *Revue du droit public* in 1928, the law professor and future Council member, Marcel Waline, argued that parliament was a *juridiction whenever* it debated what are today called motions of *irrecevabilité*.[22] Employing virtually the same definition of *juridiction* that was to be adopted by himself and other legal scholars in the 1970s,[23] Waline declared that parliament formally constituted a *juridiction* during such debates because (1) motions of *irrecevabilité*—then as now—require parliament to determine the constitutionality of a piece of legislation, and (2) the determination of unconstitutionality kills the bill. In a sentence, if the Council is to be considered a *juridiction* by virtue of the fact that it is at times charged with definitively determining the constitutionality of legislation, then so must parliament be considered a *juridiction* at times. This is the logical result of applying the extended, present-day definition of *juridiction* to an institution *other than the Council*; but, of course, public scholars never do so.

In the Fifth Republic, this argument is much more compelling than it was in 1928. Today parliamentary debates and votes on *exceptions d'irrecevabilité* are a regular part of legislative life (chapter 5). In fact, in the 1981–87 period, the National Assembly alone debated and voted on ninety-four such motions, a figure to be compared with ninety-three Council decisions. Logic, but perhaps little else, would compel us to conclude that the National Assembly behaves more often as a constitutional *juridiction* than the Council. It is important to note in this regard that these motions are written and presented in the guise of judicial decisions, employing—just as does the Council—a series of "considerations" purporting to show that a piece of legislation does not conform to one or more specific constitutional texts or principles. As important, politicians themselves view the debate on *irrecevabilité* as a kind of *juridictionnel* exercise. Jean Foyer, the law professor and former minister of justice called for and then led the debate on the *recevabilité* of the Socialist's nationalization bill, because he wanted parliament "to verify the bill's conformity to the constitution."[24]

Etienne Dailly, who led the fight against that same bill in the Senate, even asserted that parliament constituted a distinctly separate act of *juridictionnel* authority:

> I repeat: I have never said that we would refer this bill [to the Council]. I have limited myself to arguing [here] that it is unconstitutional. . . .
>
> Personally, I consider that we [in parliament] are judges of the first instance . . . [B]ut we are under the control of the Council, just as judges of first instance are under the control of the Court of Appeal and the *Cour de cassation.*[25]

Dailly's point gets to the crux of the matter. Appeals to ideal types of things judicial or things politicolegislative when debating aspects of the French system of constitutional review are hopelessly inconclusive. On one hand, the Council behaves legislatively, as a third chamber of parliament. On the other, the legislature behaves judicially, as a *juridiction* determining constitutionality. Although I am not comfortable with using the term *juridiction* with respect to any aspect of French constitutional politics, it is clear that in the terms of the French debate it is not incorrect to claim that the *degree to which any legislative process is juridicized is equivalent to the degree to which parliament behaves as a* juridiction. In juridicized debates, parliament not only debates constitutionality during motions of *irrecevabilité*; but may debate constitutionality endlessly, or at least until a bill is definitively adopted. After adoption, these debates are summarized by policymakers and then transferred to the Council.

I wish to stress that the third chamber thesis is offered here chiefly as an analytical tool, a useful conceptualization of function. It is proposed without regard to normative considerations. That said, acceptance of the notion that the Council behaves as a significant policymaker and specialized third chamber, need not necessarily destroy Council legitimacy, as French jurists argue (see chapter 4). On the contrary, acceptance of the view might lead to the opposite conclusion.

Compared to most supreme courts, the Council is relatively more vulnerable to criticism that it is political: (1) a majority of its members have always been former politicians; (2) it exercises abstract review after nonadversarial (parliamentary) processes; and (3) its offices are disconnected from the greater judicial system. These aspects can be cited in support of the third chamber thesis. But they can also be made to yield a very different perspective on the debate about the Council's legitimacy than the orthodox one in France. The judicial myth has never been accepted by politicians. (Nothing illustrates this better than the fact that politicians appoint to the Council primarily those who are both politically experienced and loyal to them.) If the Council is primarily conceptualized as a *court*, then the legitimacy problem is probably permanent. However, if the Council is accepted for what it is—a *Council* of policymakers which derives its legitimacy from the fact that its composition will eventually "follow" the electoral returns—then we need not debate the usurpation question (at least not in the same way). In fact, political loyalty and partisan affiliation become positive elements in the legitimacy debate. The a priori, abstract review mechanism, the nonadversarial process, and detachment from the judicial system might lose their debilitating impact. The Council is appointed by politicians; it only handles cases referred to it by politicians; its jurisprudence binds only politicians. Thus politics itself confers upon the Council a legitimacy as a *political* body which may be far greater than that accorded *judicial* institutions elsewhere. By framing the debate largely on the issue of the Council's "courtliness," the Council's supporters labor not only against what I view as certain insuperable obstacles, but also needlessly expose the Council to the same criticism that all constitutional courts face: the charge of usurpation. I do not expect that this argument has any possibility of gaining acceptance in France. Doctrinal commitments and orthodoxies are too deeply-held to allow much change, especially in such a (heretical) direction. My reason for making these points, however, is simply to emphasize that conceptualizing the Council as a third chamber and as a policymaker is not in itself a criticism of the Council's role or behavior. I believe, simply, that such a conceptualization yields a more realistic view of French constitutional politics than do others available.

In conclusion, the affirmation that the Council is a *juridiction* cannot be made to say that the Council's work is therefore and *by its very nature* judicial, if what is meant by this is either that the Council does not behave legislatively or that parliament's work is not therefore also "judicial." If the Council's work is more "judicial" than is the legislature's, then it is so for some other reason. My own view is that, for reasons already discussed, the Council's behavior is today more judicial only because its work has increasingly conformed to long-standing standards of conduct, of decision making, and of argumentation recognized and approved of by the doctrinal community; an important problem with such an argument, however, is that in consequence other policymakers have been forced or led to conform to these standards as well.

Constitutional development in France is not simply a matter of the Council and its supporters on one side slowly but surely defeating and converting "liberticidal" politicians on the other. The constitution is more participatory than that. A lawmaker who criticizes a Council ruling is not necessarily an opponent of constitutional review, and even less an opponent of the constitution. Such criticism is rather important evidence of the interinstitutional context in which constitutional law and legislation—the two can never be separated—is made in France. It is testimony to the uniqueness of the French review mechanism that the most effective mode of obstruction available to the French parliamentary opposition is at the same time an effective guarantor that a whole panoply of civil rights and democratic procedures will be essential terms of legislative debate. While French legal scholars regularly chastise politicians for engaging in Council-bashing, parliament, its in-house constitutional watchdogs, and the drafters of Council petitions have not been given the credit they deserve for their role in protecting fundamental rights and developing constitutional principles. In addition to transmitting issues to the Council and to formulating constitutional arguments, much of juridicized debate is consciously undertaken to improve legislation with respect to constitutionality (true of reforms in penal and judicial procedures, for example). Neither the parliament nor the Council possesses a monopoly on lawmaking or on the building of constitutional law; both are products of sustained interinstitutional interaction.

III

TOWARD A COMPARATIVE UNDERSTANDING OF JUDICIAL REVIEW

9

West European Constitutional Courts in Comparative Perspective

During the 1981–87 period, constitutional politics altered governmental processes at the very heart of the French State. Most important, the conduct of policymaking was transformed by the development of the Constitutional Council as a powerful actor, capable not only of having its policies implemented but of structuring future legislative processes with reference to those policies. As the preceding demonstrates, our understanding of institutional interaction in France—between the government and the *Conseil d'Etat*, between the executive and the legislature, and between legislative majorities and oppositions within parliament—is incomplete absent attention to constitutional politics.

It is the purpose of this concluding chapter to go beyond these ideographic concerns, employing the French case as a heuristic device whose primary utility is, in Eckstein's terms, to shed light on "important general problems" and to suggest "theoretical puzzles and insights."[1] Articulated in the form of general hypotheses, these insights can be made to structure comparative inquiry, a central objective of which is to identify and to explain meaningful regularities as well as differences among a number of cases. What follows are some first, tentative steps toward a comparative understanding of the politics of abstract review in Western Europe.

A number of hypotheses about constitutional review and its relationship to politics may be derived from the study of the French case and comparison with other European cases. These may be stated in general terms:

- The existence of abstract review leads (inevitably?) to the juridicization of policymaking processes;
- As a matter of concrete policymaking impact, constitutional courts behave as third legislative chambers whenever they engage in abstract review. Put slightly differently, when compared with traditional, accepted notions of "functions" judicial and legislative, courts which exercise abstract review behave more as "legislators" than they do as "courts," and this behavior in turn leads legislators to behave "judicially."

- Abstract review is inherently more destabilizing to a court's politicoinstitutional environment than is concrete review.

Informed by these hypotheses, this chapter is an overview and assessment of the development of abstract review in Europe. I examine the creation of constitutional jurisdictions set apart from the ordinary and administrative judicial systems. This creation had the particular advantage of allowing for the *constitutional* review of legislation by special judges while preserving the main tenets of European separation of powers doctrines, tenets which had long enshrined an uncompromising hostility to *judicial* review. The cases of Austria, France, West Germany, and Spain have been selected for their comparability because (1) each is a civil law polity in which the practice of judicial review was previously constitutionally forbidden; (2) in each, a special constitutional court was created to exercise constitutional review; and (3) each of these constitutional courts possesses the power of abstract review. Among other European constitutional courts, only the Portuguese (established in 1983) meets these criteria, but it is excluded for lack of data.[2] This analysis is seriously hindered by the paucity of work on Austria and Spain. I also describe aspects of the structure, mandate, and activity of these courts with special emphasis on the relationship between abstract review and other activities. *Abstract* constitutional review differs from American and other forms of judicial review in that it is not dependent on, or incidental to, *concrete* litigation or controversy involving a statute. The abstract review process results in a ruling on the *prima facie* constitutionality of a legislative text; a concrete tort is not a requisite condition; the process is a purely exegetical exercise. In addition, I examine the impact of constitutional review on legislative processes in those countries in which research on the matter has been undertaken—France and Germany. In these countries, at least, policymaking has been transformed, and in remarkably similar ways. Following this discussion, I suggest a number of general hypotheses about judicial–political interaction. Finally, I seek to extend existing theoretical work on courts and judicial review along lines traced by Martin Shapiro in his comparative work.[3]

Origins

In classic Continental separation of powers doctrines, the dogmatic aversion to judicial review occupies a central place. According to these doctrines, the judiciary is not a co-equal branch of government. On the contrary, judges are subservient to one or more entities which possess the sovereignty of the State itself. A vast majority of legal theory and scholarship from the last third of the nineteenth century until after World War II is devoted to this notion of sovereignty, and to the proper relationship of doctrinal authority to it. In general, statutes are held to be formal, concrete pronouncements of sovereignty; it is the function of the judiciary to apply these statutes in the course of deciding legal disputes, but not to interpret them or otherwise sit in judgment of the work of the legislator. In France, Rousseauian-Republicans, Royalists, or Bonapartists might alternate in power, but the strict rule according to which judges were bound by statute remained constitutional orthodoxy at all times. In Germany, too, the notion of *Rechtsstaat*, constructed by judicial, administrative, and doctrinal activity from the State's pronouncements, became an overarching one. Nothing illustrates the subservient nature of the judicial function in civil law systems more than the fact that judges were denied jurisdiction over higher law. In France, constitutions, including provisions touching on fundamental rights, could be amended by ordinary statute. Although German scholarship was informed by a very different tradition of state theory, similar conclusions about the relationship between political and legal power were obtained. As Carl Schmitt declared, ultimately the sovereign is whoever has the power to violate the constitution.[4] Stated somewhat differently: "The predominant view has been that the individual does not and cannot hold rights against the 'state,' for the state itself through an act of self-limitation is the source of these rights."[5] From 1780 in Germanic states and from 1791 in France, judicial interpretation of statute was explicitly prohibited by constitutions, and penalties were prescribed for any transgression in the penal codes.

During the latter half of the nineteenth century public law developed as an autonomous branch of the law in both countries. From this point onward legal scholarship proved increasingly hostile to the prohibition on judicial review. In 1863, a majority of the association of German jurists "declared itself in favor of judicial review," culminating in the work of Kantorowicz, Fuchs, and Schmitt in the early twentieth century.[6] In France, no major figure in public law after 1890 argued against judicial review *in principle*, although some feared the political backlashes which might result from such an innovation. As discussed in chapter 2, the most important French specialists of the Third Republic, Duguit and Hauriou, vigorously lobbied in favor of judicial review on the American model. Thus by 1920 at the latest, academic lawyers on the Continent had developed and achieved a remarkable consensus around doctrines radically opposed to the existing model of the politicolegal system. These doctrines, based on neo-natural law ideas, were developed largely in response to the increase in the political, and therefore the legislative, influence of unions and of working class parties within parliaments. As Neumann has it, rigid positivism—that is, subservience to the terms of statute—was viewed as no longer favoring the interests of capital, and "hence the existence of a natural law was . . . openly discussed"; in C. J. Friedrich's words, natural law functioned "as an antidote to positivism."[7] This natural law renaissance posited the existence of a supreme constitution, to be judicially interpreted and developed.

In the end, ordinary and administrative courts did not undertake review activities. The movement failed for two principal reasons. First, politicians continually and overwhelmingly reiterated their opposition to granting interpretive powers to judges, an opposition which became all the more resolute when they learned that judicial review in the United States had led to a reactionary "government of judges."[8] Second, unlike law professors, judges had internalized their bureaucratic role and were further constrained by their lack of independence from political authority. At the 1912 congress of German judges, for example, the convention declared itself in favor of the continued subordination of judicial authority to that of statute.[9] During the Weimar Republic, the German constitutional court, the *Reichtsgericht*—described by one scholar as a "highly political and highly politicized instrument,"[10]— rendered a handful of decisions which in essence nullified the application of certain laws passed by parliament between 1921 and 1925. It asserted this authority on its own (without an enabling constitutional provision) during a time when political power was too fragmented to effectively resist the judges. Each of these decisions dealt with property rights and labor law, and each benefited monopoly capital.[11] Whatever evolution this development might have had in a less reactionary direction, and whatever influence it might have had on the activities of ordinary judges, can not be gauged given the collapse of the Republic and the rise of National Socialism.

By far the most innovative pre-World War II experiment in constitutional review occurred in Austria at the instigation of Hans Kelsen, an extraordinarily influential law professor and legal theorist who had been asked to draft what became the constitution of the short-lived First Republic (1920–34). Kelsen, like many of his French and German peers, argued that if a constitution was to mean anything at all, it had to be considered superior to statute, and that this hierarchy had to be defended if the *état de droit* or *Rechtsstaat* was to be assured. But Kelsen also understood that *judicial* review, that is review by the ordinary courts on the American model, would not likely be politically accept-able, and he searched instead for another means by which the constitution could be defended. The result was the Austrian constitutional court, a special jurisdiction whose exclusive purpose was to decide constitutional controver-sies.[12] The Court possessed wide-ranging powers of abstract and concrete review. Cursed by the turbulent times into which it was born, the institution was subject to periodic, virulent attacks by right-wing political parties and its press organs, and its review powers were finally all but rescinded by govern-ment decree in 1933.[13] The Republic was engulfed shortly thereafter by fascism.

The Kelsenian Court

The Austrian precedent is considered "seminal for Western Europe,"[14] and the Kelsenian court is recognized today as the prototype of the European "model" of "constitutional review," in opposition to the American model.[15] Kelsen's ideas has proved profoundly important to legal scholars in recent years, inspiring the revival of the Austrian court, the creation of the West German court,[16] and generally functioning to bolster the legitimacy of the European model (and to counter what remains of the former doctrinal orthodoxy in favor of judicial review).[17] Kelsen himself faced the legitimacy issue principally in a 1928 article widely cited today.[18] The article deserves examination because it constitutes a kind of "tool kit" for the establishment of constitutional courts in civil law systems, and because it foresees nearly every significant variation now in place.

While convinced of the "necessity" of some mechanism to protect the supremacy of the constitution, Kelsen labored against two hostile currents of opinion: that of politicians suspicious of any judicial incursion on their powers to legislate, and that of scholarly adoration of American judicial review.[19] He therefore sought to demonstrate that effective review would neither usurp legislative sovereignty nor be mere "political review." First, Kelsen distinguished between the work of legislators—which was "creative" and "positive"—and the work of constitutional judges—which was "negative." Legislators make law freely, limited only by preestablished procedural rules and the federal division of powers. Kelsen acknowledged that the power to declare legislation unconstitutional is also the power to make law:

> To annul a law is to assert a general [legislative] norm, because the annulment of a law has the same character as its elaboration—only with a negative sign attached. . . . A tribunal which has the power to annul a law is as a result an organ of legislative power.

But judicial lawmaking power is constrained power: there is no "free creation of law," since the judges' decision making is "absolutely determined by the constitution." For Kelsen, the court is only "a negative legislator."

Undergirding the distinction between the positive and negative legislator is Kelsen's belief that constitutions should not enshrine bills of rights, what he called "norms of natural law." Indeed, he believed that constitutions should not contain such statements, unless they could be made absolutely precise and transparent in their meaning:

> Sometimes constitutions themselves refer to principles [of natural law], invoking the ideals of equity, justice, liberty, equality, morality, etc., without in the least defining what are meant by these terms. . . . But with respect to constitutional justice, these can play an extremely dangerous role. A court could interpret these constitutional provisions, which invite the legislator to honor the principles of justice, equity, equality . . . *as positive requirements for the contents of laws* [emphasis added].

Second, Kelsen advocated a number of means by which these new courts might preserve their independence from political authority. He insisted that professional judges and law professors be recruited to the court, and emphasized that "members of parliament or of the government" be excluded. The "judicial" nature of the court could be enhanced in another way: by granting to it jurisdiction over constitutional controversies originating in the administrative court system. This would both extend the court's protection of the constitution to executive acts and also anchor the court in processes of *concrete* review. Finally, Kelsen also proposed that courts, individuals, and/or a special constitutional ombudsman should have the right to refer matters to the constitutional court.

While there is significant variation, the majority of European courts conform to the most important tenets of Kelsen's model. *The crucial exception is that most Continental constitutions grant to the constitutional court jurisdic-*

tion over a written bill of rights. The post-World War II political environment in which modern constitutional courts find themselves differs fundamentally from that of Kelsen's day and before. Most important is the central place accorded to constitutions—and by extension to the constitutional courts—as institutional bulwarks against a recurrence of authoritarianism. The drafting of the Federal Republic's basic law and the decision in Austria in 1945 to revive and modernize Kelsen's constitution of 1920–29 were above all reactions, in Taylor Cole's words, to the "gloomy past" of fascism.[20] The same can be said of the drafting of the Spanish constitution of 1978. In all three cases, the founders explicitly gave to constitutional courts the burden of protecting citizens from abuses by public authorities. In Germany, an extensive bill of rights comprises the first eighteen articles of the basic law, repudiating traditional theories that the State necessarily presupposes and is responsible for the existence of individual rights. In Spain, "by far the longest section of the Constitution deals with fundamental rights and the obligation of the state to uphold and guarantee these rights."[21] In Austria, the situation is more complicated since there is no charter of rights in the constitution proper. But the constitution does require the court to protect rights and freedoms, and the court has made use of a number of texts which it has elevated to constitutional status to that end.[22] Furthermore, the desire to permanently decentralize German and Austrian state power led to the adoption of federal structures, which in turn virtually required the existence of a constitutional court. Likewise, the dominant issue confronting the Spanish framers was that of regional autonomy, and they relied heavily on the constitutional court as an instrument of supervision over what is in effect a quasi-federal system.

The French case is exceptional. The 1958 constitution does not contain a bill of rights, and the Constitutional Council was not created in order to protect fundamental rights and liberties. Moreover, the federal logic is absent. The fact that the French court is actively involved in constitutional review is due to judicial activism, and to the politicization of its offices by politicians. The Council's current role and its terms of reference therefore have virtually no relation to the framers' intentions.

Three general points should be made at this point. First, the proliferation of constitutional courts in Europe on the Austrian model is related to the fact that such institutions preserve the traditional legal order and judicial function, while at the same time enabling effective review. Second, legal scholars have embraced constitutional review because it serves to protect individual rights, and because it provides them with a stable and creative source for the building of constitutional law. The support of the scholarly community has proved enormously important in courts' struggles to appropriate power and gain legitimacy. Doctrinal activity weighs heavily on jurisprudential outcomes,[23] but it also functions—and sometimes quite consciously seeks—to remove issues from their macropolitical settings and to place them in legal ones. While attention to this activity is essential to any understanding of European constitutional politics, social scientists can not expect Continental public lawyers to produce work of significance beyond the study of law and jurisprudence. The

French resistance to treating the Council or constitutional review as important elements with the greater political and institutional environment have been documented at length in chapters 2 to 5. But this tendency is a strong one everywhere in Europe. As Blair writes, "Given the strict separation of law and politics, acknowledgement of creative decision-making with regard for political realities has been much slower and more painful than in the anglo-saxon world, where it has been taken for granted."[24] For the same reasons, no general work on Austrian or Spanish judicial politics yet exists.

Third and most important for students of judicial policymaking, the constitutional inclusion of judicially enforceable bills of rights makes of these courts positive law-makers. With respect to their policy-making impact, it may be argued that they are *more unlike than like* the Kelsenian court. It bears repeating that Kelsen's distinction between positive and negative judicial lawmaking capacity rests on the denial of jurisdiction over natural rights. Any court which exercises constitutional review powers with reference to natural rights must, in Kelsen's thinking, be said to participate intimately in the work of legislators. The distinction between lawmaking and judicial decision making breaks down and is not easily reconstituted, at least not in terms which Kelsen would recognize.

Structure and Activity

There is significant variation in the constitutional mandate and activity of European courts which exercise abstract review authority. As Table 9.1 shows, a constitutional court may possess abstract review powers alone or in combination with powers of concrete review. Further, there exist two modes of abstract review—the a posteriori (Austria, Portugal, Spain, West Germany), and the a priori (France, Spain until 1985, Portugal). In the former, laws are referred to the constitutional court immediately after promulgation; in the latter, laws are referred after final adoption by parliament, but *before* promulgation. In all cases, abstract review is initiated by politicians, who refer legislation directly to the court. Courts cannot refuse to accept a petition, and governments and legislative majorities cannot avoid having their legislation examined. *Abstract review therefore functions to extend what would otherwise be a concluded legislative process*; referrals in effect require the court to undertake a final "reading" of a disputed bill or law.

The highly partisan nature of this process places constitutional courts in delicate situations, and the possibility of explosive judicial–political confrontation might appear to be virtually permanent. However, *for every European court excepting the French, abstract review processes neither constitute a major source of caseload nor dominate public perceptions about the court's role in the political system.* Whatever impact abstract review might have on debates and controversies about a court's institutional legitimacy is counterbalanced by lower profile work. That is, in countries other than France, what constitutional courts do most of the time is not of high political (in the

Table 9.1. Structure and Mandate of European Courts Which Exercise Abstract Review*

	France (1958)	W. Germany (1951)	Austria (1920/1945)	Spain (1980)
Composition and Recruitment				
No. of members	9	16	14	12
Appointing authorities	President (3) Pres. Nat. Ass. (3) Pres. Senate (3)	Bundestag (8) Bundesrat (8)	Federal Govt (8) Nationalrat (3) Bundesrat (3)	Congress (4) Senate (4) Govt (2) Judiciary (2)
Length of term	9 yrs.	12 yrs.	Until 70 yrs. of age	9 yrs.
Age limit	None	40 yr. min. 68 yr. max.	70 yr. max.	None
Requisite qualifications	None	6/16 must be federal judges; others must be qualified to be German judges	8/14 must be judges functionaires, or law professors; others must be lawyers or political scientists	All must be judges, lawyers, or law professors with at least 15 yrs. experience
Constitutional Review Authority				
Attached to court systems	No	Yes	Yes	Yes
Abstract review				
a priori	Yes	No	No	Abolished (1985)
a posteriori	No	Yes	Yes	Yes
Concrete review	No	Yes	Yes	Yes
Power to Refer Constitutional Controversies to the Court Possessed by				
Politicians (abstract review)	President Pres. Nat. Ass. Pres. Senate 60 deputies 60 senators	Fed. Govt. Länder Govts. 1/3 of Bundestag	Fed. Govt. Länder Govts. 1/3 Nationalrat 1/3 lower houses of Länder	Prime Min. Pres. Parliament 50 deputies 50 senators Executives autonomous regions
Ombudsman (abstract and concrete review)	—	—	—	Yes
Judiciary (concrete review)	No	Yes	Yes	Yes
Individuals (concrete review)	No	Yes	Yes	Yes

*A complete list would include Portugal, whose constitutional court was established in 1983.

politico-partisan sense of the term) salience: political parties are not involved directly in these processes, and they do *not* actively question and debate the legitimacy of the work being performed.

Statistics show the extent to which abstract review constitutes only a small fraction of total activity outside of France.[25] The German court, for example, receives 99 percent of all of its cases via direct appeal by individuals—who, as in Austria and Spain where similar mechanisms exist, must demonstrate that their rights have *already* been violated. Since 1951, individuals seeking to initiate concrete review have filed on average more than 1,500 individual complaints per year, and more than 3,300 were filed in 1987. Referrals of legislation by politicians seeking abstract review average less than 3 per year.

In Austria, concrete review of cases originating in the administrative court system comprises well over 90 percent of the Vienna court's caseload. The court has been asked to decide over 1,000 such cases per year during the 1980s, and its docket is chronically backlogged (there are some 2,000 cases pending presently). The court, which also receives approximately 25 individual referrals annually, is exercised above all else by its desire and responsibility to harmonize the legal order. *Abstract review is exceedingly rare in Austria, and, indeed, is politically insignificant.* In 1975, the right of referral was granted to one-third of the deputies in the federal and state lower houses, that is, to the minority party. Whether due to the consensual nature of Austrian politics, a belief that referrals are not altogether legitimate, or both, the court has received only five referrals to date, resulting in only one ruling of unconstitutionality. In consequence, the legislative process has not been significantly altered by the existence of such review.

The work of the Spanish court, like that of its German counterpart, is dominated by individual referrals (90 percent of all of the cases which reach the court). These referrals (*amparos*) may not attack a law directly, but instead are requests that the court defend those fundamental rights enumerated in articles 14 and 30 of the constitution alleged to have been violated by administrative authorities. From 1981, when the court began its jurisprudential activity, through 1985, the court handed down 422 decisions on nearly 4,000 individual referrals. Moreover, *the court has clearly signaled that it considers the protection of individual rights to be its top priority.* As in Germany, this is largely due to the court's desire to contribute to the stability of a democratic regime created in the wake of fascist rule. And, as in Germany, it is politically unacceptable for any major political party to attack the court for its activism in the name of individual rights. Abstract review referrals for a posteriori control have averaged 8 per year, while the court received a total of 13 petitions for a priori control from 1983 to 1985. In 1985, the a priori power was rescinded because it was considered to be an illegitimate affront to parliamentary sovereignty (discussed later).

The French Constitutional Council exercises a priori abstract review exclusively, and solely upon referral by political authorities. The Council's role in the legislative process has vastly expanded: from 1974, when the power of referral was granted to any sixty deputies or senators, through 1987, the

Council received 191 referrals; in the 1958–73 period, it received a total of 9. Concrete review is forbidden: once promulgated, laws are immune from scrutiny by the Council or by any other jurisdiction. Further, not only is the Council detached from the greater judicial system, but it is cut off from direct popular contact with the citizenry. Political scientists, including myself, comparativists, and non-French legal specialists have consistently conceptualized the Council as something other than a court, and as fulfilling more a legislative than a judicial function. Unable to claim that it performs a function of harmonizing jurisprudence or administrative activity with the exigencies of the constitution, and bereft of a constituency beyond parliament, the Council and its supporters may be said to possess relatively fewer resources with which to counter criticisms of its lawmaking activities. The Council is unquestionably the constitutional court which least conforms to Kelsen's model. Perhaps not surprisingly, these criticisms occur with far greater frequency and are much more public and vitriolic than those directed at other European courts. In consequence of this, French legal specialists increasingly debate the merits of expanding the referral procedure, to the ordinary and administrative courts, for example.[26] And in 1989 the Rocard government acceded to the president of the Council's request that the constitution be amended so as to allow individuals to refer legislation directly to the Council for a ruling.[27] As chapter 2 describes, the amendment was quashed in the Senate. The revision, if it had been accepted, would have fundamentally altered the terms of the debate on the legitimacy of constitutional review in France, and the Council would have been placed, it seems, in a less exposed position.

The French Constitutional Council has also been heavily criticized for its "political" composition. As Table 9.1 shows, whereas in the German, Austrian, and Spanish cases, minimum levels of judicial expertise are requisite conditions for appointment (and would certainly be gratifying to Kelsen), there are no such formal standards in France. Of the forty-one members who have served on the Council from 1958 to 1988, 59 percent were selected from the ranks of parliamentarians and/or ministers. In Germany, the tendency has been toward greater "juridicization" of the selection process, that is, the number of members of the court continuing long careers on the bench or selected from law faculties has increased over time. Such has not been the case in France. As noted in chapter 3, in 1968 the nine-member Council contained six (67 percent) former professional politicians, increasing to seven (78 percent) in 1983, and to eight (89 percent), after 1986. Professional judges are rarely selected, but there is usually at least one law professor sitting at any given time. As I have shown, in spite (or because?) of its "political" composition, the Council makes a conscious effort to conform to judicial norms of behavior. The juridicization of the composition of other constitutional courts should not imply that the recruitment process in those countries is apolitical. On the contrary, in both Germany and Austria, formalized negotiations among the major political parties determine which party will fill vacancies on the court (allocations are roughly proportionate to parliamentary strength, conforming to Kelsen's dicta); in Spain as well, although it is too early to draw firm conclusions, the appointment process is largely one of bargaining among political parties.

Abstract Review and Policymaking

What literature exists on the impact of abstract review on policymaking in West Germany appears to confirm the essential lessons of the French experience and of the first hypothesis mentioned. The regular use of abstract review has led to a juridicization of policymaking processes, and this juridicization manifests itself in regularized behavior which is in effect institutionalized. The significant variation in the conduct of constitutional politics which does exist may be best explained, apparently, by the greater French penchant for unyielding, polarized parliamentary debate, and by the greater German tolerance for judicial solutions to political conflicts. I will return to these points shortly.

Simplifying and breaking down what is a complex phenomenon, the juridicization of policymaking processes in France and West Germany can be explained by four interrelated structural and behavioral factors: (1) the mode of constitutional review exercised by the respective constitutional courts over legislation; (2) the use by politicians of the courts' offices for political ends both during and after the legislative process; (3) judicial activism and the attendant development by courts of creative techniques of controlling legislation; and, (4) the strict application of decisions by legislators. In examining each, I have sought to generalize from my research on the French case and from that, notably, of the political scientist, Christine Landfried, on the German.

Mode of Control

The concept of judicial policymaking has been a slippery one for American political scientists. In his pathbreaking, now classic essay on conceptualizing the U.S. Supreme Court as a "national policy-maker," Dahl argued that "what is critical is the extent to which a court can or does make policy decisions by going outside established 'legal' criteria found in precedent, statute, and constitution."[28] Creative judicial interpretation will have policy impact in any political system. But Dahl's focus is too limited for our purposes, reflecting the realties of the American judicial review mechanism and a specifically American separation of powers tradition. Abstract control is typically justified as providing for a more complete, potentially systematic, and therefore efficacious defense of the supremacy of the constitution within a hierarchy of judicial norms. *Abstract review is of interest to policy studies because it requires or enables constitutional courts to intervene in and alter legislative processes and outcomes.* In comparing the American and European models, Klaus von Beyme has noted that the mechanism of abstract review "represents a further step away from the American model," and with that a "tendency for constitutional jurisdiction to become too deeply involved in dealing with political issues."[29] Whether "too deeply involved" or not, this jurisdictional intervention is virtually immediate: in France, bills must be referred to the Constitutional Council within fifteen days after their adoption in parliament, and may not be promulgated until a decision has been reached by the Council; in Germany, politicians have one month from the date of promulgation to refer legislation. Thus, it should not be surprising that the subsequent decision is viewed by politicians as the true final stage of the legislative process.

Juridicizing Legislative Processes

The remarkable development of abstract constitutional control in France and Germany is a result of, and a response to, the exploitation of the court's offices by politicians for partisan, political ends. In France, successive oppositions in the 1980s correctly viewed petitions to the Constitutional Council, or the mere threat of petition, to be their most effective means to obstruct or enforce changes in legislation proposed by the government and its parliamentary majority. Because governments cannot prevent such petitions, they are obliged to either work on the assumption that the opposition will refer important projects to constitutional judges or court censure, embarrassment, and lost time. Since 1981, such major reforms as the laws on decentralization (1982), press pluralism (1984), audiovisual communications (1986), and the Chirac government's penal code reforms (1986) were subject to massive *autolimitation* processes, as majorities sacrificed important policy objectives due to threats of referral and fear of censure. As Blair describes the West German constitutional politics, abstract review processes "can scarcely be regarded . . . as . . . ensuring observance of the constraining framework of political action. They are in reality attempts to circumvent and obstruct the democratic decision of the legislator, albeit clothed in the most respectable constitutional and legal form."[30] In West Germany, governments and their supporters may even be *more* willing to compromise with the opposition than in France, so risk-averse have they become in constitutional matters. In consequence, policymaking is "overloaded with legal arguments and considerations"[31] as the "opposition in the Bundestag [works] to attain its political goals by judicial means."[32] The bills on radicals in the civil service, codetermination, and on service for conscientious objectors are just three important examples of Social Democratic Party-Free Democratic Party (SDP-FDP) reforms (1969–76) which were substantially altered by the juridicization of the the legislative process.

In 1975, the SDP-FDP government sought to rewrite regulations governing recruitment to the civil service, and notably those enabling the exclusion of applicants judged to have connections with anticonstitutional political groups or to harbor anticonstitutional political beliefs. During the debates on the bill, it became known that the Constitutional Court was about to rule on these same regulations under concrete review procedures; the reform was then placed on hold pending the decision. In its ruling, the Court produced a detailed series of requirements which every applicant would have to meet in order not to be considered an "enemy of the constitution" and therefore be qualified for an administrative post. The government, dutifully watched by the opposition, then copied the terms of the decision into a new draft of the bill.[33] This case provides an example not only of *autolimitation*, but also of how concrete review may serve to juridicize parliament—aided of course by the threat of referral.

The process by which the codetermination law of 1976 was adopted conforms more to the French model, as opposition politicians regularly threatened referral as a means of exacting concessions from the government and majority, and without the aid of a prior decision. Reform of the historic 1951 codetermination legislation had been one of the top priorities of the SDP and of the labor movement. Most important, they sought to gain equal representation with management on supervisory boards—boards of directors—in the largest West German corporations. Debates in parliament immediately focused on the apparent opposition between two conceptions of property coexisting in the constitution: the constitution guarantees the right to property, but it also states that property must serve the public good. After nearly two years of rancorous debate (June 1984–March 1976!), during which deputies carried copies of the constitution and of the court's jurisprudence around with them, the bill was finally adopted, but without management-labor parity. *Autolimitation*—or what Landfried calls "obedience in advance" of a decision—had removed that central provision along with many others. When finally adopted, the bill bore little resemblance to the original draft.[34] It is important to note as well that elements within the SDP's coalition partner, the FDP, had strongly opposed extending codetermination.[35] As in France, juridicized processes at times provide governments with a convenient scapegoat for scrapping controversial provisions and reneging on electoral promises. In this case, the SDP could blame constitutional politics for its failure to deliver, while keeping the peace with its pro-business coalition partner.

In both France and Germany, therefore, constitutional debate is not limited to official judicial intervention, but may occur during all stages of the legislative process. In fact, policymakers in both countries have institutionalized a range of practices designed specifically to insulate bills from constitutional censure. In France, the role of the *Conseil d'Etat* as the government's official legal advisor has been enhanced, and the parliamentary oppositions employ constitutional specialists to help them prepare for juridicized debates as well as to draft petitions to the Council. In Germany, long Bundestag hearings are regularly organized during which selected legal experts, jurists, and former constitutional judges are asked to engage in what Landfried calls "Karlsruhe-astrology"[36]—attempts to predict the future position of the court. In any event, the task of insulating a bill from constitutional censure is not a simple one since official advisers, politicians, and private constitutional consultants may have radically differing conceptions of the legislator's legal obligations, and predict different rulings. During the process of adopting the codetermination law, for example, eleven different constitutional lawyers testified in committee hearings on the constitutionality of worker-management parity. After months of debate, one such expert told the deputies,

> . . . by now you have heard more or less everything which could be defended
> . . . : absolute opposition, absolute support, and everything in between.
> You'll have to form your own opinion about how legal science ought to be
> put to work.[37]

The study of the juridicization phenomenon can contribute to a better
understanding of policymaking "impact," and therefore to theories of judicial
power. If, taking Dahl's classic definition, "A has power over B to the extent
that he can get B to do something he would not otherwise do," Friedrich's "law
of anticipatory reactions" posited that B's behavior might be altered to the
extent that B anticipates A's interests and constrains his behavior accordingly.[38] Impact studies have been frustrated, not least, by difficulties in controlling for spurious correlations.[39] Feeley complains, with respect to work on the
U.S. Supreme Court, that

> few of the systematic studies of impact have been . . . concerned with the
> nature and scope of anticipated reactions, despite the fact . . . that it consti-
> tutes a major segment of the court's power on the American political process.
> Clearly one factor contributing . . . is the difficulty . . . of systematically
> identifying anticipatory reactions and adjustments.[40]

Where abstract, politically initiated control exists, such impact is far more
visible, since the specter of a court decision can hang over any given legislative
process. Thus, indirect effects can be examined and to some degree measured, as
in Part II of this book, by tracing legislation through the policymaking process
in order to determine how, why, and when it is actually altered due to anticipatory reactions, and how jurisprudence can generate or shape legislative activity.
Research on France and West Germany presented here shows that this influence
is extensive, significant, and multidimensional. Such research will contribute to
our understanding of the participatory nature of the process of building constitutional law. Scholars too often assume that constitutional interpretation is the
exclusive prerogative of the judiciary.[41] The juridicization of parliament is in
essence the formalization of an extensive and intimate form of what is called, in
American parlance, "coordinate construction." In Europe, constitutional law is
built by the complex interaction between lawmakers, legislative and constitutional texts, constitutional courts, and doctrinal authority.

Judicial Activism

Constitutional courts are intervening in legislative processes at an increasing
rate, as statistics show. In France, in the 1958–80 period, the Constitutional
Council examined forty-four laws referred to it by politicians; in the 1981–87
period, the number more than doubled—to ninety-one. In the 1974–80 period,
an average of 8.8 percent of the bills adopted by parliament were referred; since
1981, the percentage is 19.3 percent, with a high of 36.3 percent of the laws
adopted in 1986. Indeed, Council intervention in the legislative process can be
said to be systematic: *all budgets since 1974 have been scrutinized by the
Council as has virtually every major piece of legislation since 1981.* In West

Germany, the intervention is relatively limited: seventy-one laws were referred to the Constitutional Court between 1951 and 1981; In the 1981–87 period, twenty-three laws were referred. Several points should be made about the German statistics. First, in terms of the legislative process in the Bundestag, partisan battles over legislation occur, if they are to occur, at the committee stage, accounting for the fact that nine of every ten laws are adopted by unanimity.[42] The approximately three laws per year which are referred are those on which the parties were not able to achieve prior consensus.[43] The impact of the court, therefore, cannot be assessed or measured by examining referrals and decisions alone. The researcher must be willing to wade through debates in searches for *autolimitation*. Second, the power of the Länder governments to refer federal legislation has been used without reference to problems of federalism. Parties in opposition at the federal level but making up the governments of Länder have used the referral in service of the national party, in what are essentially national conflicts. Thus, the SDP used its control of state governments to refer federal legislation on rearmament (1950s) and social welfare policy (1961), and Christian Democratic Union (CDU)-Christian Social Union (CSU) Länder governments did the same, after 1969, to refer to the Court the SDP-FDP legislation on abortion (1974), and the Ostpolitik treaties with East Germany (1973).

These figures measure only the volition of politicians to use constitutional courts as a means of obtaining their political goals, and not "judicial activism." However, *there is a kind of structured complicity between opposition politicians and constitutional courts.* Petitions provide courts with opportunities to build constitutional law and—the same thing—to make policy; resulting decisions provide oppositions with a steady supply of arms, expanding the grounds of judicial debate in parliament and in future petitions. In addition, constitutional principles are most effectively enshrined when legislative choices are invalidated (or rewritten by the court)—a more acceptable raw measure of activism. Since 1981, nearly 52.7 percent of the laws referred to the French Constitutional Council were judged to be in whole or in part unconstitutional as adopted, nearly double the 27.3 percent registered in the 1958–74 period. In West Germany, where concrete control also exists, judicial invalidation has risen dramatically in recent years: in the 1951–80 period, eighty-five federal laws were judged to be in whole or in part unconstitutional; in the 1981–88 period, there were ninety-four.

As important, constitutional courts have developed a host of techniques of controlling the legislator other than declarations of unconstitutionality. The most important of these are the declaration of SROIs—that is, a declaration "that one particular interpretation of the law is the only constitutional one"[44]—and the acceptance of the principle of a reform but not of the means chosen by the legislator. These "weapons of limited warfare against constitutionality"[45] were initially developed as means of judicial self-restraint. In Germany, these declarations of SROIs "often entail precise prescriptions for its implementation and is therefore nothing else but a law-giving act of the Constitutional Court."[46] In France, lawmakers have responded to them simply by copying the terms of the courts' decisions directly into subsequent laws on the same legislative subject matter.

Lastly, constitutional judges in both countries have aroused controversy in both political and academic *milieux* by "going outside of established 'legal' criteria found in precedent, statute, and constitution." In France, as noted earlier, the Constitutional Council has willfully expanded its field of reference by incorporating into the constitution a bill of rights. In 1986, following five years of similar attacks by the Socialists, a number of ministers in the Chirac government and parliamentary leaders accused the Council of proliferating constitutional principles in order to enhance its own authority, and called for a codification of constitutional obligations to eliminate "arbitrary" rulings. The German court, for its part, has been accused of "drawing conclusions from the basic law which one can hardly relate to the text of the constitution."[47]

It is at least worth mention that judges on constitutional courts may also have their own political or policy agenda. In France, by far the greatest portion of the debate on the legitimacy of the Council and of constitutional review has centered on the fact that politicians rather than judges have made up the overwhelming majority of Council members. But given the secrecy of the deliberations and of voting records, and the prohibition against dissenting opinions, it is virtually impossible to empirically measure the extent to which partisan affiliation matters. In West Germany, where dissenting opinions have been allowed since the early 1970s, there is also great debate on the extent to which the partisan affiliation of judges influences the Court's decision-making processes. Former constitutional judge, Martin Hirsch, has written that party affiliation exercises a profound impact on the jurisprudential production of the Court, and therefore can never be ignored.[48] Landfried and others, however, have argued that this view is exaggerated, that the influence is not clearly *decisive*, but that *in certain cases, and particularly those initiated according to abstract review procedures, party affiliation clearly played an important role.*[49] In any case, the number of referrals of laws to the West German court is highest after national elections yielding an alternation in power, that is, during a new government's so-called honeymoon period, and when reform spirits are highest. Thus, in Germany in the 1970–71, 1976–77, 1983–84, and 1987 periods, the number of referrals jump significantly—from three to five or more per year. Moreover, virtually all students of German judicial politics have noted that the court demonstrated greater judicial activism when faced with reforms from the Left during the 1970s than it had previously.[50] Von Beyme, for example, notes that "the Constitutional Court . . . served in many respects as a brake on reforms by SPD governments."[51] The relationship which developed—between a newly constituted, reform-minded government, an opposition willing to use the referral mechanism to obstruct that agenda, and increased judicial activism—is obviously comparable to that described in the 1981–86 period in France. That judges are creatively building constitutional law in periods of great reform activity is undeniable, and perhaps an understandable response to the fact that many of the disputes they are asked to resolve are highly complex socially and politically, and do not fall into neat constitutionally fixed categories.

"Overdone Scrupulousness" and Corrective Revision

Theoretically, legislators would have a range of options available to them in response to constitutional censure or control: they could, on one extreme, copy word-for-word relevant jurisprudence directly into new legislation, seek creative ways to circumvent a court's dictates on the other, or strike balances between the two. What Landfried concludes with respect to West German legislators could also describe their French counterparts: "The problem is not so much the absence than the excess of obedience . . . towards the court"— there is an "overdone scrupulousness."[52] The practical effect of many of the most important decisions of unconstitutionality is to force a second legislative process, which I have called a corrective revision process—the reelaboration of a censured text in conformity with judicial prescriptions in a second legislative process. This conformity can be characterized as strict, and no legislative project has ever been censured twice in either country, despite multiple referrals.

In cases such as these, legislators simply allow constitutional courts to dictate, often word-for-word, the terms of new legislation. Policy outcomes may have no relation to initial policy preferences as expressed by the respective parliaments. Indeed, revised laws reflect the policy preferences of constitutional judges unambiguously overriding those of elected officials. A few examples will suffice. In 1982, the French Council struck down the nationalization bill on the grounds that its provision for compensation to expropriated stockholders violated property rights. It then went on to state how the government could save the bill, by employing different formulas for arriving at the valuation of the companies concerned. The government was obliged to write the formulas into the law; the bill survived a second referral, but the revision raised the cost of nationalizations by a full 25 percent. In 1986, the Chirac government was forced to revise both its press and audiovisual bills after they had been struck down because, the Council asserted, they did not adequately protect media "pluralism"—a concept which is not mentioned in any constitutional text (including in those incorporated by the Council). In both cases, the government simply copied word-for-word, comma-for-comma, long sections of the Council's decision directly into the law. In 1967, the German parliament all but unanimously passed a electoral finance law elaborated, or so it was thought, in accordance with a 1966 decision on the same topic.[53] The Court, however, struck it down as unconstitutional due to the fact that it provided for reimbursements of campaign expenses only for those parties which had received at least 2.5 percent of the vote. The Court ruled that the floor should be placed at 0.5 percent, though it could point to no constitutional text in support of such a judgment.[54] The subsequent corrective revision process enshrined the

Court's solution.[55] In 1974, the Court was asked by 193 Bundestag deputies and the CDU- or CSU-led governments of five länder to rule on the SDP-FDP's abortion law. The law would have decriminalized abortion through the first three months of pregnancy; before 1974, abortion had been forbidden by the penal codes. The Court ruled, on a 6–2 vote along strict party lines (with the two SDP appointees writing strong dissents to the effect that the court had exceeded its competence), that given the Nazi past the State had an overriding obligation to protect all forms of human life, including the embryonic. The Court then decided, among other things, that abortion could not be decriminalized, but would nonetheless be allowed when justified by the (mostly health) interests of the mother as determined by a number of criteria. The decision was written into a new revised law.[56] Again, it bears emphasis that *this result is the rule not the exception*. Indeed, Kommers reports that in Germany, strict compliance is more prevalent in cases of abstract review than for any other form of review.[57] Returning to Kelsen's distinction, *constitutional courts which exercise abstract review are both positive and negative lawmakers*, a point which Kelsen would surely recognize if alive today.[58]

One important macropolitical effect of evolving juridicization has been to close off reform routes that would otherwise be open to reform-minded governments. Said differently, because these courts have (as yet) never reversed themselves, because politicians perceive the effects of judicial review as binding upon them forever, and because lawmakers choose to incorporate constitutional court jurisprudence directly into legal regimes, many political issues are no longer open to legislative activity, as the web of constitutional obligation and enjoinment becomes increasingly "close-meshed." French ministers, during the summer of 1986, spoke of being "paralyzed" by constitutional preoccupation. German politicians complain that law may not evolve with social changes and that, once juridicized, policy outcomes tend toward the conservative. As one Bundestag deputy has it, the niceties of legal debate may overwhelm broader policy considerations: the legal experts are brought in; they draw upon past jurisprudence, often seemingly unrelated to the legislation at hand, and tell us how to rewrite the law; they then predict the future decision of the Court; finally, the Court refers to these experts in its decision.[59] Many see these developments as detrimental to representative democracy. Landfried, among other West Germans, has argued on a number of occasions that the "juridicization of parliament [is] dangerous for democracy," and that abstract control mechanisms "should be abolished."[60]

It should not be surprising that normative debate attends any discussion of abstract review and its role in juridicizing policy processes; here a complex set of political, academic, and ideological commitments intersect in the concrete world of policymaking. Tolerance for review appears to vary cross-nationally. The French are much more prone to explosive confrontation: from 1981 to 1987, a succession of ministers and parliamentarians from both the Left and the Right decried what they viewed as a dangerous development toward a "government of judges," and publicly threatened to curtail the Constitutional Council's powers. I would argue that this is in part a result of the deeply ingrained Rousseauian-Republican, ideological orthodoxy according to which absolute legitimacy is conferred by the ballot box. Opponents of this ideology—mostly law professors and politicians when they are in opposition—counter that in the Fifth Republic only behavior which conforms to the constitution may be described as legitimate. But the proponents of "constitutionalism" can at best claim only that this counterideology presently coexists with its rival.

In West Germany, *Rechtsstaat* ideology has much stronger roots than does that of representative democracy, and as a result, legalism tends to overwhelm political processes. According to Dahrendorf, Germans commonly seek "authoritative solutions" to political problems, and especially those which can later be said to have emanated from one or more institution assumed to be "the most objective authority in the world."[61] In practice, the search for such "authoritative solutions" has led to heavy reliance on law and on courts to resolve "disputes . . . which would elsewhere be considered political questions."[62] The impact of this tendency appears twofold. First, juridicization results in part from the fact that policymakers constantly refer to the *Rechtsstaat*, and draft bills according to their understanding of it.[63] Once opposition politicians can claim that they have "the god of the constitution on their side,"[64] the legislative battle has virtually been won. Second, judicial-political confrontation on the French or New Deal model is unimaginable. Both appear to be true largely because notions of *Rechtsstaat* and democracy are not opposed, but meld in the minds and in the legislative discourse of governing elites. As Brinkman puts it, in West Germany

> . . . "legitimacy" tends to become "legality," since courts determine at least indirectly the shape of society. Democracy tends to be above all defined in terms of the *rechtsstaat* . . .[65]

Attention to such cognitive structures are not sufficient in and of themselves to explain cross-national attitudes among legislators toward the influence of constitutional courts on their work. *Tolerance for constitutional review also appears to vary with respect to the mode of review being exercised.* It is striking in this regard how often abstract review itself is put on trial, nearly always on the grounds that it is inherently "undemocratic," because antimajoritarian. While calls for the abolition of abstract review have been heard wherever such review exists, concrete review has never given rise to the similar attacks. *Where they exist together, politicians and doctrinal authority view abstract review as inherently more "political" than "judicial," and therefore more legitimate.* The hypothesis that politically initiated, abstract review is inherently more destabilizing than is concrete review appears to be a valid one. This is undoubtedly due to the fact that abstract review poses the "countermajoritarian difficulty" unambiguously, from the moment it is initiated. Blair reports that the German Court readily understands this, and is thus "far more cautious" when engaging in abstract review than in other activities.[66] *The French Council, on the other hand, can engage in nothing but abstract review, and is thus placed in a much more vulnerable institutional position than are other European constitutional courts.* This undoubtedly accounts for recent proposals by the Council's president and the Council's supporters to expand its jurisdiction to include forms of concrete review. It might also lead us to conclude that the judicial–political confrontation of 1981–86 was exacerbated, and perhaps largely a result of, the consequences of the a priori review mechanism.

The Spanish case is of special interest with regard to these points because it is the only court examined here which possessed both a priori and the a posteriori abstract review powers. It also provides us with another dramatic example of the use of abstract review by oppositions to obstruct what they considered to be radical reform. Following democratic Spain's first *alternance* in 1983, the Socialist-Workers government saw its program paralyzed (quite literally) as the number of referrals made by the opposition rose dramatically.[67] A noisy confrontation erupted: between the Court and the opposition on one side, and the government and the majority on the other. Most frustrating for the government, the Court possessed the power of abstract, a priori review over all organic laws as well as any laws governing the status of the autonomous regions, upon referral by politicians. (*Organic laws* are pieces of legislation, adopted according to ordinary legislative process, which alter or establish the role and functioning of constitutionally established institutions.) Upon coming to power, the Socialist-Workers embarked on a number of wide-ranging legislative and constitutional reforms, and these required extensive organic legislation. From 1983 to early 1985, the opposition referred six laws (of a total of twenty-seven which could have been referred) to the Court according to the rules governing a priori review; three of these were judged to be in whole or in part unconstitutional.[68] Perhaps most serious, these referrals delayed the reforms for ludicrous periods of time. In France, the Council is required to rule within a maximum delay of one month, and in Germany referrals do not suspend the law's effect unless a negative decision has been rendered. The Spanish referrals suspended promulgation of these laws, but much worse for the government, in five of the six cases the Court took more than a year to render a judgment! In 1985, the majority abolished a priori review over the objection of the opposition.[69] The change had the support not only of the governing party, but of the major press,[70] and, significantly, the legal community.[71] Two main arguments were most widely heard in favor of abolition of a priori control. First, a priori control was considered to be manifestly political and not judicial: its effect being to implicate the Court directly in day-to-day parliamentary politics. Second, it was judged that the procedure was being used primarily as a means of parliamentary obstruction, and therefore could not be defended as a democratic practice.

Summing Up

A survey of existing research relevant to the policymaking impact of European constitutional courts suggests the following candidate hypotheses:

• The regular use of abstract review mechanisms during periods of intense and nonincremental legislative activity leads to a *general* juridicization of policymaking processes. In consequence, constitutional law becomes constitutive of legislative behavior, and legislative activity becomes a constituent element in the building of constitutional law.

If a controversial bill on a legislative matter already subject to constitutional control was not substantially altered by juridicized legislative debate or referred to the constitutional court, this hypothesis would be disproved.

• With respect to structural mechanisms of review: Abstract review is more prone to raise fundamental questions about the democratic legitimacy of the political role of the constitutional court than is the exercise of concrete review; a priori abstract review is more destabilizing, more prone to raise questions about the court's legitimacy, than is a posteriori abstract review.

These hypotheses are suggested in part by the regularity and greater intensity of judicial–political confrontation in France, and in part by the Spanish experience. But they are difficult to prove given the paucity of research, and must remain only working hypotheses. They also must be made more sensitive to political cultural variables: to the resilience of notions of parliamentary sovereignty, or the willingness to set aside majoritarian notions in favor of legality and rule of law values, for example. Much more comparative work needs to be done, on Austria, Portugal, Spain, and on polities like Italy, which possess concrete but not abstract review. Such research would aid in attempts to specify similarities and general processes, but also to uncover and explain cross-national differences in the conduct of constitutional politics, in political tolerance for constitutional review, and in sources of and responses to judicial activism.

In the final section of this chapter, the two salient issues of this study—the policymaking capacity of European constitutional courts and the problem of the democratic legitimacy of constitutional review—are treated comparatively, with respect to the U.S. model of judicial review.

Toward a Comparative Understanding of Abstract Review

In his book, *Courts: A Comparative and Political Analysis*, Martin Shapiro identifies what he calls a "prototype of courts," demonstrates the extent to which most courts to be found in the world do not conform to this ideal, and assesses the impact of this tension on how courts behave and how legal scholars make sense of that behavior.[72] As Shapiro readily admits, most academic lawyers are fiercely attached to this prototype, to what is in effect a model of "courtliness." In fact, the model appears to be an invention of legal scholarship. In this concluding section, I use Shapiro's work in order to derive a continuum along which any judicial institution may be placed according to the distance from which each is removed from the core prototype. At the end of this continuum, furthest removed from that core, lie appellate and supreme courts. I argue that Shapiro's analysis must be extended in order to make room for the cases examined here: that is, when courts exercise abstract review their behavior conforms even less to the judicial paradigm than when they exercise concrete, judicial review.

Shapiro grounds his analysis on what he calls the "root concept" of triadic conflict resolution:

> Cutting quite across cultural lines, it appears that whenever two person come into a conflict that they cannot themselves solve, one solution appealing to common sense is to call upon a third for assistance in achieving a resolution. So universal across time and space is this simple social invention of triads that we can discover almost no society that fails to employ it. And from its overwhelming appeal to common sense stems *the basic political legitimacy of courts everywhere*. In short, *the triad for purposes of conflict resolution is the basic social logic of courts*, a logic so compelling that courts have become a universal political phenomenon [emphases added].[73]

The political legitimacy of courts is weakened to the extent that judges are perceived as having their own interests, that is as being not wholly neutral vis-à-vis the disputants. In Shapiro's terms, anything which leads disputants or future disputants to question a judge's neutrality potentially "destabilizes" the triad, and therefore the social logic of conflict resolution. In private acts of arbitration, the issue of neutrality is minimized by virtue of the fact that disputants consent to the third party's authority, that is, *disputants themselves freely build the triad*. One fundamental distinction between courts and other conflict resolvers is that jurisdiction and coercion substitute for consent: *it is through the power of the State that the triad is completed* and conflict resolving norms are constituted.[74] In modern judicial systems, the social logic of the triad has been significantly eroded. Often litigants and their lawyers do not view courts and judges as neutral, and for good reason. Not only do legal regimes tend to benefit certain classes of people to the detriment of others, but judges in their decisions demonstrate identifiable and often well-known patterns of bias with respect to certain kinds of litigants and certain kinds of controversies.[75] The massive academic literature which seeks (1) to defend judicial independence, and (2) to elaborate and/or to affirm the existence of supposedly "neutral principles," can thus be understood as attempts to reconstitute or reaffirm judicial legitimacy.

A second distinguishing characteristic of courts is their capacity to destabilize the triad by performing functions other than conflict resolution. First, courts are engaged in social control. In performing a social control function, a court does not behave as a neutral third party, but as a party which brings to the activity of conflict resolution a third interest—that of the regime broadly conceived. Thus, the social logic is again significantly weakened. Second, when judges make decisions they often make law, by judicial discovery of legal principles, for example, or due to a felt obligation to harmonize existing legal norms.[76] Lawmaking further destabilizes the triad because the rules which are applied are not preexisting ones, but are generated by the activity of conflict resolution itself.

Starting with these premises, I wish to construct a general continuum of formal conflict-resolving institutions, as a means of grounding a comparative discussion of judicial review which is sensitive to the particularities of the European experience. If such a continuum can be said to start with private, consensual triadic arbitration, each step along it represents the extent to which courts go beyond conflict resolution and engage in social control activity and lawmaking. Each step also represents the further capacity of courts to destabilize their environments and therefore to raise questions of legitimacy. As we move further along the continuum, the potential for direct confrontation with other governmental institutions increases—because *at each successive stage courts look and behave less and less like conflict-resolvers and more and more like other political actors and, in particular, legislators*. Leaving out private forms of mediation, concentrating only on formal judicial institutions, such a continuum might look like that portrayed in Table 9.2.

It is important to recognize that traditional legal theory focuses attention on the extent to which courts are *not* like other governmental institutions. Many legal scholars and judges possess strong commitments to a fundamental distinction between political and judicial authority. French orthodoxy on this matter is representative of classic Continental legal theory, but also Anglo-Saxon ideas. According to this orthodoxy (described in chapters 2, 4, and earlier in this chapter), courts are (1) composed of judges who are (2) primarily engaged in settling disputes brought by (3) real-life litigants who (4) argue a concrete case or controversy before them according to (5) fixed, contradictory judicial procedures. This orthodoxy, dominant in civil as well as common law systems, is here called the *judicial paradigm*, comparable in most respects to what Shapiro calls the "prototype of courts." The central difference between civil and common law systems, in theory at least, occurs later on in the judicial process. In civil law courts, judicial decision making is held to be *rigidly* constrained by relatively self-evident codes, which judges simply apply to cases before them. In common law courts, judges may also appeal to the authority of precedent in adjudicating cases, and this body of law and principles is understood to be in part judge-made and therefore capable of creative development as circumstances and cases may warrant. Judicial lawmaking in common law systems too is recognized as a powerful source of destabilization. According to the dictates of the prototype, judges are expected to apply only "preexisting legal norms"[77] in their decisions. The doctrine of *stare decisis* is crucial precisely because it serves to codify judge-made law. The rule also accounts for the fact that the activities of common law scholars and practitioners are structured by case law. Both—the importance of precedent and the scholarly building of constitutional law from case law—function to preserve the prototype.

As we move left along the continuum we encounter courts which conform less and less to the judicial paradigm described, and therefore encounter courts

Table 9.2. A Continuum for Comparing Types of Courts Agains the "Judicial Paradigm"*

American Model

Courts of First Instance	Appellate Courts		Supreme Courts:	Judicial Review	
Ordinary Courts	Administrative Courts	Courts of Cassation High Administrative Courts	Constitutional Courts:	Concrete Review	Abstract Review

European Model

*The further to the right a court may be positioned along this continuum, the more it engages in social control and creative lawmaking activities, and the less it conforms to the traditional judicial paradigm.

which increasingly engage in social control and lawmaking. As Table 9.2 shows, the differences between the unified court system prescribed by the American model on the one hand, and the specialized courts systems of the European model on the other, leads to a good deal of overlap when comparing common law and civil law courts. What is clear is that when we reach the appellate stage in Europe, the *Cour de cassation* and the *Conseil d'Etat*, for example, judges are far less constrained than are their lower court counterparts. It was in these courts that European judges first resisted and then broke free of the confines of positivism, discovering and then elaborating a body of natural law (i.e., judicially discovered) norms. These norms then spread throughout the judicial system as the famous "general principles of law." *But like statutes, the decisions of administrative judges are made with respect to general norms of behavior and these are expected to generate general rules of conduct governing the formal interaction between the State and the citizenry.* What Shapiro concludes about common law appellate courts applies with no loss of relevance or meaning to the high administrative courts of Austria, France, West Germany, Italy, and so on:

> . . . most high courts of appeal are barely courts at all. That is, while in form they may be engaged in finally resolving one particular dispute between two particular litigants, their principle role may be to provide uniform rules of law. Naturally such rules must be based on considerations of public policy that may have little to with the particular litigation. At worst the litigants are irrelevant; at best they are examples or samples of the general problems to be solved.

Furthest along the continuum we encounter supreme or constitutional courts exercising the power of constitutional review. At this stage, the triad is constantly being destabilized, precisely because social control and lawmaking functions are not only inseparable from conflict resolution, but they tend to overwhelm it. It should hardly be surprising therefore that judicial review is by far the most controversial activity engaged in by the U.S. Supreme Court (or any American court); indeed the fact is so well known that it hardly needs to be restated here.[78] Bobbitt goes even further: "The central issue of the constitutional debate of the past 25 years has been the legitimacy of judicial review of constitutional questions by the U.S. Supreme Court," an issue which "has claimed more discussion and more analysis than any other . . . in constitutional law."[79] But wherever it exists, debates about review are rarely about the appropriateness of dispute settlement. They are instead about the extent to which courts ought to substitute their legislative priorities for those of democratically constituted legislatures. Without wishing to engage in a comprehensive survey of what is a vast literature,[80] debates about the legitimacy of judicial review are nonetheless crucial to comparisons of different forms of review.

Leaving aside the question of original intent, contemporary defenders of the legitimacy of American judicial review have relied on two main lines of argument. First, they have employed separation of powers theories as a means to ground the practice of review in the judicial function itself. Briefly, judicial review is viewed as legitimate—and positively required—to the extent that the constitution creates a judicial order separate from and not subservient to "political" authority, replete with final powers of judgment with respect to *judicial* matters. In theory, the judiciary is formally separated from the legislature and the administration because it is expected to perform functions which the other two do not. This performance, moreover, is governed by meaningfully different decision-making criteria, rules of procedure, and standards of conduct than those which govern the political branches. Put simply, the judicial "function" is the settlement of legal disputes, brought before the judiciary in the form of litigation, according to the dictates of the law.

Problems arise because judicial review implicates the judicial function in activities otherwise thought to be legislative or executive in nature. Review unavoidably raises the countermajoritarian difficulty. Proponents of judicial review as well as courts themselves counter charges of usurpation by arguing that conflict resolution itself unavoidably involves the judiciary in the making of law and in the overseeing of its execution. The power of judicial review is therefore *not* wished for in and of itself, but at times *must* be exercised in order to resolve a pending legal conflict. Accordingly, the U.S. Supreme Court itself has articulated a number of "doctrines of self-restraint,"[81] all of which are designed to make clearer the distinction between judicial and political powers of lawmaking: for the court to rule on a law, there must be a concrete case or controversy; there must be real litigants with real interests in the outcome; remedies in lower courts must have been exhausted; some disputes are not appropriate of judicial adjudication (are "political questions"); advisory opinions are precluded, and so on. Moreover, the founders explicitly rejected proposals to give the court abstract review powers, because, among other things, it was believed that the the power to make and the power to judge laws must be kept separate from each other.[82] Thus, *proponents of review and courts themselves seek to enhance their legitimacy by appealing back to the social logic of the triad, to the judicial paradigm, to the prototype.* Finally, even though the judiciary may at times encroach on the legislature, judicial techniques of making law are said to be meaningfully different from legislative techniques of making law. This difference, too, is related to judicial function. In theory, judicial techniques are embedded in judicial process: *judicial lawmaking is particular and retrospective*, since it is a by-product of case-by-case adjudication and applies to existing situations. *Legislatures on the other hand make law generally and prospectively.*

In the real world, as the political jurisprudence movement showed again and again, distinctions between judicial and legislative behavior, and distinctions between judicial and legislative policymaking, may not be that meaningful. But whatever difference *can* be said to exist is normally understood in the terms given. When European constitutional courts exercise concrete review, they too raise the countermajoritarian difficulty, and thus all but the French Council have access to the legitimation afforded by the judicial paradigm. But European constitutional courts are less reliant on the paradigm than is the U.S. Supreme Court. This is so because, unlike the American case, constitutional review is explicitly called for in the constitution. To say this, however, is simply to recognize the fact that *Europeans desire and expect their constitutional courts to conform less to the judicial paradigm than their other courts.* For these constitutional jurisdictions alone, they rejected traditional distinctions between "judicial" and "political," and instead granted to them unambiguous political functions to perform—both in terms of social control and of lawmaking. Thus, in addition to their constitutional review activities, these courts were given extensive powers to promote the "interests of the regime." In fact, each was as an integral *legitimacy-building instrument* of a new regime. Among many other examples, the French Council was expected to intervene on the side of the executive in a wide range of potential conflicts with what was viewed by the founders as a parliament which had lost its legitimacy; the German Court was given the power (article 21.2 of the basic law) to ban "anti-democratic" political parties in the wake of a Nazi past; each of these courts was given the responsibility to verify that elections proceed according to prescribed norms; and all but the French court were granted extensive jurisdiction over fundamental rights and liberties and explicitly required to force political authorities to respect these rights in dealing with the citizenry.

European abstract review however contrasts dramatically with that of concrete review. The abstract review process is devoid of litigation, of contradictory procedures, of "case or controversy." What conflicts these courts are asked to resolve are in no sense judicial, but instead wholly legislative in nature. Indeed, as Brinkman puts it, the "law-creating element" is more important in this work than is the "dispute-deciding element."[83] And, like legislatures, the courts' judgment about the law is abstract and general. The French media pluralism decisions are useful examples—but every case of abstract review in every country where it exists can be made to say the same thing. In 1984, the Constitutional Council not only overrode the government's and the parliament's judgments that press pluralism was then threatened, but it went on to specify in detail how the legislature could protect pluralism *in the event* that a threat *might* develop. Similarly, in 1986 the Council ruled that the majority's audiovisual law—which the latter rightly argued would enhance pluralism on its face, by transferring from a monopoly public sector to the private sector France's most popular television channel, and by creating new channels—did not do enough to protect against *potential* concentration in the industry in the *future*. In this way, courts which engage in abstract review, like parliaments, make law prospectively—for situations which may or may not develop. When these courts decide, they not only make law outside of the judicial process, but according to lawmaking techniques more legislative than judicial. This appears to be an unavoidable result of abstract review processes, and further supports the view, defended in chapter 5 and earlier in this chapter, that courts which exercise abstract review behave as third legislative chambers.

The statement that these courts may at times behave as third chambers is in and of itself neither original nor an argument for or against review. It is instead merely a convenient way to describe some essential truths about how these institutions behave in their political environments. Moreover, it can be argued—in all but the French case—that the creators of these courts were aware that they were establishing third legislative chambers. Speaking of the West German case, Golay wrote in 1959 that the framers

> frankly recognized the political character of the Constitutional Court: that in many issues on which it is called to adjudicate, it acts as a kind of third legislative chamber, whose decisions have the same effects as legislation and are usually determined by, despite a play with legal concepts, by considerations of the same order as move the legislator.[84]

Finally, as noted, there is a second important set of arguments which proponents of review employ to bolster its legitimacy in the face of charges of usurpation: namely, that review protects fundamental liberties and minority rights, and that no democracy deserves to be called by that name in the absence of this protection. This is the thrust of Rostow's influential 1952 article on the "democratic nature of judicial review."[85] Rostow's view, that judicial review inherently functions to protect fundamental rights and is therefore inherently democratic is controversial, but it was also fundamental in the movement among American constitutional lawyers toward rights and moral discourse.[86] A short comment is warranted because Rostow's argument is made constantly in Europe, and because European legal scholars are exercised above all else by this presumed "function" of constitutional courts in the protection of rights.[87]

In terms of the judicial paradigm, courts may in fact be led to protect fundamental rights to the extent that these rights are embedded in law, and because courts must apply the law in their decisions. Such protection can therefore be considered a by-product, or impact, of the judiciary's basic conflict-resolving activities. However, as courts move right along the continuum, as we leave the judicial paradigm behind, courts become much more actively engaged in cataloguing new rights, reinterpreting long-established ones, and discarding old ones. This is so because, wherever it exists, constitutional review leads to the identification of constitution text and case law: "the law is what the constitutional court says it is." (One interesting and important result of the development of constitutional review in Europe is that constitutional law—unlike other domains of the law in civil law countries—is today fundamentally case law, that is judge-made law, and is treated as such by scholars.) While this occurs with respect to other aspects of the constitutional text, it may even more important with respect to constitutional rights. First, rights have proven to less stable, more malleable, to interpretation than are provisions establishing state institutions and the rules which govern their interaction. Thus Kelsen could argue that review was essential in federal states, but then oppose granting jurisdiction over rights. Second, constitutional courts appear increasingly to rely on rights provisions in periods which might be characterized as judicial activism. Indeed, I would hypothesize that the more that courts engage in social control and lawmaking generally, the more they rely on their jurisdiction over rights to justify that behavior. In any event, to say that courts function to protect rights is also to say that courts engage in social control and lawmaking.

Such protection is, after all, only real to the extent that behavior abusive to rights is or was at one time censured. The argument according to which judicial review gains in legitimacy because it serves to protect rights, takes proponents of review much further away from the judicial paradigm than does the argument from separation of powers. In fact, it leads to repudiation. In essence, the claim is that *not only do courts make law, but that review is justified because courts make better law than do legislatures.* In Europe, with the exception of France, the framers believed that the active participation of constitutional courts defending constitutional rights within lawmaking processes would result in better laws, and regime legitimacy would be enhanced accordingly.

Conclusion

The eminent German jurist, Carl Schmitt, long opposed the establishment of an organ replete with the power of constitutional review on the grounds that it would lead either to the "judicialization of politics" or to a "politicization of justice."[88] Of course, from the perspective of policymakers, it led to both. When European constitutional courts exercise abstract review, traditional separation of powers schemes are blurred: these courts behave as third chambers of parliament, which in turn leads legislatures to behave somewhat judicially (that is, policymakers feel obliged to deliberate questions of constitutional law). In all cases, abstract review exists only to the extent that politicians seek to alter legislative outcomes, by having their policy choices ratified, or the government's and parliamentary majority's choices watered down or vetoed. While the countermajoritarian problem is inevitably raised by such constitutional review, it is somewhat mitigated when compared to American judicial review by the fact that European courts were explicitly charged with important legislative roles. In any event, the politicization, by opposition groups, of these courts' offices for political ends is inseparable from the efficacy and vitality of abstract review itself: if politicians ceased to use referrals as political weapons, abstract review would disappear, and the countermajoritarian difficulty would no longer be posed. From a doctrinal perspective, the regular exercise of abstract review serves to establish fundamental rules of politics and policymaking which, taken together, constitute a new form of constitutional law. While these rules clearly impact legislative outcomes, their cumulative effect is seen as far more important and unambiguously beneficial: they serve to strengthen respect for the constitution, protect fundamental rights, and thus contribute to regime stability. Both phenomena—the lawmaking activities of European constitutional courts and the power of these courts to enhance regime legitimacy—direct analytical and empirical attention to the complex interaction of constitutional judges and elected politicians. Such interaction merits far greater emphasis than has hitherto been accorded to it by comparative and legal scholars.

APPENDIX A

Constitution Provisions Relevant to the Constitutional Council

Composition and Recruitment

Article 56:

"The Constitutional Council is composed of nine members who serve nine year, non-renewable terms. The Constitutional Council is renewed in thirds every three years. Three of its members are named by the President of the Republic, three by the President of the National Assembly, three by the President of the Senate.

In addition to the nine members mentioned above, former Presidents of the Republic are members of the Constitutional Council for life."

Article 57:

"The functions of membership in the Constitutional Council are incompatible with those of minister or member of parliament. Other incompatibilities are fixed by an organic law."

Jurisdiction

On the distinction between loi *and* reglement:

Article 37:

"Subject-matters other than those of the domain of *la loi* are of a character *règlementaire*.

Texts in legislative form governing such matters may be modified by decree issued after consulting the *Conseil d'Etat*. After the entry into force of the present Constitution, such texts can only be modified by decree after the Constitutional Council has declared that they are of a character *règlementaire* by virtue of the preceding line."

Article 41:

"If it appears during the course of the legislative procedure that a bill or an amendment is not in the domain of *la loi* or is contrary to a delegation made according to article 38, the Government may raise a motion of *irrecevabilité*.

In the case of conflict between the Government and the President of the relevant assembly, the Constitutional Council, upon the demand of one or the other, must decide within eight days."

On the constitutionality of organic laws, treaties, and ordinary legislation

Article 46 (line 5):

"Organic laws may only be promulgated after a declaration as to their conformity to the Constitution by the Constitutional Council."

Article 54:

"If the Constitutional Council, after a referral by the President of the Republic, Prime Minister, or the President of one of the two assemblies, declares that an international agreement contains a clause contrary to the constitution, the authorization to ratify or to approve it may only occur after revision of the Constitution."

Article 61 (as revised by the constitutional law of 30 October 1974)

"Organic laws, before their promulgation, and the standing orders of the parliamentary assemblies, before their entry into application, must be submitted to the Constitutional Council, which will rule on their conformity to the Constitution.

To the same ends, ordinary laws may be referred to the Constitutional Council, before their promulgation, by the President of the Republic, the Prime Minister, the President of the National Assembly, the President of the Senate, or sixty deputies or sixty senators.

In these cases, the Constitutional Council must decide within 1 month. At the demand of the Government, after a declaration of urgency, this time limit is reduced to eight days.

A referral of any law to the Constitutional Council suspends its promulgation."

Article 62:

"A provision declared unconstitutional may not be promulgation nor may it enter into force.

The decisions of the Constitutional Council may not be appealed. They bind all public powers and all administrative and jurisdictional authorities."

On the regularity of referenda and elections

Article 60:

"The Constitutional Council supervises the regularity of the operations of referenda and proclaims the results."

Articles 7, 58, and 59, charge the Constitutional Council with supervising the election of the president of the Republic, deputies and senators.

APPENDIX B

Texts Incorporated Into the Constitution of 4 October 1958 by the Constitutional Council's Decision of 16 July 1971 (Freedom of Association)

Preamble of the Constitution of 4 October 1958 (line 1)

"The French People solemnly proclaim their attachment to the Rights of Man and to the principles of national sovereignty as defined by the Declaration of 1789, confirmed and completed by the preamble of the Constitution of 1946."

Preamble of the Constitution of 28 October 1946

"In the aftermath of the victory won by the free peoples over regimes which tried to enslave and degrade the human person, the French people solemnly proclaim anew that every human being, without distinction to race, religion or belief, possesses inalienable and sacred rights. *They reaffirm solemnly the rights and the liberties of man and of the citizen consecrated by the Declaration of Rights of 1789 and the fundamental principles recognized by the laws of the Republic* [emphases added].

They proclaim, moreover, as particularly necessary to our times, the following political, economic, and social principles:

La loi guarantees to women, in every domain, rights equal to those possessed by men.

Every man persecuted due to his activities in favor of liberty has the right to asylum in the territories of the Republic.

Everyone has a right to work and the right to obtain employment. No one may be discriminated against, in his work or employment, due to his origins, opinions, or beliefs.

Every man may defend his rights and his interests by union action, and may belong to the union of his choice.

The right to strike is exercised according to the laws which regulate it.

Every worker participates, by the intermediary of his representatives, in the collective determination of the conditions of work as well as the management of the enterprise.

Every asset, every enterprise, whose exploitation is or has acquired the character of a national public service or of a de facto monopoly, must become the property of the collective.

The nation assures the individual and his family of the necessary conditions for their development.

The nation guarantees to all, notably to children, mothers, and elder workers, the protection of health, material security, rest, and leisure. Every human being who, due to his age, his physical or mental state, or economic situation, finds himself incapable to work has the right to obtain from the collectivity the means necessary for existence.

The nation proclaims the solidarity and equality of every Frenchman.

The nation guarantees equal access to the child and the adult to instruction, to professional training, and to culture. The organization of free and secular public education at every level is a responsibility of the State.

The French Republic, true to its traditions, respects the rules of international law. It will undertake no war of conquest and will never employ its forces against the liberty of any people.

Under reserve of reciprocity, France consents to those limitations of sovereignty necessary for the organization and the defense of the peace.

France forms with the peoples of the overseas territories a Union founded on the equality of rights and responsibilities, without distinction to race or religion.

The French Union is composed of nations and peoples who dedicate and coordinate in common their resources and their efforts to develop their respective civilizations, to increase their well-being, and to assure their security.

Faithful to its traditional mission, France seeks to lead the peoples which it has taken in its charge to the freedom to administer themselves and to manage democratically their own affairs; opposing all systems of arbitrary systems of colonialism, France guarantees to all equal access to public functions and the exercising of individual or collective rights and liberties proclaimed or confirmed above."

The Declaration of the Rights of Man of 1789

"The representatives of the French People, sitting in the National Assembly, considering that the ignorance, the neglect, or the disregard of the rights of man are the sole causes of public misfortune and of the corruption of governments, have resolved to list, in a solemn declaration, the natural rights of man, inalienable and sacred, in order that this declaration, constantly presented to all of the members of the social body, reminds them continuously of their rights and responsibilities; in order that the acts of the legislature and of the executive, comparable at all times with the objectives of all political institutions, will be more respectful of them; in order that the complaints of citizens, founded henceforth on simple and incontestable principles, will lead always to the maintenance of the Constitution to the happiness of all. In consequence, the National Assembly recognizes and declares, in the presence and under the auspices of the supreme being, the following rights of Man and Citizen. [Preamble to the Declaration incorporated into the Constitution of 3 September 1791].

Article 1: Men are born and remain free, and possess equal rights. Social distinctions may only be establish for the public good.

Article 2: The goal of any political association is the protection of the natural and inalienable rights of man. These rights are liberty, property, security, and resistance to oppression.

Article 3: The principle of all sovereignty resides essentially in the Nation. No body, no individual may exercise authority which has not been expressly granted.

Article 4: Liberty consists of being able to do what does not injure others: thus, the exercising of natural rights by every man may only be limited in order to assure other members of the society the enjoyment of the same rights. These limits may only be determined by *la loi*.

Article 5: *La loi* may only forbid those actions injurious to society. That which is not forbidden by *la loi* may not be circumscribed, and no one may be forced to do what *la loi* does not command.

Article 6: *La loi* is the expression of the general will. Every citizen has the right to participate personally, or by their representatives, it is formation. *La loi* applies equally to everyone, whether it protects or punishes. All citizens being equal before it, are equally eligible to enjoy all honors, public places and employment, according to their capacity, and without distinction other than that of their own virtue and talent.

Article 7: A man may be accused, arrested, or detained only in circumstances determined by *la loi*, and according to the forms which it prescribes. Those who foster, expedite, or execute or demand the execution of arbitrary orders must be punished; but every citizen summoned or seized by virtue of *la loi* must obey immediately, or be judged guilty for resisting.

Article 8: *La loi* must establish only those punishments which are strictly and obviously necessary, and a man may be punished only by virtue of an established law and promulgated prior to the offense, and legally applied.

Article 9: Every man being presumed innocent until he has been declared guilty, if it is judged indispensable to arrest him, may not be subjected to more than that necessary to detain him. Transgression will be severely punished by *la loi*.

Article 10: No one may be harassed for their opinions, including religious ones, as long as their manifestations do not trouble the public order established by *la loi*.

Article 11: The free communication of thoughts and of opinions is one of the most precious rights of man; every citizen may therefore speak, write, and print freely, but is responsible for the abuse of this liberty in circumstances determined by *la loi*.

Article 12: The guarantee of the rights of man and of citizen necessitates public authority; this authority is therefore instituted for the advantage of everyone, and not for the particular advantage of those to which it has been confided.

Article 13: For the undertaking of public authority, and for the expenses of the administration, a communal contribution is indispensable: it must be equally divided among all citizens, according to their faculties.

Article 14: Every citizen has the right to take notice of, by themselves or by their representatives, the necessity of public contributions, to consent to them freely, to follow their employment, and to determine the quota, the means of assessment, the collection, and the duration.

Article 15: Society has the right to call to account every public agent for its administration.

Article 16: Every society in which the guarantee of rights is not assured does not possess a constitution.

Article 17: Property being inviolable and sacred, no one can be deprived of it in the absence of public necessity, legally declared, obviously warranted, and without just and prior compensation.

NOTES

Introduction: Where Judicial Politics Are Legislative Politics

1. *Lettre à la nation* (notes bleus), 7 October 1986.
2. *Débats*, National Assembly (*Constituante*), 4 August 1986, pp. 4019–4024.
3. Jacques Toubon, secretary-general of the RPR, in *Le Monde*, 5 September 1986.
4. Albin Chalandon, minister of justice, quoted in *Le Monde*, 9 August 1986.
5. *Le Monde*, 25–26 January 1987; *Le Figaro*, 28 January 1987.
6. John T. S. Keeler and Alec Stone, "Judicial–Political Confrontation in Mitterrand's France: The Emergence of the Constitutional Council as a Major Actor in the Policy-Making Process," in *The Mitterrand Experiment*, ed. Stanley Hoffmann, Sylvia Malzacher, and George Ross (New York: Oxford, 1987), pp. 161–81.
7. For reactions, see *Le Monde*, 21 February 1986.
8. Guy Carcassonne.
9. *L'Express*, 13–19 June 1986.
10. Text in *Le Monde*, 27 May 1988.
11. Roy Macridis, *The Study of Comparative Government* (New York: Random House, 1955).
12. Harry Eckstein, "Introduction: A Perspective on Comparative Politics, Past and Present," in *Comparative Politics: A Reader*, ed. David E. Apter and Harry Eckstein (Glencoe: Free Press, 1963), pp. 3–31.
13. Roy Macridis, "Comparative Politics and the Study of Government," *Comparative Politics* 1 (1968):85–86.
14. Lee Sigelman and George Gadbois, "Contemporary Comparative Politics: An Inventory and Assessment," *Comparative Political Studies* 16 (1983):293–95.
15. Harry P. Stumph et al., "Whither Political Jurisprudence: A Symposium," *Western Political Quarterly* 36 (1983):533–70.
16. Attempts at introducing "sociological jurisprudence, the jurisprudence of interests, and legal realism . . . have not gone very far. These schools of thought have not been refuted or even ignored; they simply have not penetrated into the legal consciousness." John Henry Merryman, *The Civil Law Tradition*, 2d ed. (Stanford: Stanford University Press, 1985), p. 84.
17. The West German case is the exception. See Donald P. Kommers, *Judicial Politics in West Germany* (Beverly Hills and London: Sage, 1976), and Kommers, *The Constitutional Jurisprudence of the Federal Republic of Germany* (Durham and London: Duke University Press, 1989); Philip M. Blair, *Federalism and Judicial Review in West Germany* (Oxford: Clarendon, 1981). I know of no other full-length studies in English on the other national constitutional courts in Europe.
18. Theda Skocpol, "Bringing the State Back In: Strategies of Analysis in Current Research," in *Bringing the State Back In*, ed. Peter Evans, Dietrich Rueschmeyer, and Theda Skocpol (New York: Cambridge, 1985), p. 3.

19. James G. March and Johan P. Olsen, "The New Institutionalism: Organizational Actors in Political Life," *American Political Science Review* 78 (1984):734–49.

20. Ibid., p. 738.

21. Macridis, "Comparative Politics and the Study of Government," pp. 85, 79–90.

22. Alec Stone, "Where Judicial Politics are Legislative Politics: The Birth and Development of Abstract Review in Western Europe," *Policy Studies Journal* 19 (1990):81–95; "In the Shadow of the Constitutional Council: The 'Juridization' of the Legislative Process in France," *West European Politics* 12 (April 1989):12–34; "Legal Constraints to Policy-Making: The Conseil constitutionnel and the Conseil d'état," in *Policy-Making in France, From De Gaulle to Mitterrand*, ed. Paul Godt (London: Pinter, 1989), pp. 28–41.

23. *Ordonnance 58-1067 du 7 novembre 1958 portant loi organique sur le Conseil constitutionnel, modifiée par la loi organique 74-1101 du 26 décembre 1974.*

24. While Almond characterizes the "return to the state" movement as a "polemic" and a "scholarly tantrum" organized around false claims of a "paradigmatic shift," it is rather a matter of emphasis and research strategy, and should not—and really cannot—be made to close down communication between so-called traditionalists and statists. Almond's assertion that "rigorous," "empirical" work is somehow antithetical to an institutionalist bias should be resisted: such work is all the more necessary to the extent that our understanding of institutional life is limited. Gabriel Almond, "The Return to the State," *American Political Science Review* 82 (1988):853–58.

25. In Stumph et al., "Whither Political Jurisprudence?," p. 547.

26. Glendon Schubert, *Judicial Decision-Making* (London: Free Press, 1963), p. 2.

27. In Stumph et al., "Whither Political Jurisprudence?," p. 548.

28. James L. Gibson, "From Simplicity to Complexity: The Development of Theory in the Study of Judicial Behavior," *Political Behavior* 5 (1983):7–49.

29. Glendon Schubert, "Behavioral Research in Public Law," *American Political Science Review* 57 (1963):433.

30. Walter Murphy, "Courts as Small Groups," *Harvard Law Review* 79 (1966): 1565.

31. The classic study is Martin Shapiro, *Law and Politics of the Supreme Court* (London: Free Press, 1965).

32. Stumph et al., "Whither Political Jurisprudence?," p. 536.

33. Herman C. Pritchett, "The Development of Judicial Research," in *Frontiers of Judicial Research*, ed. Joel B. Grossman and Joseph Tanenhaus (New York: Wiley, 1969), p. 42.

34. Charles L. Black, Jr., *The People and the Court* (Englewood Cliffs: Prentice Hall, 1960); Alexander M. Bickel, *The Least Dangerous Branch* (New York: Bobbs and Merrill, 1962).

35. Some contemporary scholars combine both concerns; see John H. Ely, *Democracy and Distrust: A Theory of Judicial Review* (Cambridge: Harvard, 1982), and Philip Bobbitt, *Constitutional Fate: Theory of the Constitution* (New York: Oxford, 1982).

36. "Symposium: Legal Scholarship: Its Nature and Purposes," *Yale Law Journal* 90 (Special Issue 1984).

37. John Brigham, *Constitutional Language: An Interpretation of Judicial Decision* (London: Greenwood, 1978).

38. Robert Gordon, "Critical Legal Histories," *Stanford Law Review* 36 (1984):57–125.

39. Rogers Smith, "Political Jurisprudence, the 'New Institutionalism,' and the Future of Public Law," *American Political Science Review* 82 (1988):89–109.

40. See Isaac D. Balbus, "Commodity Form and Legal Form: An Essay on the 'Relative Autonomy' of the Law," *Law and Society Review* 11 (1976–77):572.

41. Smith, "Political Jurisprudence, the 'New Institutionalism,' and the Future of Public Law," p. 96.

42. Gordon, "Critical Legal Histories," esp. pp. 100–101.

43. Ibid., p. 101.

44. Smith, "Political Jurisprudence, the 'New Institutionalism,' and the Future of Public Law," p. 104.

45. Ibid., p. 97.

46. Merryman, *Civil Law Tradition*, p. 60.

47. Ibid., p. 60.

48. Martin Shapiro, "Political Jurisprudence, Public Law, and Post-Consequentialist Ethics," *Studies in American Political Development* 3 (1989):99.

49. Smith, "Political Jurisprudence, the 'New Institutionalism,' and the Future of Public Law," p. 91.

50. The "hypothesis-generating case-study . . . is an attempt to formulate definite hypotheses to be tested subsequently among a larger number of cases. Their objective is to develop theoretical generalizations where no theory exists." Arendt Lijphart, "Comparative Politics and the Comparative Method," *American Political Science Review* 65 (1971):692.

51. "One studies a case in order to arrive at a preliminary theoretical construct. That construct, being based on a single case, is unlikely to constitute more than a clue to a valid general model. One therefore confronts it with another case that may suggest ways of amending and improving the construct to achieve better case interpretation." Harry Eckstein, "Case Study and Theory in Political Science," *Handbook of Political Science* (Reading, Mass.: Addison-Wesley, 1975), 7:104.

Chapter 1. The Historical Tension: Politics v. *le droit*

1. The term, *constitutional review*, is used throughout this book to describe the activities of *any* institution—whether ordinary court, administrative court, or nonjudicial entity such as the Constitutional Council—which possesses the power to declare legislative acts unconstitutional. It corresponds to the French *le contrôle de la constitutionnalité des lois*.

2. Louis Rougier, *La France à la recherche d'une constitution* (Paris: Sirey, 1952), p. 82.

3. "If the judge has difficulty finding the applicable provision, or interpreting and applying that provision to the fact situation, then one of the following people must be at fault: the judge, because he does not know how to follow clear instructions; the legislator, because he failed to draft clearly stated and clearly applicable legislation; or the legal scholar . . . because he has failed to instruct the legislator or judge properly on how to draft and apply statutes. No other explanation is possible." John Henry Merryman, *The Civil Law Tradition*, 2d. ed. (Stanford: Stanford University Press, 1985), p. 81.

4. René David, *French Law: Its Structure, Sources, and Methodology* (Baton Rouge: LSU Press, 1972), p. 124.

5. James Beardsley, "Constitutional Review in France," *The Supreme Court Review: 1975* (Chicago: University of Chicago Press, 1975), pp. 189–260.

6. Article 6 of the Declaration of the Rights of Man of 1789 states that: "*La loi*

is the expression of the general will," in G. Berlia, R. Bonnard, L. Duguit, and H. Monnier (hereafter cited as Bonnard), *Les Constitutions et les principales lois politiques de la France* (Paris: Librairie générale de droit et de jurisprudence, 1952), p. 2.

7. Jean Brissaud, *A History of French Law* (Boston: Little Brown, 1915), pp. 427–73.

8. A. Esmein, *Cours élémentaire d'histoire de droit francais* (Paris: Sirey, 1903), pp. 518–40; M. Petiet, *Du pouvoir législatif en France* (Paris: Sirey, 1891) p. 222; J. H. Shennan, *The Parlement of Paris* (Ithaca, N.Y.: Cornell, 1968).

9. Bonnard, *Les Constitutions*, p. 25.

10. Article 127 of the penal code, which has also never been abrogated, states that "judges shall be guilty of an abuse of their authority and punished with loss of their civil rights" for interfering with the legislature or administration "by issuing regulations containing legislative provisions, by suspending applications of one or several laws, or by deliberating on whether or not a law will be published or applied."

11. "The principle that interpretation of *la loi* could only be made by the legislator was not contested by anyone." Jean Bourdon, *La réforme judiciare de l'An VIII* (Paris: Carrere, 1942), p. 436.

12. Merryman, *Civil Law Tradition*, p. 28.

13. Donald R. Kelley, *Historians and the Law in Post-Revolutionary France* (Princeton: Princeton, 1984), p. 44.

14. Bourdon, *La réforme judiciare de l'An VIII*, pp. 432–33.

15. Bonnard, *Les Constitutions*, p. 99.

16. Franz Neumann, *The Democratic and the Authoritarian State* (New York: Free Press, 1964), p. 37.

17. Bonnard, *Les Constitutions*, p. 114.

18. Merryman, *Civil Law Tradition*, p. 36.

19. *Paulin (Cassation criminelle*, 11 May 1833), *Sirey* 1 (1833):357–60.

20. But see *Débats*, Archives parlementaires, 39 (8 August 1791):271–72.

21. Ibid., 66 (16 June 1793):576.

22. Ibid., pp. 576–77.

23. *Journal officiel*, Chambre des deputés, documents parlementaires, session ordinaire, 28 January 1903, pp. 95, 97, 99. The bills were allowed to die without ever being brought to debate, but one response was recorded: "It should be added that our colleague wants to destroy the constitution." *Annales de la Chambre des députés*, Débats parlementaires, 28 January 1903, p. 328.

24. Jeanne Lemasurier, *La Constitution de 1946 et le contrôle de la constitutionnalité des lois* (Paris: Librairie générale de droit et de jurisprudence, 1953), p. 14.

25. Edward Lambert, *Le gouvernement des juges et la lutte contre la législation sociale aux Etats-unis* (Paris: Giard, 1921), argued that judicial review would inevitably lead to a reactionary "government of judges."

26. O. R. Tayler, *The Fourth Republic of France: Constitution and Political Parties* (London: Aldon and Blackwell [Eton], 1951), pp. 1–17.

27. Maurice Duverger, *Les Constitutions de la France*, 4th ed. (Paris: Presses universitaires de France, 1961), pp. 107–10.

28. Lemasurier, *La Constitution de 1946 et le contrôle de la constitutionnalité des lois*, p. 28.

29. Rougier, *La France à la recherche d'une constitution*, pp. 116–17.

30. Taylor, *The Fourth Republic of France*, p. 74.

31. Bonnard, *Les Constitutions*, pp. 568–70.

32. Quoted in Rougier, *La France à la recherche d'une constitution*, p. 118.

33. If the lower and upper chambers agree on the terms of revision, the revision can be effected by legislation. If the chambers do not agree, the will of the National Assembly prevails. The latter then drafts the amendment according to the procedures governing ordinary legislation. If this bill is adopted by less than two-thirds of the assembly, or less than three-fifths of both chambers, then the People would have the final say.

34. The committee met on 18 June 1948 after the assembly had adopted a bill granting a loan to an airplane engine manufacturer which could not meet its payroll. The Council of the Republic voted 215–80 to ask the president of the Republic to convene the committee on the grounds that the assembly had unconstitutionally limited debate on the bill. The committee asked the two chambers for consultations, and within a week the bill was promulgated. See the *Chronique constitutionnelle*, *Revue du droit public* 65 (1949):195–98.

35. Duverger, *Les Constitutions de la France*, pp. 113–14.

36. Bourdon, *La réforme judiciare de l'An VIII*, pp. 2–44; Paul Bastid, *Les institutions politiques de la monarchie parlementaire française* (Paris: Sirey, 1954), pp. 346–48.

37. *Débats*, 16 June 1793, pp. 576–77. See also J. H. Clapham, *The Abbé Sieyès: An Essay in the Politics of the French Revolution* (London: King, 1912), pp. 173–75.

38. Maurice Deslandres, *Histoire constitutionnelle de la France de 1789 à 1870* (Paris, Colin, Sirey, 1932), 1:426–44; Jean Thiry, *Le Sénat de Napoléon, 1800–1814* (Paris: Berger-Lerrault, 1949), pp. 20–26.

39. Bonnard, *Les Constitutions*, pp. 110–11, 141–43.

40. Ibid., pp. 153–54.

41. Georges Burdeau, *Droit constitutionnel et institutions politiques* (Paris: Librairie générale de droit et de jurisprudence, 1957), p. 80.

42. Maurice Duverger, *Droit constitutionnel et institutions politiques* (Paris: Presses universitaires de France, 1956), p. 224.

43. Irene Collins, *Napoléon and His Parliaments* (London: Arnold, 1979), p. 63.

44. Paul Bastid, *Sieyès et sa pensée* (Paris: Hachette, 1939), p. 598.

45. Deslandres, *Histoire constitutionnelle de la France de 1789 à 1870*, pp. 448–51.

46. Thiry, *Le Sénat de Napoléon, 1800–1814*, pp. 359–60.

47. Merryman, *Civil Law Tradition*, p. 56.

48. Ibid., pp. 92–93.

49. Kelley, *Historians and the Law in Post-Revolutionary France*, pp. 56–71, 134.

50. L. Neville Brown and J. F. Garner, *French Administrative Law*, 2d ed. (London: Buttersworth, 1973), pp. 18–30.

51. "Bonaparte, watching the rising tide of jurisprudence, is said to have cried: 'My code is lost.'" Kelley, *Historians and the Law in Post-Revolutionary France*, p. 44.

52. Brown and Garner, *French Administrative Law*, pp. 18–30.

53. Henry Nézard argued that "... *it is certain that, provoked by the frequence of abusive and arbitrary laws made in evident violation of every judicial sense, a powerful doctrinal movement developed to bestow upon the courts the power to refuse to apply laws contrary to the Constitution.*" A. Esmein, *Droit constitutionnel*, 7th ed. (Paris: Sirey, 1927). It is unlikely that Third Republic legislation was more abusive than what had occurred in the past—by any standard. On the contrary, it is much more likely that the movement developed when it did because, and for the first time, there was a greater chance that policymakers could be influenced by doctrine.

54. F. Arnande, "Notre programme," *Revue du droit public* 1 (1884):3–4.

55. I am aware of no scholarly treatment of either.

56. Léon Duguit, "The Power of the State," *Harvard Law Review* 31 (1917):1–2.

57. Léon Duguit, "Theory of Objective Law Anterior to the State," in *Modern Legal Philosophy*, ed. Arthur W. Spencer (New York: Macmillan, 1921), pp. 247–48.

58. My discussion is based on the excellent account by Mario Einaudi, *The Physiocratic Doctrine of Judicial Control* (Cambridge: Harvard, 1938). Einaudi leaves the French quotations in their original French, the translations here are therefore my own.

59. Ibid., pp. 35–45, 71.

60. Emmanuel Sieyès, *Qu'est-ce que le tiers état* (Geneva: Droz, 1970; orig., 1789).

61. Benjamin Constant, *Cours de politique constitutionnelle* (Paris: 1819).

62. Quoted in Bastid, *Sieyès et sa pensée* p. 598.

63. Clapham, *The Abbé Sièyes*, p. 422.

64. Maurice Hauriou, *Précis du droit constitutionnel* (Paris: Sirey, 1929), p. 261.

65. Berthelémy, "Les limites au pouvoir legislatif," *Revue politique et parlementaire*, 10 December 1925, p. 355; Paul Roubier, *Théorie générale du droit*, 2d ed. (Paris: Sirey, 1951), p. 9.

66. Kenneth H. F. Dyson, *The State Tradition in Western Europe* (Oxford: Martin Robertson, 1980), pp. 172–73.

67. Maurice Hauriou, *Principes du droit public* (Paris: Sirey, 1910), p. 235.

68. Duguit, *Law in the Modern State*, p. 70.

69. Gaston Jèze, "Le contrôle juridictionnel des lois," *Revue du droit public* 40 (1924):402.

70. R. Carré de Malberg, *Contribution à la theorie générale de l'état* (Paris: Sirey, 1922) 2:545–50, 576–622. Carré de Malberg, although sympathetic to the movement's objectives and to judicial review in theory, was the most influential public law specialist to remain faithful to the traditional model. His position was that since legislative and constituent powers were fused in France, these debates were entirely academic. Still, he argued that as a matter of legal science, the French doctrine of legislative sovereignty was "unacceptable" (pp. 549–50, note 33).

71. Maurice Hauriou, *Droit constitutionnel* (Paris: Sirey, 1923), p. 298. The notion that individual rights are the basis of higher law is echoed even by those who were not ready to support the introduction of judicial review. See A. Esmein, *Droit constitutionnel* (Paris: Sirey, 1915), pp. 29–30.

72. Duguit, *Traité du droit constitutionnel*, p. 673.

73. Hauriou, *Droit constitutionnel*, pp. 297–300.

74. There were of course great differences in form and substance between the natural law as articulated in the seventeenth and eighteenth centuries and that propagated by neo-natural lawyers in the first part of the twentieth century. Neo-natural lawyers, for example, viewed the law not as fixed and unchanging across time and space, but as an evolutive product of legal science and judicial activity. See Carl Joachim Friedrich, *The Philosophy of Law in Historical Perspective*, 2d ed. (Chicago: University of Chicago Press, 1963), p. 181.

75. F. Gény, "La laïcité du droit naturel," *Archives de philosophie de droit et de sociologie juridique* (Paris: Sirey, 1930), p. 18; Roubier, *Théorie générale du droit*, pp. 182–92.

76. Roubier, *Théorie générale du droit*, p. 281.

77. Duguit, *Traité du droit constitutionnel*, pp. 660–68.

78. Duguit, "The Power of the State."

79. Roubier, *Théorie générale du droit*, p. 282.

80. In 1881, A. Saint-Girons wrote in his extremely influential *Essai sur la séparation des pouvoirs* (Paris: Larose, 1881), pp. 545–61: "If ever our country was to be so happy to enjoy a system of judicial authority as well organized as in the United States, if ever the tenacity with which revolutionary prejudices was lost, we would finally understand that judges are not the enemy to weaken, but the truest friend of public liberties."

81. I know of no exceptions. Even the great critic of the movement, Carré de Malberg (*Contribution à la théorie générale de l'état*, 2:545–50), called the American system of judicial review "the best expression of the principle of national sovereignty."

82. Hauriou, *Précis du droit constitutionnel*, pp. 267–68.

83. Ibid., pp. 281–82.

84. Duguit, *Law in the Modern State*, p. 87.

85. Ibid., p. 92.

86. Ibid., p. 89.

87. *Winkel (Conseil d'état), Sirey* 3 (1909):147, note Hauriou.

88. Hauriou, *Droit constitutionnel*, p. 319. Six years later, Hauriou wrote, "It can no longer be contested that the *Conseil d'état* was not engaged . . . in interpreting the constitution, and with great vigor, . . . based on the constitutional principle of the continuity of public service." *Précis du droit constitutionnel*, p. 286; Duguit, *Law in the Modern State*, pp. 90–91.

89. See the newspaper, *Le Temps*, 14–29 November 1925.

90. Lambert, *Le gouvernement des juges* . . .

91. Ibid., pp. 4–7.

92. Ibid., p. 227.

93. Ibid., chapter 11.

94. Lemasurier, *La Constitution de 1946 et le contrôle de la constitutionalité des lois*, p. 22.

95. Gaston Jèze, "Contrôle des deliberations des assemblées délibérantes," *Revue générale d'administration*, 2 (1895):411.

96. Jèze, "Le contrôle juridictionnel des lois."

97. Ibid., pp. 400–401, 408–11.

98. Ibid., p. 412.

99. Ibid., p. 421.

100. For a survey of this jurisprudence see Lemasurier, *La Constitution de 1946 et le contrôle de la constitutionnalité des lois*, pp. 169–72.

101. Julien Laferrière, *Manuel de droit constitutionnel*, 2d ed. (Paris: Domat, 1947), p. 952.

102. Lemasurier, *La Constitution de 1946 et le contrôle de la constitutionnalité des lois*, p. 116.

103. Gordon Wright, *The Reshaping of French Democracy* (New York: Reynal and Hitchcock, 1948), pp. 136–58; Philip Williams, *Politics in Post-War France: Parties and the Constitution in the Fourth Republic* (London: Longmans and Green, 1958), pp. 306–8.

104. Taylor, *The Fourth Republic of France*, pp. 18–19.

105. *Débats*, National Assembly (*Constituante*), 7 March 1946, p. 607.

106. Ibid., p. 617.

107. Ibid., p. 639.

108. Ibid., 20 August 1946, p. 3362.

109. Ibid., 29 August 1946, pp. 3361–62.

110. The remarks of de Tinguy, ibid., 23 August 1946, p. 3303.

111. Lemasurier, *La Constitution de 1946 et le contrôle de la constitutionnalité des lois*, p. 178, recounts a discussion of an amendment offered to the preamble, which would have bound the legislature to conform to its principles. According to Lemasurier, debate on the amendment was cut off when André Philip responded that it was unnecessary since such a requirement "was obvious." While she reports that this exchange occurred at *Débats*, National Assembly (*Constituante*), 28 August 1946, p. 3365, only the raising of the amendment is there; there is no record of the Philip response at the page or debate cited in her work. Even if such an amendment had been adopted, parliament alone would have possessed the power to ensure its respect.

112. The preamble was amended to include the FPRLR at *Débats*, National Assembly (*Constituante*), 28 August 1946, pp. 3363–68.

113. See Charles-Albert Colliard, *Précis de droit public* (Paris: Dalloz, 1950), p. 99, and G. Ripert, *Le déclin du droit* (Paris: Librarie générale de droit et de jurisprudence, 1949), pp. 13, 17. Both argued, in Austinian terms, that since violations of the preamble would incur no sanction the text could not be law, but possessed only "moral" authority. Both, however, as the title of Ripert's book testifies, expressed displeasure with having arrived at such a conclusion.

114. The exception is Lemasurier, who sums up her conclusion as follows: "The evidence contained in the *travaux préparatoires* for the constitution are very disappointing because, without being decisive, they give birth to serious doubts about the [constitutional] status of the principles edicted by the preamble." *La Constitution de 1946 et le contrôle de la constitutionnalité des lois*, p. 175.

115. Notably Burdeau, *Droit constitutionnel et institutions politiques*, pp. 346–48; Maurice Duverger, *Manuel de droit constitutionnel* (Paris: Presses universitaires de France, 1948), pp. 370–74; F. Gény, "De l'inconstitutionnalité des lois et des autres actes de l'autorité publique et des sanctions qu'elle comporte dans les droits nouveaux de la Quatrième République," *Jurisclasseur périodiques: Semaines juridiques* 1 (1947):613; F. Pelloux, "Le Préambule de la Constitution de 27 octobre 1946," *Revue du droit public* 63 (1947):347; Jean Rivéro and Georges Vedel, "Les principes économiques et sociaux et la Constitution du 27 octobre 1946," *Collection Droit social*, 31 May 1947, pp. 13, 15; Vedel, *Manuel élémentaire de droit constitutionnel*, pp. 326–27, 553; Marcel Waline, note on *Dehaene (Conseil d'Etat)*, *Revue du droit public* 66 (1950):694.

116. Bonnard, *Les Constitutions*, p. 567.

117. See *Débats*, National Assembly (*Constituante*), 20 September 1946, pp. 3908–3909. The article is there denoted as 71-L.

118. Gény, "De l'inconstitutionnalité des lois et des autres actes de l'autorité publique et des sanctions qu'elle comporte dans les droits nouveaux de la Quatrième Republique."

119. Duverger, *Manuel du droit constitutionnel*, pp. 374–78.

120. Gény, "De l'inconstitutionnalité des lois et des autres actes de l'autorité publique et des sanctions qu'elle comporte dans les droits nouveaux de la Quatrième Republique," p. 613.

121. Beardsley, "Constitutional Review in France," p. 197; Brown and Garner, *French Administrative Law*, p. 119; Lemasurier, *La Constitution de 1946 et le contrôle de constitutionnalité des lois*, pp. 187–200.

122. *Amicales des annamités de Paris, Recueil du Conseil d'état*, 11 July 1956, p. 317.

Chapter 2. From Watchdog to Policymaker: Structure, Function, Mandate

1. ". . . the alternative to institutionalized Bonapartism had become Bonapartism unlimited." Stanley Hoffmann, "The New Constitution of the Fifth Republic," *American Political Science Review* 53 (1959):348.

2. Long a central objective of Gaullist theory. Michel Debré, "Trois caracteristiques du régime parlementaire française," *Revue française de science politique* 5 (1955):21–48.

3. Didier Maus, "La Constitution jugée par sa pratique," *Revue française de science politique* 34 (1984):887.

4. François Mitterrand, *Le coup d'état permanent* (Paris: Plon, 1964).

5. Marcel Waline, "Les rapports entre la loi et le règlement avant et après la Constitution de 1958," *Revue du droit public* 75 (1959):699–717.

6. Marcel Waline, "The Constitutional Council of the Fifth Republic," *American Journal of Comparative Law* 12 (1963):483; François Luchaire, *Le Conseil constitutionnel* (Paris and Aix-en-Provence: Economica, 1980), p. 92.

7. J. E. S. Hayward, *Governing France* (New York: Norton, 1983), p. 139.

8. In Didier Maus, ed., *Textes et documents sur la pratique institutionnelle de la Ve République* (Paris: Documentation française, 1978), p. 5.

9. *Travaux préparatoires de la Constitution du 4 octobre 1958, Avis et débats du Comité consultatif constitutionnel* (Paris: Documentation française, 1960).

10. Ibid., pp. 75–76.

11. Ibid., p. 76; my discussion of this proposal is based on debates appearing at ibid., pp. 75–79.

12. The draft appears at ibid., pp. 205–22.

13. A proposal to allow the council to hear cases on appeal from the *Conseil d'Etat* and the *Cour de cassation* to determine the constitutionality of legislation was raised but elicited near total hostility. *Documents pour servir à l'histoire de l'élaboration de la Constitution du 4 octobre 1958, tome 1: Des origines de la loi constitutionnelle du 3 juin 1958 à l'avant-projet du 29 juillet 1958* (Paris: Documentation française, 1987) pp. 388, 425.

14. The Council's duties also include supervising presidential elections, parliamentary elections, and referenda, certifying the incapacity of the president of the Republic (never performed), and advising him on the exercise of emergency powers. Constitutional provisions relevant to the council are reproduced in Appendix A.

15. There is one exception: article 61 requires that the initial standing orders of both the National Assembly and the Senate, and any subsequent amendments to them, be submitted to the Constitutional Council before their entry into force.

16. *Travaux préparatoires*, pp. 101–102.

17. Ibid., pp. 164–66.

18. Members appointed to serve out the terms of those who die in office or are otherwise unable to finish their terms, may be reappointed for a full nine years.

19. Dominique Rosenberg, "Les anciens Presidents de la République, membres de droit du Conseil constitutionnel: L'impossible retraite," *Revue du droit public* 101 (1985):1263–1318.

20. *Le Monde*, 19 September 1962.

21. Palewski admits this in *La revue des deux mondes*, May 1980, p. 377.

22. *Le Monde*, 28 February 1974.

23. Quoted in *L'Express*, 7–13 April 1975.

24. Patrick Juillard, "Difficultés du changement en matière constitutionnelle:

l'aménagement de l'article 61.2 de la Constitution," *Revue du droit public* 90 (1974): 1767.

25. *L'Unité*, 23–29 June 1978.

26. François Léotard, soon to be named minister of culture, characterized the appointment as "an inadmissible politicization of the very center of our institutions"; the president of the UDF (center-Right) called it "a veritable provocation in light of the period chosen, in the middle of the electoral campaign, and of the important role that the Constitutional Council will play between 1986 and 1988." *Le Monde*, 21 February 1986.

27. Maurice Duverger, "Une fraude à la constitution?," and François Luchaire's rebuttal, *Le Monde*, 26 February 1986. The legal controversy, which was all but ignored by most politicians, concerned the terms of the organic law which fixes the procedures of naming the president of the council and the fulfillment of those functions.

28. Luchaire, *Le Conseil constitutionnel*, pp. 59–66.

29. Hoffmann, "The New Constitution of the Fifth Republic."

30. *Travaux préparatoires*, p. 76.

31. Rarely is this made explicit; nevertheless, Luchaire reports that the Gaullist veteran, Louis Joxe, was named in 1977 (at age 76 years) in order to clear the way for future Prime Minister Raymond Barre to be able to stand for Joxe's "safe" seat in the 1978 parliamentary elections. Luchaire, *Le Conseil constitutionnel*, pp. 59–60, note 1.

32. The Council jurisprudence in this area, noncontroversial and relatively technical, will not be discussed in this book, but see Bruno Genevois, *La Jurisprudence du Conseil constitutionnel: Principes directeurs* (Paris: STH, 1988), pp. 42–43, 152–58, and Louis Favoreu and Loïc Philip, eds., *Les grandes décisions du Conseil constitutionnel* (Paris: Sirey, 1988), pp. 184–207.

33. If the council rules that a clause in a treaty is unconstitutional, the constitution must be revised before the treaty may be ratified. This has, to date, never occurred. For the relationship between the Constitutional Council and international law, see Genevois, *La Jurisprudence du Conseil constitutionnel*, pp. 355–82.

34. Treaties can be referred to the Constitutional Council only by the president of the Republic, the prime minister, or the presidents of the Senate or National Assembly. The 1974 amendment expanding the referral mechanism applies only to ordinary legislation, and not to treaties.

35. The council ruled that its competence extended only to that which is expressly mentioned by the constitution, thus excluding a general advisory capacity. Documents concerning this affair are in Maus, ed., *Textes et documents sur la pratique institutionnelle de la Ve République*, pp. 116–20.

36. Michel Debré, *Débats*, National Assembly (*Constituante*), 26 May 1959, pp. 557–58.

37. Charles de Gaulle, *Mémoires d'éspoir* (Paris: Plon, 1970), 1:291.

38. *Débats*, National Assembly (*Constituante*), 27 May 1959, p. 605.

39. Ibid., 26 May 1959, p. 561.

40. Ibid., 26–27 May 1959, pp. 554–605.

41. 59-2 DC, *Recueil* (1959), p. 58; 59-3 DC, *Recueil* (1959), p. 61.

42. Put differently, the decision "illustrates clearly the general tendency of the Council to conceive in an extensive manner the Constitution, and in a restrictive manner, [parliamentary] conformity to it," Favoreu and Philip, *Les grandes décisions du Conseil constitutionnel*, p. 44.

43. *Le Monde*, 3 July 1959.

44. *Débats*, Senate, 27 October 1960, p. 1383.

45. 59-1L, *Recueil* (1959), p. 67. Favoreu and Philip, *Les grandes décisions du Conseil constitutionnel*, pp. 57–69.

46. 61-14L, *Recueil* (1961), p. 38.

47. Maus, ed., *Textes et documents sur la pratique institutionnelle de la Ve République*, pp. 189–91.

48. Louis Favoreu, ed., *Le domaine de la loi et du règlement* (Paris: Economica, 1978); Jean-Louis Pézant, "Loi/règlement: la construction d'un nouvel équilibre," *Revue francaise de science politique* 34 (1984):922–54.

49. Luchaire, *Le Conseil constitutionnel*, pp. 106–12.

50. Louis Favoreu, *La politique saisie par le droit* (Paris: Economica, 1987), pp. 115–17, 123–32.

51. In the 1974–80 period, 80 percent of all parliamentary referrals were made by deputies; in the 1981–87 period, the figure decreased to 60 percent, a change which can largely be attributed to the Senate's active opposition to Socialist rule during much of that time.

52. The most publicized of such threats concerned proposals to alter the status of New Caledonia. See *Le Monde*, 22 May 1986 and 20 February 1987; on both instances, the government watered down or dropped their proposals.

53. *Revue française de droit constitutionnel* 2 (1990) is devoted in its entirety to different aspects of the reform.

Chapter 3. From Watchdog to Policymaker: The Evolution of Constitutional Review

1. François Mitterrand, *Le coup d'état permanent* (Paris: Plon, 1964), pp. 144, 146.

2. Léon Nöel, *De Gaulle et les débuts de la Ve République* (Paris: Plon, 1976), p. 92.

3. Charles de Gaulle, *Mémoires d'éspoirs* (Paris: Plon, 1970), 1:297.

4. *La revue des deux mondes*, January 1981, p. 139.

5. François Luchaire, *Le Conseil constitutionnel* (Paris and Aix-en-Provence: Economica, 1980), p. 112.

6. Jean Boulouis, "Le défenseur de l'Executif," *Pouvoirs* 13 (1980):27–34.

7. Luchaire, *Le Conseil constitutionnel*, p. 31.

8. 60-8 DC, *Recueil* (1960), p. 25; Louis Favoreu and Loic Philip, eds., *Les grandes décisions du Conseil constitutionnel* (Paris: Sirey, 1986), pp. 86–87.

9. Didier Maus, ed., *Textes et documents sur la pratique institutionnelle de la Ve République* (Paris: Documentation française, 1978), pp. 310–12.

10. 60-11 DC, *Recueil* (1961), p. 29.

11. *Débats*, Senate, 20 October 1960, p. 1325.

12. Maus, ed., *Textes et documents sur la pratique institutionnelle de la Ve République*, pp. 312–14.

13. *Travaux préparatoires de la Constitution du 4 octobre 1958, Avis et débats du Comité consultatif constitutionnel* (Paris: Documentation française, 1960), pp. 113–14.

14. Still the government used the procedure again. 63-21 DC, *Recueil* (1963), p. 23.

15. Favoreu and Philip, *Les grandes décisions du Conseil constitutionnel*, pp. 86–87.

16. Made explicit in 28 DC, *Recueil* (1966), p. 15.

17. Maus, ed., *Textes et documents sur la pratique institutionnelle de la Ve Republique*, p. 202.

18. Léo Hamon, quoted in Favoreu and Philip, *Les grandes décisions du Conseil constitutionnel*, p. 121.

19. Quoted in James E. Beardsley, "Constitutional Review in France," *Supreme Court Review* (1975), pp. 212–13.

20. *Débats*, Senate, 10 October 1962, pp. 1305–1308.

21. *Le Monde*, 19 September 1962.

22. See G. Berlia, "Le probleme de la constitutionnalité du référendum du 28 octobre 1962," *Revue du droit public* 78 (1962):936–46.

23. *Le Monde*, 3 October 1962 and 4 October 1962.

24. Maus, ed., *Textes et documents sur la pratique institutionnelle de la Ve République*, p. 85; *Débats*, National Assembly (*Constituante*), 4 October 1962, p. 3028.

25. Maus, ed., *Textes et documents sur la pratique institutionnele de la Ve République*, pp. 315–17.

26. The tenth member was former President Auriol, who had broken his vow never again to sit on the Constitutional Council in order to fight the revision.

27. 62-20 DC, *Recueil* (1962), p. 27.

28. *Le Monde*, 8 November 1962.

29. Ibid. The council could have noted that neither article 11, which gives the president the power to submit "any bill (*loi*)" to the people in referendum, nor article 61, which simply states that "*lois* may be referred to the Council" by the competent authorities, differentiates between different *categories* of *lois*. Even more persuasive, since according to article 6 the constitution requires that the details of the president's election be established and modified only by virtue of an organic law, and since article 61 requires a ruling as to the constitutionality of such laws before their promulgation, the council could have argued that it had no choice but to review the revision. Last, there is nothing in French constitutional law that places the People above the constitution: could not the People be considered a public power which the Council, in its own words, is asked to regulate?

30. The vote of 6–4 is not really as close as it might appear at first glance. As long as de Gaulle was assured of the votes of his appointees (which must always include those appointed by the president of the National Assembly), he was assured of a majority. It may be strongly inferred that the votes of Auriol and the three appointees made by Monnerville made up the minority.

31. "La Constitution: doit-elle être revisée?," *Revue politique et parlementaire* 741 (1964):3–17, and 742 (1964):3–18; "Pour ou contre un régime présidentiel," *Revue politique et parlementaire* 757 (1965):3–14, and 758 (1965):11–24.

32. "Le Conseil constitutionnel au Parlement" (unpublished study of the Center for Constitutional Studies at the University of Aix-Marseilles III, 1976).

33. *Programme commun de gouvernement du PCF et du PS* (Paris: Editions Socialies, 27 June 1972), pp. 145–46.

34. 71-44 DC, *Recueil* (1971), p. 29.

35. George D. Haimbaugh, Jr., "Was it France's Marbury v. Madison?," *Ohio State Law Review* 35 (1974):910.

36. Jacques Robert, "Propos sur le sauvetage d'une liberté," *Revue du droit public* 87 (1971):1171–1203.

37. The text of the original bill is reproduced at ibid., p. 1201.

38. *Débats*, National Assembly (*Constituante*), 23 June 1971, pp. 3342–43, and 30 June 1971, pp. 3566–68, 3581–83.

39. *Débats*, Senate, 28 June 1971, pp. 1430–36.

40. *Le Monde*, 2 July 1971; 3 July 1971.

41. Ibid., 30 June 1971; 1 July 1971; 10 July 1971; 16 July 1971; 17 July 1971.

42. Ibid., 18–19 July 1971.

43. Ibid., 20 July 1971.

44. Jean Rivéro, "Rapport de Synthèse," in *Cours constitutionnelles européennes de droits fondamentaux* (Paris and Aix-en-Provence: Economica, 1982), p. 520.

45. Palewski, *Revue des deux mondes*, August 1979, p. 372.

46. Interviews with Louis Favoreu, November 1988, and Bruno Genevois, June 1989.

47. 73-51 DC, *Recueil* (1973), p. 25. Favoreu and Philip, *Les grandes décisions du Conseil constitutionnel*, pp. 269–86.

48. 74-54 DC, *Recueil* (1975), p. 19; Favoreu and Philip, *Les grandes décisions du Conseil constitutionnel*, pp. 291–313. The bill was referred by Gaullists and others within the rightist majority.

49. In his speech before the council in 1977, Giscard called the right of referral "an essential element of opposition status," in Maus, ed., *Textes et documents sur la pratique instituionnelle de la Ve République*, pp. 373–77.

50. Loïc Philip, "Bilan et éffets de la saisine du Conseil constitutionnel," *Revue française de science politique* 34 (1984):989.

51. Juillard, "Difficultés du changement en matière constitutionnelle: l'aménagement de l'article 61.2 de la Constitution," *Revue du droit public* 90 (1974):1733; Philip, "Bilan et éffets de la saisine du Conseil constitutionnel," p. 989.

52. *Débats*, Senate, 17 October 1974, p. 1958.

53. Ibid., 16 October 1974, p. 1313; *Débats*, National Assembly (*Constituante*), 10 October 1974, p. 4952.

54. *Débats*, National Assembly (*Constituante*), 8 October 1974, pp. 4863–64.

55. Juillard, "Difficultés du changement en matière constitutionnelle: l'aménagement de l'article 61.2 de la Constitution," 1703–1772.

56. *Débats*, National Assembly (*Constituante*), 8 October 1974, p. 4870.

57. Duverger, "Une gramme de démocratie," *Le Monde*, 11 October 1974.

58. *Débats*, Senate, 18 October 1973, p. 1426.

59. Ibid., 16 October 1974, p. 1322.

60. *Le Monde*, 10 October 1974; *L'Humanité*, 19 October 1974.

61. Duverger, "Une gramme de démocratie."

62. *Rapport #2128*, National Assembly, 20 December 1975; *Rapport #2080*, National Assembly, 17 December 1975; and *Rapport #2131*, National Assembly, 20 December 1975.

63. *Rapport #2128*; *Rapport #2131*.

64. Duverger, "Une gramme de démocratie."

65. 77-87 DC, *Recueil* (1977), p. 42; Favoreu and Philip, *Les grandes décisions du Conseil constitutionnel*, pp. 370–86.

66. *Le Monde*, 25 November 1977; 26 November 1977.

67. *Débats*, Senate, 25 October 1977, p. 2436.

68. The vote was close, 274–272, *Débats*, National Assembly (*Constituante*), 29 August 1946, p. 3433.

69. Ibid., pp. 2432–33.

70. Duverger, *Manuel du droit constitutionnel*, pp. 170–71. The law itself is probably the original source of the phrase, "the fundamental principles recognized by the laws of the Republic [FPRLR]."

71. 77-79 DC, *Recueil* (1977), p. 35; 77-92 DC, *Recueil* (1977), p. 21; 77-83 DC, *Recueil* (1977), p. 39.

72. 79-105 DC, *Recueil* (1979), p. 33. Favoreu and Philip, *Les grandes décisions du Conseil constitutionnel*, pp. 421–38.

73. *Débats*, National Assembly (*Constituante*), 26 April 1979, p. 3189.

74. Ibid., pp. 3161–165; *Débats*, Senate, 21 June 1979, pp. 2081–84.

75. *Débats*, National Assembly (*Constituante*), 26 April 1979, pp. 3165–69.

76. Ibid., p. 3169.

77. Ibid., 26 June 1979, pp. 5657–59; *Débats*, Senate, 27 June 1979, p. 2389.

78. *Débats*, National Assembly (*Constituante*), 26 April 1979, p. 3169.

79. Ibid., 26 June 1979, p. 5659.

80. Ibid., p. 5663.

81. *Débats*, Senate, 27 June 1979, p. 2388.

82. 80-117 DC, *Recueil* (1980), p. 42.

83. *Le Monde*, 14 June 1980.

84. *Law #80-572*, 25 July 1980, *Journal officiel* (*Lois . . .*), 26 July 1980, p. 1882.

85. Maus, ed., *Textes et documents sur la pratique institutionnelle de la Ve Republique*, pp. 353–56.

86. 76-75 DC, *Recueil* (1976), p. 33; Favoreu and Philip, *Les grandes décisions du Conseil constitutionnel*, pp. 361–75.

87. The reasons cited by Poher for his decision to refer the 1971 legislation to modify the law of association are found in *Le Monde*, 3 July 1971.

88. *Débats*, Senate, 15 December 1976, pp. 4481–90; *Débats*, National Assembly (*Constituante*), 25 November 1976, pp. 8697–99.

89. Perhaps the earliest and clearest such case occurred during debates on a finance law in 1975, when after the threat of referral, the Senate removed a provision desired by the government and the government subsequently made no attempt to restore it. *Débats*, Senate, 11 September 1975, p. 2670.

90. The best is Stanley Hoffmann, Sylvia Malzacher, and George Ross, eds., *The Mitterrand Experiment* (New York: Oxford, 1987).

91. John T. S. Keeler and Alec Stone, "Judicial–Political Confrontation in Mitterrand's France: The Emergence of the Constitutional Council as a Major Actor in the Policy-Making Process," *The Mitterrand Experiment*, pp. 161–81.

92. The government was actually a coalition government, since it originally included four communist ministers.

93. *Le Monde*, 15 September 1981.

94. *Le Monde*, 20 January 1982.

95. *Le Figaro*, 26 August 1981; *La Croix*, 29 October 1981.

96. *Quotidien de Paris*, 20 January 1982; *L'Humanité*, 20 January, 1982.

97. Hughes Portelli, "Le juge constitutionnel et le pouvoir," *La Croix*, 19 October 1984.

98. 81-132 DC, *Recueil* (1982), p. 18; Favoreu and Philip, *Les grandes décisions du Conseil constitutionnel*, pp. 516–58.

99. *Le Monde*, 19–20 January 1982.

100. Ibid., *L'Humanité*, 19 January 1982; *Quotidien de Paris*, 20 January 1982.

101. Roger Pinto, "Un recours improbable," *Le Monde*, 7 January 1982.

102. *Le Monde*, 19–20 January 1982.

103. 82-139 DC, *Recueil* (1982), p. 31.

104. *Le Figaro*, 20 January 1982.

105. 82-146 DC, *Recueil* (1982), p. 66.

106. *Le Monde*, 3 February 1979.

107. See Daniele Loschak, "Les hommes politiques, les 'sages' (?) . . . et les femmes (à propos de la décision du Conseil constitutionnel du 18 novembre 1982)," *Droit social*, February 1982, pp. 131–37.

108. *Le Monde*, 21–22 November 1982; 24 November 1982; 25 November 1982.

109. 82-147 DC, *Recueil* (1982), p. 70.

110. Favoreu and Philip, *Les grandes décisions du Conseil constitutionnel*, pp. 580–91.

111. *Le Figaro*, 4–5 December 1982.

112. *La Libération*, 5 December 1982.

113. *Le Monde*, 16 December 1982.

114. 83-165 DC, *Recueil* (1984), p. 30; Favoreu and Philip, *Les grandes décisions du Conseil constitutionnel*, pp. 626–43.

115. *Le Monde*, 13 December 1983.

116. Ibid., 24 January 1984.

117. 84-181 DC, *Recueil* (1984), p. 73; Favoreu and Philip, *Les grandes décisions du Conseil constitutionnel*, pp. 644–64.

118. *Le Monde*, 14 September 1984.

119. Ibid., 15 October 1984.

120. 85-196 DC, *Recueil* (1985), p. 63; 85-197 DC, *Recueil* (1985), p. 70; Favoreu and Philip, *Les grandes décisions du Conseil constitutionnel*, pp. 676–98.

121. *Le Monde*, 1 June 1985; 4–5 August 1985; *The Economist*, 17 August 1985.

122. *Le Monde*, 10 August 1985; 14 August 1985.

123. Ibid., 23 August 1985; 25–26 August 1985.

124. See *Rapport #111*, National Assembly, 15 May 1986.

125. *Le Monde*, 21 February 1986; *Le Figaro*, 20 February 1986.

126. *Le Monde*, 21 February 1986.

127. Olivier Duhamel, "L'histoire extravagante du Conseil constitutionnel," *L'Express*, 27 June–3 July 1986, pp. 70–78; "What is the Constitutional Council?," *Le Monde*, 6 September 1986, pp. 10–11.

128. *Le Monde*, 21 January 1982.

129. Ibid., 9 August 1986.

130. Ibid., 7 October 1986.

131. Ibid., 5 September 1986.

132. Ibid., 9 August 1986; *La Libération*, 13 August 1986.

133. 86-207 DC, *Recueil* (1986), p. 61; 86-208 DC, *Recueil des lois* (1986), p. 87.

134. See *Le Monde*, 16 July 1986.

135. Text and commentary by Louis Favoreu in *Le Figaro*, 17 November 1986.

136. 86-210 DC, *Recueil* (1986), p. 110; 86-217 DC, *Recueil* (1986), p. 141.

137. *Débats*, National Assembly (*Constituante*), 10 June 1986, p. 2029.

138. Stone, "In the Shadow of the Council: The 'Juridicisation' of the Legislative Process in France."

139. *Le Monde*, 11 December 1986.

140. Ibid., 22 December 1986.

141. 86-225 DC, *Recueil* (1987).

142. *Le Figaro*, 26 January 1987.

143. *Le Monde*, 25–26 January 1987; *Le Figaro*, 28 January 1987.

144. In a long and unprecedented exposée of the internal debates on a decision within the Council, *Le Nouvel observateur*, 6–12 February 1987, reported that the vote was 4–3 with 1 abstention, with all four socialist appointees voting to annul. The report of one abstention is in error: the vote was 4–4.

145. *La Libération*, 26 January 1987.

146. *Le Monde*, 14 May 1987.

147. Ibid., 11 December 1987.

Chapter 4. Understanding French Constitutional Politics

1. Charles L. Black, Jr., *The People and the Court* (Englewood Cliffs: Prentice Hall, 1960), p. 24.

2. Alexander M. Bickel, *The Least Dangerous Branch* (New York: Bobbs and Merrill, 1962), p. 29.

3. The only articles on the Constitutional Council to have appeared to date in the *Revue française de science politique*, France's leading political science journal, were written by the law professors Louis Favoreu and Loïc Philip for a special issue devoted to the 1958 constitution. *Revue française de science politique* 34 (1984).

4. For example, those by: 1) former Constitutional Council members, such as Georges Vedel, "Le Conseil constituionnel, gardien du droit positif ou défenseur de la transcendance des droits de l'homme," *Pouvoirs* 45 (1988), and Vedel, "Neuf ans au Conseil constitutionnel," *Le Débat* 55 (1989):49–56; 2) the present secretary-general of the council and *conseiller d'Etat*, Bruno Genevois, "L'influence du Conseil constitutionnel," *Pouvoirs* 49 (1989):47–56; or 3) legal advisors to political parties, such as Guy Carcassonne, "A propos du droit d'amendment : les errements du Conseil constitutionnel," *Pouvoirs* 41 (1987):163.

5. Loic Philip, "Les attributions et le rôle du Conseil constitutionnel en matière d'élections et de référendums," *Revue du droit public* 78 (1962):101.

6. Maurice Duverger, *Institutions politiques et droit constitutionnel* (Paris: Presses universitaires de France, 1962), pp. 634–35.

7. For a review, see Jacques Georgel, "Aspects du Préambule de la Constitution du 4 octobre 1958," *Revue du droit public* 76 (1960):85–101.

8. Ibid., p. 101.

9. Jacques Robert, "Propos sur le sauvetage d'une liberté," *Revue du droit public* 87 (1971):1171–1203.

10. Patrick Juillard, "Difficultés du changement en matière constitutionnelle: l'aménagement de l'article 61.2 de la Constitution," *Revue du droit public* 90 (1974): 1704–1705.

11. Maurice Duverger, "Un gramme de démocratie," *Le Monde*, 11 October 1974.

12. *Débats*, National Assembly (*Constituante*), 10 October 1974, p. 4952.

13. Ibid., p. 4859.

14. Ibid., pp. 4863–64.

15. Quoted in Francois Luchaire, "Le Conseil constitutionnel: est-il une juridiction?," *Revue du droit public* 95 (1979):31.

16. Marcel Waline, "Préface," in Favoreu and Philip, eds., *Les grandes décisions du Conseil constitutionnel* (Paris: Sirey, 1986), pp. xi–xx; Luchaire, "Le Conseil constitutionnel; est-il une juridiction?," p. 31.

17. Quoted in Michael H. Davis, "The Law/Politics Distinction, the French Constitutional Council, and the U.S. Supreme Court," *American Journal of Comparative Law* 34 (1986):71.

18. "The essential element which . . . characterizes a *juridiction* is the fact that its decisions are final. . . . [T]he only other condition is that its judgments are based on law." Waline, "Préface," p. xii.

19. Luchaire, "Le Conseil constitutionnel: est-il une juridiction?," p. 37.

20. *Revue du droit public* 91 (1975):164.

21. More than a dozen public law specialists spoke to the issue in *Commentaire* 9 (1986).

22. Louis Favoreu, "L'apport du Conseil constitutionnel au droit public," *Pouvoirs* 13 (1980):17–26.

23. Louis Favoreu, "La décision de constitutionnalité," *Revue de droit comparé* 1986, pp. 628–33.

24. Ibid., p. 630.

25. In itself, this is unremarkable: the *Conseil d'Etat* is bound by the terms of statute, and since a council decision is the final step in the making of many statutes its effect must be respected.

26. Louis Favoreu, "L'application des décisions du Conseil constitutionnel par le Conseil d'état at le Tribunal des conflits," *Revue francaise du droit administratif* 3 (1987):240–80. Favoreu's conclusion—a minority one—is that the *Conseil d'Etat* is indeed applying the council's jurisprudence.

27. Jean Vincent, Gabriel Montagnier, and André Varinard, *La justice et les institutions* (Paris: Dalloz, 1985) has 8 of some 500 pages devoted to the Constitutional Council.

28. Yves Bot, *Les institutions judiciares* (Paris: Berger-Levrault, 1985), pp. 35–39, 264.

29. 74-54 DC, *Recueil* (1975), p. 19.

30. 80-127 DC, *Recueil* (1981), p. 15, 84-176 DC, *Recueil* (1984), p. 55.

31. 85-197 DC, *Recueil* (23 August 1985).

32. *Le Monde*, 14 August 1986.

33. 80-127 DC. The decision contains more than four times the number of considerations as any previous one, was an intricate partial annulment, and contained a number of detailed SROIs. It was also one of the first decisions of the Constitutional Councl with Georges Vedel as a member.

34. Vedel's influence in "juridicizing" the council's work is recognized as crucial. *Le Monde*, 27 February 1989; Louis Favoreu in "Le droit constitutionnel jurisprudentiel (mars 1986–mars 1989)," *Revue du droit public* 105 (1989):411.

35. Favoreu, "1977, l'année charnière: le développement de la saisine parlementaire et la jurisprudence relative aux libertés et droits fondamentaux," *Revue du droit public* 94 (1978):839.

36. Ibid.

37. François Luchaire, *Le Conseil constitutionnel* (Paris and Aix-en-Provence: Economica, 1980), pp. 179–83.

38. See also Danielle Loschak, "Le Conseil constitutionnel, protecteur des libertés," *Pouvoirs* 13 (1980):43 criticizing the council for relying on "principles impossible to find . . . whose content was wholly elastic."

39. Loïc Philip, "Le développement du controle de constitutionnalité et l'accroissement des pouvoirs du juge constitutionnel," *Revue du droit public* 99 (1983):401–18.

40. Quoted in Louis Favoreu, "Les cent premières annulations prononcées par le Conseil constitutionnel," *Revue du droit public* 103 (1987):446.

41. See the roundtable discussion in Robert Etien, "Le Conseil constitutionnel sous la VIIe législateur (1981–1986)," *La revue administrative* 229 (1986):33–42.

42. Jacques Robert, *La Croix*, 3 September 1986.

43. Favoreu, "Les cent premières annulations prononcées par le Conseil constitutionnel," pp. 443–54, updated in Favoreu, "Le droit constitutionnel jurisprudentiel (mars 1986–mars 1989)," pp. 427–28.

44. Favoreu, "Les cent premières annulations prononcées par le Conseil constitutionnel," p. 443.

45. Vedel, "Neuf ans au Conseil constitutionnel," p. 49.

46. Laurent Cohen-Tanugi sees this as a general French trait. *Le droit sans l'état* (Paris: Presses universitaires de France, 1985), p. 53.

47. Martin Shapiro, *Law and Politics of the Supreme Court* (London: Free Press, 1965), p. 26.

48. Cohen-Tanugi, "Qui a peur du Conseil constitutionnel?," *Le Débat* 43 (1987): 58.

49. Favoreu, "Les décisions du Conseil constitutionnel dans l'affaire des nationalisations," *Revue du droit public* 98 (1982):382.

50. Favoreu, "Le droit constitutionnel jurisprudentiel (mars 1983–mars 1986)," 102 (1986):408.

51. Favoreu, "Les décisions du Conseil constitutionnel dans l'affaire des nationalisations," p. 382.

52. Louis Favoreu, "Conseil constitutionnel: mythes et réalités," *Regards sur l'actualité*, June 1987, p. 19.

53. Louis Favoreu, "Une grande décision," in *Nationalisation et Constitution*, ed. Louis Favoreu (Paris and Aix-en-Provence: Economica, 1982), 55:23; Jean Rivéro, "Ni lu, ni compris," *Actualité juridique, Droit administratif*, 20 April 1982, p. 209; Jacques Robert, *Le Monde*, 23–24 December 1984.

54. Favoreu, "Conseil constitutionnel: mythes et réalités," p. 19.

55. Favoreu, "Une grande décision," p. 23.

56. Shapiro, *Courts* (Chicago: University of Chicago Press, 1980), p. 29.

57. Philip Bobbitt, *Constitutional Fate: Theory of the Constitution* (New York: Oxford, 1982), p. 17.

58. Louis Favoreu, *La politique saisie par le droit* (Paris: Economica, 1988), p. 97.

59. Ibid., p. 137.

60. Favoreu and Robert, in Etien, "Le Conseil constitutionnel sous la VIIe législateur (1981–1986)," *La revue administrative*, no. 221 (1984):35.

61. Louis Favoreu, "La mythe du gouvernement des juges" (Paper presented at the Colloque sur les aspects nouveaux des institutions de la Veme Republique, Oxford University, October 1987), p. 15.

62. Ibid., p. 16.

63. See especially, Favoreu, *La politique saisie par le droit*, pp. 105–11.

64. Guy Carcassonne, "A propos du droit d'amendement : les errements du Conseil constitutionnel," *Pouvoirs* no. 41 (1987):163.

65. The expression is Jerome Frank's, *The Courts on Trial* (Princeton: Princeton, 1949), chapter 18.

66. Favoreu, *La politique saisie par le droit*, p. 95.

67. The assessment of Autin, "Les exceptions d'irrecevabilité soulevées par les parlementaires," *Revue du droit public* 99 (1983):737. There has been some limited attention to the body's policymaking impact in France. See notes to chapter 5.

68. I am not suggesting that political scientists never adopt interior perspectives.

69. Favoreu, *La politique saisie par le droit*, pp. 30, 35.

70. Favoreu, "Actualité et legitimité du contrôle juridictionnel des lois en Europe occidentale," *Revue du droit public* 100 (1984):1196.

71. Favoreu, *La politique saisie par le droit*, pp. 30–39, 117–18.

72. Ibid., pp. 15, 128.

73. Black, *The People and the Court*, p. 223.

74. Ibid., pp. 61–65.

75. Christine Landfried, "The Impact of the German Constitutional Court on

Politics and Policy-Outputs," in *Constitutional Review and Legislation: An Internal Comparison* (Baden-Baden: Nomos, 1989), p. 537.

76. David Adamany, "Legitimacy, Realigning Elections, and the Supreme Court," *Wisconsin Law Review*, 1973, pp. 790–846.

77. Ibid., p. 807.

78. Ibid., pp. 845–46.

79. In fact, the Council does not declare legislation "constitutional," but only that it is "not contrary" or, less often, that it "conforms" to the constitution.

80. Favoreu, *La politique saisie par le droit*, pp. 20, 35, 46, 77.

81. Vedel, "Le Conseil constitutionnel, gardien du droit positif ou défenseur de la transcendance des droits de l'homme," p. 151.

82. Adamany, "Legitimacy, Realigning Elections, and the Supreme Court," p. 807.

83. Ibid., p. 791.

84. Bobbitt, *Constitutional Fate: Theory of the Constitution*, pp. 190–91.

85. Adamany, "Legitimacy, Realigning Elections, and the Supreme Court," pp. 808–15.

86. Newspapers feel obliged to provide readers with histories and explanations of the Constitutional Council's role; e.g., the article, "What is the Constitutional Council?," *Le Monde*, 6 September 1986.

87. Favoreu, "La décision de constitutionnalité," p. 631.

88. *Le Monde*, 21 January 1982.

89. Carcassonne, "A propos du droit d'amendement : les errements du Conseil constitutionnel," p. 163.

90. Bickel, *The Least Dangerous Branch*, pp. 190–91.

91. Ibid., p. 29.

92. Favoreu, "Europe occidentale," *Le contrôle juridictionnel des lois*, p. 62.

93. Ibid.

94. Favoreu, *La politique saisie par le droit*, pp. 19, 39.

Chapter 5. The Juridicized Policymaking Process

1. Jean-Marie Garrigou-Lagrange, "Les partenaires du Conseil constitutionnel," *Revue du droit public* 102 (1986):665.

2. Guy Carcassonne, "La résistance de l'Assemblée nationale a l'abaissement de son role," *Revue francaise de science politique* 34 (1984):910–21, and Guy Carcassonne, "Réhabiliter le Parlement," *Pouvoirs* 49 (1989):37–45.

3. The percentage of laws of parliamentary origin has remained remarkably stable over time, usually hovering at around 10 percent. See Olivier Duhamel, "The Fifth Republic Under Francois Mitterrand: Evolution and Perspectives," in *The Mitterrand Experiment*, ed. Stanley Hoffman, Sylvia Malzacher, and George Ross (New York: Oxford, 1987), p. 148.

4. Statistics on parliamentary activity here and elsewhere are taken from the annual *Statistiques, Bulletin de l'Assemblée nationale*, cited hereafter as the *Statistical Bulletin*.

5. Jean-Louis Pézant, "Contribution à l'étude du pouvoir législatif selon la Constitution de 1958," *Melanges Burdeau* (Paris: Librairie générale de droit, 1977), p. 477. The term *autolimitation* appears to have been used in this sense first by Louis Favoreu, "Décentralisation et Constitution," *Revue du droit public* 98 (1982):1268.

6. Louis Favoreu and Loic Philip, eds., *Les grandes décisions du Conseil constitutionnel* (Paris: Sirey, 1988), pp. 361–75.

7. The Senate debated the bill extensively only once, when it passed the first of two *motions d'irrecevabilité, Débats*, Senate, 15 December 1976, pp. 4481–90.

8. *Débats*, National Assembly (*Constituante*), 25 November 1976, pp. 8697–99.

9. Ibid., p. 8697.

10. The *Conseil d'Etat* may also identify and study judicial and administrative aspects of social problems on its own, and make policy recommendations to governments based on these studies. See generally G. Braibant, "Les nouvelles fonctions du Conseil d'état," *Revue administrative* 239 (1987):415–21.

11. *Rapport annuel 1982, Conseil d'Etat*, 1982, p. 15.

12. *Rapport annuel 1987, Conseil d'Etat*, 1987, p. 54.

13. *Rapport annuel 1982*, pp. 9–10.

14. *Le Monde*, 23 October 1986; *Rapport #102*, Senate, *Commission de lois* 10 December 1986, pp. 18–22; *Le Figaro*, 26 January 1987.

15. Interviews with staff members of legislative committees at the National Assembly, February 1987; *Le Monde*, 23 October 1986.

16. *Le Monde*, 6 November 1986; 9–10 November 1986.

17. Ibid., 22 May 1986; 20 February 1987.

18. *Règlement de l'Assemblée nationale*, Bureau de l'Assemblée, April 1986, 7th ed., p. 94.

19. In the National Assembly, only one such motion has been adopted; this occurred when Jean Foyer successfully argued against a government move to harmonize tax codes with European Economic Community (EEC) directives after declaring urgency—the vote was 332–132. *Débats*, National Assembly (*Constituante*), 30 November 1978, pp. 8567–75.

20. Jean-Louis Autin, "Les exceptions d'irrecevabilité soulevées par les parlementaires," *Revue du droit public* 99 (1983):728, 731; Jean-Louis Pézant, "Le contrôle de la recevabilité des initiatives parlementaires, Eléments pour un bilan," *Revue française de science politique* 31 (1981):168.

21. This appears to be a record for a law passed in the Fifth Republic. National Assembly statistics, however, show that an increased number of laws are passed after being extensively amended. Whereas from 1974 to 1981 the average number of laws adopted after acceptance of 50 or more amendments was less than 10 per year, from 1982 to 1985 the average number is 21.5. In 1984, 3 bills were successfully amended more than 300 times, and 10 more between 100 and 300 times; in 1986–87, the average number drops to 6, but 5 (of 12) had been amended over 100 times. The source is the *Statistical Bulletin*.

22. Favoreu, "Décentralisation et Constitution," p. 1265.

23. Carcassonne, "La résistance de l'Assemblée nationale à l'abaissement de son role," p. 220.

24. Robert Etien, "L'Application des décisions d'annulation du Conseil constitutionnel sur saisine parlementaire," *La revue administrative* 221 (1984):473, note 20.

25. The information for this section was obtained in interviews with Guy Carcassonne, February 1987, Louis Favoreu, June 1988, and Bruno Genevois, June 1989. A shorter summary of procedures is contained in Louis Favoreu, "La décision de constitutionnalité," *Revue internationale de droit comparé* 1986, pp. 613–16.

26. There are also ten specialists who help the council to fulfill its role as appellate judge of electoral conflicts: five *maître de requêtes* from the *Conseil d'Etat*, and five from the *Cour de comptes*.

27. *Le Figaro*, 5 May 1986.

28. Bruno Genevois, *La Jurisprudence du Conseil constitutionnel: Principes directeurs* (Paris: Editions STH, 1988).

29. Didier Maus, ed., *Textes et documents sur la pratique institutionnelle de la Ve République* (Paris: Documentation francaise, 1978).

30. Favoreu, "Les cent premières annulations prononcées par le Conseil constitutionnel," *Revue du droit public* 103 (1987):449.

31. See *Le Monde*, 21 June 1986.

32. Secretary-general of the government to the Constitutional Council, 30 June 1987. I obtained my copy of the letter directly from the prime minister's office.

33. Daniel Labetoulle, "Les méthodes du travail au Conseil d'état at au Conseil constitutionnel" (Paper presented at the conference, "Conseil constitutionnel et Conseil d'état," Luxemburg Palace, January 1988), p. 3.

34. The leading decision is DC 75-57, *Recueil* (1975), p. 24, in which the Council announced that: "The Constitutional Council, when a law voted by Parliament . . . has been referred to it according to article 61 of the Constitution, possesses the power not only to rule on the conformity of the provisions of this law to the Constitution, but also to examine if it has been adopted with respect for the rules of *valeur constitutionnel* relative to the legislative procedures." Technical aspects of Council control over parliamentary procedure will not be treated in any systematic way in this dissertation, but see Philippe Terneyre, "La procédure législative ordinaire dans la jurisprudence du Conseil constitutionnel," *Revue du droit public* 101 (1985):691–749.

35. *Le Monde*, 23 December 1974.

36. 79-110 DC; 79-111 DC, *Recueil* (1979), p. 36; 39. Favoreu and Philip, *Les grandes décisions du Conseil constitutionnel*, pp. 439–63.

37. Moreover, to date and in spite of doctrinal advocacy, ordinary judges have not sought to apply or otherwise use SROIs in their decisions. See Favoreu, "La décision de constitutionnalité," p. 630.

38. *Le Monde*, 4 July 1986.

39. 86-208 DC; 86-218 DC, *Recueil* (1986), p. 78; 167.

40. The decision, according to *Le Monde*, not only "imposed a line of conduct, and only one, on the government," but it gave to Mitterrand "a judicial basis for refusing to sign the ordonnances." *Le Monde*, 28 June 1986.

41. *Le Monde*, 16 July 1986.

42. Ibid., 31 July 1986.

43. Ibid., 25–26 January 1987; *La Libération*, 26 January 1987.

44. 86-220 DC, *Recueil* (1986), p. 177.

45. The referral is at *Journal officiel* (*Lois . . .*), 23 December 1986, p. 15501.

46. *Rapport #101*, Senate, 10 December 1986, pp. 11–12.

47. 86-221 DC, *Recueil* (1986), p. 179.

48. Guy Carcassonne, "A propos du droit d'amendement : les errements du Conseil constitutionnel," *Pouvoirs* 41 (1987):163.

49. Louis Favoreu, *Le Figaro*, 19 January 1987.

50. Olivier Duhamel, "Les droits du parlement," *L'Express*, 6 February 1987, p. 8 (international edition).

51. The judgment of J. M. Sorel, "De l'administratif au judiciaire," *Revue administrative* 241 (1988):29.

52. Pézant, "Contribution à l'étude du pouvoir législatif selon la Constitution de 1958," p. 473.

53. *Statistical Bulletin 1985*. A plurality of all amendments are proposed by the

opposition. In 1987, for example, the Socialists proposed over one-fourth of all amendments. *Statistical Bulletin 1987*.

Chapter 6. The Council Legislates: Nationalization and Privatization Policy

1. George Ross and Jane Jenson, "Political Pluralism and Economic Policy," in *The French Socialist Experiment*, ed. John S. Ambler (Philadelphia: Institute for the Study of Human Issues, 1985), p. 39.

2. Didier Linotte, "Les nationalisations de 1982," *Revue du droit public* 98 (1982):435-56. Technical aspects and bibliographies are at "*Dossier nationalisation*," *Actualite juridique*, *Droit administratif*, 20 April 1982; Michel Durupty, *Les entreprises publiques, Rôle economique, Cadre juridique* (Paris: Thémis, Presses universitaires de France, 1986).

3. The stated objectives of the *Programme commun de gouvernement du parti socialiste et du parti communiste*.

4. *Le Monde*, 10 July 1981; 26 September 1981.

5. The Auroux laws went forward in 1983 with the law on the "democratization of the public sector." Although the Right threatened referral to the Constitutional Council (e.g., *Rapport #1659*, National Assembly, 28 June 1983, p. 4), it never developed solid constitutional arguments for opposing the bill, and in the end it was not referred.

6. For Usinor and Sacilor—the two iron and steel concerns of which the State already owned a significant percentage (about 70 percent of each)—and for two aerospace and electronics manufacturers specializing in armaments, Matra and Dassault, the government guaranteed at least majority ownership by appropriating money, for purchases on the stock market, in revisions of the finance law for 1981. Three other companies, Honeywell-Bull (computers, electronics), Roussel-Uclaf (pharmaceuticals), and CGCT (telecommunications), were in large part foreign owned, or subsidiaries of foreign-based companies. For these companies, complex negotiations with owners were required before proceeding by decree.

7. *Rapport #456*, National Assembly, 1981, p. 129.

8. Paul Fabra, "Banking Policy Under the Socialists," *Economic Policy and Policy-Making Under the Mitterrand Presidency, 1981–1984*, p. 176.

9. *Rapport #456*, p. 129. There were also exceptions made for institutions not otherwise considered banks under most circumstances, such as real estate holding companies and discount houses.

10. Lionel Zinson, *Le fer de lance* (Paris: Olivier Orban, 1985), pp. 69–71.

11. Oscar Schacter, "Compensation for Expropriation," *American Journal of International Law* 78 (1984):121. The international legal aspects of the bill are examined in M. H. Mendelson, "Valuation of French Shares: Two French Decisions," *International and Comparative Law Quarterly* 34 (April 1986):284–96, and in Geneviève Burdeau, "Les nationalisations françaises de 1982," *Revue générale de droit international public* 89 (1985):23–25.

12. "Les nationalisations de 1982," *Documentation française* 4721–22 (1983):34.

13. *Le Monde*, 11 September 1981.

14. The administrative details of compensation are much more complicated than described here, since they impinge on tax codes, accounting practices, and literally thousands of regulations for a wide range of stockholders in very different individual and collective situations.

15. *Rapport #456*, p. 202.

16. "Consultation des professeurs Robert et Luchaire," in *Nationalisation et Constitution*, ed. Louis Favoreu (Paris and Aix-en-Provence: Economica, 1982), pp. 93–104.

17. André Siegfried, *De la IIIe a la IVe Republique* (Paris: Grasset, 1956), p. 141.

18. See *Débats*, National Assembly (*Constituante*), 7 March 1946, esp. pp. 606–19.

19. Ibid., p. 607.

20. G. Wright, *The Reshaping of French Democracy* (New York: Reynal and Hitchcock, 1948), p. 136.

21. Debats, National Assembly (Constituante), 28 August 1946, p. 3375.

22. Philip argued that certain principles contained in the 1789 document were outmoded, and that this was "especially true" for article 17. "La valeur juridique de la Déclaration des droits de l'homme et du citoyen du 26 aout 1789 selon la jurisprudence du Conseil constitutionnel," *Mélange Kayser* 2 (1979):317.

23. The argument in LR is a curious one in this regard. After stating that "it is . . . difficult, in 1981, to consider that the right to property is a constitutent element of the rights of man," and after denying the constitutional status of article 17 (1789), LR go on to locate the source and the precise legal terms of the obligation to compensate in that same article. Presumably, LR would argue that the terms of article 17 have been absorbed by the greater legal system, as a general principle, perhaps.

24. Jean-Maxime Leveque, *En première ligne* (Paris: Albin Michel, 1986).

25. *Le Monde*, 23 October 1981.

26. Ibid., 25 September 1981.

27. *La nouvel économiste* 296 (17 July 1981):48–49.

28. *Le Monde*, 20–21 September 1981.

29. *Financial Times*, 18 September 1981; *Le Monde*, 20–12 September 1981.

30. *Le Monde*, 15 September 1981.

31. Ibid., 20–21 September 1981.

32. Ibid., 12 September 1981; answered point-by-point by the Socialist, André Laignel, *Le Monde*, 18 September 1981.

33. Ibid., 19 September 1981; 20–21 September 1981.

34. Ibid., 25 September 1981.

35. *Rapport #456*, 1:250.

36. For companies whose shares were not traded publicly, worth was to be evaluated accordingly: 50 percent representing by the average dividends paid between 1978 and 1980 multiplied by fifty, and 50 percent representing the net accounting assets.

37. Jacques Delors, minister of finance, *Le Monde*, 20–21 September 1981.

38. *Rapport #456*, 1:262.

39. *Débats*, National Assembly (*Constituante*), 13 October 1981, p. 1732.

40. *Le Monde*, 18–19 October 1981.

41. Charles Millon, *Débats*, National Assembly (*Constituante*), 26 October 1981, p. 2593.

42. *Rapport #56*, Senate, 3 (1981):18.

43. Bernard Saint-Girons, "La loi du 11 février 1982 et l'indemnisation des actionnaires des sociétés nationalisée," *Revue des sociétés* 100 (1982):266.

44. *Rapport #456*, pp. 282–84.

45. Ibid., p. 262.

46. *Rapport #456*, 2:26–27.

47. Ibid., pp. 5–6.

48. Ibid., p. 63.

49. Ibid., pp. 103–6.

50. *Rapport #700*, National Assembly, 22 January1982, p. 6. The spin-offs became the subject of subsequent legislation.

51. *Débats*, National Assembly (*Constituante*), 13 October 1981, p. 1713.

52. References which follow this debate are at ibid., pp. 1720–37.

53. Loussouarn, Drago, and Delvolve, "Consultation," *Nationalisation et Constitution*, pp. 105–93.

54. As Foyer put it, "Nationalization is good for one's adversaries, but one takes care to protect one's friends [i.e., the mutuals and coops]"—"C'est la République des Copains" ("It's the Republic of Our Pals"), someone called out.

55. *Le Monde*, 15 September 1981.

56. Foyer, *Débats*, National Assembly (*Constituante*), 1 December 1981, p. 4284.

57. *Le Monde*, 16 October 1981; 23 October 1981.

58. Ibid., 17 October 1981; 15 October 1981.

59. Ibid., 18–19 October 1981; the Sofres poll is reported at ibid., 14 October 1981.

60. Ibid., 22 October 1981; 23 October 1981; 27 October 1981.

61. Ibid., 28 October 1981.

62. *Débats*, National Assembly (*Constituante*), 18 October 1981, pp. 2150–51.

63. Ibid., p. 2111.

64. Ibid., p. 2088.

65. Ibid., p. 2095.

66. *Le Monde*, 14 October 1981; 28 October 1981.

67. The opposition, for example, attacked certain articles employing the language of "direct and indirect subsidiaries," for being judicially incorrect, since the codes use the terms "majority or minority participations." An amendment, offered by Millon, was accepted after the government spokesman stated, "We think the proposed amendment . . . ameliorates the text," leading to the following exchange: FOYER: "Miracle." LE GARREC: "And we hope that it will be adopted." SÉGUIN: "That's too much to believe." MILLON: "I am tempted to ask for a suspension of the meeting so that we can all go together and drain a bottle of champagne at the bar." *Débats*, National Assembly (*Constituante*), 17 October 1981, p. 1990.

68. Ibid., 1 December 1981, pp. 4283–86; 18 December 1981, pp. 5170–71; 18 December, p. 5170.

69. Ibid., 18 December 1981, p. 5171.

70. Ibid., 3 December 1981, pp. 4398–99.

71. *Débats*, Senate, 16 December 1981, p. 4290.

72. Ibid., 20 November 1981, pp. 2917–23. Article 13 lists those banks to be nationalized and provides for exceptions. The vote was 184–109, and thus the bill itself could not be discussed, ibid., p. 3014.

73. Ibid., 16 December 1981, pp. 4276–90.

74. Reproduced in Favoreu, ed., *Nationalisation et Constitution*, pp. 197–251, 253–314.

75. Published in ibid., pp. 315–28.

76. *Le Monde*, 7 January 1982.

77. Ibid., 16 January 1982, pp. 1, 27.

78. Interviews with (permanent) committee staff in the National Assembly, February 1987. My own view is that this practice occurs not irregularly, and that such considerations were, at least in 1986, built into the government's deliberations and management of the *autolimitation* process.

79. 81-132 DC, *Recueil* (1982), p. 18; Louis Favoreu and Loïc Philip, eds., *Les grandes décisions du Conseil constitutionnel* (Paris: Sirey, 1986), pp. 516–59.

80. *Le Monde*, 19 January 1982. The date of the decision, 16 January, was in fact the latest possible date, since the constitution states that the council must reach a decision within a thirty-day limit (except in cases when the government makes a declaration of urgency, which shortens the delay to eight days).

81. Jean Rivéro, "Ni lu, ni compris," *Actualité juridique, Droit administratif*, 20 April 1982, p. 210.

82. This is not to imply that the notion makes no sense; see Laurent Habib, "L'erreur manifeste d'appréciation," *Revue du droit public 101 (1986):695*-730.

83. Favoreu, ed., *Nationalisation et Constitution*, p. 320.

84. *Le Monde*, 21 January 1982.

85. The Council had itself made 1 January 1982 the reference point for "the day of the property transfer."

86. *Le Monde*, 21 January 1982.

87. See ibid., 19 January 1982.

88. Reported in ibid., 20 January 1982.

89. Ibid.

90. *Rapport annuel, Conseil d'état*, 1981–82, pp. 55–67.

91. *Débats*, National Assembly (*Constituante*), 26 January 1982, p. 550.

92. John T. S. Keeler and Alec Stone, "Judicial Confrontation in Mitterrand's France," in *The Mitterrand Experiment*, ed. Stanley Hoffman, Sylvia Malzacher, and George Ross (New York: Oxford, 1987), p. 170.

93. *Rapport #700*, pp. 3–13.

94. *Débats*, National Assembly (*Constituante*), 26 January 1982, pp. 550–51.

95. Ibid., pp. 534–52.

96. Ibid., p. 533.

97. Ibid., pp. 550–51.

98. "Commentaire de M. François Luchaire," in *Nationalisation et Constitution*, p. 75.

99. *Le Monde*, 20 January 1982. For companies not traded publicly, an administrative body was established to make the evaluation of worth as of 31 December 1981.

100. 82-139 DC, *Recueil* (1982), p. 31. The deputies argued that article 13 continued to violate the principle of equality, and that compensation would not be adequate or fair.

101. Martin Shapiro, *Law and Politics of the Supreme Court* (London: Free Press, 1965), pp. 17–32.

102. Rivéro and Vedel, "Droit social," quoted in Loussouarn, Drago, and Delvolve, "Consultation," p. 115.

103. *Le Monde*, 15 September 1981.

104. Ibid., 23 October 1981.

105. Favoreu, ed., *Nationalisation et Constitution*, pp. 197–99.

106. *Rapport #700*, pp. 14–18.

107. "Opinion de Gustavo Zagrebelsky," in *Nationalisation et Constitution*, pp. 87–90.

108. Stockbrokers noted that their clients were celebrating the unexpected windfall. *Le Monde*, 19 January 1989. Uri called the settlement "exhorbitant." Pierre Uri, "Un privilège pour les actionnaires," *Le Monde*, 24–25 January 1982.

109. "Commentaire de M. François Luchaire," pp. 77–78.

110. *Le Monde*, 20 January 1982.

111. See ibid., 22 January 1982.

112. *Débats*, National Assembly (*Constituante*), 26 January 1982, p. 550.

113. Jean-Maxime Leveque, *En premiere ligne* (Paris: Albine, Michel, 1986), p. 179.

114. Ibid., p. 181.

115. Louis Favoreu, *La politique saisie par le droit* (Paris: Economica, 1985), pp. 30–39, 117–18.

116. *Débats*, National Assembly (*Constituante*), 28 January 1982, p. 647.

117. Ibid., p. 644.

118. "Comentaire de M. François Luchaire," pp. 68–70.

119. Louis Favoreu, "Une grande décision," *Nationalisation et Constitution*, p. 41; and Rivéro, "Ni lu, ni compris," p. 210.

120. C. Millon, *L'extravagante histoire des nationalisations* (Paris: Plon, 1984), p. 185.

121. Alexander M. Bickel, *The Least Dangerous Branch* (New York: Bobbs and Merrill, 1962), pp. 29–33.

122. Pierre-Emmanuel Guillet (Socialist) explained the overwhelming vote to reject inclusion of the 1789 text this way: "Certain people would wish . . . , taking a detour into the past, to take up again, purely and simply, the declaration of 1789 . . . This is the very definition of what we called the reactionary spirit." *Débats*, National Assembly (*Constituante*), 7 March 1946, pp. 606–19.

123. *Le Monde*, 18 December 1981.

124. *Annex, Loi #86-793*, 2 July 1986, *Receuil des lois*, 1986, pp. 12–13; *Actualité legislative Dalloz* 1987, pp. 21–28.

125. 76-72 DC, *Recueil* (1977), p. 31. *Le Monde*, 23 April 1986.

126. *Rapport #10*, National Assembly, 22 April 1986, p. 31.

127. Ibid., pp. 82–83.

128. Ibid., p. 9.

129. *Le Monde*, 23 April 1986.

130. *Journal officiel* (*Lois . . .*), 27 June 1986, pp. 7984–90.

131. 86-207 DC, *Recueil* (1986), p. 61.

132. *Le Monde*, 16 July 1986.

133. *Rapport #298*, National Assembly, 1986, p. 4.

134. Ibid., p. 9.

135. *Le Monde*, 7 July 1986; *Débats*, National Assembly (*Constituante*), 28 July 1986, p. 3963.

136. Interview with Guy Carcassonne, February 1987.

Chapter 7. The Council Legislates: In Search of Media Pluralism

1. Reported later.

2. The decisions on the 1984 press law and the 1986 audiovisual reform law contained 103 and 101 considerations, respectively, to be compared with the 76 considerations contained in the 1980 security and liberty decision, and the 75 in the 1982 decision on nationalizations.

3. "Special Issue on the Politics of the Communications Revolution in Western Europe," *West European Politics* 9 (1986); Dennis McQuail and Karen Siune, eds., *New Media Politics: Comparative Perspectives in Western Europe* (London: Sage, 1987).

4. "La presse française," *Documentation française: notes et études* 4729-30 (1985):31. For a historical overview, see Pierre Albert and Fernand Terrou, *Histoire de la press*, 4th ed. (Paris: Presses universitaires de France, 1985).

5. J. W. Freiberg, *The French Press: Class, State, and Ideology* (New York: Praeger, 1981), pp. 23–24.

6. P. Williams, *Politics in Post-War France* (London: Longmans and Green, 1958), p. 389. Freiberg reports that of the thirty-one dailies published in Paris in 1939, only ten were allowed to publish after the liberation. *The French Press: Class, State, and Ideology*, p. 24.

7. Georges Vedel, report to the Economic and Social Council, adopted 23 May 1979, p. 80 (citations refer to a copy on file at the National Assembly, hereafter cited as the *Vedel Report*); Charles Debbasch, Guy Drouot, "La loi du 23 octobre 1984 et la liberté de la presse," *Actualité législative Dalloz* 1985, p. 50.

8. Nicolas Brimo, *Le Dossier Hersant* (Paris: Maspero, 1977); Dominique Pons, *Dossier H . . . comme Hersant* (Paris: Moreau, 1977).

9. Freiberg, *The French Press: Class, State, and Ideology*, pp. 64–81.

10. *Le Monde*, 17 May 1972.

11. The paper had supported Allende's election.

12. Pons, *Dossier H . . . comme Hersant*, p. 277. Pons also reports that the purchase was highly irregular; among other things, it was made in cash brought in suitcases.

13. Freiberg reports that before the takeover, the editorial staff at *Le Monde* had examined and discussed the contents of *Le Figaro* religiously every morning, but that by 1978 the habit virtually ceased. *The French Press: Class, State, and Ideology*, p. 73.

14. Brimo, *Le Dossier Hersant*, p. 99.

15. "La presse francaise," p. 7.

16. In addition to using front men and paper corporations, Hersant rotated ownership among cronies and family members. Michel Mathieu, *La presse quotidien régionale*, 2d ed. (Paris: Presses universitaires de France, 1986), p. 19.

17. The *Vedel Report*, pp. 8–17, 99–100.

18. *Le Monde* called Vedel the "spiritual father of the press legislation." *Le Monde*, 13–14 November 1983.

19. Ibid., 16 December 1983.

20. *Le Monde* characterized the group's activities as "systematic obstruction." *Le Monde*, 15 November 1983.

21. Ibid., 4 June 1983.

22. Ibid., 16 December 1983; 4 June 1983; 13–14 November 1983.

23. Ibid., 13–14 November 1983.

24. Penal sanctions were later specified for failure to comply.

25. *Le Monde*, 26 October 1983.

26. Ibid., 15 December 1983.

27. The lamentation of Maurice Duverger, ibid., 30 November 1989.

28. The opposition is allowed only one motion of censure to be raised each legislative session. The censure motion of 12 December was raised on the grounds that the government's bill would "seriously violate public liberties," namely, freedom of information and the press, and the right to property and of enterprise. *Débats*, National Assembly (*Constituante*), 12 December 1983, p. 6270.

29. Characterized by the majority as "parliamentary terrorism." *Débats*, National Assembly (*Constituante*), 15 December 1983, p. 6543.

30. Such a procedure violates constitutional provisions requiring full committee debate and a published report on legislation before first reading may proceed. The government and the Socialist majorities in the committees involved agreed to pass the bill on to the full National Assembly after the Right's campaign of obstruction—

including the boycott of proceedings—had paralyzed debate. The Right claimed that the reason for the delays was the concern of the committees' *rapporteurs* about constitutionality. Ibid., pp. 6535–36. After preliminary discussions in December, both the Cultural Affairs and the Laws Committee were obliged to meet a second time in mid-January. The bill was ultimately debated a total of 145 hours in committee for first reading, shattering the previous such record of 63 for the 1981 nationalization bill. Ibid., 24 January 1984, p. 21.

31. Ibid., 13 February 1984, p. 1041.

32. Ibid., 15 December 1983, pp. 6547–48.

33. The deputies were censured and fined one month's pay for impugning the wartime record of François Mitterrand, after debate had focused on the collaborationist record of Hersant. Ibid., 4 February 1984.

34. *Rapport #1885*, National Assembly, 14 December 1983, p. 62.

35. *Débats*, National Assembly (*Constituante*), 16 December 1983, p. 6583.

36. Ibid., 15 December 1983, pp. 6547–48.

37. Ibid., 14 December 1983, p. 6488.

38. Ibid., 16 December 1983, p. 6605.

39. Ibid., 3 February 1984, p. 525.

40. Ibid., 15 December 1983, pp. 6555–57.

41. Ibid., 16 December 1983, p. 6592. The bill, however, did allow for regional editions of national papers.

42. Ibid., p. 6590.

43. Jean Foyer, *Rapport #1963 (Annex - Lois)*, National Assembly, 14 December 1983, p. 41.

44. Debbasch and Drouot, "La loi du 23 octobre 1984 et la liberté de la presse," pp. 59–60.

45. *Le Figaro*, 24 November 1983.

46. *Débats*, National Assembly (*Constituante*), 15 December 1983, pp. 6535–36.

47. *Le Monde*, 13 January 1984.

48. Ibid., 9 February 1984.

49. *Rapport #1963 (Annex - Lois)*, pp. 32–33.

50. As Table 7.1 shows, the government had already compromised its original position as stated by Mauroy. The bill sent to parliament was internally inconsistent, title II restating the one-newspaper/one-man rule for national publications in the first sentence, and repudiating it in the second. This is best interpreted as an open invitation to the National Assembly to amend.

51. *Rapport #1963 (Annex -Affaires culturelles)*, pp. 155–64.

52. *Rapport #1963 (Annex - Lois)*, pp. 31–32; *Le Monde*, 12 December 1983.

53. *Rapport #1963 (Annex - Lois)*, pp. 29–32.

54. In the government's bill a *national* paper was that which possessed a "national audience" and was "distributed nationally." The committee's version is much more precise: any newspaper which enjoys at least 20 percent of its distribution outside of its three largest regions of distribution is considered a national paper.

55. *Rapport #1963 (Annex - Affaires culturelles)*, pp. 180–86.

56. Ibid., p. 181; *Rapport #1963 (Annex - Lois)*, p. 11.

57. *Rapport #1963 (Annex - Affaires culturelles)*, pp. 180–86.

58. Ibid., pp. 262–63.

59. Ibid., pp. 236–51.

60. "We will no longer be able to say that France is still a liberal democracy. After the long road of our history, after the vote of this law and particularly of articles 10, 11,

and 12 [the antitrust provisions]—this trilogy of . . . oppression . . . our country will cease to be a free democracy, and will enter that deathly zone of authoritarian democracies." Emmanuel Hamel, *Débats*, National Assembly (*Constituante*), 6 February 1983, p. 613.

61. After one detailed defense by the Socialists of the constitutionality of parts of title II, Toubon suggested that the majority "would be better off writing directly to the president of the Constitutional Council." Ibid., 6 February 1984, p. 610.

62. The so-called sarcastic amendments, ibid., 13 February 1984, p. 1039.

63. *Débats*, Senate, 24 May 1984, pp. 1160–65.

64. *Rapport #2194*, National Assembly, 14 June 1984, pp. 4–25.

65. *Débats*, Senate, 24 May 1984, pp. 1067–1068.

66. According to the Senate's version, the CTPP would be composed of twenty members, ten appointed by management, seven by politicians, and three by judges. Since decisions were to be made by majority vote, owners could, on their own, block any CTPP measure.

67. *Débats*, Senate, 11 September 1984, pp. 2503–508.

68. Ibid., p. 2508.

69. *Journal officiel* (*Lois . . .*), 13 October 1984, pp. 3206–212.

70. *Le Monde*, 11 October 1984. Hersant's lawyer argued that *any* regulation of the press would violate his client's constitutional rights, and he identified thirteen different reasons why the bill was unconstitutional. Hersant wrote, "For the first time in the history of five republics, a law . . . is targeted at one man."

71. 84-181 DC, *Recueil* (1984), p. 73. Favoreu and Philip, *Les grandes décisions du Conseil constitutionnel*, pp. 644–64.

72. Genevois, *La jurisprudence du Conseil constitutionnel*, p. 205.

73. Hughes Portelli, "Le juge constitutionnel et le pouvoir," *La Croix*, 19 October 1984.

74. Of course, such hypotheses can never be proved or disproved.

75. Favoreu and Philip put it this way: "It is true that, in its judicial terms, the decision is not easy to understand on first reading." *Les grandes décisions du Conseil constitutionnel*, p. 653.

76. In 83-165 DC, *Recueil* (1984), p. 30, the Constitutional Council had ruled that lawmakers could only change such a regime if the proposed one protected the public liberty concerned to at least an equivalent extent; Favoreu and Philip, *Les grandes décisions du Conseil constitutionnel*, pp. 626–43.

77. Consideration #44.

78. Sylvie Hubac and Jean-Eric Schoettl, "La situation des groupes de presses à la suite de la décision des 10 et 11 octobre du Conseil constitutionnel et de la promulgation de la loi du 23 octobre 1984," *Revue de science criminelle et droit penal comparé*, 1985, pp. 12–13.

79. *Le Monde*, 13 October 1984.

80. Promulgation also allowed the government to claim that its intent had not been to punish one man, but to protect a general liberty.

81. *La Croix*, 9 November 1984.

82. *Le Monde*, 15 October 1984.

83. Ibid., 13 October 1984.

84. Ibid., 2–3 December 1984, p. x.

85. *Débats*, Senate, 17–18 December 1985, pp. 4130–35.

86. *Le Monde*, 5–6 January 1986.

87. *Le Figaro*, 6 January 1986.

88. *Le Monde*, 7 January 1986. The Committee of Cultural Affairs gave Hersant 38.7 percent of the national and 13.5 percent of the regional market, pre-1984 numbers which curiously did not reflect the purchase of the *Dauphine-liberé* group, *l'Union*, and *le Progrès*. *Rapport #193*, National Assembly, 6 June 1986, pp. 49–50.

89. *Le Monde*, 1 August 1986.

90. The bill is one of the longest and most complex ever adopted by the French parliament, and had engendered an enormous literature in journals devoted to French politics and administrative law. See the special issues of the *Revue politique et parlementaire*, no. 929, May–June 1987; *Revue française d'administration publique* 44 (1987).

91. *Rapport #420*, Senate, 26 June 1986, pp. 5–10.

92. *Rapport #193*, p. 107.

93. *Rapport #98*, National Assembly, 28 April 1986.

94. *Rapport #193*, pp. 119–21. Five amendments offered by the Left were adopted. *Débats*, National Assembly (*Constituante*), 10 June 1986, p. 2022.

95. Ibid., pp. 97–98.

96. The salient part of this debate occurs at ibid., pp. 132–35.

97. Ibid., 17 June 1986, p. 2287.

98. Ibid., p. 2285.

99. Interviews conducted in February 1987.

100. *Débats*, National Assembly, 17 June 1986, p. 2287.

101. *Débats*, Senate, 17–18 December 1985, p. 4135; *Débats*, National Assembly (*Constituante*), 10 June 1986, p. 2046.

102. "The majority wraps up their gift-law to Hersant" was the headline of *La Libération*, 20 June 1986. "Mr. Hersant, who served well the ex-opposition for 5 years, is now receiving his dividends. He will now have his hands free, if they had not been already." *Le Monde*, 20 June 1986. The president of the largest French journalist's union called the bill "a law custom-made for the Hersant group," and a "royal gift." *Le Monde*, 13 June 1986.

103. Ibid., 14 June 1986.

104. *Débats*, Senate, 26 June 1986, p. 2035.

105. *Journal officiel* (*Lois . . .*), 30 July 1986, pp. 9396–98.

106. For the period up to 1982, see Michael Myerson, "The Pursuit of Pluralism: Lessons From the New French Audiovisual Communications Law," *Stanford Journal of International Law*, 1985, pp. 102–11.

107. Raymond Kuhn, "France and the 'New Media,'" *West European Politics* 8 (1985):51.

108. After extensive modification by the Senate, which among other things raise the number of NCCL members from nine to thirteen, the final bill fixed recruitment to the body as follows: two each to be designated by the presidents of the Republic, the National Assembly and the Senate; one member each to be elected by colleagues at the *Conseil d'Etat*, the *Cour de cassation*, and the *Cour des comptes*; one to be elected by and from the ranks of the *Academie française*; and three members from the industry selected by the first ten members above.

109. *Débats*, Senate, 11 July 1986, p. 2749.

110. The bill's first reading takes up more than 1,000 pages in the *Journal officiel*, and the Senate was ultimately obliged to wade through a total of 1,934 amendments, a record for that chamber.

111. See chapter 6.

112. *Débats*, Senate, 11 July 1986, pp. 3276–77.

113. *Débats*, National Assembly (*Constituante*), 12 August 1986, p. 4281.

114. *Rapport #339*, National Assembly, 4 August 1986, vol. 1, pp. 283–84.

115. *Rapport #415*, Senate, 25 June 1986, vol. 2, pp. 68–69.

116. *Débats*, Senate, 11 July 1986, p. 2730.

117. Ibid., 19 June 1986, pp. 2747–756; *Rapport #415*, pp. 75–81.

118. *Débats*, National Assembly (*Constituante*), 4 August 1986, p. 4289; *Le Monde*, 21 July 1986.

119. *Le Monde*, 12 August 1986.

120. *Débats*, Senate, 12 August 1986, p. 3823.

121. *Le Monde*, 12 August 1986.

122. "La télévision en 1987," *Dossier et Documents - Le Monde*, 1988, pp. 14–19.

123. *Le Point*, 22–28 September 1986, p. 69.

124. *Débats*, National Assembly (*Constituante*), 4 August 1986, pp. 4017–4030.

125. Ibid., p. 4025.

126. Ibid., pp. 3988–89.

127. Ibid., 12 August 1986, pp. 4287–88.

128. *Le Point*, 22–28 September 1986, p. 69.

129. *Journal officiel* (*Lois . . .*), 19 September 1986, pp. 11302–306.

130. *Rapport #371*, National Assembly, 7 October 1986, p. 26.

131. *Le Monde*, 23 October 1986.

132. *Rapport #19*, Senate, 21 October 1986, p. 18.

133. *Rapport #371*, p. 19.

134. *Rapport #19*, pp. 3, 7.

135. *Rapport #371*, p. 26.

136. Ibid., pp. 38–39.

137. Ibid., pp. 41–42.

138. *Débats*, Senate, 21 October 1986, p. 3983.

139. Ibid., pp. 3986–88.

140. *Rapport #19*, p. 22.

141. Favoreu and Philip, *Les grandes décisions du Conseil constitutionnel*, p. 664.

142. Georges Vedel, "Neuf ans au Conseil constitutionnel," *Le Débat*, 1989, pp. 48–49.

143. Favoreu and Philip, *Les grandes décisions du Conseil constitutionnel*, pp. 656–58.

144. Guillaume Pépy, "La réforme du régime juridique de la presse," *L'actualité juridique, Droit administratif*, 10 October 1986 (doctrine), pp. 527–40.

145. Favoreu, "Europe occidentale," *La contrôle juridictionnel des lois*, p. 53.

146. *Débats*, National Assembly (*Constituante*), 9 October 1986, p. 4499.

Chapter 8. The Third Chamber Model: A Review and Defense

1. 86-211 DC, *Recueil* (1986), p. 120; 86-213 DC, *Recueil* (1986), p. 122; 86-214 DC, *Recueil* (1986), p. 128; 86-215 DC, *Recueil* (1986), p. 130; 86-216 DC *Recueil* (1986), p. 135.

2. Loïc Philip, "La constitutionalisation du droit pénal francais," *Revue de science criminelle et de droit pénal compare*, no. 4, 1985.

3. *Débats*, National Assembly (*Constituante*), 26 June 1986, p. 2546.

4. Ibid., 1 July 1986, pp. 2792–98.

5. Ibid., 3 July 1986, p. 2854.

6. 86-211 DC, *Recueil*, p. 120.

7. 80-127 DC, *Recueil* (1981), p. 15. Louis Favoreu and Loïc Philip, eds., *Les grandes décisions du Conseil constitutionnel* (Paris: Sirey, 1986), pp. 477-515.

8. *Le Monde*, 7 January 1982.

9. Favoreu, "La mythe du gouvernement des juges" (Paper presented at Oxford University, Oxford, October 1987), p. 11. The citations which follow are at Ibid., p. 12.

10. 74-54 DC, *Recueil* (1975), p. 19; 81-127 DC, *Recueil* (1981), p. 15; 84-176 DC, *Recueil* (1984), p. 55.

11. And elsewhere: Louis Favoreu, *La politique saisie par le droit* (Paris: Economica, 1988), pp. 109, 138.

12. Nelson Polsby, "Legislatures," in *Handbook of Political Science*, eds. N. Polsby and F. I. Greenstein (Reading, Mass.: Addison, Wesley, 1975), 5:277.

13. Richard Rose, "The Roles of Laws in Comparative Perspective," *Studies in Public Policy*, no. 106, 1982 (Centre for the Study of Public Policy, University of Strathclyde), p. 21.

14. Favoreu, *La politique saisie par le droit*, p. 31.

15. Quoted in Alexander M. Bickel, *The Least Dangerous Branch* (New York: Bobbs and Merrill, 1962), p. 148.

16. J. H. Merryman, *The Civil Law Tradition* (Stanford: Stanford University Press, 1985), p. 42.

17. Vedel, in his assessment of this debate, denies all of this, appealing apparently to the self-evident nature of the constitutional text and propagating a radical distinction between what the Council does and what parliament does, declaring that "the Council is not a third political chamber [because] constitutional texts serve as the bases for its decisions." Georges Vedel, "Neuf ans au Conseil constitutionnel," *Le Débat*, 1989, p. 50.

18. Guy Carcassonne, "The Fifth Republic After Thirty Years," in *Constitutions in Democratic Polities*, ed. Vernon Rogdanor (Gower: Aldershot, 1988), p. 249.

19. Pierre Pascallon, "Le Conseil constitutionnel: un deuxième parlement," *Revue politique et parlementaire* 925 (1986):3.

20. *Le Monde*, 5 September 1986.

21. Michel de Villiers, commentary on the decision on the 1984 press law, note 16, *Revue administrative*, November-December 1984, p. 587.

22. Marcel Waline, "Eléments d'une theorie de la juridiction constitutionnel," *Revue du droit public* 44 (1928):449. In the Third Republic these debates were undertaken under the general rubric of the *quéstion préalable*.

23. I do not know if contemporary legal scholars are aware of this fact. In his enormously influential preface, Waline does not mention that he applied the same definition to parliament fifty years earlier. "Préface," in Favoreu and Philip, *Les grandes décisions du Conseil constitutionnel*.

24. *Débats*, National Assembly (*Constituante*), 26 January 1982, p. 653.

25. *Débats*, Senate, 20 November 1981.

Chapter 9. West European Constitutional Courts in Comparative Perspective

1. Harry Eckstein, "Case Study and Theory in Political Science," *Handbook of Political Science* (Reading, Mass.: Addison-Wesley, 1975), pp. 104–105.

2. The structural attributes of the Portuguese court are listed in Louis Favoreu, *Les Cours constitutionnelles* (Paris: Presses universitaires de France, 1986), pp. 110–13.

3. Martin Shapiro, *Courts: A Comparative and Political Analysis* (Chicago: University of Chicago Press, 1980).

4. Discussed in Glenn Schram, "Ideology and Politics: The Rechtsstaat Idea in West Germany," *Journal of Politics* 33 (February 1971):139.

5. John Ford Golay, *The Founding of the Federal Republic of Germany* (Chicago: University of Chicago Press, 1958), p. 166.

6. This advocacy is examined by Neumann, *The Democratic and the Authoritarian State* (New York: Free Press, 1964), chapter 2.

7. Ibid., p. 53; Friedrich, *The Philosophy of Law in Historical Perspective* (Chicago: University of Chicago Press, 1963), pp. 178–79.

8. See chapter 1 for the French case. In West Germany, Friedrich reports that the Christian Democrats were in favor of establishing judicial review but that the Socialists, "obsessed by the memory of Roosevelt's struggle with the Supreme Court . . . were determined to avoid any mechanism which might obscure future social and economic reforms." Carl J. Friedrich, *Constitutional Government and Democracy: Theory and Practice in Europe and America* (Waltham, Mass.: Blaisdell, 1968), pp. 262–63.

9. Neumann, *The Democratic and the Authoritarian State*, p. 45.

10. H. W. Koch, *A Constitutional History of Germany* (London: Longman, 1984), p. 270.

11. Neumann, *The Democratic and the Authoritarian State*, p. 45.

12. Eisenmann, *La justice constitutionnelle et la haute cour constitutionnelle d'Autriche* (Paris and Aix-en-Provence: Economica, 1986).

13. Charles Gulick, *Austria between Habsburg and Hitler* (Berkeley: University of California, 1948), pp. 785–86, 877–78, 1075–77.

14. Mauro Cappelletti, "Rapport general," in *Le contrôle juridictionnel des lois*, ed. Louis Favoreu and John-Anthony Jolowicz (Paris and Aix-en-Provence: Economica, 1986), pp. 301–14.

15. The best statement of the differences is Favoreu, *Les Cours constitutionnelles*, pp. 5–32.

16. Klaus Von Beyme, *America as Model: The Impact of American Democracy in the World* (Boston: Boston University Press, 1987), p. 94.

17. In France, Kelsen's influence comes by way of Eisenmann; *La justice constitutionnelle et la haute cour constitutionnelle d'Autriche*, is Eisenmann's doctoral thesis. See also Louis Favoreu, "La modernité des vues de Charles Eisenmann sur la justice constitutionnelle," in ibid., pp. 367–83; and Paul Amselek, ed., *La pensée de Charles Eisenmann* (Paris and Aix-en-Provence: Economica/PUAM, 1986).

18. Kelsen, "La garantie juridictionnel de la constitution," *Revue de droit public* 44 (1928):197–257.

19. Citations which follow are at ibid., pp. 221–41.

20. Taylor Cole, "Three Constitutional Courts: A Comparison," *American Political Science Review* 53 (1959):983.

21. Peter J. Donaghy and Michael T. Newton, *Spain: A Guide to Political and Economic Institutions* (Cambridge: Cambridge University Press, 1987), p. 13.

22. Namely, an 1867 law on the "general rights of citizens," the principle of equality in the constitution proper, and the European Convention of the Rights of Man which the court has given the rank of constitutional status.

23. Blair, *Federalism and Judicial Review in West Germany* (Oxford: Clarendon, 1981), pp. 14–15.

24. Ibid., p. 36.

25. The statistics which follow were obtained directly from the respective courts. I know of no general source for such information.

26. *Commentaire* 9 (Autumn and Spring 1986).

27. *Le Monde*, 3 March 1989; 11 August 1989.

28. Robert Dahl, "Decision-Making in a Democracy, The Supreme Court as a National Policy-Maker," *Journal of Public Law* 6 (1957):279–80.

29. Von Beyme, *America as Model: The Impact of American Democracy in the World*, p. 95.

30. Philip Blair, "Law and Politics in West Germany," *Political Studies* 26 (1978):354.

31. Christine Landfried, "Legislation and Judicial Review in the Federal Republic of Germany," in *Constitutional Review and Legislation: An International Comparison*, ed. Christine Landfried (Baden-Baden: Nomos, 1989). I cite from the forthcoming manuscript.

32. Christine Landfried, "The Impact of the German Constitutional Court on Politics and Policy-Outputs," in *Constitutional Review and Legislation*, p. 541.

33. See Christine Landfried, *Bundesverfassungsgericht und Gesetzgeber* (Baden-Baden: Nomos, 1984), pp. 75–85. See also Peter J. Katzenstein, *Politics and Policy in West Germany: The Growth of a Semi-Sovereign State* (Philadelphia: Temple University, 1987), pp. 254–95.

34. Landfried, *Bundesverfassungsgericht und Gesetzgeber*, pp. 52–63.

35. See Katzenstein, *Politics and Policy in West Germany: The Growth of a Semi-Soverign State*, pp. 125–67.

36. Landfried, "Legislation and Judicial Review in the Federal Republic of Germany."

37. Landfried, *Bundesverfassungsgericht und Gesetzgeber*, p. 54.

38. Following Malcolm Feeley, "Power, Impact, and the Supreme Court," in *The Impact of Supreme Court Decisions: Empirical Studies*, ed. Theodore Becker and Malcolm Feeley (New York: Oxford, 1973). See Robert Dahl, "The Concept of Power," *Behavioral Science* 2 (1957):201–15, and Carl Friedrich, *Constitutional Government and Democracy* (Boston: Ginn, 1946), pp. 589–90.

39. Stephen L. Wasby, *The Impact of the United States Supreme Court* (Homewood, Ill.: Dorsey, 1970); Stephen L. Wasby, "The Supreme Court's Impact: Some Problems of Conceptualization and Measurement," in *Compliance and the Law: A Multi-Disciplinary Approach*, ed. Samuel Krislov (Beverly Hills: Sage, 1972).

40. Feeley, "Power, Impact, and the Supreme Court," p. 226.

41. Louis Fisher, *Constitutional Dialogues: Interpretation as Political Process* (Princeton: Princeton University Press, 1988), p. 231.

42. R. Rose, "The Roles of Laws in Comparative Perspective," *Studies in Public Policy*, no. 106, p. 21.

43. The high degree of consensus around policy is a result of the constraints of coalition government, the Bundesrat's veto over legislative matters of concurrent jurisdiction, and—simply—the high value accorded consensus among West German politicians. Katzenstein, *Politics and Policy in West Germany: The Growth of a Semi-Sovereign State*, pp. 15–79.

44. Landfried, "The Impact of the German Constitutional Court on Politics and Policy-Outputs," pp. 531–32.

45. Mauro Cappelletti and William Cohen, eds., *The Modern Systems of Judicial Review: Comparative Constitutional Law* (New York: Bobbs-Merrill, 1979), p. 94.

46. Landfried, "The Impact of the German Constitutional Court on Politics and Policy-Outputs," p. 532.

47. Landfried, "Legislation and Judicial Review in the Federal Republic of Germany."

48. Martin Hirsch, "Zum Problem der 'Grenzuberschreitungen des Bundesverfassungsgerichte der Bundesrepublik Deutschland," *DRIZ* (1977), p. 225.

49. Landfried, "Legislation and Judicial Review in the Federal Republic of Germany."

50. See Klaus Von Beyme, *The Political System of the Federal Republic of Germany* (Hants, UK: Gower, 1983), p. 186; Blair, "Law and Politics in West Germany," p. 354.

51. Klaus von Beyme and Manfred G. Schmidt, eds., *Policy and Politics in the Federal Republic of Germany* (New York: St. Martins, 1985), p. 21.

52. Landfried, "Legislation and Judicial Review in the Federal Republic of Germany."

53. The law was referred by Lander authorities.

54. The court relied on constitutional provisions guaranteeing the freedom to organize into political parties and rights to equal political participation.

55. Landfried, *Bundesverfassungsgericht und Gesetzgeber*, pp. 102–108.

56. Ibid., pp. 87–95.

57. Kommers, *Judicial Politics in West Germany*, p. 275.

58. Not least because these courts rely heavily on bills of rights in their decisions.

59. Landfried, *Bundesverfassungsgericht und Gesetzgeber*, p. 123.

60. Landfried, "The Impact of the German Constitutional Court on Politics and Policy-Outputs," p. 541.

61. Ralf Dahrendorf, *Society and Democracy in Germany* (Garden City: Doubleday, 1969), p. 131.

62. Blair, "Law and Politics in West Germany," p. 352. Nevil Johnson, "Law as the Articulation of the State in Western Germany: A German Tradition Seen from a British Perspective," *Western European Politics* (1971), p. 246.

63. Schram, "Ideology and Politics: The Rechtsstaat Idea in West Germany," p. 150.

64. Blair, "Law and Politics in West Germany," p. 349.

65. Gisbert Brinkman, "The West German Federal Constitutional Court: Political Control through Judges," *Public Law* (Spring 1981), p. 104.

66. Blair, "Law and Politics in West Germany," p. 358.

67. Weber, "Le Controle juridictionnel de la constitutionnalité des lois dans les pays d'Europe occidentale," p. 50.

68. By comparison, prior to Socialist rule only one such law had been referred to the court.

69. See P. Bon and F. Moderne, "Chronique," *Annuaire international de justice constitutionnelle* (1985), pp. 339–67.

70. *El Pais*, 29 July 1984; 25 May 1985.

71. M. Alba Navorro, "El Recurso Previo de Inconstitucionalidad contra Proyectos de Ley Organica," *Revista de Derecho Politico* 16 (Winter 1982–1983):167; P. Cruz Villalon, "El Control Previo de Constitucionalidad," *Revista de Derecho Publico* 82 (Jan–Mar 1981):5; F. Santaolalla Lopez, "Problemos del Recurso Previo de Inconstitucionalidad y Adicion Sobre la I.O.A.P.A.," *Revista de Derecho Politico* 18–19 (Summer–Winter 1983):177. No defense of the a priori review was published in any of the major public law journals.

72. Shapiro, *Courts*, chapter 1.

73. Ibid., p. 1.

74. Ibid., p. 8.

75. Ibid.

76. Ibid., pp. 28–37.

77. Ibid., p. 1.

78. Abraham, *The Judicial Process* (New York: Oxford University Press, 1980), pp. 295, 333.

79. Philip Bobbitt, *Constitutional Fate: Theory of the Constitution* (New York: Oxford, 1982), p. 3.

80. Leonard W. Levy, ed., *Judicial Review and the Supreme Court* (New York: Harper, 1967); Albert P. Malone and George Mace, eds., *Judicial Review and American Democracy* (Ames: University of Iowa, 1988).

81. Abraham, *The Judicial Process*, pp. 373–400.

82. Saul K. Padover, *To Secure These Blessings: The Great Debates of the Constitutional Convention of 1787, Arranged According to Topics* (New York: Washington Square, 1970), pp. 410–19.

83. Brinkman, "The West German Federal Constitutional Court: Political Control through Judges," p. 88.

84. Golay, *The Founding of the Federal Republic of Germany*, p. 183. Johnson calls the court "a supplementary organ of public policy-making." Neil Johnson, "The Interdependence of Law and Politics: Judges and the Constitution in West Germany," *West European Politics*, 1 (1978):245.

85. Eugene Rostow, "The Democratic Nature of Judicial Review," in *Judicial Review and the Supreme Court*, ed. L. W. Levy (New York: Harper, 1967), pp. 74–104.

86. John Agresto, *The Supreme Court and Constitutional Democracy* (Ithaca: Cornell, 1984); Gary McDowell, *Curbing the Courts: The Constitution and the Limits of Judicial Power* (Baton Rouge: LSU Press, 1988).

87. Louis Favoreu, ed., *Cours constitutionnelles européennes et droits fondamentaux*; Louis Favoreu and John-Anthony Jolowicz, eds., *Le contrôle juridictionnel des lois: légitimité, effectivité, et développements récents; Droit constitutionnel et droits de l'homme* (Paris and Aix-en-Provence: Economica, 1987).

88. Carl Schmitt, "Das Reichsgericht als Huter der Verfassung," in *Verfassungsrechliche Aufsätze* (Berlin: Duncker and Humboldt, 1958), pp. 63–100.

REFERENCES

Council Decisions

[Decisions are cited according to French custom. *59-2 DC Recueil*, (1959), p. 58 signifies that the decision was rendered in 1959, was the second decision of the Constitutional Council based on its article 61 constitutional review jurisdiction, and that it can be found in the *Recueil du Conseil constitutionnel* of 1959 beginning on page 58. The *Recueil* is the official record of the Constitutional Council's activity, published annually. *DC* denotes a decision enabled by jurisdiction conferred by articles 54 and 61 of the constitution; *L* denotes a decision enabled by jurisdiction conferred by article 37; *FNR* denotes a decision enabled by jurisdiction conferred by article 41.]

59-2 DC, *Recueil*. 1959: 58.
59-3 DC, *Recueil*. 1959: 61.
59-1 L, *Recueil*. 1959: 67.
59-1 FNR, *Recueil*. 1959: 71.
59-5 DC, *Recueil*. 1960: 15.
60-8 DC, *Recueil*. 1960: 25.
60-11 DC, *Recueil*. 1961: 29.
61-14 L, *Recueil*. 1961: 38.
62-20 DC, *Recueil*. 1962: 27.
63-21 DC, *Recueil*. 1963: 23.
66-28 DC, *Recueil*. 1966: 15.
71-44 DC, *Recueil*. 1971: 29.
73-51 DC, *Recueil*. 1973: 25.
74-54 DC, *Recueil*. 1975: 19.
76-75 DC, *Recueil*. 1976: 33.
77-79 DC, *Recueil*. 1977: 35.
77-83 DC, *Recueil*. 1977: 39.
77-87 DC, *Recueil*. 1977: 42.
77-92 DC, *Recueil*. 1977: 21.
79-105 DC, *Recueil*. 1979: 33.
80-117 DC, *Recueil*. 1980: 42.
80-127 DC, *Recueil*. 1981: 15.
81-132 DC, *Recueil*. 1982: 18.
82-139 DC, *Recueil*. 1982: 31.
82-144 DC, *Recueil*. 1982: 61.
82-146 DC, *Recueil*. 1982: 66.
82-147 DC, *Recueil*. 1982: 70.
83-165 DC, *Recueil*. 1984: 30.
84-176 DC, *Recueil*. 1984: 55.
84-181 DC, *Recueil*. 1984: 73.

85-196 DC, *Recueil*. 1985: 63.
85-197 DC, *Recueil*. 1985: 70.
86-207 DC, *Recueil*. 1986: 61.
86-208 DC, *Recueil*. 1986: 78.
86-210 DC, *Recueil*. 1986: 110.
86-211 DC, *Recueil*. 1986: 120.
86-213 DC, *Recueil*. 1986: 122.
86-214 DC, *Recueil*. 1986: 128.
86-215 DC, *Recueil*. 1986: 130.
86-216 DC, *Recueil*. 1986: 135.
86-217 DC, *Recueil*. 1986: 141.
86-218 DC, *Recueil*. 1986: 167.
86-225 DC, *Recueil*. 1986: 13.

Judicial Decisions

Paulin (*Cassation criminelle*). 1833. In Sirey. 1 (1833): 357.
Gauthier (*Cassation, Chambre criminelle*). 1851. In Dalloz. 1 (1851): 142.
Gent (*Cassation, Chambre criminell*). 1851. In Dalloz. 1 (1851): 333.
Winkel (*Conseil d'Etat*). 1909. In Sirey. 3 (1909): 147.
Amicales des annamités de Paris (*Conseil d'Etat*). 1956. In *Recueil du Conseil d'Etat*. 11 July 1956, p. 317.

Referrals to the Constitutional Council

All referrals to the Constitutional Council in the 1959–82 period are published in Maus, D., ed., *Textes et documents sur la pratique institutionnelle de la Ve Republique* (Paris: Documentation française, 1978). After that date, referrals are published immediately following the Constitutional Council's decision in the *Journal officiel* (*Lois . . .*).
Referrals of the 1981 nationalization bill. 1982. In *Nationalisation et Constitution*. Paris and Aix-en-Provence: Economica. 197–251, 253–314.
Referrals of the 1984 Press Law. In *Journal officiel* (*Lois . . .*). 1984: 3206.
Referrals of the 1986 privatization bill to the Constitutional Council. In *Journal officiel* (*Lois . . .*). 1986: 7984.
Referrals of the 1986 Press Law. In *Journal officiel* (*Lois . . .*). 1986: 9396–98.
Referral of the 1986 Audiovisual Law. In *Journal officiel* (*Lois . . .*). 1986: 11302–1306.
Referral of the "Séguin Amendment." In *Journal officiel* (*Lois . . .*). 1986: 15501.

Parliamentary Documents

Archives parlementaires (1st series, 1787–99).
National Assembly Committee Reports (*Rapports*): 1975: numbers 2128, 2080, 2131; 1981–84: numbers 456, 700, 779, 1659, 1885, 1963, 2194; 1986: numbers 10, 98, 111, 193, 298, 339, 371.
National Assembly Debates (*Journal officiel*): 1907, 1946, 1959, 1962, 1971, 1974, 1975, 1976, 1977, 1978, 1979, 1980, 1981, 1982, 1983, 1984, 1985, 1986.

Senate Committee Reports (*Rapports*): 1981: numbers 56; 1986: numbers 19, 101, 102, 415, 420, 481.
Senate Debates (*Journal officiel*): 1959, 1962, 1971, 1973, 1974, 1975, 1976, 1977, 1979, 1980, 1981, 1982, 1983, 1984, 1985, 1986.

Other Documents

Documents pour servir à l'histoire de l'élaboration de la Constitution du 4 octobre 1958, tome 1: Des origines de la loi constitutionnelle du 3 juin 1958 à l'avant-projet du 29 juillet 1958. 1987. Paris: Documentation française.
Lettre a la nation. 7 October 1986.
Programme commun de gouvernement du parti socialiste et du parti communiste. 1981. In *Régards sur l'actualité.* Number 74.
Le programme Mauroy. 1981. In *Regards sur l'actualité.*
Rapport annuel: Commission pour la transparence et le pluralisme de la press. 1985–86.
Rapport annuel: Conseil d'Etat. 1981, 1982, 1987.
Statistiques: Bulletin de l'Assemblée nationale. 1958–87.
Textes et documents sur la pratique institutionnelle de la Ve République. Maus, D., ed. 1978, 1982, 1986. Paris: Documentation française.
Travaux préparatoires de la Constitution du 4 octobre 1958, Avis et débats du Comité consultatif constitutionnel. 1960. Paris: Documentation française.
Vedel Report. 1979. Conseil économique et social.

Books, Articles, and Papers

Actualité juridique, Droit administratif. 20 April 1982 (special issue on the 1982 nationalizations).
Adamany, D. 1973. *Wisconsin Law Review*, pp. 790–846.
Agresto, J. 1984. *The Supreme Court and Constitutional Democracy.* Ithaca: Cornell.
Albert, P., and Terrou, F. 1985. *Histoire de la presse.* Paris: Presses universitaires de France.
Almond, G. 1988. *American Political Science Review* 82: 853.
Amselek, P., ed. 1986. *La pensée de Charles Eisenmann.* Paris and Aix-en-Provence: Economica.
Andrews, W. 1982. *Presidential Government in Gaullist France.* Albany: State University of New York.
Apter, D. E., and Eckstein, H., eds. 1963. *Comparative Politics: A Reader.* Glencoe: Free Press.
Arnande, F. 1884. *Revue du droit public* 1:1.
Autin, J-L. 1983. *Revue du droit public* 99: 687.
Balbus, I. D. 1976–77. *Law and Society Review* 11: 572.
Bastid, P. 1939. *Sieyès et sa pensée.* Paris: Hachette.
——— . 1954. *Les institutions politiques de la monarchie parlementaire française.* Paris: Sirey.
Beardsley, J. 1972. *American Journal of Comparative Law.* 20: 431.
——— . 1975. *Supreme Court Review*, p. 189.
Berlia, G. 1962. *Revue du droit public* 78: 931.
——— ; Bonnard, R.; Duguit, L.; and Monnier, H. 1952. *Les Constitutions et les*

principales lois politiques de la France. Paris: Librairie générale de droit et de jurisprudence.

Beyme, K. von. 1983. *The Political System of the Federal Republic of Germany.* Aldershot: Gower.

———. 1987. *America as Model: The Impact of American Democracy in the World.* Boston: Boston University Press.

———, and Schmidt, M. G., eds. 1985. *Policy and Politics in the Federal Republic of Germany.* New York: St. Martins.

Bickel, A. M. 1962. *The Least Dangerous Branch.* New York: Bobbs and Merrill.

Black, Jr., C. L. 1960. *The People and the Court.* Englewood Cliffs: Prentice Hall.

Blair, P. M. 1978. *Political Studies* 26: 348.

———. 1981. *Federalism and Judicial Review in West Germany.* Oxford: Clarendon.

Bobbitt, P. 1982. *Constitutional Fate: Theory of the Constitution.* New York: Oxford University Press.

Bon, P., and Moderne, F. 1987. Chronique. In *Annuaire international de justice constitutionnelle, 1985,* p. 339. Paris and Aix-en-Provence: Economica.

Boulouis, J. 1980. *Pouvoirs* 13: 27.

Bourdon, J. 1942. *La réforme judiciare de l'An VIII.* Paris: Carrere.

Braibant, G. *Revue administrative* 239: 415.

Brigham, J. 1978. *Constitutional Language: An Interpretation of Judicial Decision.* London: Greenwood.

Brimo, N. 1977. *Le Dossier Hersant.* Paris: Maspero.

Brinkman, G. Spring 1981. *Public Law,* p. 104.

Brissaud, J. 1915. *A History of French Law.* Boston: Little Brown.

Brown, G. D. 1966. *Boston University Law Review* 46: 491.

Brown, L. N., and Garner, J. F. 1973. *French Administrative Law.* London: Buttersworth.

Burdeau, Gen. 1985. *Revue générale de droit international public* 89: 23.

Burdeau, Geo. 1957. *Droit constitutionnel et institutions politiques.* Paris: Librairie générale de droit et de jurisprudence.

Cappelletti, M. Rapport general. 1986. In *Le contrôle juridictionnel des lois.* Paris and Aix-en-Provence: Economica.

Cappelletti, M., and Cohen, W., eds. *The Modern Systems of Judicial Review: Comparative Constitutional Law.* New York: Bobbs-Merrill, 1979.

Carcassonne, G. 1984. *Revue française de science politique* 34: 910.

———. 1987. *Pouvoirs* 41: 163.

———. 1988. The Fifth Republic After Thirty Years. In *Constitutions in Democratic Polities,* p. 241. Aldershot: Gower.

———. 1989. *Pouvoirs* 49: 37.

Carre de Malberg, R. 1922. *Contribution à la théorie générale de l'état.* Paris: Sirey.

Center for Constitutional Studies at the University of Aix-Marseilles III. 1972. *Le Conseil constitutionnel au Parlement.*

Clapham, J. H. 1912. *The Abbé Sieyès: An Essay in the Politics of the French Revolution.* London: King.

Cohen-Tanugi, L. 1985. *Le droit sans l'état.* Paris: Presses universitaires de France.

———. 1987. *Le Débat* 43: 58.

Cole, T. 1959. *American Political Science Review* 53: 963.

Colliard, C. A. 1950. *Précis de droit public.* Paris: Dalloz.

Collins, I. 1979. *Napoleon and His Parliaments.* London: Arnold.

Constant, B. 1819. *Cours de politique constitutionnelle.* Paris.

Dahl, R. 1957. *Behavioral Science* 2: 201.

——— . 1957. *Journal of Public Law* 6: 279.

Dahrendorf, R. 1969. *Society and Democracy in Germany*. Garden City: Doubleday.

David, R. 1972. *French Law: Its Structure, Sources, and Methodology*. Baton Rouge: LSU Press.

Davis, M. H. *American Journal of Comparative Law* 34: 45.

Debbasch, C., and Drouot, G. 1985. *Actualité législative Dalloz*. 1985, p. 50.

Debré, M. 1955. *Revue française de science politique* 5: 21.

Deener, D. 1952. *American Political Science Review* 46: 1079.

Delion, A., and Durupty, M. 1982. *Les nationalisations: 1982*. Paris: Economica.

Demichel, A., and Lalumiere, P. 1985. *Le droit public*. Paris: Presses universitaires de France.

Deslandres, M. 1932. *Histoire constitutionnelle de la France de 1789 à 1870*. Paris: Colin, Sirey.

Donaghy, P. J., and Newton, M. T. 1987. *Spain: A Guide to Political and Economic Institutions*. Cambridge: Cambridge University Press.

Dossier et Documents—Le Monde, 1988.

Duguit, L. 1917. *Harvard Law Review* 31: 1.

——— . 1919. *Law in the Modern State*. New York: Huebsch.

——— . 1921. Theory of Objective Law Anterior to the State. In *Modern French Legal Philosophy*. New York: Macmillan.

——— . 1923. *Traité du droit constitutionnel*. Paris: Sirey.

Duverger, M. 1948. *Manuel de droit constitutionnel*. Paris: Presses universitaires de France.

——— . 1956. *Droit constitutionnel et institutions politiques*. Paris: Presses universitaires de France.

——— . 1961. *Les Constitutions de la France*. Paris: Presses universitaires de France.

——— . 1962. *Institutions politiques et droit constitutionnel*. Paris: Presses universitaires de France.

Durupty, M. 1986. *Les entreprises publiques, Rôle economique, Cadre juridique*. Paris: Themis, Presses universitaires de France.

Dyson, K. H. F. 1980. *The State Tradition in Western Europe*. Oxford: Martin Robertson.

Eckstein, H. 1975. *Handbook of Political Science* 7: 79.

Einaudi, M. 1938. *The Physiocratic Doctrine of Judicial Control*. Cambridge: Harvard University Press.

Eisenmann, C. 1986 (orig. 1928). *La justice constitutionnelle et la haute cour constitutionnelle d'Autriche*. Paris and Aix-en-Provence: Economica.

Ely, J. H. 1982. *Democracy and Distrust: A Theory of Judicial Review*. Cambridge: Harvard University Press.

Esmein, A. 1903. *Cours élémentaire d'histoire du droit français*. Paris: Sirey.

——— . 1915. *Droit constitutionnel*. Paris: Sirey.

——— , and Nezard, H. 1903. *Droit constitutionnel*. Paris: Sirey.

Etien, R. 1984. *La revue administrative* 221: 472.

——— . 1986. *La revue administrative* 229: 33.

Favoreu, L. 1975. *Revue du droit public* 91: 801.

——— , ed. 1978. *Le domaine de la loi et du règlement*. Paris: Economica.

——— . 1980. *Pouvoirs* 13: 17.

——— . 1982a. *Revue du droit public* 98: 377.

——— . 1982b. *Revue du droit public* 98: 1259.

——— . 1982c. Une grande décision. In *Nationalisation et Constitution*, p. 55. Paris and Aix-en-Provence: Economica.

——— . 1984. *Revue du droit public* 100: 1147.

——— . 1986a. Europe occidentale. In *Le contrôle juridictionnel des lois*, p. 17. Paris and Aix-en-Provence: Economica.

——— . 1986b. *Les cours constitutionnelles*. Paris: Presses universitaires de France.

——— . 1986c. *Revue du droit public* 102: 395.

——— . 1986d. *Revue du droit public* 102: 399.

——— . 1986e. *Revue internationale de droit compare*, p. 613.

——— . 1987a. *Régards sur l'actualité*, p. 19.

——— . 1987b. *Revue du droit public* 103: 442.

——— . 1987c. *Revue française du droit administratif* 3: 240.

——— . 1987d. La mythe du gouvernement des juges. Paper presented at Oxford University, October 1987.

——— . 1988. *La politique saisie par le droit*. Paris: Economica.

——— , and Philip, L. 1975. *Revue du droit public* 91: 201.

——— . 1986. *Les grandes décisions du Conseil constitutionnel*. Paris: Sirey.

Feeley, M. 1973. Power, Impact, and the Supreme Court. In *The Impact of Supreme Court Decisions: Empirical Studies*. New York: Oxford University Press.

Fisher, L. 1988. *Constitutional Dialogues: Interpretation as Political Process*. Princeton: Princeton University Press.

Frank, J. 1949. *The Courts on Trial*. Princeton: Princeton University Press.

Freiberg, J. W. 1981. *The French Press: Class, State, and Ideology*. New York: Praeger.

Friedrich, C. J. 1946. *Constitutional Government and Democracy*. Boston: Ginn.

——— . 1963. *The Philosophy of Law in Historical Perspective*. Chicago: University of Chicago Press.

——— . 1968. *Constitutional Government and Democracy: Theory and Practice in Europe and America*. Waltham, Mass.: Blaisdell.

Funston, R. 1975. *American Political Science Review* 69: 795.

Garrigou-Lagrange, J-M. 1986. *Revue du droit public* 102: 647.

Gaulle, C. de. 1970. *Mémoires d'éspoir*. Paris: Plon.

Genevois, B. 1988. *La Jurisprudence du Conseil constitutionnel: Principes directeurs*. Paris: Editions STH.

——— . 1989. *Pouvoirs* 49: 47.

Gény, F. 1930. *Archives de philosophie de droit et de sociologie juridique*. Paris: Sirey.

——— . 1947. *Jurisclasseur périodiques: Semaines juridiques*, p. 613.

Georgel, J. 1960. *Revue du droit public* 76: 85.

Gibson, J. L. 1983. *Political Behavior* 5: 7.

Golay, J. F. 1958. *The Founding of the Federal Republic of Germany*. Chicago: University of Chicago Press.

Gordon, R. 1984. *Stanford Law Review* 36: 57.

Gulick, C. 1948. *Austria between Habsburg and Hitler*. Berkeley: University of California Press.

Habib, L. 1986. *Revue du droit public* 102: 695.

Haimbaugh, G. D., Jr. 1974. *Ohio State Law Review* 35: 910.

Hauriou, M. 1910. *Principes du droit public*. Paris: Sirey.

——— . 1923. *Droit constitutionnel*. Paris: Sirey.

——— . 1929. *Précis du droit constitutionnel*. Paris: Sirey.

Hayward, J. E. S. 1983. *Governing France*. New York: Norton.

Hirsch, M. 1977. *DRiZ*, p. 225.

Hoffmann, S. 1959. *American Political Science Review* 53: 332.

Hubac, S., and Schoettl, J-E. 1985. *Revue de science criminelle et droit pénal comparé*, p. 12.

Jenson, J., and Ross, G. 1985. Political Pluralism and Economic Policy. In *The French Socialist Experiment*, p. 25. Philadelphia: Institute for the Study of Human Issues.

Jeze, G. 1895. *Revue générale d'administration* 2: 411.

——— . 1924. *Revue du droit public* 40: 400.

Johnson, N. 1978. *West European Politics* 1: 177.

Juillard, P. 1974. *Revue du droit public* 90: 1703.

Katzenstein, P. J. 1987. *Politics and Policy in West Germany: The Growth of a Semi-Sovereign State*. Philadelphia: Temple University.

Keeler, J. T. S. 1988. *Pouvoirs* 47: 145.

——— , and Stone, A. 1987. Judicial-Political Confrontation in Mitterrand's France: The Emergence of the Constitutional Council as a Major Actor in the Policy-Making Process. In *The Mitterrand Experiment*, p. 161. New York: Oxford.

Kelley, D. R. 1984. *Historians and the Law in Post-Revolutionary France*. Princeton: Princeton University Press.

Kelsen, H. 1928. *Revue du droit public* 44: 197.

Kommers, D. P. 1976. *Judicial Politics in West Germany*. Beverly Hills and London: Sage.

Kuhn, R. 1985. *West European Politics* 8: 50.

Kurland, P. *University of Chicago Law Review* 28: 223.

Labetoulle, D. 1988. Les méthodes du travail au Conseil d'état at au Conseil constitutionnel. Paper presented at the conference, "Conseil constitutionnel et Conseil d'état," Luxemburg Palace, Paris, January 1988.

Laferrière, J. 1947. *Manuel de droit constitutionnel*. Paris: Domat.

Lambert, E. 1921. *Le gouvernement des juges et la lutte contre la législation sociale aux Etats-unis*. Paris: Giard.

Landfried, C. 1984. *Bundesverfassungsgericht und Gesetzgeber*. Baden-Baden: Nomos.

——— . 1985. *Government and Opposition* 20: 522.

——— , ed. 1989. *Constitutional Review and Legislation: An International Comparison*. Baden-Baden: Nomos.

Leben, C. 1982. *Revue du droit public* 98: 295.

Lemasurier, J. 1953. *La Constitution de 1946 et le contrôle de la constitutionnalité des lois*. Paris: Librairie générale de droit et de jurisprudence.

Leroy, M. 1908. *La loi. Essai sur la théorie de l'autorité dans la démocratie*. Paris: Sirey.

Leveque, J-M. 1986. *En premiere ligne*. Paris: Albin Michel.

Levy, L. W., ed. 1967. *Judicial Review and the Supreme Court*. New York: Harper.

Lijphart, A. 1971. *American Political Science Review* 65: 682.

Linotte, D. 1982. *Revue du droit public* 98: 435.

Lopez, S. 1983. *Revista de Derecho Politico* 18–19: 177.

Loschak, D. 1980. *Pouvoirs* 13: 35.

——— . 1983. *Droit social*, p. 131.

Luchaire, F. 1979. *Revue du droit public* 95: 27.

——— . 1980. *Le Conseil constitutionnel*. Paris and Aix-en-Provence: Economica.

——— . 1982. Commentaire. In *Nationalisatoin et Constitution*, p. 65. Paris and Aix-en-Provence: Economica.

——— , and Robert, J. 1982. Consultation. In *Nationalisation et Constitution*, p. 93. Paris and Aix-en-Provence: Economica.

Lussouarn, Y.; Drago, R.; and Delvolve, P. 1982. Consultation. In *Nationalisation et Constitution*, p. 105. Paris and Aix-en-Provence: Economica.

Macridis, R. 1955. *The Study of Comparative Government*. New York: Random House.

———. 1968. *Comparative Politics* 1: 78.

Malone, A. P., and Mace, G., eds. 1988. *Judicial Review and American Democracy*. Ames: University of Iowa.

March, J. G., and Olsen, J. P. 1984. *American Political Science Review* 78: 734.

Mathieu, M. 1986. *La presse quotidien régionale*. Paris: Presses universitaires de France.

Maus, D. 1984. *Revue française de science politique* 34: 875.

McCarthy, P. *The French Socialists in Power, 1981–1986*. Westport, Conn.: Greenwood.

McDowell, G. 1988. *Curbing the Courts: The Constitution and the Limits of Judicial Power*. Baton Rouge: LSU Press.

McQuail, D., and Siune, K., eds. 1987. *New Media Politics: Comparative Perspectives in Western Europe*. London: Sage.

Mendelson, M. H. 1986. *International and Comparative Law Quarterly* 34: 284.

Mény, Y. 1987. *Politique comparée*. Paris: Montchrestien.

Merryman, J. H. 1985. *The Civil Law Tradition*. Stanford: Stanford University Press.

Millon, C. 1984. *L'extravagante histoire des nationalisations*. Paris: Plon.

Mitterrand, F. 1964. *Le coup d'état permanent*. Paris: Plon.

Myerson, M. 1985. *Stanford Journal of International Law*, p. 102.

Navorro, M. A. 1983. *Revista de Derecho Politico* 16: 167.

Neumann, F. 1964. *The Democratic and the Authoritarian State*. New York: Free Press.

Nicholas, B. 1970. *Public Law*, p. 255.

Noel, L. 1976. *De Gaulle et les débuts de la Ve Republique*. Paris: Plon.

Ohlinger, T. 1982. Objet et portée de la protection des droits fondamentaux en Autriche. In *Cours constitutionnelles européennes et droits fondamentaux*, p. 335. Paris and Aix-en-Provence: Economica.

Padover, S. K. 1970. *To Secure These Blessings: The Great Debates of the Constitutional Convention of 1787, Arranged According to Topics*. New York: Washington Square.

Pascallon, P. 1986. *Revue politique et parlementaire* 925: 2.

Pelloux, F. 1947. *Revue du droit public* 63: 347.

Pépy, G. 1986. *L'actualité juridique, Droit administratif* 10 October 1986, p. 527.

Perrot, R. 1986. *Institutions judiciares*. Paris: Montchrestien.

Petiet, M. 1891. *Du pouvoir législatif en France*. Paris: Sirey.

Pézant, J-L. 1981. Contribution a l'étude du pouvoir législatif selon la Constitution de 1958. In *Mélanges Burdeau*, p. 477. Paris: Librairie générale de droit.

———. 1981. *Revue française de science politique* 31: 140.

———. 1984. *Revue française de science politique* 34: 922.

Philip, L. 1962. *Revue du droit public* 78: 46.

———. 1979. La valeur juridique de la Déclaration des droits de l'homme et du citoyen du 26 août 1789 selon la jurisprudence du Conseil constitutionnel. vol. 2. In *Mélange Kayser*.

———. 1983. *Revue du droit public* 99: 401.

———. 1984. *Revue française de science politique* 34: 988.

———. 1985. *Revue de science criminelle et de droit pénal comparé* 1985: 711.

Polsby, N. 1975. *Legislatures. Handbook of Political Science* 5: 277.

Pons, D. 1977. *Dossier H . . . comme Hersant*. Paris: Moreau.

Pritchett, H. C. 1969. The Development of Judical Research. In *Frontiers of Judicial Research*. New York: Wiley.

Revue française d'administration publique (special issue on the 1986 audiovisual reform. 1987, no. 44.

Revue politique et parlementaire. 1964. 741: 3.

Revue politique et parlementaire. 1964. 742: 3.

Revue politique et parlementaire. 1965. 757: 3.

Revue politique et parlementaire. 1965. 758: 11.

Revue politique et parlementaire (special issue on the 1986 audiovisuval reform). 1987, no. 929.

Ripert, G. 1949. *Le déclin du droit*. Paris: Librairie générale de droit et de jurisprudence.

Rivéro, J. 1982. *Actualité juridique, Droit administratif* 20 April 1982, p. 209.

——— . 1986. *Actualité juridique, Droit administratif* 20 October 1986, p. 580.

——— , and Vedel, G. 1947. *Collection droit social* 31: 13.

Robert, J. 1971. *Revue du droit public* 87: 1171.

Rose, R. 1982. The Roles of Laws in Comparative Perspective. *Studies in Public Policy*, no. 106. Centre for the Study of Public Policy, University of Strathclyde.

Rosenberg, D. 1985. *Revue du droit public* 101: 1263.

Rostow, E. 1967. The Democratic Nature of Judicial Review. In *Judicial Review and the Supreme Court*, p. 74. New York: Harper.

Roubier, P. 1951. *Théorie générale du droit*. Paris: Sirey.

Rougier, L. *La France à la recherche d'une constitution*. Paris: Sirey.

Rousseau, J-J. (Roger D. Masters, ed.). 1978. *On the Social Contract*. New York: St. Martin's.

Rudelle, O. 1984. *Revue française de science politique* 34: 687.

Saint-Girons, A. 1881. *Essai sur le séparation des pouvoirs*. Paris: Larose.

Sartori, G. 1970. *American Political Science Review* 64: 1033.

Schacter, O. 1984. *American Journal of International Law* 78: 121.

Schmitt, C. 1958. Das Reichsgericht als Huter der Verfassung. In *Verfassungsrechliche Aufsätze*, p. 63. Berlin: Duncker and Humboldt.

Schram, G. 1971. *Journal of Politics* 33: 133.

Schubert, G. 1963. *American Political Science Review* 57: 433.

——— . 1963. *Judicial Decision-Making*. London: Free Press.

Shapiro, M. 1964. *Kentucky Law Journal* 52: 294.

——— . 1965. *Law and Politics of the Supreme Court: New Approaches in Political Jurisprudence*. London: Free Press.

——— . 1980. *Courts: A Comparative and Political Analysis*. Chicago: University of Chicago Press.

——— . 1990. *Studies in American Political Development* 3 1989: 88–104.

Shennan, J. H. 1968. *The Parlement of Paris*. Ithaca: Cornell.

Siegfried, A. 1956. *De la IIIe à la IVe République*. Paris: Grasset.

Sieyès, E. 1970 (orig. 1789). *Qu'est-ce que le tiers état*. Geneva: Droz.

Sigelman, L., and Gadbois, G. 1983. *Comparative Political Studies* 16: 293.

Skocpol, T. 1985. Bringing the State Back In: Strategies of Analysis in Current Research. In *Bringing the State Back In*, p. 3. New York: Cambridge.

Smith, R. 1988. *American Political Science Review* 82: 89.

Sorel, M. 1988. *Revue administrative* 24: 29.

Soto, J. de. 1959. *Revue du droit public* 75: 240.

Stone, A. 1989. Legal Constraints to Policy-Making: The Conseil constitutionnel and the Conseil d'état. In Paul Godt, ed., *Policy-Making in France, From De Gaulle to Mitterrand*, p. 28. London: Pinter.

———. 1989. *West European Politics* 12: 12.

———. 1991. *Policy Studies Journal* 19: 81.

Stumph, H. P.; Shapiro, M.; Danelski, D. J.; Sarat, A.; and O'Brien, D. M. 1983. *Western Political Quarterly* 36: 533.

Taylor, O. R. 1951. *The Fourth Republic of France: Constitution and Political Parties.* London: Aldon and Blackwell.

Terneyre, P. 1985. *Revue du droit public* 101: 691.

Thiry, J. 1949. *Le Sénat de Napoléon, 1800–1814.* Paris: Berger-Lerrault.

Toqueville, A. de. (J. P. Mayer, ed.). 1969. *Democracy in America.* Garden City: Anchor Doubleday.

Vedel, G. 1947. *Manuel élémentaire de droit constitutionnel.* Paris: Sirey.

———. 1988. *Pouvoirs* 45: 151.

———. 1989a. *Le Débat* May 1989, p. 48.

———. 1989b. *Revue du droit public* 105: 11.

Vier, C. L. 1972. *Revue du droit public* 88: 165.

Villalon, P. C. 1981. *Revista de Derecho Publico* 82: 5.

Villiers, M. de. 1983. *La Revue administrative* 213: 247.

———. 1984. *La revue administrative* 222: 581.

Vincent, J.; Montagnier, G.; and Varinard, A. 1985. *La justice et les institutions.* Paris: Dalloz.

Waline, M. 1928. *Revue du droit public* 44: 441.

———. 1950. *Revue du droit public* 66: 694.

———. 1959. *Revue du droit public* 75: 699.

Wasby, S. L. 1970. *The Impact of the United States Supreme Court.* Homewood, Ill.: Dorsey.

———. 1972. The Supreme Court's Impact: Some Problems of Conceptualization and Measurement. In Samuel Krislov, ed., *Compliance and the Law: A Multi-Disciplinary Approach.* Beverly Hills: Sage.

Williams, P. 1958. *Politics in Post-War France: Parties and the Constitution in the Fourth Republic.* London: Longmans and Green.

Wright, G. 1948. *The Reshaping of French Democracy.* New York: Reynal and Hitchcock.

Zinson, L. 1985. *Le fer de lance.* Paris: Olivier Orban.

Interviews

Guy Carcassonne, February 1987.
Louis Favoreu, June 1988.
Jean Foyer, March 1987.
Bruno Genevois, June 1989.
Committee Staff of the National Assembly, February–March 1987; February–June 1988.

INDEX

A posteriori review, 8, 38, 231, 232t, 233, 244–45
A priori review, 8, 105, 209, 215, 220, 231, 232t. *See also* Abstract review
Abbé de Sieyès, 30, 35
Abstract review
  definition, 8, 226
  general, 219, 220, 225–31, 232t, 233–47, 248t, 249–53
  policymaking impact, 225, 235–45, 251
Audio-visual law (1986)
  decision of Constitutional Council, 199–200
  general, 89–90, 191–95, 196t, 196–200
  and National Commission on Communication and Liberties (CNCL), 194–95, 196t, 196, 200
  notion of pluralism, 193–95, 196t, 197–200, 204–7
Auriol, Vincent, 50, 66n.30
Auroux laws, 143, 143n.5
Austria
  constitutional court, 228–31, 232t, 233–35
  legal system, 228
Autolimitation phenomenon
  and audiovisual law (1986), 191, 195, 196t, 197–99
  and decentralization law, 128–29
  definition, 78, 122
  general, 78, 78n.89, 122–29, 138, 236–39
  in Germany, 236–39
  and nationalization law, 152, 158
  penal law, 210–11
  and press law (1984), 181–82, 182t, 184–86
  and press law (1986), 191–93
  and privatization law, 159
  see also Juridicization

Badinter, Robert
  appointment to the Council, 52, 53
  as law professor, 67, 69
  as Minister of Justice, 156
  as President of the Constitutional Council, 4, 58, 88, 91, 129, 131, 136
Barre, Raymond, 53n.31, 134, 177, 198, 211
Bickel, Alexander, 114, 169
Black, Charles, Jr., 93, 110–14, 167
Blum, Léon, 52, 157
Bolo, Alexandre, 70
Bonapartism, 26, 30–31, 46, 54

Caillevet, Henri, 75
Carcassonne, Guy
  as consultant to Socialist Party, 88, 130, 216
  as doctrinal analyst, 108, 114, 128, 137
Carré de Malberg, 36n.70, 37n.81
Chalandon, Albin, 3, 87, 103, 197
Chirac, Jacques
  as head of the RPR, 52
  as opposition leader, 81, 87, 170, 176, 180
  as Prime Minister, 71, 87, 197
Chirac government
  attacks on the Constitutional Council, 3–4, 86–91, 100, 104, 197, 240
  attitude on judicial status of constitutional review, 132
  legislative program, 86–89, 89t, 90–91, 135, 168–72, 174, 191–208, 210, 236, 241
Civil law, 14, 23n.3, 25n.10, 97, 226–28, 247, 251
Cognitive structures, 13–15. *See also* Legal discourse
Cohabitation, 52, 121, 199
Commission of the Stock Exchange (COB), 151, 159, 165
Common law, 247
Communist Party (French), 66, 71, 113, 146
Concrete review
  compared to abstract review, 8, 226, 245, 248t
  and the Constitutional Council, 58–59
  definition of, 8
  and European constitutional courts, 226–31, 232t, 233–35, 244–47, 248t, 249–53
Conseil d'état
  Amicales decision (1956), 45
  Arrighi decision (1936), 40
  and Constitutional Committee, 28
  and the Constitutional Council, 48n.13, 58–59, 69, 99, 124–25, 129n.26, 189–90, 225
  and constitutional status of the 1946 preamble, 44–45, 67–69
  creation of, 26
  nationalization law, 150, 151, 156, 159, 160, 162, 165
  Paulin decision (1833), 25
  and policymaking process, 30, 124–25, 126, 127, 237
  and press law (1984), 179, 185, 189–90

307